D0028493

Chasing Stars

Chasing Stars

The Myth of Talent and the Portability of Performance

BORIS GROYSBERG

PRINCETON UNIVERSITY PRESS | *Princeton and Oxford*

Copyright © 2010 by Princeton University Press

Published by Princeton University Press, 41 William Street, Princeton, New Jersey 08540
In the United Kingdom: Princeton University Press, 6 Oxford Street, Woodstock,
Oxfordshire OX20 1TW

press.princeton.edu

All Rights Reserved

Sixth printing, and first paperback printing, 2012
Paperback ISBN 978-0-691-15451-0

The Library of Congress has cataloged the cloth edition of this book as follows

Groysberg, Boris.
    Chasing stars : the myth of talent and the portability of performance / Boris Groysberg.
        p.   cm.
    Includes bibliographical references and index.
    ISBN 978-0-691-12720-0 (alk. paper)
    1. Investment advisors—United States.   2. Wall Street (New York, N.Y.).   3. Labor turn-
over—United States.   I. Title.
    HG4928.5.G76 2010
    332.6068'3—dc22   2009052992

British Library Cataloging-in-Publication Data is available

This book has been composed in Minion and Myriad
Design and composition by Tracy Baldwin
Printed on acid-free paper. ∞
Printed in the United States of America

10

To my parents and my wife

My biggest supporters

Contents

Part Three
Implications for Talent Management:
Developing, Retaining, and Rewarding Stars

Acknowledgments

No one works alone. That is the premise of this book, and it makes these acknowledgments no mere courtesy but in a very real way the heart of the book. How convincing can the book's findings be if I overlook others' contributions to my own work? The authorial voice in this book is "we," not "I," to acknowledge the contributions of my colleagues, coauthors, interviewees, and others.

My research interests in stars, portability, and mobility started when I was pursuing my doctorate in business policy. Thus, my first thanks go to my dissertation committee: George Baker, Paul Healy, Ashish Nanda, and Nitin Nohria. They made profound contributions to my work, and this book would not exist without them.

Ashish Nanda took me under his wing when I was a first-year doctoral student and taught me about research and case writing. From the outset we have worked shoulder to shoulder developing ideas. Ashish has been a true mentor and guided me through the ins and outs of the doctoral program. Our collaboration on several projects about portability and mobility of stars has been truly rewarding.

Nitin Nohria taught me how to ask big questions, how to combine rigor and relevance, how to do interdisciplinary work, and how to write for both academics and executives. For ten years Nitin has been a patient advisor, and he has occasionally had very rough raw material to work with: he once spent six hours walking me word by word through the roughest of rough drafts of an article—drafted by me. He has been my biggest motivator. Nitin has also been a great advisor both professionally and personally. This book would not have happened without his continual support and encouragement.

Few people comment on work as meticulously and insightfully as Paul Healy. During our ten years of collaboration on research projects and cases, he has taught me to ask the right questions and how to do careful empirical work. Paul also encourages unconventional thinking. At his urging I learned a completely new field, financial accounting, which has greatly enriched my understanding of analysts, the focus of this book. Paul has supported me every step of the way.

From George Baker I learned how to frame and develop my work. His ability to pinpoint what was most compelling in a project honed my focus and clarified my thinking. George taught me to dig ever deeper to understand a phenomenon as thoroughly as possible. It has served me well in all my projects.

When I met Linda-Eling Lee at Harvard Business School, we found that our research interests coincided and began to collaborate on several papers. We have worked hard together to understand the mobility-and-portability phenomenon; ours has been a true partnership.

My heartfelt thanks go to Ann Goodsell. I can't even describe how grateful I am for her contributions. She helped prepare the manuscript with as much enthusiasm, curiosity, skill, and dedication as if it were her own. She was relentless in asking insightful questions that tested and pushed my logic. From shaping its structure to fixing my mistakes, she has made this book readable. I learned a great deal from her.

Anahita Hashemi has been a friend and supporter for fifteen years. She has welcomed my ideas and patiently watched them develop. I cannot imagine a better confidante and cheerleader. At times when I was down, she raised my spirits. Anahita suffered through frequent requests for feedback—and has consistently given me honest and detailed feedback even when I didn't want it. Anahita kept my hope alive and always pointed out the light at the end of the tunnel.

I cannot say enough about Robin Abrahams's contribution. She has become much more than a research associate; she has been instrumental in developing ideas, framing, and editing. We have also collaborated on several of the articles and cases that I have drawn on for the book. Her signature question, "Why would the reader care about this point?" has made this a better book. The research associates who helped with the manuscript, some for only one month and others for longer periods, are Gabrielle Fraenkel, Geoff Marietta, and Michael Slind.

Current and former colleagues in my department read the manuscript and helped transform vague notions into fully articulated ideas. I could not ask for better colleagues: Julie Battilana, Michael Beer, Tiziana Casciaro, Thomas DeLong, Robert Eccles, Robin Ely, Ranjay Gulati, Monica Higgins, Linda Hill, Robert S. Kaplan, Rakesh Khurana, Jay Lorsch, Joshua Margolis, Chris Marquis, Laura Morgan Roberts, Leslie Perlow, Joel Podolny, Jeff Polzer, Scott Snook, David Thomas, and Michael Tushman have all been important intellectual contributors. Many read this book more than once, and they're still speaking to me!

Many other Harvard colleagues helped shape and clarify my thoughts, offered valuable insights, and introduced me to scholarly work I might not otherwise have encountered. Special thanks to Teresa Amabile, Bharat Anand, Lynda Applegate, Carliss Baldwin, David Bell, Joseph Bower, Hannah Bowles, Clayton Christensen, Dwight Crane, Srikant Datar, Frank Dobbin, Thomas Eisenmann, Benjamin Esty, Lee Fleming, Richard Hackman, Brian Hall, David Hawkins, Paul Healy, Andrew Hill, Tarun Khanna, Rajiv Lal, Kathleen McGinn, Krishna Palepu, Andre Perold, Toby Stuart, Stefan Thomke, and Peter Tufano.

The quality of this book was greatly enhanced by colleagues outside Harvard who read and commented on drafts of particular chapters. They provided constructive feedback and valuable insights; they all have been instrumental in shaping my thinking. Thanks to Emily Amanatullah, Joel Brockner, John Boudreau, Peter Cappelli, Jennifer Chatman, Daniel Feldman, Roberto Fernandez, Morten Hansen, Chip Heath, Mark Huselid, Herminia Ibarra, Duane Ireland, Kevin Kelly, Thomas Kochan, Kathy Kram, Ed Lawler, Chris Leavy, Will Mitchell, Michael Morris, Jone Pearce, Jeff Pfeffer, Huggy Rao, Denise Rousseau, Amy Schulman, Zur Shapira, Don Sull, Kathleen Sutcliffe, Robert Sutton, Pamela Tolbert, and Dave Ulrich.

Significant portions of this book are based on cases written for teaching purposes, usually with talented coauthors. Thanks to the colleagues who participated in the interviews for this book. I appreciate their insightful questions. None of those cases, nor this book, could have been written without the extraordinary insight and openness of the research directors, equity analysts, *Institutional Investor* editors, and executive recruiters I interviewed. I am also grateful to all those, from CEOs to junior analysts and search consultants, who gave me access to their firms as well as their time. I am especially indebted to Claudio Fernandez Araoz, Steve Balog, Fred Fraenkel, Jack Rivkin, and Lisa Shalett. I interviewed each of them several times (as many as eight); they also helped me gain access to investment banks and commented on cases, research papers, and this manuscript. I learned a lot about what analysts do from Josie Esquivel, whose story encapsulates many of the book's themes. Their practical suggestions were invaluable in my work. Most of those quoted in this book are identified by name; others did not want their names used. You know who you are: please accept my thanks for sharing your knowledge.

I also thank Capco, Harvard Business School Publishing, Harvard Business School, the *Wall Street Journal,* the publishers of *Journal of Financial Transformation, Journal of Organizational Behavior, Management Science,* and *Organizational Science,* the Institute for Operations Research and the Management Sciences, and Wiley for permission to use material in articles, papers, and cases.

I thank Harvard Business School for the financial support of the Division of Research, as well as the research directors whose encouragement was critical in the writing process. To work at Harvard Business School is astonishing. The quality of its resources is beyond compare, and the intellectual curiosity and passion for excellence of my colleagues, from senior professors to faculty assistants, has made "firm-specific human capital" more than an abstraction. I thank all the transcribers, librarians, word-processing professionals, case-service people, and others at the school who helped me. In particular, I would not survive without my assistant: Tasha Miller pushed the process along by obtaining permission from journals, reserving conference rooms on "a different planet" so no one could disturb me, and forcing me to eat lunch. Prior to Tasha, Meredith Cook helped with scheduling field interviews. I also thank Linda Olsen for helping get approvals for field cases that might not otherwise have seen the light of day.

At Princeton University Press, Tim Sullivan took an interest in the project before anyone else. The press and its reviewers saw promise in the book proposal; their insightful feedback made this a better book. Seth Ditchik took over from Tim and has been a great supporter. Jenn Backer, Janie Chan, and Kathleen Cioffi helped in many ways.

With such an astonishing range of intellectual, logistical, technical, literary, and emotional support, it might seem that I could not stumble. But flaws are inevitable, and they belong only to me. A book that is the culmination of over a decade of research becomes, early on, more than an intellectual pursuit; it is also a matter of emotional endurance. I could not have persevered without my family and the friends who helped me keep my sense of humor. They survived endless conversations about portability. Many watched the kids, bolstered my confidence, brought lunch, and prayed for me.

My thoughts turn first to my parents, who sacrificed to come to this country and to offer me its opportunities. I am very grateful. They have also been my greatest supporters emotionally. My sister, Natalia, who worked in the investment-banking industry, helped me understand the institutional context and even read papers and cases; isn't that what little sisters are for? Her motivational technique was to ask, "Why is it taking you so long?" Once she calculated that I wrote less than a paragraph a day. It became a family joke: whenever I inscribed more than three sentences on a birthday card, the family would declare that I had had an unusually productive day.

None of this would have been possible without my wife, Liliya. She has stood by me through the ups and downs of writing this book and helped me maintain some balance. She is my joy. This book became our fourth child; it was a very long pregnancy. In fact, the idea of the book was born right after our first son, Joshua. Over time, it learned to crawl, walk, and run. The manuscript acquired a voice of its own; it even went through the terrible twos and developed a fleeting attitude problem. To my wife's dismay, our daughter Liana's first word was "portability." Tali was born during my revisions of the manuscript. He made sure his father was productive by waking up every morning at 4 A.M. Joshua was a big help, too; he learned numbers by putting chapters in order and began learning to read with this book. I probably violated child-labor laws by asking him to help me on Sundays, but he seemed to enjoy it. My family has always been an everyday part of my life!

Chasing Stars

Introduction

Many knowledge-based firms view their employees as their most valuable resource. At such companies, where it is virtually an article of faith that settling for "B" players is a recipe for mediocrity, managers work hard to attract the best and the brightest. When companies do find first-rate talent, they're often willing to offer those stars huge salaries, signing bonuses, stock options—in short, whatever it takes. The value of stars is a powerful idea, one that numerous books and management gurus have popularized over the past decade by invoking a so-called war for talent. This assumption is the cornerstone of many companies' people-management strategies. On its face, the star hypothesis makes sense. After all, a firm can sustain a competitive advantage only if its strategic resources are valuable, rare, lacking substitutes, and difficult to duplicate.[1]

But reliance on stars is a highly speculative managerial policy because we don't really know very much about what drives outstanding individual performance. Little clear-cut evidence supports or refutes prevailing beliefs about why some people excel. Both stars and their employers often assume that outstanding performance is the result of a combination of innate talent and good educational preparation. But is this the entire story? And if not, what is missing?

Another hazard of an unexamined reliance on stars is that the portability of talent—or, more accurately, the prevailing belief in such portability—cuts two ways. A prize-winning scientist may be a unique resource, for instance, but unless he or she is deeply embedded and loyal, the attractiveness of his or her talents makes that scientist an unreliable source of sustainable competitive advantage.[2] And there is also a risk for the firm that lures that star scientist away: instead of continuing to excel, he or she might turn out to resemble a comet, quickly fading out in a new setting.

The extent to which skills are portable is also a compelling question for individual knowledge workers whose stock-in-trade is information and intellectual activity, whether or not they are stars in their fields. Knowledge workers are encouraged by popular career-guidance literature to think of themselves as resourceful free agents with portable stores of knowledge and skills. Determining whether the skills of knowledge workers are in fact portable from one firm to another—or to what degree and under what circumstances they are portable—can potentially shed light on the accuracy of this formulation and the wisdom of building one's career on it.

Almost fifty years ago, human-capital theory posed a challenge to the free-agent thesis by suggesting that a part of individual performance is specific to a particular workplace and not readily transferable elsewhere. Though this is not a new idea, it has gained very little traction, or even recognition, beyond the confines of academia. For one thing, its proponents until recently concentrated on manual labor. Also, human-capital theory has not yet generated the texture and nuance necessary to make it usefully applicable to the practical world of work: it has remained largely abstract and ideological, and the question of whether human capital is primarily generalizable or firm-specific is still being debated as if there were only two possible answers. Nor has the human-capital literature thoroughly explored the impact of firms' capabilities on individual performance.

Thus, the question of portability continues to offer a promising point of entry into the longstanding debate about the fundamental nature of exceptional performance. If we can determine whether stars' performance is indeed portable from one employer to another, we may learn something fundamental about the origins and drivers of such performance. Are those who excel in the workplace mobile free agents with highly portable skills, or is their performance primarily driven by adept use of the resources of the organization in which they thrive? An answer to this question, even an answer less cut-and-dried than popular wisdom or theoretical formulations, could shed new light on pressing managerial questions about how to hire, develop, compensate, and retain talent.

Though this is a book about a specific profession, it presents evidence drawn from other positions and professions, ranging from CEOs to football players, to maximize the applicability of its findings. And though the book addresses a longstanding academic debate about human capital, it is also intended for practitioners on the corporate front lines and for individual professionals with a personal stake in questions about career management and workplace success.

Finding a Population to Study

Chasing Stars began with an effort to identify a suitable labor market in which to compare the performance of exceptional workers before and after a move to a new employer. If conducted rigorously, a study of this kind could reveal a good deal about the portability of talent and even about talent itself. But such a labor market would have to fulfill several requirements.

The first such requirement, and the hardest to meet, was shared, objective, and publicly available criteria for measuring performance. Very few professions outside of individual sports pit their members against each other in a systematic and public way. Who is to say whether a brain surgeon in Albuquerque is more or less skilled than her counterpart in Cleveland? How would we go about comparing physicists or litigators or software engineers or even basketball coaches? We systematically considered a number of professions, including academics, accountants, advertising creatives, architects, athletes, consultants, engineers, inventors, lawyers, money managers, and programmers. Some professions proved unsuitable because of a lack of reliable mobility and performance data, or because jobs that sound comparable actually differ. Two lawyers or two accountants with identical job titles, for instance, may perform very different jobs. Creatives in advertising are rated competitively by their clients, but their jobs are not strictly comparable; also, some ratings reward creativity while others emphasize an ad's effectiveness. Athletes were an appealing population because of the wealth of statistics on their performance, but they are not a good proxy for knowledge workers. Academics were also attractive from the perspective of data, but the long interval between completing research and publishing it (during which a job change would make it tricky to decide which university to credit for contributing to an individual's success) and the impact of tenure on publication both represent confounding factors.

We finally found a suitable labor market on Wall Street. For a handful of reasons that we will explore more fully in chapter 2, investment banks' research departments turned out to be a near ideal real-world laboratory for assessing the portability of talent. Wall Street equity analysts, who follow companies and stocks in particular industries and share their insights with their firms' institutional clients, are assessed annually according to standardized measures. Since 1972 a respected trade journal, *Institutional Investor*, has compiled and published an annual ranking of the best stock analysts in each industry. *Institutional Investor* awards its rankings by asking hundreds of institutional investors to rank the analysts on whose research they have relied in the preceding year. These rankings are viewed on Wall Street and by academics as a reliable proxy for performance. Research departments collect voluminous data of other kinds about their analysts, as do information intermediaries like Thomson Financial, allowing for simultaneous examination of the impact of various variables on performance. Detailed data on moves between employers is also readily available for top-rated analysts.

Furthermore, the labor market for analysts, though large enough to produce valid and reliable observations, is small and concentrated enough to lend itself well to study. It is remarkably compact compared to professions like law, medicine, biochemistry, or information technology: to be specific, many top stock analysts work in Manhattan. This geographic concentration eliminates complicating factors, like family upheaval, in job changes; analysts who change employers typically move across the street or down the block. When analysts move, furthermore, both their clients and the content of their work typically remain unchanged, eliminating further potentially confounding factors.

Finally, belief that individual talent is the prime determinant of performance is deeply entrenched among research analysts and others on Wall Street. Fully 85 percent of the individuals we interviewed asserted that analysts' performance is independent of the companies they work for and thus highly portable. The prevailing belief in innate talent has generated an enormous expenditure of effort on the part of research departments to identify the traits of exceptional analysts.

For all these reasons, Wall Street equity analysts appeared to be an excellent test case. We believe that the labor market for research analysts offers an extremely rigorous test of nonportability of performance. Thus if outstanding performance on the part of stock analysts turns out not to be portable, performance in most other knowledge-based professions is unlikely to prove otherwise.

Our research sample consisted of over 1,000 star analysts (that is, those ranked by *Institutional Investor*) at 78 investment banks. For comparative purposes, we also employed data on about 20,000 non-star analysts at approximately 400 investment banks. To flesh out our findings and shed light on both the mechanics and the culture of the profession, we conducted in-depth interviews with more than 200 stock analysts; with research directors, traders, salespeople, investment bankers, and executives at 37 investment banks; and with the institutional investors who are analysts' clients. This book draws liberally on these frank and detailed interviews to supplement our hard data with enlightening accounts of the inner workings of research departments and the experiential dimensions of mobility and performance. (Some chapters also draw on previously published papers; the quantitative findings in particular have been reported elsewhere. For reasons of space, certain previously published statistical methodologies, endogeneity and robustness checks, regressions, and exhibits are not included; these materials are included in the endnotes to each chapter.)

The investment-banking landscape of 2010, when this book was finished, looks very different than it did in 1988–96, the years of our study. During the most recent financial crisis, several large firms collapsed or were acquired as this manuscript moved toward publication. These tumultuous events do not undermine our findings. The period of our study represents an optimal time to examine equities research. The *Institutional Investor* rankings, initiated in 1972, had had sufficient time to permeate the industry and shape practices. Equity analysts' involvement in investment-banking deals was also rarer than it became later in the 1990s. (The practice ultimately led to a 2003 agreement among ten investment banks and regulators, called the Global Research Analyst Settlement, to eliminate conflicts of interest by insulating research from investment banking. However, recent research questioned this agreement. In fact, the government might have punished the wrong banks.)[3] If anything, the shifting fortunes of the industry make the book's findings more deserving of attention. The more turbulent the business landscape, the more crucial it becomes to think strategically about performance and talent management.

Nor is this book merely a study of star analysts' performance and the degree to which it is portable. It is also an extended examination of the management of high-performance knowledge workers. As subjects of study, Wall Street research departments are in their way as rewarding as the analysts they employ: their competitive mission and market-driven budgets make many research directors zealous about building strong departments. The relatively self-contained nature of their departments gives them the maneuverability and agility to put their points of view into practice. And their varied approaches to hiring, training, retention, evaluation, compensation, and other fundamentals of human-resource management offer rich material for insight.

No prior study has empirically examined the simultaneous effects of individual, departmental, firm-specific, and market-performance variables on mobility and performance. *Chasing Stars* draws on several disciplines—human resource management, organizational behavior, and strategy—to analyze the effects of these variables thoroughly and multidimensionally, and to spell out the possible implications of our findings for other professions.

The Flow of the Book

Chasing Stars is in three parts. Part 1 presents the basic building blocks of our study: prior work on the question of portability, the population we examined, and our central findings about the effects of job changes on individual performance and on the destination firm.

Chapter 1 traces the meteoric career of Josie Esquivel, a star apparel-and-textiles analyst on Wall Street, and uses Esquivel's story to introduce the profession and the book's basic concepts. The chapter discusses the idea of knowledge workers as free agents and human-capital theory's alternative hypotheses, and surveys unresolved controversies about the nature of exceptional performance, the sources of human capital, and the portability of job performance.

Chapter 2 explains the world of Wall Street equity analysts, describing their work and outlining the structural characteristics of the profession that make its practitioners an ideal population among whom to explore questions about the portability of job performance.

Chapter 3 presents our most central and global finding about the effects of changing employers on star analysts' performance: in short, exceptional performance is far less portable than is widely believed. Mobile stars experienced an immediate degradation in performance. Even after five years at a new firm, star analysts who changed employers underperformed comparable star analysts who stayed put. Thus the tests we performed captured performance differences (delta) between "switchers" and "stayers" (i.e., the control group). Our tests also controlled for a range of factors including individual, firm, sector, and macroeconomic. The appendix explains our research approach, data, variables, model specifications, robustness checks, endogeneity analysis, and results. The endnotes provide references to our published articles for readers interested in more detailed information behind our tests and results. Thus the exceptional performance of stars at their prior employer appears to have been more firm-specific—more dependent on the firm's resources and capabilities—than is generally appreciated. This is a finding with many implications and nuances, which part 2 explores. "Can you take it with you?" turns out to be an insufficiently nuanced question; more productive formulations might be "Under what conditions can you take it with you?" or "Should you try to take it with you?" Chapter 3 also describes the experiential aspects of changing employers—what is lost when an individual changes employers and what the newcomer experiences at the new firm. Finally, the chapter looks at the effect on post-move performance of the relative quality (that is, the capabilities) of both the firm of origin and the new employer.

Chapter 4 examines whether or not firms benefit by hiring stars. In doing so, a firm risks paying more than the individual turns out to be worth to the firm. The chapter describes the dynamics and operation of the labor

Figure I.1. A conceptual overview of the contents of parts 1 and 2.

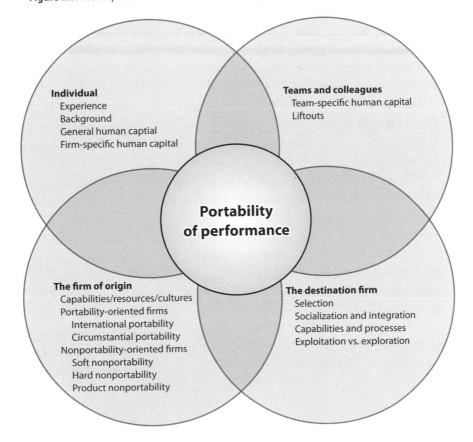

Individual
  Experience
  Background
  General human captial
  Firm-specific human capital

Teams and colleagues
  Team-specific human capital
  Liftouts

**Portability
of performance**

The firm of origin
  Capabilities/resources/cultures
  Portability-oriented firms
    International portability
    Circumstantial portability
  Nonportability-oriented firms
    Soft nonportability
    Hard nonportability
    Product nonportability

The destination firm
  Selection
  Socialization and integration
  Capabilities and processes
  Exploitation vs. exploration

market for stars and the effects on the acquiring company's stock price of hiring a star.

Part 2 examines our findings in a more fine-grained way, devoting a chapter to each of the factors we found to contribute to variance in performance portability. The sequence begins with firm-specific factors (at both origin and destination firms) followed by team-specific and individual factors. Figure I.1 is a conceptual overview of the contents of parts 1 and 2.

Chapter 5 profiles research departments, some whose star analysts' post-exit performance proved portable and others that successfully fostered nonportability. These profiles depict the range of ways in which departmental cultures and resources shape the subsequent portability of their employees. The chapter looks in detail at four firms—Goldman Sachs, Merrill Lynch, Sanford C. Bernstein, and Lehman Brothers—as illustrations of specific types of nonportability: *hard nonportability* (dependent on proprietary information systems and the like), *product-related nonportability* (linked to a unique product), and *soft nonportability* (relational and cultural). The chapter also looks longitudinally at several research departments' efforts to foster nonportability in the form of a unique culture, loyalty, collaboration, and a firm-specific training program.

Chapter 6 turns to the destination firm, examining the effects of organized efforts at socialization and integration by comparing the records of star analysts hired into different situations: to exploit (reinforce existing activities) and to explore (initiate new activities). Stars hired to exploit were less likely to suffer performance shortfalls because the firm resources and capabilities to support them were already in place. Stars hired to explore were in a vulnerable position and far more likely to fail. We also examined how various kinds of hiring and integration capabilities affect the portability of stars' performance.

Chapter 7 looks at the phenomenon of hiring entire teams, known colloquially on Wall Street as "block trading in people" or "liftouts." Compared to stars who moved alone, those who moved in teams did not suffer a performance decline, suggesting that team-specific skills have a marked effect on performance. The loss of firm-specific human capital inevitable in a move can apparently be recouped to some degree by taking valuable colleagues along. This chapter also examines the four stages of a successful team move, which our findings suggest must be meticulously managed: courtship, leadership integration, operational integration, and cultural integration.

Chapter 8 looks at portability of performance in individual terms by examining the role of gender. Our data produced an unexpected finding:

star women's skills were more portable than those of their male counterparts. Women in a male-dominated profession appeared to nurture stronger external (and therefore portable) professional relationships in the face of institutional barriers to creating strong in-house relationships. When they moved, therefore, they could take their outside (not firm-specific) network with them. They suffered less from the loss of firm-specific relationships that never developed in the first place. Also, women were apparently more strategic than men about changing jobs: acutely aware that Wall Street culture was not a particularly female-friendly environment, women tended to do far more rigorous due diligence on a company before accepting an offer. Female stars have developed these strategies in response to structural conditions, but their approach (external relationships and intensive research) could also benefit men who wish to protect their own portability.

With part 3 the book's focus broadens to examine what firms can do to effectively develop, retain, and leverage their best and brightest. It also explores the applicability of our findings to other labor markets. Figure I.2 is a conceptual overview of the contents of part 3.

Chapter 9 looks in detail at the efforts of several Wall Street research departments to develop homegrown stars using a variety of approaches to

Figure I.2. A conceptual overview of the contents of part 3.

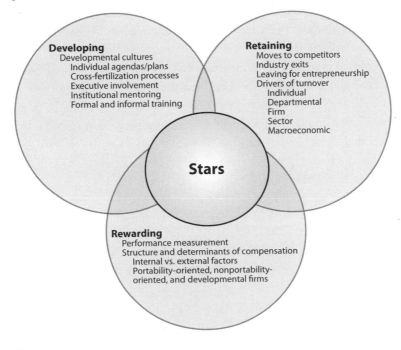

Developing
Developmental cultures
Individual agendas/plans
Cross-fertilization processes
Executive involvement
Institutional mentoring
Formal and informal training

Retaining
Moves to competitors
Industry exits
Leaving for entrepreneurship
Drivers of turnover
  Individual
  Departmental
  Firm
  Sector
  Macroeconomic

Stars

Rewarding
Performance measurement
Structure and determinants of compensation
Internal vs. external factors
Portability-oriented, nonportability-
oriented, and developmental firms

mentoring and training. To capture the methods and flavor of differing types and intensities of mentoring, the chapter draws heavily on interviews. It then describes a legendary training program used at three investment banks in succession, as well as alternative approaches to formal training employed successfully at other firms. We found that firms with what we call developmental cultures were far more successful than other firms at producing and retaining stars. The chapter also quantifies the effects of developmental cultures on performance, turnover, and compensation.

Chapter 10 looks at the question of whether stardom promotes turnover. One school of thought predicts high turnover because stars are highly visible; another asserts that stars are less apt to change jobs because they are well matched with their firms and have accumulated abundant firm-specific human capital. We found stars less likely than their more ordinary colleagues to change employers, but turnover rates differed markedly from firm to firm. We looked at factors at every level from individual to macroeconomic and at possible drivers of turnover by destination (moving to a competitor or leaving the industry).

Chapter 11 looks at entrepreneurship as a special case of turnover. The chapter examines the success records of analysts who left investment banks to strike out on their own. We found that stars were more likely than other analysts to choose entrepreneurship and more likely to succeed at it. The transition to entrepreneurship differs strikingly from a conventional move to a competitor. This chapter also looks at some factors affecting analysts' success at creating their own firms.

Chapter 12 examines performance evaluation and compensation. When it comes to evaluating analysts' performance, the *Institutional Investor* rankings are just the beginning; the industry employs multiple mechanisms for external evaluation of analysts, and research directors also generate voluminous internal data about their employees' activities. The chapter looks at how internal evaluation is performed, and its purposes. The chapter also examines several different approaches to determining individual compensation. We found that being ranked by *Institutional Investor* was the strongest predictor of compensation.

Chapter 13 surveys several studies of other professions—from corporate general managers to inventors, from surgeons to football players—that extend the conclusions suggested by our findings and thus their potential reach. The chapter ends with a discussion of the applicability of our findings to other professions and labor markets, and practical guidelines for employers and individual professionals about how to use our findings about the nature of exceptional professional performance and the crucial importance of context and fit.

Part One | Talent and Portability

1 | Moving On

In 1994, Josie Esquivel was in her seventh year at Lehman Brothers.[1] Though barely forty, Esquivel was a legend on Wall Street: having arrived at Lehman in 1987 with almost no experience, she had been voted one of the best equity analysts in her industry a mere eighteen months later. And a few weeks earlier she had finally achieved the goal she had set for herself upon first arriving in New York: she had been named the number-one apparel-and-textiles analyst on Wall Street. Yet here she was, pondering a move to Morgan Stanley.

"I never would have even considered such an offer before," Esquivel said at the time. "I am very loyal to Lehman Brothers. In the past, I have never even taken calls from headhunters or gone to interviews. I've seen a lot of people go to other firms. They received an increase in salary, but it wasn't worth trading in the privileges they had in Lehman's research department. We have always been given the freedom to be ourselves and create our own style. As long as I was producing, my style didn't matter."

But over the previous couple of years Lehman's research department had been rocked by cost cutting, defections, and the abrupt firing of Esquivel's mentor, research director Jack Rivkin. Two weeks earlier a client had warned Esquivel that her franchise would deteriorate unless she found a new employer. Another client had remarked that she deserved "a better firm than Lehman." After days of weighing the pros and cons, Esquivel had to decide. "Should I stay or move?" she asked herself repeatedly. "Can I move my franchise from Lehman to another firm? What should I look for in another firm if I decide to leave?"

☆ ☆ ☆

Over the last few decades, an increasing number of employed Americans have been, like Esquivel, knowledge workers.[2] And the growth of this employment sector is expected to continue: the Bureau of Labor Statistics reports that professional occupations will grow most quickly and add more jobs than any other employment category in the United States between 2002 and 2014.[3]

The individuals who hold such jobs—consultants, engineers, software developers, scientists, professors, physicians, technicians, attorneys, and the like—view themselves as free agents with portable skills. They attribute their job performance largely to their own talent, skills, and knowledge, and thus regard themselves as equipped to be equally productive in any appropriate workplace. This outlook has been endorsed and promulgated by scholars. Knowledge workers "own the means of production," as the management visionary Peter Drucker memorably put it, unlike manual workers whose skills are likely to be specific to a particular employer or production process. "They carry that knowledge in their heads and can therefore take it with them."[4] In the words of economist Oliver Williamson, knowledge-based workers such as artists, researchers, and administrators have "unique skills [that] are rarely of a transaction-specific kind. On the contrary, most of these individuals could move to another organization without significant productivity loss."[5]

The concept of an elite workforce composed of free agents with portable talent gained currency in the 1990s.[6] Books and articles on the *protean* career, the *boundaryless* career, the *career-resilient workforce, career pluralism, self-centered career management,* and the *free-agent career* all emphasized career flexibility.[7] Consultants urged talented knowledge workers to view themselves, in the words of one such book, as "free agents using different jobs and organizations as stepping stones in their self-managed careers."[8]

The free-agent outlook places a premium on portable skills that can be put to use in a series of jobs, and in which validation and marketability derive not only from the employee-employer relationship but from external networks of clients and peers.[9] Thus knowledge workers who expect to change jobs frequently—from one firm to another, between occupations, or by switching to self-employment—have been repeatedly advised to acquire a portfolio of flexible skills transferable to other work situations and to cultivate extensive external networks.[10]

More and more workers appear to be making employment choices on the strength of these propositions.[11] Thus Josie Esquivel's caution about how moving set her apart from most knowledge workers. One outcome of the tendency for knowledge workers to view themselves as free agents with portable intellectual talent is a fundamental shift in prevailing employment patterns from long-term employment to short-term transactional relationships between knowledge workers and their employers.[12] The transferability of talent is particularly alarming to employers in businesses where the bond between top performers and their clients renders an individual's client base mobile as well.[13] As a result, firms have become increasingly willing to poach top talent from rival firms.[14] In the New Economy, as Peter Cappelli has insightfully argued, companies must find ways of hiring and retaining workers who are increasingly far more committed to an occupation than to an employer.[15]

☆ ☆ ☆

Josie Esquivel grew up in Miami. Her mother, a former high school teacher, and her father, an entrepreneur, had emigrated from Cuba in 1952, two years before she was born. "My mother set equally high educational standards for me and my younger brother Raul," Esquivel recalled. "Another important family value was meritocracy. We were taught that if we worked hard to meet our goals in life, we would be rewarded." The day after her high school graduation, Esquivel went to work as a sales clerk at Burdines, a Florida department-store chain. That fall she entered the University of Miami. Her original goal had been clinical psychology, but her experience at Burdines piqued an interest in business management: "Despite my father's protests that 'no daughter of mine will have a job,' I retained my position at Burdines so that I could have my own money," Esquivel said. "I also loved my job at Burdines. I was very inquisitive, and I had a great manager, an older gentleman who took the time to explain purchasing, sales, and inventory to me. He also encouraged me to take management and economics courses."

Esquivel graduated in two and a half years and stayed on at Burdines. "I thrived on trying new layouts for the floor," she later recalled, "and beating the previous year's figures for sales and profit." Her zeal led to promotions, first to assistant buyer and then to manager of the juniors' department in Orlando where she increased profitability 55 percent by introducing a contemporary "Miami-style" look. After three years without another promotion, Esquivel asked herself what had happened to the rewards of hard work and began to notice that most of those who were promoted were men.

In 1980 she took a sales position at Borden's Dairy, responsible for the firm's dairy and frozen foods account with the large grocery chain Winn-Dixie. In this position, too, she took a hands-on approach: "No one had ever called on these accounts to ask them, 'What do you need from us?' The bigwigs would always play golf together but no one talked to the store managers who stocked the cases. . . . The store managers were surprised when I began to call on their accounts."

Esquivel performed well at Borden's, but at age twenty-six she left for Harvard Business School (HBS). Her brother was at HBS and had urged her to apply. She arrived apprehensive but determined.

> Since I had set this goal of succeeding at HBS, I absolutely could
> not fail. I was really nervous about my first case discussion, the
> Fieldcrest–St. Mary's Blankets case in Marketing. The case protago-
> nist, David Tracy, came to our class. At that time Tracy was the CEO
> of Fieldcrest; he had engineered a remarkable turnaround for the
> company. I studied hard to prepare for that case discussion and I was
> eager to get into the conversation. I waited and waited, until finally
> Professor Ben Shapiro called on me. I remember that I brought up
> the fact that women were the primary consumers of Fieldcrest's
> products, which no one had mentioned yet.

Esquivel made an impression on Shapiro and Tracy. "Josie had an interesting combination of intelligence and street savvy. She was average in smarts for HBS but had a better understanding of how people behave and more nerve than most people," Shapiro recalled. "She played well in that environment because she wouldn't let anyone push her around. She wasn't hard-hearted but she was tough-minded."

As president of the HBS Marketing Club, Esquivel invited Tracy back to HBS as a guest speaker shortly after he had left Fieldcrest for J. P. Stevens. He in turn invited Esquivel to interview for a job. "Josie had a great combination of tenacity and a drive to achieve," Tracy later said. "She also had a great reputation on the job market, so we put on the full-court press to hire her." Esquivel joined J. P. Stevens and was assigned a $16 million department-store towel brand that was losing market share.

☆ ☆ ☆

Prevailing business wisdom suggests that Tracy's intense wooing of Esquivel was warranted. "The basic resource in any company is the people," Nobel Prize–winning economist Gary Becker observed in a 2001 interview. "Remember Bill Gates' famous comment that if you took away the top 30 employees at Microsoft, it would be a pretty ordinary company. . . . In the New Economy, the reliance on people hasn't fallen, but has increased. We are much more a human capital based economy than the economy was even thirty years ago."[16] It has become almost commonplace, in fact, for professional firms to hail their employees as their most fundamental and valuable asset.[17] Sometimes this is mere lip service or cheerleading, but countless knowledge-based firms today are treating their human resources as, in essence, their business strategy, seeking to build competitive advantage on the skills and talents of their most productive employees. In a study of eight companies, management scholars Charles O'Reilly and Jeff Pfeffer wrote that the best companies concentrate hard on fostering the talents of their employees and went on to argue that developing and leveraging talent is the most sustainable source of competitive advantage.[18]

But a competitive strategy constructed on a faulty premise could spell disadvantage rather than the advantage the firm is seeking. In *Hard Facts, Dangerous Half-Truths, and Total Nonsense*, Jeff Pfeffer and Bob Sutton have demonstrated that many popular management practices (including star systems) are simply wrong, arguing that organizations must base their decisions on hard evidence.[19] Specifically, as we will see, talented workers can only be a source of sustained competitive advantage if their talents are imperfectly mobile. Thus, a sound grasp of what factors are responsible for the performance of talented employees has obvious urgency for employers of knowledge workers. And an empirical inquiry into the true extent of free agency could produce useful lessons for employees as well. Employees who attribute their success entirely to their own talent and effort might seek to sell their services to the highest bidder. But if part of that success is based on the capabilities of the firm, employees would do well to think strategically about factors other than compensation when contemplating a job offer. A star performer receives many attractive offers, but what will those companies do to keep the star at the top?

☆ ☆ ☆

A year after Josie Esquivel joined J. P. Stevens, her brand's sales and profit had increased substantially. Esquivel described her tactics:

I would go to the mills in North Carolina early in the morning with coffee and doughnuts and talk to the guys about sports and other topics of interest to them. Then I would ask them, "How can I make my towels more exciting?" and we would come up with lots of new ideas. I realized that we all really wanted the same goal—to make a difference and to increase sales. My toughest challenge was that, at age thirty-one, I had to fight with the head of the plant about why he needed to run my $24 million specialty towels for department stores in his $500 million mass-production plant. Department stores were on the bottom of his list, behind Wal-Mart, Sears, the military, and industrial customers.

Tracy described Esquivel's style as appealing but occasionally unnerving: "Josie always stuck her head out. She had a fiery personality, and she was highly critical of everything, including herself. She never hesitated to call something exactly as she saw it. . . . She did a terrific job on both the marketing and production sides. Josie always had a target, lots of drive, and she wanted to make a heck of a lot of money."

Four years after Esquivel joined J. P. Stevens, the firm ran into financial problems. Indignant at a 6 percent pay increase, which she viewed as scant reward for transforming a $16 million money-losing operation into a profitable $24 million business, she also saw little likelihood of better compensation, more visibility, or professional growth. Her brother, who had become a Wall Street research analyst, encouraged her to consider the same career. She knew the textile industry so well, he predicted, that she could succeed even with little knowledge of capital markets and portfolio management. Esquivel began interviewing on Wall Street.

Her business-school roommate, Lynda Davey, who had become an investment banker at Salomon Brothers, helped Esquivel prepare for interviews: "I remember thinking Josie was more exotic and fashion-forward than anyone on the Street. In 1987 on Wall Street, women wore very conservative business suits. Josie didn't look like Wall Street. For example, she had really long nails with red nail polish. . . . I recommended that she be more conservative. I told her she needed to cut her nails and lose the red polish. Josie's initial reaction to my suggestion about her nails was 'Absolutely not!' She did trim her nails for the interview, but she kept the red nail polish. . . . That was Josie's style. She wouldn't totally conform."

Esquivel joined E. F. Hutton in 1987 as an equity analyst in the apparel and textiles sector. An equity analyst at a brokerage house studies companies in a particular industry by analyzing financial data, keeping abreast of industry-wide and company-specific developments, and talking to management, customers, and suppliers. Analysts use this information to produce predictive models, research reports on firms' strategies and prospects, competitive earnings forecasts, and buy and sell recommendations. The recipients of their research are institutional investors like money-management firms, mutual funds, pension funds, and hedge funds; a typical analyst covers about a dozen companies[20] and may have hundreds of institutional clients. Because these clients have similar relationships with analysts at other investment banks, competing for their attention and trust is critical.

On a typical day Esquivel made thirty phone calls to clients and insiders in the apparel industry; she also traveled heavily to meet with both key investors and heads of major apparel companies. Her workday began with a 7:30 A.M. meeting at which she competed for the attention of the sales force and traders—analysts need the sales staff and traders to help draw clients' attention to their work—and she was often at her desk long after Wall Street had closed for the day.

Four months after Josie Esquivel joined E. F. Hutton, the stock market crashed. The Dow lost 22.6 percent of its value, or $500 billion, on "Black Monday" in October 1987. Hutton, already in financial trouble, could not weather the crash. The firm was snapped up by Lehman Brothers, an old-line but aggressive investment bank.

Jack Rivkin, Lehman's blunt, restless, energetic director of equity research, had joined the firm only ten months earlier. Rivkin, who had previously transformed Paine Webber's research department into a powerhouse, promptly declared his intention to build the best research department on Wall Street. Best, it was understood on the Street, meant highest-ranked in the annual poll that the trade magazine *Institutional Investor* (*II*) had been publishing since 1972. *II* asked institutional clients to name the analyst in each industry whose work had proven most helpful in the preceding year. First, second, third, and runner-up rankings were awarded in each sector (fewer than 3 percent of U.S. analysts were ranked in any given year). The magazine's rankings gave voice to and quantified the opinions of institutional clients, and its methodology was thorough; Wall Street viewed its findings as a measure of quality. *II*'s stamp of approval translated into credibility, power, visibility, and money; a top-ranked analyst could easily earn $1–2 million a year. *II* called its winners the "All-America Research Team," but ranked analysts were routinely referred to on Wall Street as "stars."

The overall rankings of research departments were based on the composite rankings of their individual analysts. Determined to lift Lehman out of its mediocre fifteenth-place position, Rivkin and his second in command, Fred Fraenkel (the former head of global research at Prudential), aimed to populate the department with ranked and high-potential analysts. To take advantage of the Hutton acquisition, they interviewed every Hutton analyst to determine whether he or she had the potential to become—or remain—a star.[21] Esquivel had not had time to prove herself; her first report was still in production. As Fraenkel later recalled: "Josie was very nervous during the interview because she thought that her career was over. But you could tell that she had what it takes to be an analyst. First, she knew the apparel industry really well. Second, she was very articulate. Third, whereas she was an inexperienced analyst, she demonstrated continuous improvement. To be honest, she was not a big-risk hire." Esquivel immediately buckled down to prove herself to her new superiors, but she worried that her dealings with Rivkin had gotten off to a rocky start:

> When I first joined Lehman, I felt that Jack did not care for me very much. . . . Jack had written some critiques on my research reports. I did not mind his critiques, but I just did not understand how to make the report better. I went to Jack's office and said, "Your comments tell me that my report isn't good, but they don't tell me how to change it. What should I do to make it better?" His initial response was, "It is just not a good report!" I knew that Jack was a very smart man who could help me. So I said, "Look, I'll work on making it better if you can tell me exactly what I need to do. Or at least tell me the book where I can look it up." Jack thought that was really funny, because, of course, there was no book. Finally he said, "The butler did it! You analysts think you're novel writers, so you make people wait until the end of the book to find out what to do with a stock. The butler did it!" I never forgot that advice. Very few of my reports did not start with "The butler did it." First I would give my stock recommendation, and then I would give my explanation.

She also looked to other analysts for help. Esquivel described an overture to Helane Becker, a star airline analyst:

> I had heard that she once pulled the phone out of a wall socket to prevent her competitors from calling their clients. I always thought, "I'd never do that, but this woman really has guts and I'm going to

befriend her." So I knocked on her door one day and said: "I was told that you're a very successful analyst and I really, really, really want to make II. I was hoping maybe you would teach me how to do that." . . . She pointed at the chair in front of her. I was older than she, and had worked in two businesses already, but I took notes like a schoolchild.

☆ ☆ ☆

Ever since Adam Smith, researchers have argued that workers' performance is largely a function of individual talent and that individuals of exceptional abilities outperform their less able counterparts.[22] General intelligence, which psychologists sometimes call "g,"[23] is often cited as a self-evident explanation for success. According to traditional psychological theories of human learning, knowledge determines job performance, and people who are more intelligent can acquire more job-pertinent knowledge faster than others. (The fact that Esquivel was able to complete a bachelor's degree in two and a half years is a textbook example of high g.) A series of empirical studies appears to confirm that intelligence is the key determinant of job performance.[24] The performance-intelligence link has been found to be especially strong in professional and managerial jobs, where higher intelligence consistently correlates with better job performance.[25]

Intelligence, itself a slippery concept,[26] is not the only individual factor that affects performance. "Emotional intelligence," conceptualized by popular author and psychologist Daniel Goleman as consisting of an array of attributes including self-awareness, self-regulation, motivation, empathy, and social skill, has also been shown to be a key factor in workplace success.[27] Emotional intelligence can be taught, but effective training is a lengthy process resembling therapy more than straightforward knowledge transfer. David McClelland identified deep motivational structures (such as need for achievement or for socialized power) as well as "competencies" (e.g., conceptual thinking, information seeking, organizational awareness, and developing others) as crucial to success.[28] Personality and temperamental attributes, such as energy, persistence, and a low anxiety threshold, have also been shown to contribute to high achievement.[29]

Research on star performance seems to indicate that stars differ from ordinary performers in how they approach their work.[30] Superior pattern-recognition ability has been shown to account for expert performance in a variety of domains.[31] A study of Bell Labs engineers—a uniformly high-IQ group—found that the key differences between outstanding and ordinary workers was not cognitive ability but behaviors such as taking initiative, self-management, leadership, and networking.[32] The motivations and competencies identified by McClelland and others—need for achievement, information seeking, and the like—have been used successfully to predict executive success and to discriminate between typical and outstanding performers. And feedback on competencies has also been shown to help performance.[33] Esquivel's work ethic, self-awareness, and eagerness to learn from others—from mill workers to senior star analysts—suggest that she would rank high in many of the less easily measurable elements of intelligence.

☆ ☆ ☆

Jack Rivkin and Fred Fraenkel developed a training program to teach promising Lehman analysts how to win clients' business and thus become stars. The program was limited to the twenty analysts Rivkin and Fraenkel thought would make the most of it, and Josie Esquivel was invited to participate. She spoke glowingly of the experience:

> The training sessions were invaluable. We covered every aspect of our job, from stock picking to dealing with the press, salespeople, retail brokers, clients, and company management. We also discussed how to make our reports interesting and different, so that clients would read them before reading any other analysts' reports. In each session, we were learning how to build a franchise that was molded to our strengths. Jack and Fred believed that you could develop a franchise in a number of different ways; there was no right way to do it. This view differentiated them from other research directors. I remember talking to our competitors at Merrill. They were shocked that we had programs to develop people into great analysts, because the traditional strategy was to just hire existing stars from other firms.

Esquivel was determined to use what she had learned to live up to Rivkin's battle cry, "*II* or die!" Of her quest to become a ranked analyst, she later said, "Ever since my brother had told me about *II*, I walked onto Wall Street saying, 'I want to be one of those stars.' I knew my industry, and since the goal was placed before me, I had to achieve it. Part of me thrived on that kind of challenge."

The effort paid off. *II* named Esquivel runner-up in the apparel industry less than eighteen months after she arrived on Wall Street. Very few analysts had ever made the grade so quickly.

Lehman's team structure helped analysts succeed. Lehman was among the first Wall Street firms whose analysts worked in teams and wrote joint cross-sector reports. "One of the things Jack and Fred were trying to do was to build individual superstars, but they were trying to build them around teams," Esquivel said. "They were always trying to get people to communicate across sectors or to do things with strategists. You just knew that working together was much more efficient than not."

As more and more veterans of the training program became ranked, Lehman rose from fifteenth in the *II* rankings in 1987 to seventh in 1988 and then to fourth in 1989. Among its stars were a higher percentage of women than at any other firm. Rivkin emphasized equal opportunity in the research department and encouraged female analysts to participate in recruiting. "Jack and Fred had a blind eye toward hiring," Esquivel said. "That is, they just wanted to hire the best analyst across industries."

☆ ☆ ☆

Another line of inquiry into the sources of outstanding professional performance focuses not on intelligence and other personal characteristics but on acquired skills: arrays of capabilities acquired through education, both formal and informal, and via on-the-job experience and training. The most fertile exploration of this set of abilities is human-capital theory, first articulated over forty years ago by Gary Becker.[34] In a nutshell, human-capital theory holds that more education, experience, and skill lead to higher productivity, which in turn increases earnings.

An individual's human capital—the fruits of his or her education and experience—is a set of assets that he or she owns and employs to earn income. Human capital can be invested in through the mechanisms of education and training; such investments may be made by individuals themselves or by their employers (and by governments and other dispensers of services as well). "The most successful companies and the most successful countries will be those that manage human capital in the most effective and efficient fashion—investing in their workers, encouraging workers to invest in themselves, provide a good learning environment . . . as well as skills and training," Becker said in a 2001 interview.[35] Human-capital theory, therefore, posits that work performance is driven by education and experience in addition to intelligence.[36] By and large, according to its proponents, individuals with higher levels of education and longer tenure will outperform their less-educated and less-experienced counterparts.

One of Becker's most fruitful insights has proven to be his distinction between two types of human capital: general skills, which are of potential value to numerous employers, and firm-specific skills useful only to a single employer.[37] General human capital, such as literacy, mathematical fluency, initiative, or efficient work habits, raises workers' productivity at many potential places of employment. (Esquivel's education, organizational, writing, and communication skills, and keen marketing sense would, and did, serve her well in many circumstances, not only at Lehman Brothers.) Firm-specific human capital, such as mastery of a proprietary computer system, increases workers' productivity at only one firm. The firm specificity of workers' skills is the degree to which their human capital is unique to a particular workplace and therefore not transferable to other firms. (Esquivel's in-depth knowledge of the firm's products, services, organizational processes, unique systems, idiosyncratic research reports, and teammates served her well at Lehman Brothers, but it was not transferable to other firms.) Becker's provocative distinction has generated disagreement, in academia and in the world of work, about the relative contribution of general and firm-specific skills to job performance, and to exceptional performance in particular. Forty years after Becker first introduced the concepts, this debate remains lively and unsettled.[38]

Because the decisive difference between general and firm-specific skills has to do with their value to more than one employer, much of this debate centers on the portability of job performance between one employer and another. Those who assign little importance to firm-specific human capital tend to assume that a given worker will be equally productive in comparable workplaces. Those who emphasize the firm-specific component of human capital argue that changing employers will cause a decline in performance until an employee develops skills specific to the new firm.

☆ ☆ ☆

A few months after ranking for the first time, Esquivel released a "buy" recommendation for Nike, a footwear company scorned by her counterparts. In fact, everyone else had released a more cautious "hold" on Nike stock. Esquivel remembers this episode with pride.

> When I made the Nike buy recommendation, I had just become
> ranked. So my name wasn't really out there yet. I caught a lot of flak
> for my Nike recommendation over the next few months. I was lam-
> basted by the Lehman sales force as the stock continued to decline

for several weeks; the stock price didn't start to rise for another five months. This was the kind of pressure that could make or break an analyst. Many analysts would hide when their prediction about a company was not confirmed. But I stood my ground. . . . I truly believed that Reebok's marketing success and stock price had peaked, and Nike had gotten its act together with a strong product lineup and clear brand strategy that were worth considering. It turned out that 1990 was the beginning of a seven-year run for Nike.

Lehman encouraged innovative reports, and Esquivel became known for "Clothes Line," a monthly summary of data on the Consumer Product Index, productivity, and the cost of cotton and polyester. She was the only analyst in her sector to compile such data for clients.

At the end of the year Esquivel ranked second in her sector. Meanwhile Jack Rivkin's ambition for his analysts was more than fulfilled: Lehman was the number-one research department on Wall Street. "If Lehman could have achieved top-five status, senior management would have considered that a job well done. So when we were ranked number one, it was remarkable!" said Greg Nejmeh, a Lehman building-and-construction analyst. "Perhaps Jack in his private moments had visions, but I don't think any member of the department had expected that to happen."[39] Recalling the research department's stunning achievement, Esquivel said, "We had done it together, and the camaraderie that Jack and Fred built was unbelievable. We were so ahead of everybody. It was truly special." Esquivel remained in second place for three years.

But in mid-1992 Lehman announced Jack Rivkin's departure due to "differences over the future direction of the equities business."[40] Esquivel recalled hearing this news:

I was in Ireland with my fiancé meeting my future in-laws when I got a call that Jack was leaving. I turned pale. I didn't know what to do. I remember feeling, "Now the golden run of our department is really over." Jack was the biggest mentor any of us had. . . . He was the one who would fight for the resources we needed. He was such a phenomenal leader. . . . Jack's departure was a very big deal for me because we had a great working relationship.

Though worried about the department, Esquivel consoled herself that Fred Fraenkel was sticking around: "Fred was hands-on, very smart, and likable. He had always been there for the younger analysts. I was personally very loyal to him, so I kept my nose to the grindstone." Even so, Esquivel dropped to third place in 1993.

But the next year, after she had made yet another accurate analysis of Nike, *II* finally named Esquivel number one. Fraenkel credited her ability to raise her ranking to eagerness to learn: "She went from a Harvard MBA to number one in her industry in a very short period of time just by following the training program. I mean, she followed it exactly. She used to write everything in her little black book, and with each year the book would get bigger and bigger. It had everything from what to say when no one picks up the phone to her calling schedule. She was a great student. She made a science of becoming a great analyst."

☆ ☆ ☆

The performance of any worker is clearly made up of some mix of innate, acquired, and organizational capabilities. But when so much strategic advantage can be gained by hiring, developing, and retaining stars, the question of how the performance of stars differs from that of the merely competent is a matter of great interest.

The phenomenon of stardom—of performers whose productivity massively outstrips that of their colleagues—is well documented. One study found that the top 1 percent of employees in highly complex jobs outperform average performers by 127 percent.[41] Another reported an eight-to-one productivity difference between star computer programmers and average programmers.[42] The top 1 percent of inventors was found to be five to ten times as productive as average inventors.[43] Data from different eras and disciplines have consistently shown that a small number of scientists account for a large number of publications.[44] Using citations in others' work as a measure of scientists' productivity generates an even more highly skewed distribution.[45]

The mythology of free agency and portability of performance also operates most resonantly in beliefs about stars. "The notion that some people are born with more talent than others is firmly ingrained in everyday psychology," as psychologist Dean Keith Simonton pointed out.[46] Americans and members of other individualistic cultures are particularly likely to attribute success to personal factors like intelligence, creativity, or talent. This tendency can be seen in sharpest relief in the contrast with more collectivist Asian cultures. "Self-enhancement biases," which cause individuals to recall or interpret events in a manner flattering to themselves, are more common in competitive, individualistic cultures than in collectivistic societies like

Japan.[47] Certainly, disinclination to claim responsibility for success may be more of a self-presentation style than a belief: members of collectivist cultures may believe themselves to be above average and responsible for their own success but consider it impolite or vulgar to say so. Intercultural studies suggest, however, that Asian cultures attribute much less importance to innate ability; motivation, learning, effort, and practice are seen as paramount.[48]

Although the prevalent belief that stars are innately better endowed than ordinary performers may be a cultural artifact, the existence of stars in individualistic cultures is not in doubt. More than a century ago Alfred Marshall's classic *Principles of Economics* first pointed out the emergence of superstars, whom Marshall characterized as individuals of extraordinary innate ability who capture high rewards for their services.[49] A stream of scholarly research has endorsed the high premium that the marketplace puts on exceptional performers. Almost a hundred years after Marshall, Sherwin Rosen even asserted that market forces would ensure that "relatively small numbers of people earn enormous amounts of money and dominate the activities in which they engage," even if the talent differences were small.[50]

If a star's performance is predominantly a function of his or her individual talent, or of learned but generally applicable skills, it is by definition readily portable to another employer. The problem for employers, as a series of theorists have pointed out, is that a resource that represents a potential source of sustained competitive advantage must possess four attributes: it must be valuable, it must be rare, it must be imperfectly imitable (and lack close substitutes), and it must be imperfectly mobile.[51] Exceptionally able employees are certainly rare and valuable resources with no ready substitutes, but as we have noted, they can only represent a source of sustained competitive advantage if they are not perfectly mobile.[52] In other words, if such employees' talent is readily portable from one firm to another, they cannot represent a sustainable source of competitive advantage for an organization because they can pick up and leave at any time.[53] If, on the other hand, their outstanding performance depends in part on resources and unique characteristics of the firm, and is thus attributable as much to the firm itself as to its stars, such a firm is well positioned to create a sustainable competitive advantage.[54]

One business-strategy theorist has spelled out the point memorably: "A brilliant, Nobel Prize–winning scientist may be a unique resource, but unless he has firm-specific ties, his perfect mobility makes him an unlikely source of sustainable advantage. Managers should ask themselves if his productivity has to do, in part, with the specific team of researchers of which he is a part. Does it depend on his relationship with talented managers who are exceptionally adept at managing creativity? Does it depend on the spirit of the workers or the unique culture of the firm?"[55]

These questions have immediate practical applicability to the workplace and the labor market. Individualized versions of these questions are worried over in corner offices and cubicles alike, and alternative answers are acted out every time a skilled professional like Esquivel faces the choice of changing employers or staying put. They have direct relevance as well to virtually every facet of managing knowledge workers, from hiring, training, and motivation to deployment, retention, and compensation.

☆ ☆ ☆

Esquivel reached top ranking at a turbulent time for Lehman Brothers: the firm had cut $200 million in expenses to prepare for an initial public offering, resulting in a 30–40 percent cut in bonuses. For two years, she had accepted that explanation for management's inability to compensate analysts competitively. She trusted Lehman's performance-evaluation system as fair because management relied on objective criteria but felt underpaid in view of her stellar performance. Though promised suitable compensation the following year, she was skeptical. Some colleagues and salespeople who had championed her work had left, as had some of her counterparts in trading. Esquivel commented at the time:

> How do you get things done in a service organization? You leverage your relationships, the relationships it took you years to build. They're based on trust, and trust is not easy to come by on Wall Street. For example, it took me about five years to be taken seriously by investment bankers. . . . As the firm went through cost cutting, many of my relationships were disappearing. Years and years of work were gone with each cost-cutting effort.

Esquivel felt that she was being expected to maintain her top ranking despite a heavier workload, fewer resources, and scant appreciation. She also kept in mind what someone had said when her number-one ranking was announced: "Your life just got worse. Once you make number one, you want to stay number one, and that's harder." Esquivel concurred: "I was always looking out for my next competition, to see who could really nail me." And the sense of mission that had made Lehman an exciting place to work in the late 1980s had evaporated.

Two weeks after her first-place ranking became public, Esquivel was invited to interview at Morgan Stanley, one of Wall Street's most respected investment banks. Both demand for research analysts and compensation were soaring, she had heard, and she knew that she had other options as well: more than a half-dozen investment banks would jump at a top-rated apparel-and-textiles analyst. Average compensation for a top-ranked analyst that year exceeded $1 million.

Morgan Stanley was known for a growing global presence.[56] A widely admired former investment banker, Mayree Clark, had just taken the helm of its research department. Clark was determined to improve the department's rankings, Esquivel learned when she interviewed, and her strategic plan included hiring top analysts.[57] Morgan Stanley had also recently adopted a global approach to research, creating twenty-one international teams and pioneering shared coverage of the same companies by multiple analysts. "[Morgan Stanley] put smart people in various parts of the world," one client commented, "and pulled together their coverage to make it comprehensible."[58] Historically, Morgan Stanley had very low turnover: its analysts embraced the firm's clubby culture and were cautious about outside hires. "Morgan Stanley is not for individual performers," one former star observed. "Many simply cannot get assimilated into its culture." Another had a different take: "Morgan Stanley is the rocket that can take your franchise to new highs. It might take time, but if you embrace its culture no other firm can give you a better platform."

Morgan Stanley had thirty-seven ranked analysts, and the department ranked sixth. But it had no one covering textiles and apparel, a sector of high strategic importance. The firm saw Esquivel as the cornerstone of its global coverage of textiles and pursued her eagerly and persistently.

☆ ☆ ☆

In the absence of hard answers to questions about the drivers of outstanding performance, employers tend to act on the assumptions embodied in their corporate cultures. Companies that embrace the view of knowledge workers as free agents with thoroughly portable skills tend to give short shrift to training and to deemphasize company-specific skills. Instead of developing their own stars, they reason that they can simply hire talented individuals from an efficient labor market. Some management theorists even explicitly recommend that managers shrink their investments in workers and in their firms' unique capabilities. Others advise employees in turn to minimize their efforts to master firm-specific skills.[59]

If performance is predominantly a function of individual talent and general skills acquired through education, changing employers should not influence individuals' short-term or long-term performance. But if professional performance is largely driven by firm-specific skills in conjunction with the firm's resources and capabilities, a decline in performance can be expected when an individual changes jobs because it takes time to develop skills specific to the new firm. When Josie Esquivel was at the top of her career at Lehman Brothers, how could she know how much credit to give herself and how much to give the company?

This book seeks to answer an apparently simple question—can you take it with you?—by looking at the job histories and performance records of the population of knowledge workers represented by Josie Esquivel: star Wall Street research analysts. As we will see in chapter 2, star research analysts appear more likely than members of most other professions to qualify for status as free agents. Thus they represent an ideal profession with which to perform a hard test of the portability of exceptional knowledge workers' skills.[60] If analysts' talents are as portable as many scholars and informal observers believe they are, practitioners of dozens of other professions from management consultants to CEOs to attorneys may also qualify as free agents.[61] If, on the other hand, skill specificity and dependence on their firms' resources characterize a profession so strongly qualified for free-agent status, the same is likely to be true of other knowledge-based professions as well. In short, if star research analysts' skills are not portable to other workplaces, it is highly unlikely that outstanding performance will prove to be readily portable in other knowledge-based professions. This question has profound implications for how organizations hire, develop, retain, compensate, and deploy their best performers. And it also has a direct bearing on the decisions that millions of individuals will make about their own careers.

☆ ☆ ☆

Josie Esquivel gazed at her computer screen. With forty-eight hours left to respond to Morgan Stanley's offer, she weighed the possible advantages of a move against a colleague's warning that she would never get the privileges at Morgan Stanley that she had enjoyed at Lehman. Years later she recalled her thoughts that night.

> I have to go back to the old question: What makes a great analyst?
> There are a number of attributes: organization, communication, and
> marketing. There are also my relationships with other people at the

firm—institutional salespeople who filter out information for the investors, traders who share information about stocks—and with clients. It makes me smarter as an analyst to have these relationships and communication flows. My relationship with the companies is the strength of my franchise. My institutional clients are my top priority, but my approach has always been to also focus on building relationships with company management. Finally, I need to determine if I will still be able to use my creative talents and independence in a firm with such a strong culture. Morgan Stanley seems to be so "white-shoe," so different from Lehman. The great thing about being an analyst is that I can work to my strengths. I don't have to be a certain kind of person. Going to Morgan Stanley might bring great career and financial opportunities, but will it require that I leave a piece of myself behind at Lehman Brothers?

We will return to Josie Esquivel's decision and its consequences in chapter 3 and subsequent chapters.

2 | Analysts' Labor Market

An ordinarily level-headed veteran of Wall Street, asked to explain how a security analyst becomes a star, answered, "This is a little like asking what it was that made Rembrandt or Van Gogh great artists. If there's an answer, it's probably that the greats in any profession are driven by an inner fire, and are gifted with a special spark."[1] This seasoned financial pro went on to describe an outstanding security analyst as "Diogenes with a lamp making rounds of New York, Boston, Detroit, Chicago, Los Angeles, and some tank towns in between."[2] Another observer of the profession characterized a skilled analyst as a "Renaissance man" with a "course fixed on truth."[3] Others have characterized analysts as financial detectives and wizards of odds.

A straightforward job description will seem pallid next to rhetoric about artistry and quests for truth. The security analysts we studied worked for investment banks, where they tracked firms in a particular industry and developed hypotheses about the economic futures of the companies they covered, typically ten to eighteen companies per analyst. Analysts write reports on these companies and issue recommendations on whether investors should buy, sell, or hold the companies' securities. The information and predictions analysts generate—earnings forecasts, detailed reports, stock recommendations—are in turn used by institutional investors, such as money-management firms, mutual funds, hedge funds, and pension funds, to guide their investment decisions.

This job description may sound more prosaic than glamorous, but the most admired Wall Street security analysts do indeed fulfill virtually every definition of stardom short of celebrity-level fame. For one thing, they are highly influential: it is not unusual for over eight hundred institutional clients to receive an analyst's reports and to seek out his or her advice. Analysts' opinions carry enormous weight and can create or destroy stockholder value by moving stock prices.[4] Analysts are celebrated for their brilliance. Newspapers and television newscasts solicit their opinions, and their own firms boast about them in newspaper and magazine ads. Powerful CEOs curry favor with them.

Analysts put a lot on the line in the ordinary course of their work. The flip side of their influence and visibility is peer pressure and the ever-present possibility of public humiliation. According to Steve Balog, a star analyst at Prudential and research director at Lehman Brothers, analysts are lucky if they make the right call two times out of three. "A lot of people can't handle being wrong that often, especially in front of everyone," Balog said. "Somebody's going to be right and somebody's going to be humiliated. Everyone knows—his entire firm knows, his competitors, his clients. It might even be in the *Wall Street Journal*. Everything you do is public. An analyst has to be a certain personality type to deal with occasional humiliation. People who think that the analyst's job is to quietly read, write, and run models are dead wrong." As Sidney B. Lurie, a former president of the New York Society of Security Analysts, put it in an influential article over forty years ago, "Every good analyst has to survive getting his nose bloodied in the stock market at one time or another. We only learn from experience."[5]

Analysts also work prodigiously hard and under a lot of pressure. "The analyst is a juggler. He has a lot of balls and he is trying to keep them all in the air," said veteran research executive Fred Fraenkel. "Eventually one of them is going to fall. . . . Juggling is the best thing that he can do." Lawrence Ross, a former analyst at Paine Webber, observed, "I think everybody feels, to some extent, like a victim of information overload. There is more information than ever before and less time to make sense of it."[6] A typical hard-charging analyst also spends approximately one-third of his or her time traveling, often on marathon trips to multiple cities and hard-to-reach corporate headquarters. Eighteen-hour days are routine. Analysts make dozens of phone calls a day to sources and clients. And they work under extreme pressure. "You'd like to do a month of research but you have to decide now," Steve Balog explained. "There are a lot of people that cannot do that, emotionally cannot do that. It just tears them up so much that they eventually quit. You're going to be very bothered. You're never going to be able to do it right." And analysts serve a multitude of masters—their institutional clients, investment bankers, salespeople, and traders—and have to weigh their competing interests. (Exhibit 2.1 describes a typical day in the life of a star analyst.)

Exhibit 2.1
A Star Analyst's Day

This feature story, reprinted from the *Wall Street Journal*, captures the time pressure, performance demands, and public exposure that typify the life of a ranked equity analyst. It only alludes in passing to the profession's intellectual demands.[7]

It's 7 A.M. on a recent Wednesday, and Nicholas Lobaccaro is back in the office he left only five short hours ago at Lehman Brothers' downtown headquarters overlooking the Hudson River.

Mr. Lobaccaro, who worked deep into the night preparing a report on the auto industry, is rushing to the morning conference call. The 30-year-old analyst is a new face at Lehman, having been lured away from Merrill Lynch in March with his teammate, auto-parts analyst Darren Kimball, 29. But his reputation has preceded him: Respected as a keen auto analyst, he was a runner-up on *Institutional Investor*'s All-America Research Team last fall, and he's the No. 2 auto-stock picker in this year's *Wall Street Journal* All-Star Survey.

Now, as he takes a seat at the head of a conference table next to Mr. Kimball, who won All-Star awards in this year's survey for stock picking and earnings-estimate accuracy, Lehman's entire sales force will be hanging on his every word. After explaining the reasoning behind a series of upgrades on auto stocks, the duo faces a barrage of questions about how an interest-rate increase would affect the auto industry. . . .

Don't worry if you missed something. Mr. Lobaccaro will repeat this spiel countless times throughout the day in conference calls, meetings with clients and interviews with the press. "It does get to be redundant," he says of the seemingly endless repetition.

Such is the life of an equity research analyst: early mornings followed by late nights, with lots of phone calls and meetings in between. Then there's the heavy travel schedule. Analysts typically spend a good deal

Exhibit 2.1 (continued)

of their time in the air, flying to one city after another to meet with clients, to visit the companies the analysts cover and to attend industry conferences. . . .

After a quick coffee break, Mr. Lobaccaro starts working the phones. He calls a few reporters to alert them about his latest research note. He also makes several unsuccessful attempts to reach CNBC anchor Maria Bartiromo, but settles for leaving two detailed phone messages summarizing his revisions.

Between calls to clients and reporters, Mr. Lobaccaro fields a call regarding his choice of car for a weekend jaunt to the Hamptons. "One of the perks of following the auto industry is that the auto companies have fleets of press vehicles. For this weekend I was trying to get a Jaguar, but they offered me a Mustang," he says. . . .

Mr. Lobaccaro sent out a mass voice-mail message late last night to about 150 clients briefing them on his report, and early this morning he will send those same clients a copy of the research note via e-mail. But "at the end of the day, there is no substitute for face-to-face meetings," he says.

Soon it's 11:30, time to hail a cab for a dash to a midtown meeting with Circle T Partners LP, a $230 million hedge fund. The co-managers grill Messrs. Lobaccaro and Kimball on the merits and shortcomings of their stocks, the outlook for the industry and some good stocks to short. Forget what you've read about posh Manhattan restaurants where the power elite meet—lunch is a quick sandwich in the office.

Then it's back downtown to make a 2 P.M. conference call. The two analysts, who met in 1990 during their senior year at the University of Pennsylvania's Wharton School, once again discuss their forecast for the industry, this time with clients listening in on the line.

When the conference call ends, Mr. Lobaccaro is soon inundated with calls from clients. After one particularly trying conversation, he hangs up the phone, takes a deep breath and says: "I'm tired." Ah, the first signs of wear and tear on this All-Star analyst.

But don't fret for Nick Lobaccaro. Sure, he puts in 18-hour days and often has to work on weekends. But he certainly makes the most of his downtime.

"When we do have the time off . . . we like to have as much fun as possible," Mr. Lobaccaro says. And when he can make it, that means a trip to Brazil. . . . There is no Latin American fest scheduled for tonight. After more phone calls and some clowning around with co-workers, it's off to dinner at a swanky Upper East Side Italian restaurant to meet with an analyst from Tiger Management, a big-time hedge fund. Mr. Lobaccaro calls it a day after the meal ends at 8:30. Tomorrow, it starts all over.

Most star analysts arrive on Wall Street via the traditional business-school route or from the industries they cover. Others are graduates of doctoral programs in technical specialties ranging from economics to geochemistry to mathematics. But unconventional backgrounds are far from rare. The ranks of analysts include former journalists, a former Latin teacher, a Ph.D. in medieval art history, and a taxi driver studying for a doctorate in philosophy. One analyst was an intelligence officer in the Marine Corps; another was an intelligence analyst at the National Security Agency. The mix of highly specialized advanced education and idiosyncratic backgrounds probably contributes to the profession's collective reputation for raw brilliance and irrepressible ambition.

Finally, star analysts are exceedingly well paid. Because renowned analysts help to attract underwriting and trading business to their firms, they are extremely valuable to their employers. In 1998 top analysts typically earned from $2 million to $5 million annually, and a handful were said to earn as much as $25 million.[8]

■ Investment banks, also known as brokerage houses, make money from underwriting, merger-and-acquisition advisory services, proprietary trading, and trading securities for institutional clients. These institutional clients are money-management firms like Fidelity Investments or TIAA-CREF or pension funds, which invest their clients' money by purchasing stocks. Wall Street calls investment banks "the sell side" of the investment process and money-management firms "the buy side."

Sell-side research analysts follow companies and stocks in specific industries to help their buy-side clients make sound investment decisions. The investment bank's institutional sales force promotes its analysts' research to institutional clients. Sell-side analysts' reports are also often disseminated to the financial community at large.

Buy-side money-management firms also employ their own research analysts, whose job description resembles that of their sell-side counterparts.

(continued)

But buy-side analysts track more companies, often as many as one hundred at a time; such a large portfolio prevents them from performing in-depth analyses. Buy-side analysts thus depend heavily on sell-side analysts' more thorough reports when making recommendations to the portfolio managers who ultimately make buy-side investment decisions. This book focuses exclusively on sell-side analysts.

Sell-side research is not sold directly to the buy side. Instead, institutional clients pay indirectly, through trading commissions, for the research they value most. In other words, the allocation of trading commissions is a mechanism for rewarding valuable research and service. Part of the revenue from commissions is used to fund research. This process will be discussed in more detail in chapter 12. ∎

Are Star Research Analysts the Ultimate Free Agents?

Star research analysts are widely regarded on Wall Street as free agents. Wall Street considers itself a meritocracy, and outstanding performance of any kind tends to be attributed to personal traits like raw intellectual power, knowledge, and effort. But even in this competitive and self-congratulatory culture, research analysts' skills are considered uniquely portable. "Analysts are one of the most mobile Wall Street professions because their expertise is portable," said research director Fred Fraenkel, explaining perceptions on Wall Street. "I mean, you've got it when you're here and you've got it when you're there. The client base doesn't change. You need your Rolodex and your files, and you're in business."

Analysts themselves agree wholeheartedly: they typically view themselves as free agents with fluid and mobile skills. Some even boast quite openly that they are better free agents than professional athletes. They compare themselves to golfers rather than baseball or basketball players in that their performance rests entirely on their own shoulders. Of the individuals we interviewed on Wall Street, 85 percent maintained that analysts' performance is independent of the companies they work for and thus thoroughly portable. Wall Street insiders also believe that talented analysts draw more heavily on the social capital they acquire outside the firm—their networks of external information providers—than on the resources of the firm itself.[9] Wall Street's near universal consensus on this point is evident in the fact that star analysts in hot industries receive as many as two overtures a month from competing firms.

Nature and Nurture?

What accounts for outstanding performance in knowledge-based professions? Are such job skills and performance records portable? To put the question another way, to what degree are exceptional performers like star equity analysts really the free agents they think they are?

Economists and sociologists have been examining these questions for almost a century. But they have provided no clear-cut answers, mainly because of inadequate data but also because the two research traditions have approached the question from fundamentally different vantage points, using different kinds of data. Empirical studies in economics have relied mostly on data about individuals, while sociologists and social psychologists have trained their attention on groups and organizations. Meanwhile, no one really knows for certain why star performers excel, notably including stars themselves. Stars almost unanimously attribute their success to their own skill and hard work, and few think strategically about the nonportable resources that might have helped them reach—and remain at—the top of their profession.

In the absence of hard data, managers have typically adopted one of two competing explanations for outstanding performance, which for the sake of brevity we will call *nature* and *nurture*. Those who attribute excellence to nature typically either hire in large numbers, hoping that a few stars will emerge from the crowd, or try to lure proven performers away from other firms.[10]

Adherents of nurture theory, on the other hand, maintain that stars can be homegrown through a mix of training, mentoring, incentives, and a resource-rich and supportive environment.[11] These managers and firms try to retain and spur on their best and brightest by providing constant training and mentoring, fostering loyalty and a long-term perspective, closely monitoring performance, and offering an achievement-nurturing environment.[12]

How can we attempt to sort out what drives star performance? As it happens, the labor market for security analysts exhibits a set of unusual characteristics that make it a remarkably suitable real-life laboratory for examining the sources of outstanding workplace performance. The unique features of this labor market may even make it possible to resolve some of the most pressing questions about the nature of stellar performance.

Unique Features of the Analysts' Labor Market

We have already noted one striking feature of analysts' profession and culture: a strong prevailing belief in free agency, and thus in the portability of outstanding performance. Six other features of analysts' labor market are in themselves unusual and in combination unique.

Standardized Measures of Performance

The performance of security analysts was assessed annually, according to clear standardized measures, and publicly reported. The trade journal *Institutional Investor*, familiarly known as *II*, has compiled and published an annual ranking of the best stock analysts since 1972.[13] The magazine ranked the top analysts in each industry, awarding them first-, second-, and third-place status plus a runner-up (it was possible for analysts to tie, making for more than four ranked analysts in a given sector). The magazine called its winners "the All-America Research Team," but on Wall Street they were casually referred to as first-teamers, second-teamers, and so on, as ranked analysts, or simply as stars or superstars. (We will use the terms *ranked analyst* and *star analyst* interchangeably.) According to research director Jack Rivkin, "The shorthand for figuring out who had the expertise pretty quickly became the *Institutional Investor* poll." In 1996, fewer than 3 percent of all U.S. analysts were ranked by *II*.

II awarded its rankings by asking institutional money managers to assess the analysts whose research on U.S. equities they had found most helpful in the preceding twelve months. Respondents were asked to evaluate analysts on six criteria: earnings forecasts, industry knowledge, overall service, accessibility and responsiveness, stock selection, and quality of written reports. Each analyst in each industry sector received a single overall numerical score. Votes were weighted in keeping with the relative size of the voting institution. The identities of the respondents were kept confidential. A small percentage of analysts achieved rankings in multiple sectors. Some stars in a given year continued to be ranked in subsequent years.

"We were using as objective a methodology for a subjective measure as you could," explained David Wachtel, *II*'s former publisher, "by breaking it down into six real areas of what these people were interested in." In 1996, the last year covered by our study, analysts were ranked in eighty industries, such as telecom services, automobiles, health-care services/managed care, media, and information technology. *Institutional Investor* based its ratings that year on responses from roughly 1,300 analysts' clients, or approximately 68 percent of the 300 largest financial institutions in the United States, and other investment-management enterprises.[14]

The *II* rankings were influential because they were comparative, public, efficient, and standardized, and because they represented the aggregated responses of hundreds of buy-side firms. But the *II* poll was fundamentally a public proxy for a parallel mechanism that was functionally embedded in the system by which securities are bought and sold on Wall Street. It was this system that linked the research a firm provided its institutional clients to the revenues that the firm collected from those clients.

This system, known on Wall Street as *client votes, broker votes,* or *the vote-gathering system,* was the method by which large buy-side entities— such as Fidelity, TIAA-CREF, the Ohio State Teachers' Retirement System, and their many counterparts—chose where to place orders to buy and sell securities. These institutional buy-side clients polled their own analysts (as well as portfolio managers and traders), at intervals ranging from quarterly to annually, about which sell-side analysts' work they had found most useful in the preceding period. These internal polls were then used to allocate trading commissions during the next period. In other words, the most valuable research and service were rewarded with trading commissions.

The client-vote system was initiated in the 1970s as a way for the buy side to leverage its power to increase the then-mediocre quality of sell-side research departments' service. Buy-side firms rated sell-side analysts to elicit good service by stimulating competition for their votes. "The CIO of Fidelity can call up the head of sales or research here and tell us that he's not receiving the level of service that he expects," explained an insider at a large firm. "He can then tell us that if we don't improve the level of business, he's taking his business elsewhere. It allows us to be held accountable." Some client firms also forwarded their votes and accompanying comments to the various research departments with whom they did business, but this number was small—about fifty or so—and did not provide a representative or reliable sample of overall buy-side opinion. Obviously, banks could tell how well their research was received overall by assessing how their trading commissions were rising and falling, but this was a blunt instrument for assessing the quality of a department. The allocation of trading commissions did not provide information about specific analysts (a client might be highly pleased with, say, an automotive analyst but might not have occasion to trade in that sector in a given quarter), nor did it provide information about exactly what aspects of the analysts' skills were valued or in need of improvement. Trading commissions were also affected by the quality of institutional salespeople and traders. Because of the relative opacity of the client-vote system, *Institutional Investor* quickly established itself as an arbiter of analyst talent by capturing thorough, systematic, transparent data from a much larger portion of the client base.

Wachtel called the *II* rankings "as close to getting an objective picture of what institutions are looking for as you can get," and the *II* rankings were indeed regarded, both on Wall Street and by scholars, as a reliable proxy for performance.[15] According to Fred Fraenkel, Shearson Lehman Brothers' research director, "Before *II*, you didn't know who the best analysts were. . . . *II* had an unbelievable effect. It started knighting people as *the* experts. . . . You could be seventh best in the United States and you're nothing. It's either one, two, three, runner-up, or nothing." One former director of global equity research explained the motivational aspect of the rankings: "What it represents is a standard of excellence and a goal for people to shoot at, so that when they walk out these double doors every day they know what they're supposed to do. They're supposed to be top three in their respective sectors. And 99 percent of the behavior that you need to have to achieve that is good for the firms—good for the revenue and the franchise enhancement of the firm."

Studies have confirmed that ranked analysts exhibit superior performance.[16] Ranked analysts' reports have also been found to be less likely to follow the crowd and less predictable,[17] and star analysts' forecasts have a greater impact on security prices than those of their unranked peers.[18] Thus investment banks that employed star analysts were able to offer their clients both more accurate and more influential research reports.[19] Analysts who made the All-America Research Team regularly earned far more than also-rans.

Few other professions have such quantifiable measures of success or make such systematic and transparent distinctions between outstanding and ordinary performers.[20] In the words of Mike Skutinsky, who developed electronic systems for analysts at Paine Webber, Lehman Brothers, and Salomon Smith Barney, "What job do you know that gets rated every year? . . . I don't think engineers are ranked. I don't think accountants are ranked. Could you ever tell who has the best accountants? . . . You're out there, you're measured every year for the industry you follow. . . . Your name is either in that book or it's not in the book." Fred Fraenkel concurred: "The poll is a good representation of where customers find value from research analysts.

There aren't many other jobs in America where people's performances are externally rated so specifically."[21]

A Compact and Transparent Labor Market

In 1996 there were about ten thousand sell-side equity analysts in the United States. Very few investment banks employed more than one hundred domestic equity analysts. The compactness of this population made it possible to collect reliable data on the entire roster of ranked analysts and on virtually the entire population of unranked equity analysts, rather than having to rely on a statistical sample.

And the small size of this population, in combination with the clear distinction between outstanding and ordinary performers provided by the *II* rankings and the public nature of analysts' work as manifested in their reports, also meant that equity analysts' performance was readily visible to outsiders. In other professions, as a rule, the quality of an employee's performance was far more apparent to his or her employer than to other potential employers, affecting who left and who stayed.[22] In the labor market for equity analysts, such information asymmetries were minimal.

Economists would be likely to predict unusually high turnover among analysts, in keeping with the principle that individuals in high-visibility professions are more likely to change jobs. According to this principle, turnover occurs only when a worker is worth more to an outside employer than to the worker's own employer, and an outsider needs information in order to recognize the worth of an individual employed by a rival firm.[23] In the security-analyst job market, as Steve Balog pointed out, "There's a tremendous amount of information about who the good ones are. Every time you write a research report, essentially three thousand copies of your résumé go out. You can have a great investment banker somewhere in the bowels of Lehman Brothers and nobody knows. But a research analyst—they're out there. They're voted for; their picture's in a magazine, maybe their name's in a magazine. . . . It's very, very liquid." The same reasoning would predict higher turnover among star analysts than among their unranked colleagues. In the words of one scholar, "It is individuals from the top of the distribution who get raided."[24] Our data will enable us to determine whether or not star analysts did in fact change employers more frequently than did their unranked counterparts.

Complete and Reliable Data

Thanks to rich and thorough data, we can examine analysts' achievements at many different levels: demographic, departmental, firm, sector-specific, and intertemporal. Research on performance in other professions has typically been restricted to single variables, either about knowledge workers or about their work environments, due to incomplete data and the lack of objective measures of productivity.[25]

Another virtue of the data available on security analysts is that it is archival rather than self-reported, and thus more trustworthy. Detailed mobility data were available for all analysts: analysts' quarterly earnings forecasts identified their employers, and press coverage of star analysts' moves from one employer to another provided exact move dates. Such data made it possible to examine the impact on performance of all these variables simultaneously and to control for a wide range of potential drivers of performance.

Minimal Interference from Extraneous Factors

Compared to most professionals, security analysts encountered few external distractions when they changed employers. Nearly all star U.S. analysts—about 90 percent—worked in the New York City metropolitan area. Thus they rarely relocated when they switched jobs and did not have to contend with moving and related distractions that could negatively affect performance.

Analysts who moved from one firm to another did not experience a change in the industries they tracked. An analyst who specialized in biotechnology at Morgan Stanley would cover the same sector if he or she joined Goldman Sachs. Their new employers hired them for the knowledge they had already accumulated, and they rarely needed to acquaint themselves with entirely new companies or sectors. Analysts also relied heavily on external networks—management at the firms they covered and industry associations—that did not change when they moved.[26] And they ran their own financial models, which were easily transferable between one brokerage house and another.

Nor did their clients change. Institutional investors subscribed to the reports of numerous analysts, from multiple investment banks, about a particular industry. An analyst whose services were valued developed a following and did not lose clients in the course of moving from firm to firm.

Institutional clients' loyalty to individual analysts was evident in their responses to *Institutional Investor*'s surveys.[27]

For all these reasons, many analysts continued to repeat the well-worn Wall Street saying that the only thing that changed when they moved from one firm to another was the letterhead. And for the same reasons, it was uniquely feasible when examining the employment histories of star equity analysts to attribute changes in the job performance of those who changed employers mainly to the effects of a change in organizational setting.

Participation of Search Consultants in Hiring

Virtually without exception, top jobs on Wall Street were filled with the help of search consultants, colloquially known as headhunters. The role of recruiters is particularly intriguing in the labor market for equity analysts, whose transparency thanks to the *Institutional Investor* rankings would theoretically suggest that intermediaries are unnecessary. That is, if everyone knew who the best automotive analysts were, why would a firm in need of an automotive analyst pay hundreds of thousands of dollars for help hiring one? What did search consultants contribute to the dynamics of skill portability across jobs?

Search consultants functioned as matchmakers. They created a more efficient marketplace for both client banks and job candidates by facilitating the allocation of talent. They provided their clients with real-time market intelligence on candidates and their firms. They provided the information about candidates that didn't appear on a résumé—including information about how best to attract that candidate. They also prepared candidates for interviews by providing specific preparation points and advice about what the hiring firm was looking for. And they often continued to provide assistance after the placement had been made and the analyst was acclimating to the new firm.

In the analyst labor market, search consultants enjoyed an unusual degree of integration into the workings of the research departments that were their clients, due in part to the economic model governing the relationship between recruiters and investment banks: search firms were typically hired on retainer.[28] Retained search was a client-driven process; job candidates did not hire retainer firms. Thus recruiters who worked on retainer were highly motivated to keep longstanding clients happy by conducting exhaustive searches. And given the time they spent learning the ins and outs of the industry sector they specialized in, search consultants accumulated greater knowledge of both the talent market and the job market than any other player was likely to possess.

Scholars who have studied the role of intermediaries in the job market speak of clientelization, a term borrowed from anthropologist Clifford Geertz.[29] Clientelization occurs when a customer develops a long-term relationship with a service provider rather than considering new providers for each transaction. Search consultants in the equities-analyst labor market had achieved a high level of clientelization.

Given the small number of large investment banks and their concentration in New York—all six of the largest investment banks were located within a few miles of each other—a search consulting firm could only accept one or two as clients without cutting too deeply into the pool of potential candidates. (Poaching from one's own clients was prohibited.) And having only a few client banks motivated headhunters to keep the relationships well-tended. Other factors also contributed to the high degree of embeddedness enjoyed by analyst recruiters. Many had begun their careers in investment banking, and thus possessed insider knowledge.

Search consultants' unusual degree of embeddedness in the industry gave them acute insight into individual and environmental factors that conditioned the fit between an analyst and a bank. It also both positioned and motivated them to maximize the likelihood of a good match culturally—and thus, at least theoretically, to enhance portability of performance.

A Mechanism for Registering External Reaction to Star Analysts' Moves

Finally, many investment banks were companies whose stock was publically traded. Many institutional investors' money managers tended to follow internal developments at the banks very closely, and star analysts' job changes were reported prominently in the financial press.

Thus it was feasible for investors to register their reactions to a given analyst's job change by buying or selling shares in the original or destination firm. We collected data in an effort to determine whether or not this in fact occurred and, if so, to capture the market's reactions.

☆ ☆ ☆

Because of this unique constellation of job-market characteristics, Wall Street equity analysts appeared to be not merely a suitable population to scrutinize but a near ideal test case for the proposition that outstanding performance in knowledge-based professions is portable from one employer to another. Analysts' career moves also offered a rare opportunity to learn more about the nature of exceptional job performance in general.

This book will look at what happened to the job performance of star Wall Street security analysts when they moved from one employer to another. By doing so, we will offer new answers to long-debated questions about the nature of work performance among educated professionals whose job skills are knowledge based.

Our study examined the careers of 1,053 star analysts at 78 investment banks.[30] For comparative purposes, we also employed data on non-star analysts at approximately 400 investment banks. To flesh out our findings and shed light on the mechanics and culture of the profession, we conducted in-depth interviews with over 200 analysts, with research directors, traders, salespeople, and investment bankers at 37 investment banks, and with the institutional investors who are analysts' clients. These interviews supplement hard data with accounts of the inner workings of research departments and the experiential dimensions of mobility.

3 | The Limits of Portability

When an analyst changes employers, his or her education and innate abilities, general skills, and relationships with clients and outside contacts are readily portable to another employer.[1] But the supportive relationships and resources at the analyst's former employer, which represent sources of performance-enhancing information and insight, are immediately lost. Figure 3.1 illustrates the nature of an equity analyst's human capital by depicting Josie Esquivel's professional relationships, resources, and skills at Lehman Brothers as multiple spokes on a wheel. Though specific to equity analysts, most of these relationships and resources have close analogues in other knowledge-based professions. For many professionals, for instance, outstanding performance is not solely a matter of expertise; it also calls for attentiveness to relationships with clients and a certain amount of self-promotion. Figure 3.1 also specifies which of the various components of an analyst's human capital are portable to another employer and which are nonportable.

In the course of surveying the spokes on the human-capital wheel—the drivers of an analyst's performance—this chapter will explain a bit further how analysts perform their jobs. Then we will report what we discovered about the nature of outstanding job performance and what happened to the performance of star analysts who moved to new employers. Overall, star performance declined, sharply and for a prolonged period of time, following a move. As we will see, however, there is no simple answer to the

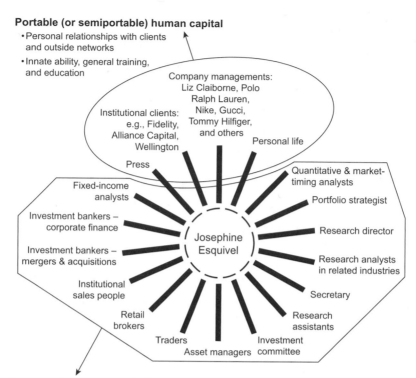

Portable (or semiportable) human capital
- Personal relationships with clients and outside networks
- Innate ability, general training, and education

Company managements:
Liz Claiborne, Polo
Ralph Lauren,
Nike, Gucci,
Tommy Hilfiger,
and others

Institutional clients:
e.g., Fidelity,
Alliance Capital,
Wellington

Personal life

Press

Fixed-income analysts

Quantitative & market-timing analysts

Portfolio strategist

Investment bankers – corporate finance

Josephine Esquivel

Research director

Investment bankers – mergers & acquisitions

Research analysts in related industries

Institutional sales people

Secretary

Retail brokers

Research assistants

Traders

Investment committee

Asset managers

Nonportable human capital
- Firm's supporting capabilities and reputation
- Routines and procedures, teammates, managers
- Knowledge and skills gained from in-house training programs and on-the-job experience that have no value outside the firm
- Internal formal and informal networks, which take years to develop, and firm's capabilities, which take years to learn how to successfully leverage

Figure 3.1. Portable and nonportable resources and human capital. Source: Boris Groysberg and Laura Morgan Roberts, "Leading the Josie Esquivel Franchise (A), (B), & (C)" (Harvard Business School teaching note, 5-405-028).

question "Are stars portable?" A better question would be "Which stars are portable under which circumstances—and why?"

The Drivers of Analysts' Job Performance

Chapter 1 briefly presented economist Gary Becker's penetrating distinction between general and firm-specific human capital, which the accompanying sidebar discusses in more detail. Broadly speaking, general human capital is understood to be portable between one firm and another. An analyst's relationships with contacts at the companies he or she covers are portable, for instance, as are relationships with clients and external information networks. By contrast, firm-specific human capital is, by definition, not portable. The distinction between portable and nonportable human capital is thus the central conceptual underpinning of this inventory of equity analysts' human capital.

■ General Human Capital

Knowledge workers have been described as textbook examples of employees whose value resides in their endowment of general human capital, both innate and acquired over time via formal education and work experience.[2] Knowledge workers' rich endowments of general human capital are also invoked to explain why they are in a position to function as free agents. Newly minted lawyers, to take one example, bring to entry-level legal jobs the fruits of sixteen years of general education plus a fundamental familiarity with legal concepts and statutes acquired in law school; they then acquire further general skills on the job. That they provide their services directly to clients, rather than exclusively to their employer, gives them additional transferable skills, both substantive and interpersonal, that can be employed in a variety of settings.[3] To the extent that knowledge workers' networks of professional contacts are external, they, too, are readily transferable to rival firms.

Because knowledge workers now expect to change firms often, the argument continues, and because a portfolio of transferable skills is crucial to future success,[4] they deliberately invest in general skills[5] and external networks of colleagues. Some economists assert that human capital has become more portable in recent years in response to increased rates of job loss and declines in job security, phenomena that have tended to make the employment relationship for white-collar workers more fragile.[6]

From an economic standpoint, dependence on general human capital has consequences for firms. Competing firms tend to bid up wages for high-performing workers whose skills are not firm-specific. Thus highly skilled knowledge workers can extract most of the value they contribute to their firms; in other words, the profits on their work flow largely to themselves rather than their employers.[7]

Firm-Specific Human Capital

Job skills and tacit knowledge specific to a particular firm equip an individual to make the most of that firm's resources, methods, and culture—

(continued)

its information system and other technologies, in-house training, as well as informal networks, supportive supervisors, and talented coworkers.[8] According to proponents of human-capital theory, mastery of the idiosyncrasies of a particular work setting is a sine qua non of high productivity, but the set of skills that constitutes such mastery has no value outside the firm. Economist Gary Becker used his own workplace as an example.

> The culture at the University of Chicago is very different from the culture of competitors like Stanford or Harvard. If I were to leave Chicago, I would lose that knowledge and I would have to acquire something comparable at another university. These differences can be found in pretty much all companies now, and the distinction also applies to particular technologies and the knowledge required to apply them. . . . If you leave that company, that knowledge becomes obsolete.[9]

The main explanatory mechanism proposed by human-capital theory is job tenure: more on-the-job experience increases the firm-specificity of workers' skills, which in turn increases productivity. Empirical studies have found close links between tenure and performance.[10] And studies of many occupations have confirmed the decisive importance of accumulated firm-specific human capital.[11] One such study attributed workplace success to superior ability to leverage intrafirm resources strategically. The top-performing knowledge workers were those who figured out how to make the most of the intrafirm networks and other capabilities available to them.[12] The investigators emphasized the non-transferability of such knowledge and its link to job tenure.[13]

Empirical studies have also confirmed the firm specificity of management skills. One study documented the struggles of newly hired managers to acquire skills specific to the new workplace and how long—two to three years—it took them to do so.[14] Another found that newcomers' performance tends to suffer, particularly if success depends on contributions from others in the organization.[15]

Human-capital theory ascribes efficacy to firm-specific training and employee-development programs, and empirical studies in turn have found a link between such training and productivity.[16] Researchers have also found that job-specific investment (on the part of both employees and employers) increases dramatically with job tenure, seniority, and rank.[17]

Portable Human Capital: What Mobile Analysts Take with Them

Star analysts often assert that they enjoy portable franchises primarily because they can carry with them their relationships with the companies they cover and the clients whose informational needs they fulfill.

Relationships with Companies

Access to management of the companies they track is crucial to analysts' work. A close relationship with top management gives an analyst an edge, and many analysts cultivate the CEOs of the companies they track. (Prior to the Fair Disclosure era, beginning in October 2000, companies could play favorites among analysts, giving some better information and access than they did to others.)

When star analysts move, their corporate relationships move with them. This is not only a universal expectation; it is sometimes a selling point. When Morgan Stanley approached Josie Esquivel with an offer, for example, the firm hoped to acquire many of her corporate relationships, including such big-ticket names as Gucci, Polo Ralph Lauren, Kenneth Cole, Tommy Hilfiger, Nine West, and Coach. Many companies want to be covered by high-profile star analysts in order to get the attention of institutional investors. Also, thanks to their contacts, analysts can often spot up-and-coming companies that need capital. "Most of the new business is being driven by research," explained Gary Goldstein of Whitney Group, a Wall Street recruiting firm. "Analysts are being seen as integral to developing relationships with companies and getting business from potential clients."[18]

Relationships with Buy-Side Clients

After joining a new firm, a star analyst performs the same job and covers the same companies, and his or her contacts at Fidelity or Putnam Investments and their counterparts almost always remain the same. Star analysts have proven track records, and they know and cater to their clients' preferences and requirements. "I called, I wrote, I visited," said star airline analyst Helane Becker. "I wrote at least one report a day. I called at least ten to twelve people a day. And I was on the road at least one week a month, visiting clients." Occasionally, an analyst will lose a small regional client that was served by his or her former employer but not by the new employer. Otherwise, it is rare for star analysts to lose clients when they switch firms.

External Information Networks

Analysts seek out relationships with suppliers and other sources of information and insight about the industry they cover. Health-care and pharmaceutical analysts, for instance, cultivate relationships with doctors who can offer educated opinions on the potential of new products.

Analysts also cultivate the press as a source of information and to promote their name recognition. "I developed my relationship with reporters at the *Wall Street Journal, USA Today,* and the *New York Times,*" said Becker. "If people in Wichita or Omaha or Seattle saw me quoted in the *Wall Street Journal,* which is a reputable paper, they would be more likely to give me credit for my knowledge of the industry. And then I potentially get to foster a relationship with them, and build my clients that way." These relationships, too, are thoroughly portable.

General Training

Much of the on-the-job training that Wall Street analysts are offered can be employed at any comparable firm and will raise participants' productivity to a roughly equal degree no matter where they work. Technical analytic skills, effective report writing, presentation skills and salesmanship, and advice on dealing with companies, clients, and the press are not firm-specific. (Chapter 9 will describe several Wall Street training programs designed to impart general skills.)

Nonportable Human Capital: What Mobile Analysts Leave Behind

Whether or not analysts recognize their relationships with other in-house professionals as interdependencies, they are essential to performance and can contribute materially to analysts' success. These relationships exemplify the spectrum of interactions that also characterize other professionals' work lives: managing laterally (colleagues and teammates), managing down (junior analysts), managing across functions (the sales force and traders), managing up (the research director), consulting specialists (the portfolio strategist and technical analysts), complying with processes and rules (the investment committee), and using technology platforms and corporate systems.

Managing Laterally: Colleagues, Teams, and Networks

Many stars readily acknowledge that working with first-rate colleagues sparks ideas and stimulates productivity.[19] Colleagues and teammates foster each other's success by sharing resources, coaching, encouraging, and serving as role models. The desire to earn and retain the esteem of longtime colleagues is also highly motivating. Some firms overtly promoted a culture of teamwork: Lehman Brothers stipulated in the 1990s that every presentation to clients had to mention at least two colleagues, and Goldman Sachs's legendary co-leader, John Whitehead, once cautioned an employee, "At Goldman Sachs, we never say 'I.'"[20] (These corporate cultures will be discussed in greater depth in chapter 5.)

Access to a capable colleague who covers a closely related sector matters most. When Lehman Brothers was rated the best research department on Wall Street in the 1990s, its analysts benefited from team-based research processes that heightened their awareness of developments in related sectors and their ability to evaluate such developments knowledgeably. Analysts working within the same sector were particularly interdependent. For example, international oil, domestic oil, exploration oil, gas, and energy analysts all study the energy markets. Thus analysts at team-oriented departments drew liberally on each other's expertise and knowledge. "Business is becoming more and more interrelated," explained Steve Balog. "If you're a great oil analyst, you really want to be working with other great oil and gas analysts. It makes your research so much better." Greg Nejmeh, a star analyst at Lehman Brothers, confirmed the value of knowledge-sharing in sector teams: "We would get together in industry sectors to have breakfast and discuss forces affecting our industries, and try to draw inferences about larger trends where some commonality seemed to exist."[21]

In every workplace, even the most entrepreneurial and individualistic, people gather information and get work done by means of informal networks. These networks operate on trust, mutual benefit, and sociability rather than formal reporting relationships, and they take time to germinate and flourish. In well-oiled and familiar networks, substantive interactions simply take less of busy analysts' time than do new relationships that need to be built from scratch.

Managing Down: Associate (Junior) Analysts

"The senior analyst needs strong associates," says Andrew Melnick, director of global research at Merrill Lynch. "And part of their job is to make the star look like a star. If the senior analyst is in Asia for a week, the firm needs someone back home who can respond to the sales force and investors, and who has the confidence of both of those groups. They [associates] are critical to maintaining our research franchise and the franchise of the superstars."[22] Our interviews with analysts and research directors confirmed that junior analysts contributed more to star analysts' performance than any other single resource, and that star analysts' single most interdependent relationship was with their juniors.

Junior analysts covered subsections of the analyst's industry, typically helping to track some companies. They collected raw data, ran financial models, wrote reports, and contacted clients. "Your junior analysts do a lot of the 'nitty-gritty' work for you," explained a Merrill Lynch analyst. "It allows stars to spend more time with important institutional clients, companies' CEOs, and focus on a big picture." Many stars viewed their juniors as their competitive advantage, crediting them for distinguishing the analyst from his or her rivals. Mary Meeker, the most influential Internet analyst on Wall Street in the 1990s, assembled a crack junior research team that enabled her to cover multiple technology and Internet-related stocks. One analyst claimed that the junior analysts she managed had enough talent to function as the nucleus of any research department. Mobile star analysts often persuade their juniors to move with them. Of the mobile stars in our study, 27 percent moved with teams, and the most constant member on those teams was junior analysts.

Managing across Functions: The Sales Force

The Wall Street tenet that a competent sales force can sell a run-of-the-mill analyst as a superstar is an exaggeration, but it speaks volumes about analysts' dependence on sales. "Salespeople's influence is huge on whether or not a research analyst's message gets out," said Steve Galbraith, a star analyst at Sanford C. Bernstein. Many analysts are heavily dependent on salespeople while others make a point of developing independent relationships with clients.

Alex Cobb, a former analyst at a buy-side client firm, elaborated: "If the firm has a great analyst but a bad institutional sales rep, the clients would have a difficult time finding out that this star analyst exists. It's not enough to build a better mousetrap; someone has to sell it." A skilled salesperson filtered and interpreted an analyst's recommendations to suit each client's needs. Salespeople kept clients abreast of changes in analysts' assessments, communicated buy and sell recommendations, helped provide backup coverage when analysts traveled, and reported back clients' decisions.

Departments that fostered teamwork between analysts and the sales force helped analysts deliver better results. And high-quality sales reps also taught inexperienced analysts about clients' needs. "I'll take one [new analyst] to lunch with a client to show them what the clients are interested in—that it's more than sitting down and talking about stocks," said Brian Raabe, a salesperson at Sanford C. Bernstein. "I help new analysts appreciate . . . what the infrastructure of a mutual fund is all about, how particular analysts' messages resonate with the portfolio managers and analysts."[23]

Star analysts who moved sometimes found that they missed their old sales force. Chris Kotowski, research director at CIBC Oppenheimer and a former star analyst, characterized a troubled relationship with the sales force at a new firm as the central ingredient in a failed move: "[Hiring stars] didn't always work out. People got used to working with one sales force [and] didn't hit it off with the next sales force."

Managing across Functions: Traders

Traders buy and sell stocks for institutional clients, and can pass on news from the trading floor of possible pertinence to analysts' short-term action reports. Information from their buy-side counterparts whose institutions plan to buy or sell a given stock can also be valuable to analysts. And traders help analysts interpret earnings reports and assess their impact on the short- and long-term performance of a company's stock. Brokerage houses take pains to promote trust, familiarity, and free information exchange between analysts and traders. Some use meetings, formal or informal; others assign traders to specific industries, just as analysts are assigned, with performance measures aligned between the two functions to encourage teamwork and coordination.

Managing Up: The Research Director

At the firms we studied, research directors had enormous sway over the performance of their departments and that of individual analysts. The research director decided how analysts allocated their time. He or she also decided how to allocate the budget, how to staff the department, and how to compensate each analyst.

The research director tended to be a lightning rod for analysts. When Lehman Brothers' equity research department was the best on Wall Street (1990–92), its star analysts credited their success to the direction and support of research director Jack Rivkin and his deputy Fred Fraenkel. At the other extreme, as the president of a money-management firm pointed out, "These guys [research directors] are working with a team of analysts who are essentially prima donnas and often wrong—and everyone is always blaming [research directors] for the mistakes."[24] One research director's wife gave him a red plastic fire hydrant to remind him that "a research director is to analysts what a fire hydrant is to dogs."[25]

Intellectual freedom mattered to many analysts, and it was up to the research director to protect that freedom.[26] As former Prudential research director Greg Smith put it, "The research director has to be the ethics director of the firm."[27] When a rival firm fired an analyst who had questioned the financial stability of Donald Trump's casino empire, provoking Trump to threaten a lawsuit, Jack Rivkin of Lehman Brothers wrote to the *Wall Street Journal* condemning the firing. The message to analysts in Rivkin's own department was clear: here, you can think independently. A number of Lehman analysts pointed to Rivkin's letter as a decisive contribution to how they performed their jobs. A research director could also protect analysts from pressures on their time and independence.[28] Barry Tarasoff, director of research at Schroder Wertheim, commented, "The toughest part of the job is to maintain the integrity of the research—and unless the organization understands the importance of that integrity at the highest level, it's doubly hard."[29]

Managing Specialists: The Portfolio Strategist

Portfolio strategists help construct portfolios by determining the asset/specialty mix to achieve the highest return for a given risk tolerance level, and adjust the mix accordingly as the market outlook changes. Skilled analysts integrate portfolio strategists' analyses into their own reports, a service valued by their clients.[30] Vladimir Zlotnitkov, chief investment strategist at Sanford C. Bernstein, explained how a portfolio strategist helped shape an analyst's stock evaluations, especially when the analyst proposed a change in a stock's rating: "[The portfolio strategist's] objective is to test the internal logic of your argument and to craft the message. . . . You're trying to anticipate clients' reactions and make sure there is closure to your logic." Outstanding work by a firm's portfolio strategists thus contributed directly to the quality of analysts' performance by providing clients extra information of particular value.

Managing Specialists: Technical Analysts

Many star analysts leverage the work of their departments' technical analysts by integrating market timing into their reports. Technical analysts use statistical analysis of past market data to forecast the future direction of prices. Analysts claim that clients appreciate research reports that combine company/industry fundamentals with market timing. Regis Schultis, a chemical analyst at Smith Barney, claimed that detailed technical analysis performed by the firm's top market strategist, Alan Shaw, gave him more confidence in his own work.[31] Richard Keating, Smith Barney's institutional sales manager, agreed: "When the chemical stocks were getting clobbered, Alan Shaw was right there. Regis [the chemical analyst] kept us informed on fundamentals, and Alan on the technical postures, and we were really on top of the situation."[32]

Managing Processes and Rules: The Investment Committee

In most departments, an analyst who wants to issue a new recommendation or establish coverage of a new stock must convince the investment committee that the underlying reasoning is sound. This gatekeeping committee usually consists of the department's big guns—the research director, the investment strategist, several senior analysts—plus salespeople and traders. The committee aggressively critiques the analyst's presentation and may send the report back to the drawing board. "Meeting with the investment committee was more than just defending stock picks," said one ranked analyst. "I can't say that I've ever learned more at any place or time on how to do my job as an analyst than during these meetings." At some firms, long-tenured analysts with solid track records were occasionally allowed to circumvent the formal presentation process. But newly hired analysts, even those with stellar track records elsewhere, were typically expected to make presentations to the investment committee, both to establish their credibility and to socialize them to the culture of the firm. Newcomers from firms without investment committees, and stars accustomed to bypassing their firms' processes, often balked and had trouble satisfying the committee's expectations.

Managing Capabilities: Information-Technology Platforms and Corporate Systems

Though Microsoft Windows is standard on Wall Street, corporate IT systems varied widely in versatility, nimbleness, thoroughness, and power during the years of our study and continue to do so today. When Lehman Brothers' research department ranked first in 1990, its star analysts publicly praised the company's computer system, which enabled analysts to deliver reports faster than their rivals. They also lauded the company's sophisticated evaluation system, which kept analysts up-to-date on how well they were performing and serving clients. "Measurement and goals help you see whether you're going in the right direction, whether you've arrived or whether you've missed by a country mile," observed Michael Skutinsky, the system's creator.

Because it is hard to recognize one's reliance on routine infrastructure, a star may only realize after leaving a company that its platform and internal processes enabled operations that mattered to outcomes. "I spent three days trying to get the investor relations people at a company to give me some information that would have taken my assistant at Merrill less than an hour to obtain," said a star analyst who left Merrill Lynch for a smaller firm. "Then I tried to populate a spreadsheet with some sector data that was available at my fingertips at Merrill but was nonexistent at the new company."

Efficient corporate procedures also streamline routine processes, putting useful information at employees' fingertips and making it unnecessary to reinvent the wheel. Many top-rated research departments have adopted formal processes that create an uninterrupted flow of strategic information between analysts and the firm's sales force and traders.

Firm-Specific Training and Firm-Specific Outcomes of General Training

Customized in-house training programs aim to familiarize employees with corporate resources and demonstrate how to make the most of them.[33] Such programs are often reserved for the most promising employees, promoting solidarity and a sense of specialness among their participants—and further enhancing their firm-specific (nonportable) human capital relative to that of their less able colleagues. Lehman Brothers' stars praised a thirteen-week training program that the company created to teach them, among other things, how to structure the reports they disseminated to their institutional clients. One of the participants described the program as "the rocket that took [us] to stardom." (Chapter 9 will offer more detail on the Lehman program and the effect of in-house training in general.)

This phenomenon thus appears to be circular rather than linear: the most promising employees were singled out for extra training on the firm's customized offerings, and they then applied their enhanced abilities to exploit the firm's resources in pursuit of supercharged performance. Evidence from other studies suggests that what most sharply distinguishes the best-performing knowledge workers is their ability to leverage intrafirm networks and supportive functions.[34] A firm's customized resources may account for a sizable fraction of its stars' performance.

Some firms trained their analysts to produce unique research products. Sanford C. Bernstein was known for its analysts' encyclopedic "blackbooks," rigorous and lavishly documented reviews of industries and companies that offered multiple long-term forecasts. The skills that went into compiling black books were unlikely to be applicable at another firm.

It is of the utmost importance to point out, too, that even training in general skills, like interpreting balance sheets or writing conventional reports, can have nonportable outcomes. Generic group-based training can have a powerful cohort effect—a bond created by shared experience—on members of the group, particularly if participation is selective and the training involves collaborating on joint projects. Done well, training of this kind creates a common language and a sense of shared enterprise, generating spillover effects like ongoing casual exchanges of information and joint projects.

The Price of Leaving: What the Data Reveal

To test whether ranked analysts' performance was portable, we set out to examine whether changing employers affected their *II* rankings, controlling for individual, firm, sector, and intertemporal variables. Using *Institutional Investor*'s annual rankings of the best equity analysts for 1988–96, we collected data on every ranked analyst who departed or joined a firm within one year of ranking. We identified 546 such moves, and then eliminated analysts who transferred to non-research positions or left investment banking entirely. The remaining 366 ranked analysts who joined competitors' research departments represented the core population for the study. Ranked analysts were employed by 78 different investment banks, but the top 24 firms accounted for fully 96 percent of all ranked analysts. Throughout the book, we only report coefficients for our independent variables. Our statistical tests controlled for a range of factors including individual, firm, sector, and macroeconomic. For a far more detailed description of the study's methodology, statistical findings, control variables, robustness check, and analysis relating to endogeneity, see the sources in the note and the appendix.[35] In qualitative analysis that will provide additional insights into statistical findings, we will almost always limit our attention to these 24 banks, because including the others would be more unwieldy than enlightening.

In short, our findings from the models in table 3.1 reveal that star analysts who switched employers paid a high price for jumping ship relative to comparable stars who stayed put: overall, their job performance plunged sharply and continued to suffer for at least five years after moving to a new firm. This evidence refutes the prevailing belief in the industry that analysts' skills are thoroughly portable—independent of the particular firm where they work— and that analysts can move without suffering a decline in performance.

Table 3.1

Effect of Switching Firms on Ranked Analysts' Short-Term and Long-Term Performance

	1988–96 Ordered probit regressions				
	M1	M2	M3	M4	M5
Variable	Rank $(t+1)$	Rank $(t+2)$	Rank $(t+3)$	Rank $(t+4)$	Rank $(t+5)$
Analyst move	−0.340 ***	−0.263 ***	−0.229 **	−0.218 **	−0.263 **
	(0.076)	(0.089)	(0.098)	(0.111)	(0.130)
Predicted probabilities for analysts who do not move					
First rank	0.106	0.150	0.156	0.157	0.154
Second rank	0.234	0.215	0.199	0.186	0.187
Third rank	0.356	0.279	0.237	0.211	0.193
Runner-up	0.238	0.252	0.258	0.256	0.258
Unranked	0.066	0.105	0.150	0.191	0.207
Marginal change in probabilities for analysts who move					
First rank	−0.050	−0.053	−0.049	−0.047	−0.054
Second rank	−0.064	−0.040	−0.033	−0.029	−0.036
Third rank	−0.013	−0.008	−0.010	−0.011	−0.014
Runner-up	0.071	0.046	0.031	0.022	0.022
Unranked	0.056	0.056	0.060	0.065	0.083
Avg. Effect	0.051	0.041	0.036	0.035	0.042

Source: Adapted from Boris Groysberg, Linda-Eling Lee, and Ashish Nanda, "Can They Take It with Them? The Portability of Star Knowledge Workers' Performance: Myth or Reality," *Management Science* 54, no. 7 (July 2008): 1213–30, p. 1223.

Notes: The marginal effect of the *Analyst move* variable is calculated as the discrete change in F(x) as this variable changes from 0 to 1: $F(x=1) - F(x=0)$. The categorical and ordinal dependent variable ($Rank_t$) is represented by first rank, second rank, third rank, runner-up, and unranked. Models 1–5 examine the impact of switching firms on ranked analysts' short-term and long-term performance. Each model is a robust cluster ordered probit specification with ranked analysts as clusters in which the dependent variable is analysts' *Institutional Investor* rankings. This table presents coefficients for the *Analyst Move* variable for ranked analysts, controlling for individual, firm, sector, and intertemporal variables (not reported). Only adjusted robust standard errors are reported.

$^*p < .10; ^{**}p < .05; ^{***}p < .01$

Another way to interpret the data is to focus on the overall probability of achieving a particular outcome. For a ranked analyst who did not change employers, for example, the probability of being ranked first the subsequent year was 0.106. For those who changed firms, the same probability declined

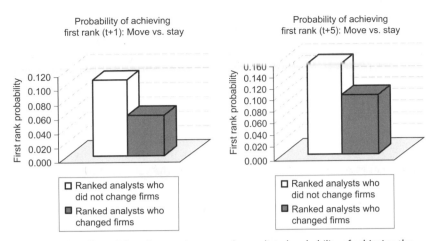

Figure 3.2. The effect of changing employers on the predicted probability of achieving the first rank, one and five years post-move.

to 0.056, a significant decrease. Over time the performance gap between the two groups narrowed but persisted. Figure 3.2 illustrates these results for two intervals, one and five years after ranking. (Using a single rank makes it possible to illustrate this finding in graphic form.)

Another illustrative way to look at the effect on performance of moving is to examine the probability of being ranked again the next year. Specifically, for nonmobile analysts ranked by *Institutional Investor* in a given year—that is, those who stayed put—the probability of being ranked again the next year was 84.9 percent. The probability of ranking again dropped to 69.4 percent for analysts who moved to a new firm.

Josie Esquivel, whom we met in chapter 1 as she was deciding whether or not to leave Lehman Brothers for Morgan Stanley, ultimately made the move in 1995. Esquivel's colorful and unconventional research reports met with resistance from Morgan Stanley's publishing department, where they did not conform to the firm's more conservative standards. As Esquivel reflected on her time at a new firm, "I was always known for my reports. My initial shock was taking a 100-page report entitled 'Oh, What a Tangled Web We Weave' to be printed. I got a dissertation from the head of editorial that I wasn't using this pun correctly! I was thinking: 'It's a textile report! I'm known for unique, creative reports. Let's add some pizzazz here.' This was so new to Morgan Stanley. I was given a lot of grief for a number of my reports."[36] Esquivel managed to maintain her number-one standing in the 1995 and 1996 *II* polls based on the strength of her external networks, but subsequently her ratngs declined. In 2000 her standing declined further, to runner-up. Esquivel reflected on whether she should have adjusted more to Morgan Stanley's culture: "I am not sure the end result would have been much different, though, even if I had sat back and played a little more to the culture. I would have had to become completely non–Josie Esquivel."[37]

"It's a bit like a baseball pitcher traded away from the Yankees," two distinguished observers of the nonportability phenomenon wrote. "These people often are totally unaware of the enormous support system they had going for them in the excellent company, and are at the very least initially lost and bewildered without it."[38] All of these individuals remained just as intelligent and capable after changing employers, and no doubt just as hard-working— probably more so, given the demands of switching firms. In fact, our interviews with analysts and research directors confirmed that stars worked hard after switching firms. They all covered the same industry and to a large extent the same companies before and after moving, and the same clients' and contacts' phone numbers remained in their Rolodexes. Even their commute remained unchanged; they simply moved across, or up, or down the street. But clearly they lost something crucial, and something they didn't expect would matter so decisively, in the course of changing employers.

What they left behind, in short, were the capabilities of the old firm and the practiced, seamless fit between their own skills and the resources of the company. When they moved, their mastery of the firm-specific aspects of their jobs and workplaces suddenly became moot. An analyst who left a firm where he or she achieved stardom lost access to colleagues, teammates, and internal networks that can take years to develop. Firm-specific skills acquired through in-house training programs and on-the-job experience had no applicability outside the firm. Proprietary electronic programs and databases were no longer accessible. Neither were supportive managers nor, usually, capable support staff familiar with the analyst's needs, quirks, and work habits. New and unfamiliar ways of doing things took the place of routines and procedures and systems that over time had become second nature.

It is conceivable, of course, that stars' performance simply deteriorates over time. Our research looks, however, at performance differences between two groups; systematic decline would not explain why stars who change firms do worse than stars who stay put. Another possible explanation also needs to be ruled out: that stars who anticipate poorer performance move before their decline becomes apparent. This scenario can be modeled statistically, and the tests we performed ruled it out as an explanation. (In fact, based on observable characteristics, movers and stayers were very similar.) We also ruled out the possibility that our results were driven by newly ranked stars who realized they had merely gotten lucky and moved to cash in before losing their stardom the following year. Robustness checks and tests to rule out additional explanations and provide support for our results and explanations are explained in other publications.[39]

It is perhaps unsurprising that many stars who left the firms where they initially made their reputations did not stay long at their new companies. Ultimately, not many ranked analysts who joined new firms remained in place five years after making the move. Once stars began job-hopping, they tended to keep moving on to the highest bidder instead of allowing their new employer to build businesses around them.

We measured performance by looking solely at the effect of the first move a star analyst made. Our analysis excludes observations about analysts' subsequent moves and thus might be biased toward those who remain with their new employers even if they underperform, but some of our interviews with research directors indicate that a number of those who left the industry were forced out for underperformance. If analysts who were forced to switch employers again after suffering a performance decline moved to lower-paying jobs or had to leave the industry, changing firms might be even more damaging than our results indicate. This pattern of subsequent job changes suggests that job-switching has further negative consequences on performance that we did not measure.

There may have been individuals who recognized the risk that changing employers posed to their performance and were willing to accept that risk in exchange for higher compensation, but we did not encounter them in our interviews. For the star analysts in our sample, whose average age was forty-one, going for the money would not have been a sustainable strategy: the significant short- and long-term decrease in performance was likely to affect their later career outcomes.

The number of analysts who realized their mistake right away and did U-turns back to their old firms was fairly high. Two of the fastest about-faces in Wall Street research history were those of James Clark, a 1995 second-teamer in domestic and international oils, and Gordon Hall, a first-teamer in oil services and equipment, both of whom returned to Credit Suisse First Boston after just a few hours at Morgan Stanley, despite higher salaries and heavy publicity. Jack Kirnan returned to Salomon Brothers in less than a week. Jim Crandall, director of U.S. equity research at Salomon, explained that Kirnan had realized how much he liked Salomon and all of the people at the firm, and what a tremendous mistake he had made.

To underline our central finding: outstanding individual performance is far more context-dependent than it appears to star performers themselves, who are apt to take full personal credit for their accomplishments. Star performers' achievements were partially attributable to the quality and resources of their firms, to their ability to make the most of the firm's supportive resources, and to the benefits of collegial cross-fertilization. The loss of these assets in turn had the effect of making professionals who had viewed themselves as free agents less portable than they thought they were. This primary finding argues for shifting the focus of both managers' and researchers' attention from individual star performers to the interplay between an individual and the colleagues and resources that the firm offers him or her. It also generates numerous questions and observations about the strategies, resources, and practices of employers and employees.

It is important news for researchers, managers, and individual knowledge workers that many mobile stars failed to maintain their outstanding performance after moving. Equally revealing, however, are the variations we found in portability: whose performance proved to be portable and whose did not. The rest of this chapter and the chapters that follow will examine those nuances and their implications in detail.

Firm Quality and Other Factors in Performance Portability: What Makes a Difference?

Our evidence revealed a handful of features of individual firms and patterns of job mobility that conditioned the fundamental relationship between firm-specific skills and performance. These findings suggest some further intriguing hypotheses about the characteristics and orientations of firms that most successfully promote outstanding performance on the part of their employees. They also suggest strategies for companies eager to pursue competitive advantage on the strength of their roster of talented employees.

Individual Performance and the Quality of the Firm

As we will see, the findings about stars' performance at their firms of origin suggested that they owed a substantial portion of their superiority to familiarity with how the firm operates and their own skills at making the most of its resources. But we also found compelling evidence that a firm's quality had a strong effect on an analyst's performance. In fact, the effect on individual performance of firm-quality variables—the overall quality of the department, of the analyst's colleagues, of the portfolio strategist, and of the firm's salespeople—was strong.[40] What is more, quality also moderated the relationship between experience and performance: analysts who worked for better departments, alongside better coworkers, achieved superior performance faster than their counterparts who worked for weaker departments.[41] Each of these aspects of firm quality separately contributed measurably to the rapidity of analysts' rise to stardom.[42] The better a department's capabilities and quality, the faster its analysts distinguished themselves.[43] In other words, the higher the quality of an organization, the higher the payoff for time spent there.

This finding has implications that resonate beyond the confines of Wall Street. If even the highest-flying individuals in a profession with a strong claim to free-agent status depend heavily on the capabilities of the firms where they work in order to excel, the same thing is likely to be true in other knowledge-based professions. The embeddedness and interconnectedness that characterize even analysts' jobs strongly suggest that there is likely to be no such thing as a pure free agent within an organization. Our findings about portability reinforce this observation.

The Relative Quality of the Two Firms

We found consistent evidence that the quality of an analyst's new firm relative to that of his or her former firm was an important factor in post-move performance.[44] To designate moves as lateral, upward, or downward, we distinguished between what Wall Street calls "bulge-bracket"[45] investment-banking firms and all others. Lateral mobility consists of a move from one bulge-bracket firm to another, or from one non-bulge-bracket firm to another; a move to a bulge-bracket firm from a non-bulge-bracket firm constitutes an upward move, and the reverse is a downward move.

Table 3.2 compares the short- and long-term performance of these different categories of mobile analysts (moving to a comparable firm, moving to a better firm, and moving to a weaker firm) to that of analysts who stayed put. We report only the coefficients for the different categories of firm qualities. Figure 3.3 provides graphical interpretation of these results for moves to comparable firms for two intervals, one and five years after ranking.

Table 3.2
Effect of Switching Firms on Ranked Analysts' Short-Term and Long-Term Performance by Type of Move

Category	Independent variable	1988–96 Ordered probit regressions				
		Rank $(t+1)$	Rank $(t+2)$	Rank $(t+3)$	Rank $(t+4)$	Rank $(t+5)$
Firm quality/capability direction	**Moving to a weaker firm**					
	Coefficient	-0.338 **	-0.407 **	-0.312 *	-0.590 ***	-0.480 *
	Robust standard error	(0.163)	(0.172)	(0.191)	(0.212)	(0.280)
	N	90	81	64	48	32
	Moving to a comparable firm					
	Coefficient	-0.409 ***	-0.250 **	-0.199	-0.064	-0.137
	Robust standard error	(0.099)	(0.121)	(0.132)	(0.145)	(0.163)
	N	209	176	145	122	98
	Moving to a better firm					
	Coefficient	-0.144	-0.083	-0.187	-0.128	-0.358
	Robust standard error	(0.148)	(0.164)	(0.167)	(0.191)	(0.247)
	N	67	64	55	45	35

Source: Adapted from Boris Groysberg, Linda-Eling Lee, and Ashish Nanda, "Can They Take It with Them? The Portability of Star Knowledge Workers' Performance: Myth or Reality," *Management Science* 54, no. 7 (July 2008): 1213–30, p. 1224.

Notes: The marginal effect of the *Analyst move* variable is calculated as the discrete change in F(x) as this variable changes from 0 to 1: F(x = 1) − F(x = 0). N represents the number of mobile star analysts. The categorical and ordinal dependent variable (*Rank*) is represented by first rank, second rank, third rank, runner-up, and unranked. Models 1–5 examine the impact of switching firms on ranked analysts' short-term and long-term performance by whether they move to (1) a weaker firm, (2) a comparable firm, or (3) a better firm. Each model is a robust cluster ordered probit specification with ranked analysts as clusters in which the dependent variable is analysts' *Institutional Investor* rankings. This table presents coefficients for the independent variables for ranked analysts, controlling for individual, firm, sector, and intertemporal variables (not reported). Only adjusted robust standard errors are reported.

*p < .10; **p < .05; ***p < .01

Moving to a Comparable Firm

Ranked analysts who made lateral moves—moves between firms with similar capabilities—experienced a post-move decline in performance. Their performance suffered for only two years, however, in contrast to the five-year decline typical of ranked analysts who changed jobs.

This comparison is particularly telling: if the performance of analysts who moved laterally were no different than that of their counterparts who did not change firms, the evidence that the loss of firm-specific human capital had a detrimental effect would be unconvincing. The fact that such analysts

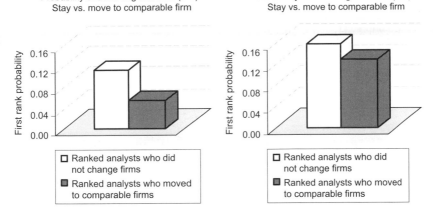

Probability of achieving first rank (t+1): Stay vs. move to comparable firm

Probability of achieving first rank (t+5): Stay vs. move to comparable firm

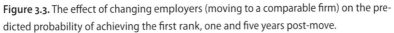

☐ Ranked analysts who did
   not change firms
■ Ranked analysts who moved
   to comparable firms

☐ Ranked analysts who did
   not change firms
■ Ranked analysts who moved
   to comparable firms

Figure 3.3. The effect of changing employers (moving to a comparable firm) on the predicted probability of achieving the first rank, one and five years post-move.

did in fact perform worse for two years strongly suggests that it was not the loss of resources—which are similar at similar firms—but the inapplicability of their firm-specific skills that undermined performance.

The fact that lateral moves had a relatively short-lived impact on performance compared to the impact of downward moves also testifies to the important role in performance of firm resources, which were not lost in lateral moves as they were in downward moves. During the first two years at the new firm, it appears, analysts successfully acclimated themselves to the formal and informal ways things were done there. They developed new firm-specific human capital. Ultimately, the long-term performance of stars who moved laterally was not statistically different from that of counterparts who did not move.

Moving to a Better Firm

Stars who moved to better firms had the most to gain by moving. These analysts experienced no significant decline in either short-term or long-term performance compared to that of star analysts who stayed.

Having worked at firms whose capabilities were relatively modest, and whose specialized offerings to their employees were likely to be meager compared to those at bulge-bracket firms, these analysts had to learn to rely on their own personal capabilities and general job skills more than their counterparts at resource-rich firms did. When such analysts found themselves at a firm with lavish resources, the combination of those resources and their well-honed general skills could prove to be a winning combination. Given time, they acquired the new firm-specific human capital that they needed to become successful.

Moving to a Weaker Firm

Analysts who left resource-rich firms for weaker firms had the most to lose. They experienced the sharpest declines in performance of the configurations we identified.

The evidence that the quality of the working environment is a strong predictor of performance, in combination with evidence that stars from better firms depend more heavily on their firms' capabilities than do their counterparts at weaker firms, goes a long way toward explaining why stars who moved to weaker (less resource-rich) firms underperformed for so long. To be successful, ranked analysts who moved to firms with weak, star-poor, or less reputable departments had to rely more exclusively on their own innate and general human capital and less on the supportive capabilities of the firm.

The fraction of an analyst's performance that is attributable to departmental and firm capabilities is not portable, nor is the analyst's firm-specific human capital. Only the fraction of a worker's performance that is attributable to individual ability and general human capital is portable across firms. Hence it should not be surprising that star analysts suffered a performance penalty upon moving from one firm to another. Moreover, the effect of mobility on performance depends on departments' and firms' characteristics, such that ranked analysts from star-rich departments, departments with better portfolio strategists, and firms with top-rated sales professionals have the most to lose when they switch firms.

These findings represent a partial answer to the question, raised in the pages of *Institutional Investor* as early as 1978, as to "whether an analyst's reputation goes with him when he changes firms or whether it's really the broker he works for and the institutional sales support he gets from his employers that account for the bulk of his reputation (answer: it usually depends on *which* firm he works for)."[46]

The Orientation of the Analyst's Original Firm

Another provocative finding from our study is that stars from certain investment banks suffered no performance penalty when they moved. These banks, which include Credit Suisse First Boston, Donaldson, Lufkin & Jenrette (DLJ), and Salomon Brothers, were those that viewed themselves as offering, in effect, an organizational umbrella for individual analysts' entrepreneurial franchises. At DLJ, for example, stars had their own profit-and-loss statements, as if they were proprietors of freestanding businesses. Because firms that operated according to this hands-off philosophy did not make a point of customizing the resources they offered their analysts, the analysts' skill sets tended to remain generalized, fluid, and mobile, as well as less idiosyncratically firm-specific than at more teamwork-oriented companies. By contrast, analysts who left Bear Stearns, Goldman Sachs, and Merrill Lynch were considerably worse-off after moving. At these firms, the star analyst and the firm were in essence a team, and the post-move uselessness of firm-specific human capital eroded performance. (The significance of the former employer's orientation will be explored fully in chapter 5.)

The Choosing and Integrating Capacities of the New Firm

The characteristics of the destination firm could also have a powerful impact on a star analyst's performance after changing jobs. One intuitive way to look at the integration successes of hiring firms is to examine what percentages of analysts continue to be ranked at a new firm. Of ranked analysts who joined Goldman Sachs, 94 percent were ranked again one year later. By contrast, only 17 percent of ranked analysts who joined Montgomery Securities were ranked the year after moving.

Furthermore, some newly hired stars joined a new firm to *explore* a sector that the firm had never covered before, and others were hired to *exploit* the firm's existing capacities in a particular sector. Our analysis suggests that this distinction between exploration and exploitation (developed in the field of organizational learning)[47] has implications for mobile stars' ability to maintain their outstanding performance after moving. (We will look in detail at the impact of the destination firm's characteristics and hiring roles in chapter 6.)

Leaving Solo versus Leaving with a Team

Some star analysts moved in teams, a phenomenon known in the industry as "block trading in people" or liftouts. Out of 366 moves, 100 were undertaken with other ranked analysts, junior analysts, institutional salespeople, or traders.

Moving with an intact team enabled a star to retain some firm-specific human capital even after moving, with performance-protective effects. We found that stars who changed firms along with teammates experienced no decline in either short- or long-term performance. Those who moved solo (without other star analysts, junior analysts, salespeople, or traders) experienced sharper declines in performance. (Chapter 7 will look further at the effects of solo and team moves.)

The Effect of Gender on Portability

The star women in our study turned out to enjoy far more portable performance than did their male counterparts. This finding demonstrates forcefully that the patterns we found are not deterministic and offers a window into the role of individual choices and institutional barriers in portability. In exploring the reasons for women's portable performance, we found that female analysts deliberately and strategically cultivated portable (i.e., external) relationships, resources, and sources of information, and also thought more strategically about the repercussions of moving than did their male counterparts. (Chapter 8 will look at why and how women cultivated portable skills and more broadly at the interface between institutional orientations and individual choices.)

Lessons for Star Analysts and Other Exceptional Knowledge Workers

As we have seen, 85 percent of the analysts and research directors we interviewed asserted that they possessed no firm-specific skills and that their job performance was entirely independent of their employers' resources and capabilities. The central lesson of our findings for people with this mentality could not be clearer. Individuals who are stars in the workplace have a strong and persistent—and potentially career-damaging—tendency to undervalue the importance to their success of their employers' capabilities and resources—and their own practiced ability to make use of these resources.

For individuals who intend to stay put at their current employers, coming to grips with this central truth may be little more than a character-building exercise in modesty and in giving credit where credit is due. But for stars who contemplate switching allegiances, such an undertaking has considerably more practical urgency. Whether contemplating an imminent move or one in the indeterminate future, these individuals should try to undertake a dispassionate and systematic assessment of the drivers of their past performance before taking any other steps. And they should carefully weigh an increase in compensation—which is likely to be their prime motivation for changing jobs—against the probability of a future performance decline, and possibly a precipitous and long-term one.

The other important component of such strategizing is a clear-eyed assessment of the quality of one's current firm relative to that of likely future employers. This assessment can turn out to be considerably more difficult in other industries than it is in investment banking, where the *Institutional Investor* rankings make firms more transparent than is typical in the economy as a whole. It is worth reiterating that moving to a firm likely to offer fewer resources and less accomplished colleagues is apt to have a debilitating effect on performance, no matter how talented one is or how hard one works.

Lessons for Firms Pursuing Competitive Advantage

A cascade of articles and books proclaims the existence of a war for talent and asserts that the increasingly technological and knowledge-based tilt of advanced economies is creating a more efficient labor market and an army of footloose free agents with portable skills. Some writers declare that a large-scale paradigm shift is occurring from long-term to short-term employment, and that the most talented employees move most often. A logical corollary of this hypothesis is that the kind of company-specific knowledge that was once valuable to both employer and employee no longer retains much value for either party. Because talent is flighty, the argument goes, managers need to get talented employees up to speed fast so they can begin contributing to the firm. An alternative scenario asserts that firms should lure stars with attractive offers and retain them with individualized career customization. Few of these prescriptions are based on empirical evidence.

The initial premise that post-industrial economies are increasingly dominated by knowledge-based work has been amply demonstrated. It is thus rational for companies whose services or products are knowledge-dependent to stake their competitive advantage largely on the talents of their employees. But the evidence generated by our study suggests a set of very different conclusions about how to pursue competitive advantage in a knowledge-based field, which the remainder of this book will explore.

4 | Do Firms Benefit from Hiring Stars?

Investment banks pursue two broad approaches to acquiring top performers.[1] Some firms make a practice of picking off highly rated employees from specific competitors. Others commit to nurturing and leveraging home-grown talent. (A certain number of these firms successfully cultivate their employees' skills but are unable to hang onto them.)

Many investment banks that make a practice of hiring outstanding analysts from other firms resemble the baseball and football teams that rely on free agents. Underperforming firms seek out stars in an attempt to quickly reverse their fortunes. Departments unable to develop stars internally, or disinclined to try because of their preoccupation with short-term results, rely on luring stars away from their competitors. Many regard doing so not as a sign of failure but as the key to a successful research department. Foreign and domestic brokerage houses trying to break into the circle of major players in equity research have resorted to the shortcut strategy of hiring stars to populate or upgrade their research departments. Other firms hire stars intermittently or opportunistically: departments that experience turnover among their best employees, perhaps because of raids by other companies, need talented replacements fast to maintain uninterrupted first-rate service to the firm's clients.[2]

Is the acquisition of a star performer value-enhancing for a firm? Some management theorists advocate hiring outsiders for the fresh perspectives and creativity they can contribute. One study claimed that the "ability to recruit talented people is the obvious first step to winning the talent war."[3] Another made an analogy to genetics, praising the benefits of cross-breeding and alteration of the organization's genetic code.[4] Other researchers have advocated recruitment of outsiders in the interests of improving the performance of veteran employees and promoting competitiveness.[5] Our evidence, however, shows that building capability by hiring stars does not work well. Three undesirable outcomes can ensue. As we have seen, the star's performance can suffer in the wake of the move. In addition, the much-publicized outside hire can cause resentment in the department, with accompanying breakdown in morale, teamwork, and communication. Finally, the firm can find that it paid more for its new star than is justified by the results.

The Dynamics of Hiring Stars

In the hunt for talent, many firms overpay the stars they hire. Replacing star analysts can be an expensive proposition. In 1998, for example, Steven Levy, a star analyst, accepted a contract for $2.5 million annually from Lehman Brothers. His previous employer, Salomon Smith Barney, had been paying him $1.5 million. Salomon immediately began a search for Levy's replacement and ended up hiring Alex Cena from Bear Stearns for $3.5 million.

"With the growing importance of research and the limited supply of analysts," pointed out Andrew Melnick, director of global equity research at Merrill Lynch, "you have a situation where demand exceeds supply."[6] Another research director blamed competition for the best talent for driving compensation to "unbelievable if not obscene" extremes.[7] Alan Johnson, managing director of Johnson Associates, a compensation consultancy, agreed that salaries had reached "insane" levels. Johnson claimed that a tacit ceiling on salaries had existed as recently as 1993, when most people still considered it unseemly to pay an analyst millions of dollars: "It was somewhere around $1.5 to $2.5 million," Johnson said.[8]

That ceiling was shattered in 1994. Bidding for talent heated up when some firms began to upgrade their research departments by poaching analysts from other firms, creating a domino effect when the poached analysts' former employers had to fill their open positions.[9]

The Operation of the Market for Stars

Over the nine years of our study, the top twenty-four research departments hired 82 percent of star analysts who switched jobs, and the same twenty-four departments accounted for 94 percent of all exits. A handful of firms routinely raided each other, in other words, but few firms experienced a balance between exits and entries.

Unsurprisingly, the most active seekers of star analysts were firms unsuccessful at developing their own talent or less interested in doing so than in pursuing short-term performance. Merrill Lynch acquired thirty-four ranked analysts. JP Morgan, at the other extreme, preferred to develop its own talent and did not hire ranked analysts from its competitors.

Timing of Exits and Entrances

The timing of job changes revealed an intriguing pattern: departing star analysts tended to quit their jobs at a point in time when their firms of origin were underperforming the market and to join firms that were also underperforming, but to a less extreme degree. Overall, their timing was impeccable; they changed employers at a juncture when their original firms were likely to be highly resource-constrained and the firms courting them were most eager to land them and most likely to outperform their original firms. On the part of the acquiring firm, the governing agenda was to better its performance by stealing talent from firms experiencing significantly worse performance.[10]

The Domino Effect and Other Reasons for Hiring Stars

Investment banks pursued a range of strategies in hiring ranked analysts. Fully 61 percent of the star hires were undertaken to reinforce coverage of a sector the bank was already researching (exploitation activity). The remaining 39 percent of hires were made to initiate coverage of a new sector (exploration activity).

Research departments that experienced turnover were naturally anxious to find a replacement. When a position remained open for months, other analysts were typically asked to step in to cover their departed colleague's companies. This stopgap could alarm clients and threaten the rankings of the overworked fill-ins trying to do their own jobs along with that of the departed analyst. Over 50 percent of hires by Credit Suisse First Boston and Prudential filled empty slots created by the exits of ranked analysts. These firms all resorted to the labor market, in other words, to maintain the quality of their departments in the face of attrition.

In contrast, UBS and Deutsche expanded the scope of their research departments by hiring ranked analysts to start new franchises. "If a sector is hot, every shop feels it had better be there," said Debra Brown of the executive search firm Russell Reynolds, surveying the various explanations for hiring frenzies. "If an analyst is recruited away or a competitor is establishing a stronger foothold in that sector, no firm can afford the opportunity cost of not filling the position. Everyone has to be in the game."[11]

The Winner's Curse

In a market of this kind—characterized as it is by high salaries, prestige seeking, a preoccupation with reputation, steadfast belief in individual talent, time pressure, and intense competition for both big names and results—the likelihood is high that a firm will overestimate the value of an outside star and pay more for the star's services than he or she will ultimately contribute to the firm's performance.

In its classic form, a winner's curse is an undesirable outcome of an auction or bidding war for a good whose value is uncertain. The bidder who has estimated the good's value most liberally wins, but in retrospect the winner may reevaluate the good's worth downward in light of rival bidders' more restrained bids. To put it another way, the very act of winning may deflate the winner's appraisal of the value of the good, and the winner might ultimately regret winning the auction.[12]

In bidding wars, the pressures and impulses that promote overbidding—competitiveness, gamesmanship, and the will to win—are so hard to resist that even expert bidders who understand the phenomenon in one setting consistently reproduce it in other situations.[13] First identified and studied in bidding on oil leases, the winner's curse has also been traced in book publishers' bids for manuscripts that fail to earn back their advances, and in the hiring of free agents in baseball and of supposedly "bankable" movie stars.[14] It has even been shown to characterize some corporate takeovers and acquisitions.[15]

Several studies of the winner's curse in corporate mergers and acquisitions reached a conclusion that may well be applicable to the phenomenon of acquiring a star away from a rival company. In corporate acquisitions, it was found, the shareholders of the acquiring firm benefited very little or not at all while the acquired firms benefited handsomely.[16] Similarly, one study found that though star analysts do have a positive impact on a firm's gross performance, they do not contribute to its bottom line, as measured by pre-tax operating income, because they appropriate the revenue they will generate.[17]

Other studies suggest that corporate prestige-seeking and individual misjudgments play a role in irrational overpayment. One study found that companies are willing to pay a premium to hire the most prestigious external auditors and outside counsel as a way of signaling their probity and credibility.[18] And a study of corporate acquisitions found that acquiring firms overpay for companies when their managers' excessive self-confidence causes them to overestimate their ability to manage new units gainfully.[19]

A firm can suffer a winner's curse whether or not the new star's performance suffers in the course of changing employers, and whether or not the star's arrival demoralizes incumbent employees and undermines their performance. The winner's curse is commonplace in environments characterized by asymmetric information. Hiring managers often have difficulty determining a star's real value because of incomplete information (even in an information-rich environment like the analyst market), emotion, and other factors. In fact, winners tend to overpay and to be "cursed" in one of two ways: either the star's compensation exceeds the value he or she brings to the new firm, or the star's value is less than the hiring company anticipated. As we saw in chapter 3, however, a change of employers does typically undermine star-quality performance, at least temporarily. And as we will see here, the arrival of a new star from outside the company tends to have harmful effects on the performance and morale of others in the department.

Star Newcomers' Effects on Departmental Productivity

Few companies are good at integrating newcomers. In their eagerness to begin reaping the benefits of the newly hired rainmaker, many firms entirely overlook his or her need to learn the ropes during a ramp-up period.[20] "A new person cannot simply arrive, read the files, and get to work. They need to build a network and make use of a wealth of knowledge that can only build over time," one writer pointed out.[21] "The higher up the organization one goes, the truer it becomes that people cannot simply be 'parachuted in' to key posts. They need to go through a lengthy socialization process or risk being rejected by the culture of the organization."[22] Another writer noted that "a dynamic player inserted into the firm can upset team dynamics, [which could be] destructive to the firm's reputation in the long run."[23]

The other side of the coin is that thorough integration of a newcomer is costly for an employer in several ways. Peers, coworkers, mentors, and bosses invest time in teaching the new hire about the firm's operations and personalities. And a star may prove to be unusually slow to make the transition from newcomer to insider. Arrogance about prior accomplishments can make stars particularly resistant to social learning and prickly about adapting to the norms of the new organization.[24] Meanwhile, disproportional managerial and financial expenditures on integrating a highly valued newcomer can shortchange other employees by depriving them of attention and resources.

Perceived Inequity, Disaffection, and Disrupted Team Dynamics

"Hiring a star resembles an organ transplant," observed the head of research at a distinguished Wall Street investment bank. "First, the new body can reject the prized organ that operated so well inside another body. . . . On some occasions, the new organ hurts healthy parts of the body by demanding a disproportionate blood supply. . . . Other parts of the body start to resent it, ache and . . . demand attention . . . or threaten to stop working. You should think about it very carefully before you do [a transplant] to a healthy body. You could get lucky, but success is rare."[25]

Most managers realize that hiring a star is likely to damage the morale of incumbents, but they tend to underestimate the magnitude of the upheaval and aftershocks. Compensation is typically the first bone of contention. It rarely takes long for the particulars of the newcomer's deal to make the rounds; confidentiality is breached by newspapers or inside sources. "Everyone knows how much the other person is making, plus or minus 5 percent," said Steve Balog. "And if they hear about a new analyst getting paid like he's the number-one analyst on Wall Street, it really ticks existing stars off."

If senior management lavishes dramatically higher pay and more desirable resources on a newly hired star than on a company stalwart who has performed equally well, both the stalwart and other employees are likely to become more or less instantly demoralized.[26]

Companies eager to please stars also award them other coveted resources, like support staff, as part of the hiring package. Loyal employees can quickly become embittered: without comparable resources they cannot possibly perform as well as the hired gun. And resources also function as a proxy for status.[27] "Managing a research department is like managing a movie set with a hundred Jack Nicholsons," said Michael Skutinsky, a research executive for Paine Webber, Lehman Brothers, and Salomon Smith Barney. "The word *anal* isn't in *analyst* by mistake. Analysts know how many more erasers a new person three offices down has than they do: 'Why do they have a better plant in their office than I have? Are you trying to tell me something?'"

A perception of unfairness and inconsistency may spread quickly. People typically use individuals similar to themselves as points of comparison when assessing whether their rewards match their contributions and whether they are being treated fairly.[28] If they conclude that they are underpaid and undervalued, they are apt to waste time complaining or infighting or to retaliate passively by expending less effort and withdrawing commitment.[29] Indignant incumbents may refuse to cooperate with a resented newcomer. They may even actively seek to leave.[30]

The money and resources that stars command also function as a signal that is subject to multiple interpretations, all corrosive. Incumbents are prone to interpret hiring from outside as "a sign of a lack of commitment to those people who are growing and developing within the organization." The effect can be as if the newcomer has preempted a position that many in the department had been aiming at.

Other star analysts are particularly likely to view a star newcomer as direct competition for resources and for status and attention, provoking bitterness, envy, and refusals to cooperate. The blow to motivation associated with a sense of having been treated unfairly can have a greater impact on the performance of high-ability people than on that of employees of lower ability.[32]

A high-profile hire is also an unwelcome development for the firm's up-and-coming analysts, who characteristically view outside hiring as a signal that the firm is lukewarm about building their franchises. By capturing management's attention, a glamorous new hire can disrupt the momentum of up-and-coming analysts and make them restless. Up-and-comers may quickly conclude that they will have to look outside the company if they hope to be appropriately valued and singled out for comparable treatment.

Meanwhile junior analysts—who traditionally work for a senior analyst for two to three years in anticipation of being awarded their own sectors to cover—are apt to become discouraged about their prospects of promotion and may start to look around outside the firm. Junior analysts are likely to interpret the star's hiring as a strong signal about the company's lack of interest in developing their potential.

All of these responses to the arrival of a star newcomer can result in demoralization, stress, dissatisfaction, disruption of a sense of teamwork, infighting, sagging effort, erosion of performance, and turnover. When hostility to the newcomer is widely shared, active or passive resistance is commonplace. If existing employees withhold cooperation from a newly hired star, two things happen: his or her chances of success drop, and team dynamics suffer.[33]

Steve Balog described the effects on the collective psyche of the research department: "There's this corrosive aspect to hiring stars with big guarantee contracts, because it gobbles up some of the bonus pool and depresses other analysts. . . . So what you have is a lot of conflicts. You screw up the budget. You screw up your culture. . . . The firm sends a negative signal to its up-and-coming analysts. . . their firm doesn't care about building their franchises anymore. . . . The results are that, first, they stop working really hard, and then they all leave for a firm that fully commits to them and helps them maintain and develop their star franchises."

Market Reactions to the Hiring of Stars

Despite the upbeat publicity that invariably accompanies the hiring of a star analyst, we found consistent evidence that investors viewed such appointments with a jaundiced eye and perceived them as value-destroying.

Measuring the Stock Market's Reactions to Acquisitions

We decided to look for measurable stock market reactions to acquisitions of ranked analysts. Such hirings were announced with fanfare in the *Wall Street*

Journal and trade publications like *Securities Week*, and also involved substantial amounts of money and the future performance of research departments on which large institutional investors depend. Institutional investors' money managers were known to follow reports of star analysts' job changes closely and to take an interest in the internal workings of investment banks. Such investors could readily react to a given analyst's job change by buying or selling shares in the analyst's original or destination firm.

The stock market reaction methodology has been an accepted way of measuring ex-ante value effects of mergers, acquisitions, and joint ventures, and has been successfully used in accounting, economics, finance, and law.[34] Its only previous application to the hiring of individuals has been to measure market reactions to announcements of appointments of corporate CEOs.[35] We conducted a short window study of daily excess returns over the event period of −1 to +1 days (the date on which the hiring announcement appeared—the event date—plus the days prior to and following the event date).[36] The data set consisted of 269 observations for ranked analysts leaving public firms and 228 observations for analysts joining public firms. After excluding subsidiaries of larger diversified firms that made less than 50 percent of the parent companies' revenues, the reduced data set consisted of 188 departures and 156 acquisitions. Because a successful event study calls for identifying possible confounding effects of "event smearing" or event reinforcement, 64 departures and 47 acquisitions were deleted for confounded effects.[37] Further, 13 departures and 8 hires were excluded because they coincided closely in time and involved identical companies.

The final data set consisted of 111 exit announcements and 101 hiring announcements for ranked analysts. Stock returns data were provided by the Center for Research in Security Prices (CRSP) at the University of Chicago.

In aggregate, the stock market viewed exit announcements as negative but not significant events. When we looked at 101 acquisitions of star analysts by investment banks traded on the New York Stock Exchange, we found that announcements of such acquisitions were accompanied by an immediate average loss in the value of the bank's stock of 0.74 percent, as table 4.1 shows. This negative stock market reaction was consistent with studies of corporate takeovers, which have found that acquiring companies tend to suffer negative market reactions following the takeover announcement. A loss of three-quarters of a percentage point over a three-day period may seem inconsequential, but it corresponds to an immediate reduction in investors' equity averaging $24 million.

Table 4.1

Aggregate Abnormal Stock Market Returns to Destination Firms around Announcements of Star Analysts' Moves, 1988–96

Category		Abnormal returns Event window (-1, $+1$)	t-statistic	Sample size
Firm	Exiting	−0.14%	(−0.56)	111
	Entering	−0.74%[a]	(−3.07)	101
Entering firm				
Firm quality/ capability direction	Moving to a weaker firm	−1.67%[a, d, e]	(−4.38)	20
	Moving to a comparable firm	−0.63%[b]	(−1.79)	53
	Moving to a better firm	−0.26%	(−0.57)	28
Moves to[f]	Stronger department	−0.22%	(−0.67)	59
	Weaker department	−1.94%[a, c]	(−4.97)	29

Source: Adapted from Boris Groysberg, Linda-Eling Lee, and Ashish Nanda, "Can They Take It with Them? The Portability of Star Knowledge Workers' Performance: Myth or Reality," *Management Science* 54, no. 7 (July 2008): 1213–30, p. 1226.

Notes: This table presents stock market reactions to announcements of movements by ranked analysts. A short window study of daily excess returns over the event window of −1 to +1 days (market model) was conducted. Stock returns data were provided by Center for Research in Security Prices (CRSP) of the University of Chicago.

[a] Different from 0 at 1% level of significance.

[b] Different from 0 at 10% level of significance.

[c] Abnormal returns for Moves to a weaker department is different from abnormal returns for Moves to a stronger department at 1% level of significance.

[d] Abnormal returns for Moving to a weaker firm is different from abnormal returns for Moving to a better firm at 5% level of significance.

[e] Abnormal returns for Moving to a weaker firm is different from abnormal returns for Moving to a comparable firm at 5% level of significance.

[f] No data are available for thirteen analyst-year observations for fixed-income research departments.

Market Reactions and What They Signify

Interpretations of the thinking behind investors' reactions to hiring announcements are of necessity only speculative. But the market's responses appeared to be discriminating and capable of distinguishing among different sets of circumstances. Thus they suggest a consistent point of view, rather than mere knee-jerk hostility to expenditures or to change.

It is striking that though the market delivered a strong negative reaction to acquisitions of star analysts (−0.74 percent), the corresponding stock market reaction to stars' departures was nonsignificant (−0.14 percent). Apparently the stock market does not view stars' exits, in the aggregate, as either value-enhancing or value-reducing.

Investors appear to believe that rival firms are willing to overpay stars relative to their likely future performance. "When a firm has a demonstrated banking franchise and needs a top analyst to drive that franchise," noted James Crandell, Salomon Brothers' U.S. research head, in 1997, "it has stepped up and paid what it takes to hire that top analyst."[38] Shareholders may also anticipate that downward-bound stars' performance will decline after they join a new firm, and that the arrival of a new star can distract and dismay other employees in ways that will impair their performance as well.

Investors may also interpret the recruitment of a star as a signal that the company has started on a star shopping spree. It is well-known that star analysts are often hired to function as magnets around whom new enterprises are organized. When Robertson Stephens lured away Steven Yanis, Salomon Brothers' top analyst in wireless services, one industry insider confided, "Robertson brought in a well-respected senior analyst like Steve as a magnet, to attract analytical and banking talent. You use one to attract the others, because you need a team."[39]

Investment banks intending to establish coverage in a new sector typically start by hiring a ranked analyst. Doing so makes it easier to attract bankers, traders, institutional salespeople, and unranked and junior analysts eager to work with an analyst with an established reputation. Press coverage of complementary hires often acknowledges this relationship. This report in *Securities Week* is typical: "County NatWest Securities has hired Ken Sheinberg, a block position trader specializing in pharmaceutical companies, as a trader in its New York office. . . . Sheinberg's abilities trading drug stocks are expected to complement the research talent the firm has in Denise Gilbert. Gilbert joined County NatWest this summer from CL GlobalPartners Securities Corp. in New York. She is primarily a biotechnology analyst."[40]

One of the investment banks we studied hired twenty-one people within six months of recruiting and overpaying a star analyst—and, according to insiders, overpaid many of them as well. Such ancillary acquisitions were not widely reported in the financial press, so the stock market anticipated the impact of the associated future expenditures on the company's wage bill by punishing the acquiring firm when it announced the hiring of the keystone star analyst.[41]

Because the abnormal market reaction to exit announcements was not significant compared to the stock price impact of hiring announcements, the rest of this section focuses exclusively on stock market reactions to hiring announcements.

Market Reactions by Departmental and Firm Strength

We also examined market reactions in light of the relative strength of research departments and that of their parent firms.

We first categorized research departments as strong or weak.[42] Acquisitions on the part of weak departments of analysts from stronger departments evoked a marked and statistically significant negative stock market reaction for the acquiring firms (−1.94 percent). Otherwise, acquisitions on the part of strong departments of analysts from weak departments generated a small and insignificant market reaction. Apparently the stock market took a dim view of acquisitions of stars from strong departments by weaker departments.

Building on chapter 3, we examined differences in stock market reactions by the quality of an analyst's new firm relative to that of his or her former firm. This analysis took into consideration the strength of the firm, rather than that of the department. Moving to a weaker firm—a move from a bulge-bracket firm to a non-bulge-bracket firm—elicited the most extreme market reaction, a loss of 1.67 percent, as shown in table 4.1. Moving to a comparable firm (a move from one bulge-bracket firm to another, or from one non-bulge-bracket firm to another) was associated with a -0.63 percent significant return. The market's reactions to moving to a better firm (a move to a bulge-bracket firm from a non-bulge-bracket firm) were insignificant. The market's negative reaction to acquisitions of stars by lower-rated firms and weaker research departments may again express suspicion that such firms have to overpay to acquire a star.

We can presume from the market's nuanced reactions to acquisitions of star analysts that the market was clearly uneasy about expenditures it feared were foolhardy and not likely to pay off for stockholders. But it may have also grasped some basic truths about hiring, compensation, and job performance better than some companies' managers did.[43]

Reevaluating the Hiring of Stars

Hiring a star should be a well-thought-out strategic decision, not a knee-jerk reaction to a perceived opportunity or emergency. Generally speaking, a firm should contemplate hiring a star only to fulfill a specific operational aim: to raise standards or introduce fresh ways of doing business or to fill a critical slot when there is no time to train anyone internally.

Even when a firm has such a clear-cut goal in mind, the potentially corrosive effects on morale and dedication of bringing in a newcomer need to be acknowledged and carefully weighed. There is no avoiding transplant shock. It is also hard to avoid scuttlebutt about the newcomer's salary or up-and-comers' preoccupation with what the new hire means for their own opportunities to advance.

Due diligence and pre-acquisition research are imperative. Effort should be expended on developing accurate projections of growth and profit margins, using outside information alongside in-house analyses to minimize bias. It is important to look hard at a spectrum of possible problem areas: the magnitude of the firm's expected gains, the strength of the competition, the culture of the department, the attitudes of the newcomer's future colleagues, the candidate's personality, and the capital requirements of support functions on which the newcomer will rely.

The goal of negotiation should be to make sure that the gains anticipated to arise from the competitive advantage of hiring outstanding performers are not all captured by the stars themselves, leaving no advantage for firms. If the firm's stars are positioned to appropriate all of the added value they create, the firm may be better served by hiring, developing, and working to retain a cadre of up-and-coming employees who would ultimately contribute greater value to the firm.

A clear strategy for integrating the newcomer into the department is crucial. Will the star operate a stand-alone franchise or be integrated completely into existing operations? In general, setting aside questions of personality, newcomers who bring less firm-specific baggage from their former firms will be easier to integrate into existing departmental operations. In recruitment, it is imperative to keep in mind the larger truth that what ultimately adds value to the firm is the net contribution of all its employees. We will look further at the hiring firm's selection and integration of star newcomers in chapter 6.

Part Two | Facets of Portability

5 | Stars and Their Galaxies

Firms of Origin and Portability

Firms appear to confer differing levels of portability on their workers.[1] Analysts who moved to new employers from certain investment banks actually performed quite well after making that transition. Analysts who left other firms suffered notable performance declines after their moves.

Figure 5.1 shows the effect of moving on the performance of analysts who left one of the top investment banks for a brokerage of comparable quality. (The figure shows only such lateral moves, in order to screen out resource discrepancies between firms of origin and destination firms. Only firms for which the statistical estimates were possible to calculate are reported.) The lower a given firm on the axis, the greater the average performance penalty incurred by analysts who left that firm. As the figure indicates, analysts from firms like DLJ and Dean Witter found that their performance declined minimally or not at all when they switched firms. By contrast, analysts who left Bear Stearns, Goldman Sachs, and Merrill Lynch suffered sharp performance drop-offs after making a lateral move.

As we saw in chapter 1, the portability of individual performance hinges on the distinction between general human capital and firm-specific human capital. Theoretically, firms that build their businesses around general human capital will produce employees whose entire skill set is readily portable to other firms. By contrast, the employees from firms that encourage the development of firm-specific human capital will have relatively nonportable skills.

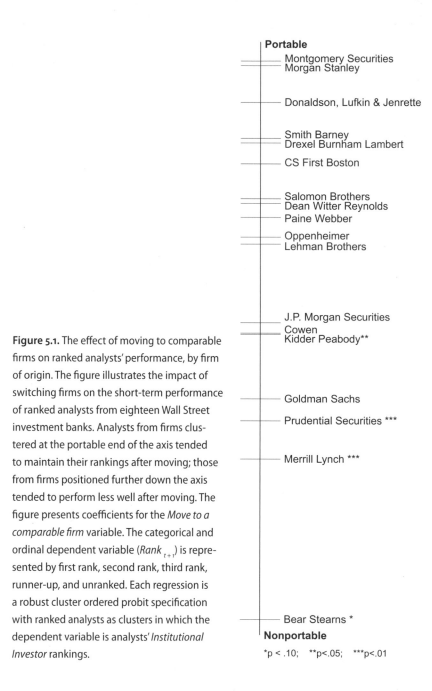

Portable
—— Montgomery Securities
—— Morgan Stanley

—— Donaldson, Lufkin & Jenrette

—— Smith Barney
—— Drexel Burnham Lambert
—— CS First Boston

—— Salomon Brothers
—— Dean Witter Reynolds
—— Paine Webber

—— Oppenheimer
—— Lehman Brothers

—— J.P. Morgan Securities
—— Cowen
—— Kidder Peabody**

—— Goldman Sachs

—— Prudential Securities ***

—— Merrill Lynch ***

—— Bear Stearns *
Nonportable

*p < .10; **p<.05;   ***p<.01

Figure 5.1. The effect of moving to comparable firms on ranked analysts' performance, by firm of origin. The figure illustrates the impact of switching firms on the short-term performance of ranked analysts from eighteen Wall Street investment banks. Analysts from firms clustered at the portable end of the axis tended to maintain their rankings after moving; those from firms positioned further down the axis tended to perform less well after moving. The figure presents coefficients for the *Move to a comparable firm* variable. The categorical and ordinal dependent variable (*Rank $_{t+1}$*) is represented by first rank, second rank, third rank, runner-up, and unranked. Each regression is a robust cluster ordered probit specification with ranked analysts as clusters in which the dependent variable is analysts' *Institutional Investor* rankings.

In-depth research on the cultures, capabilities, and human-resources practices of firms in our study bears out this theory. Firms like DLJ and Credit Suisse First Boston, either by design or through benign neglect, possessed cultures that encouraged analysts to concentrate on acquiring general human capital. When those analysts changed firms, they easily carried with them the skills that had made them stars. At Goldman Sachs, Sanford C. Bernstein, and like-minded firms, however, star analysts grew accustomed to relying on resources and engaging in practices specific to those employers. Arriving at other firms, they tended to experience adjustment difficulties that impaired performance. None of these firms expressly set out to enhance or impair the portability of their stars, but their pursuit of strategies that shaped human-capital formation had precisely that effect.

This chapter will explore the various ways that firms promote one or another kind of human capital. Though the focus here is on firms, the implications of our findings for individuals will be apparent. As our data make clear, stars who emerged from certain corporate cultures were better equipped to enact a "free-agent" strategy than those from other firms.

This chapter draws on detailed interviews with analysts, research directors, traders, salespeople, and executives at the top twenty-four investment banks. Each section portrays the culture and organizational practices of a single illustrative firm or handful of firms. Most of these portraits examine the culture and practices of an entire investment bank; in interview after interview, sources told us that the culture and organizational practices of a given research department almost always reflected those of the parent firm (we note when they are different).

We will look first at firms that encourage their analysts to rely on general human capital, and then turn to firms whose strategies lead them to instill firm-specific human capital in their employees. Next we will examine at length a single firm, Lehman Brothers, and its impressive but uneven history of building a research department around high-level firm-specific human capital. Finally, we will briefly look at the relationship between firms of origin, performance portability, and retention.

Firms That Foster General Human Capital

Several of the investment banks in our study treated their human capital as fluid and non-firm-specific. When they hired successful veteran analysts on the labor market, as they often did, neither they nor the newly hired analysts expected the research department to contribute substantially to the analysts' performance. All parties assumed that an incoming analyst would be given a computer, a telephone, and some staff support, and then be expected to produce. Beginning analysts at these firms typically learned on the job, without the benefit of firm-specific training; at best, they received some general training. Analysts who performed well could expect generous compensation; those who didn't would soon be gone.

Many of these firms shared certain attributes with respect to how individual analysts functioned. Each analyst, along with a support staff, typically occupied a "silo," an organizational space distinct from that of other analysts. Substantive interaction between silos was rare: management did not encourage or promote joint projects or information sharing. Interaction with the firm's traders and its sales force was mostly opportunistic and transactional. Analysts' most intense working relationships were with sources at the firms they covered and with their clients—relationships they could maintain after moving elsewhere. These firms used nonproprietary information systems of a kind employed by many other research departments. Likewise, the products that such firms offered to investors closely resembled those produced at other firms.

Above all, what firms of this type had in common was what they did *not* do. They did not aim to build unique cultures and capabilities, or to deploy analysts' skills in idiosyncratic ways. They did not channel analysts' energies into collaborative projects, or harness them to specialized information systems, or expect unique work products. By and large, their goal was to do what other research departments did, in more or less the same fashion, but to do so more competitively. Insofar as analysts at these firms acquired new human capital, that capital was general in nature—and therefore readily portable to a new workplace.

Though these firms shared many attributes, they can be assigned to two distinct categories. Some intentionally embraced policies, values, and cultures that fostered reliance on general human capital. The others—for reasons of inconsistent business strategy, internal turmoil, or mismanagement—inadvertently created environments in which the only option available to analysts was to develop non-firm-specific human capital.

Intentional Portability

Some investment banks deliberately cultivated a hands-off, "fend-for-yourself" mind-set among their analysts. DLJ epitomized this stance.[2] DLJ's star analysts—routinely referred to and treated as franchises—were considered entrepreneurs, and their operations exhibited many of the characteristics of small entrepreneurial enterprises. Most strikingly, the firm produced a profit-and-loss statement for each ranked analyst, and paid them accordingly. "Here, you don't have the business card that allows a mediocre person to be successful," said Tony James, head of investment banking. "Our people need to have individual strengths. It helps tremendously if you are a brand in the context of DLJ."[3]

In keeping with this entrepreneurial ethos, the firm was unbureaucratic and relatively free of internal politics. *Institutional Investor* characterized DLJ as a "collection of fiefdoms run by powerful barons."[4] But baronial power did not translate into arrogance, according to DLJ star analyst Ed Comeau: "There were no prima donnas allowed, and there was no bullshit. . . . I never saw anybody raise their voice at the analyst meetings, at trading calls—even to analysts that have gotten things dead wrong. There was no screaming and yelling. Everybody did their job. If there were ever any issues, management kind of stepped right in and took care of it."

Management focused primarily on driving efficiency and otherwise did not interfere in analysts' work. "It was not political; it was not bureaucratic,"[5] said managing director Jill Greenthal, explaining why she moved to DLJ from Lehman Brothers in 1996. And Comeau described DLJ as an environment that catered to analysts:

> They allowed the best analysts to really flourish at the place. . . .
> Coming in the door, they gave you their propaganda, for lack of a
> better word, that the director of research is a former analyst, the head
> of sales is a former analyst, the head of banking is a former analyst,
> and the head of the firm is a former analyst. So they gave you . . . this
> whole this-is-the-house-that-research-built type of thing. . . . From
> the time I got there to the time I left, I felt like I had a very friendly
> work environment—not just for me, because I was a star or whatever
> you want to call it—but for everyone at the firm. They treated every-
> one really well, and you just felt really comfortable there. You didn't
> want to go somewhere else and have to fight your way up the sales
> chain or that type of stuff. . . . They all would sit you down and kind
> of give you what you need to succeed and tell you what's going on at
> the firm and treat you well.

DLJ's work practices, though friendly, were not firm-specific. And, as Comeau pointed out, research methods tended to be tried-and-true rather than firm-specific: "Nothing I did was new or different. You learn what the clients are doing. I had a lot of good contacts in the industry that I was able to tap and discuss things with. Company managements would like to have me come in from time to time and talk to their management. And you'd get a lot out of that. And a lot of analysts used these techniques. I think I probably pounded the pavement a little more on the research side than maybe some of the others."

A harsher entrepreneurial culture distinguished Montgomery Securities, where analysts needed not just a strong independent streak but also a thick skin.[6] Montgomery, a small firm focused on the emerging-growth sector, cultivated a driving, aggressive style and an intimidating intensity level. Some insiders referred to it as "a jock shop." "No matter how much business you do," a former trader recalled, "you're always uncomfortable about your job."[7]

Partner and founder Thomas Weisel was largely responsible for the firm's high-stakes, sink-or-swim atmosphere. Weisel was well-known in the industry for his cutthroat style, and his management team embodied the same quality. Head equity trader Robert Kahan, for example, earned a reputation for tirades. The CEO of a securities firm recalled a disagreement with Kahan over a trade: "Kahan screamed over the phone—not just during trading, which a lot of guys do, but he called back again and kept screaming after the close."[8]

The firm's hard-driving environment was complemented by its laser-like focus on building strong relationships with clients. "Thomas Weisel will put a knife in his teeth every morning for any client at Montgomery," one client said.[9] As a consequence, analysts built strong relationships with their clients. The firm's support functions in non-client-facing roles were weak, however, and analysts had to rely on themselves to build business.

Circumstantial Portability

Several firms experienced upheavals or serious mismanagement during the period of our study. Managers who had their hands full maintaining stability or handling problems of their own were unlikely to initiate sustained investments in team building, ambitious training programs, or other efforts to create firm-specific human capital. Likewise, analysts at turbulent firms were less likely to invest in acquiring firm-specific human capital; the value of such effort, they reasoned, was apt to disappear if restructuring occurred. As a result, due to circumstances largely beyond anyone's control, analysts at these firms were left to hone general, relatively portable skills on their own.

Even before it experienced serious turmoil, Credit Suisse First Boston (CSFB) was known as a place that hired stars and then let them run free. CEO Allen Wheat encouraged that approach. "He likes the example of a star. He likes the competitive dynamic," one CSFB investment banker said.[10] As *Institutional Investor* put it, CSFB's culture "encouraged prima donna behavior, discouraged cooperation, and depressed profitability."[11] Meanwhile, turmoil at the firm fed that dynamic. The partnership of Credit Suisse and First Boston, dating from 1978, was characterized from the start by discord between wheeling-and-dealing Americans and conservative Swiss corporate bankers. Virtually every year, CSFB opted for a change in strategy and a management shake-up. New leadership teams were plagued by internal squabbles. Individual departments designed their own business cards. The firm's freewheeling culture flourished, essentially, because of weak controls.

CSFB's research department thus failed to develop either a consistent strategy or permanent systems. Analysts considered themselves free agents and behaved accordingly. "You build relationships, invest time and effort just to see the strategy, systems, and reporting relationships being changed year after year," one CSFB insider said. "There is no stability. People get demoted; people leave. You feel like you're lost. The bigger the change, the less communication comes from the top. The key is just to sit quietly and wait for the reversal of strategies."

Salomon Brothers was another entrepreneurial firm that found itself embroiled in circumstances that compelled employees to cultivate transferable skills.[12] Its CEO, John Gutfreund, ran Salomon as a personal fiefdom, establishing only the most casual of systems and allowing a permissive culture to flourish. In his best-selling memoir *Liar's Poker*, Michael Lewis captured the firm's freewheeling culture well: "That they let me—and other drifters like me—in the door at all was an early warning signal. Alarm bells should have rung. They were losing touch with their identity. They had once been shrewd traders of horseflesh. Now they were taking in all the wrong kinds of people."[13]

In 1991, Salomon Brothers disclosed that it had uncovered irregularities in its bond-trading department. Gutfreund resigned, along with the firm's president and two of its managing directors. The firm was mired in legal and regulatory proceedings for years, and for a time its survival remained in doubt. The lack of processes and structures that had enabled misconduct to occur also reinforced an every-man-for-himself culture, promoting an opportunistic attitude among employees.

The research group at Salomon was in constant flux. Managerial processes changed repeatedly. Internal communication was unsystematic. Information systems were inadequate and received scant attention. Control and compliance functions were weak or nonexistent, as were systems to monitor performance. Teams formed and disbanded quickly. Though the department did develop some star analysts in-house, turnover among them was high. Whatever human capital they had acquired was solely their own.

Firms That Instill Firm-Specific Human Capital

Several investment banks in our study sought to mold or customize their analysts' skills in ways, and in pursuit of initiatives, that were highly firm-specific. These firms did not do so deliberately to lessen the portability of their star analysts, any more than the firms described in the previous section intended to make it easy for star analysts to leave. Their agenda was always to improve the performance of their research departments—and to raise the quality of the information that analysts provided to institutional clients. By insisting that their analysts participate in collaborative or cross-sector projects, master proprietary information systems, or produce unique research products, firms like Goldman Sachs and Sanford C. Bernstein aimed to create competitive advantage in the investment-banking industry.

In so doing, these firms generated firm-specific human capital. Such capital, we have argued, effectively translates into nonportability on the part of any employee who comes to depend on it. In our survey of firms that excel at instilling firm-specific human capital, we identified three types of nonportability: *soft, hard,* and *product-based.* By *soft nonportability*, we mean all unique aspects of firm culture and all human-resources practices that affect an employee's work life: recruitment, training, evaluation, motivation, culture, and collaboration. *Hard nonportability* flows from mastery of a firm's computerized information systems and idiosyncratic platforms, along with the data and capabilities contained in those systems. *Product-based nonportability* is embodied in skills learned to produce goods and services that no other firm sells.

Distinguishing among these categories helps specify the rich variety of firm-specific human capital. In practice, though, these types of nonportability often coexisted and reinforced one another. The firm strategy to promote differentiated products gave rise to customized hard systems; unique systems in turn supported firm culture with its differentiated human-resources practices, and so forth. Thus, though each firm discussed in this section stood out for its ability to instill one particular type of nonportability, it usually fostered other types as well.

Soft Nonportability

Goldman Sachs, known for its clubby corporate culture, excelled at integrating its employees into a web of "soft" practices and procedures unmatched at other firms.[14] "In a lot of cases, we have the same clients as our competition," said Goldman Sachs's managing director John Rogers. "When it comes down to it, it's a combination of execution and culture that makes the difference between us and other firms. Behavior is shaped by it—that's why our culture is necessary. It's the glue that binds us together."

Globalization and Collaboration

Like other investment banks, Goldman discovered in the 1990s that changes in the world economy were creating a demand among its clients for new kinds of research that the traditional silo-driven model could not support. With a globalization initiative launched in 1993 to capitalize on the firm's international reach, Goldman encouraged analysts to collaborate in novel ways. "We would have analysts in different regions of the world who could interact with each other in a global context about their industry," explained Steve Einhorn, head of global research. Analyst Abby Joseph Cohen offered an example of internationally integrated research: "We publish a monthly report on flat-panel screens, which includes input from all our analysts across Europe, Asia, and the U.S. They all work together to get a sense of global demand for flat-panel screens, who's producing, and where they're distributing." Cohen called the result of global collaborative research "incredibly powerful." Such research took time to develop, but Goldman clients valued it highly.

Einhorn called this intense interaction between analysts, domestically and internationally, a "connect-the-dots" strategy. If a chemicals analyst noticed that plastic prices had dipped unexpectedly, for example, he would inform colleagues who covered industries that could be affected by the price differential. The beneficial effect on research quality was enormous. "When a company reported, the analyst would think horizontally across the analytical staff about who would be impacted," Einhorn explained. "And that provided a bond between various analysts."

A Team-Based Culture

Globalization led to a premium on collaboration, but Goldman already took pains to foster an all-for-one/one-for-all sensibility. Bob Steel, a member of Goldman's management committee, described how a firm that bristled with talent managed to keep egos in check: "We have what we call 'pronoun education.' Someone would come to me and say, 'I just did so and so.' I say, 'Excuse me?' 'I just did a big trade,' they'd repeat. I would say, 'Stop. Wrong pronoun. *We* just did a big trade. Try again.' First-person singular is only used to describe a mistake, not an accomplishment. . . . Little things like that are quite significant. I've never heard a boss at Goldman Sachs say, 'I just did this.' If I ever did, I'd be embarrassed."

Deeply collaborative practices followed from this orientation. Steel elaborated:

> We were always taught that the odds are high you'll have bet-
> ter outcomes with a shared work effort than with that of a single
> individual. . . . If a client wants to accomplish something and there
> are ten different ways to finance it, you aren't offering the client the
> optimum solution if you don't get the benefit of all the different ways
> of financing it across all markets—and no one person can do that. So
> in a meeting you say, "Before we make a left turn here, let's call Mary
> or Fred and check it off with them." It's leaders who say that, and do-
> ing so sets the tone.

An oft-repeated anecdote illustrates the degree to which a collaborative spirit pervaded the firm. At a dinner for twenty-five partners in the mid- to late 1980s, a recent $100 million loss by the fixed-income department dominated the conversation. "What have you done to the partners managing the department and the trader responsible for the loss?" one partner asked senior partner John Weinberg. Weinberg reportedly replied, "Look, we're a partnership. The partners responsible were in my office today in tears. We will support our partners because that's the essence of a partnership. Next question."

Goldman's team-based culture not only created firm-specific human capital; it also led Goldman analysts to appreciate the firm-specificity of their performance.[15] When asked what accounted for their success, Goldman stars typically credited the partnership between themselves and Goldman Sachs. "We never thought of ourselves as stars," Einhorn said. "We didn't encourage celebrity. We didn't have celebrity analysts."

Recruitment and Training

Indoctrination into Goldman's collaborative culture began early—during recruitment, in fact. Instead of looking for established stars, Goldman mostly concentrated on bringing in analysts who fit its culture. "We were looking to bring good people into the organization who could do good research, who could leverage the resources of the department and firm, and who would be team players," Einhorn said. "We always felt that if we brought in two good people and they worked together, one plus one would equal three." Einhorn added that the firm incorporated a spirit of collaboration into the recruitment process itself: "People were not only interviewed by research, but also by sales, equity trading, fixed income, commodities, currencies, and investment banking."

Fewer than 10 percent of candidates received an offer. "Our people are what my wife calls gold-star types," said CEO Henry Paulson (who was later appointed U.S. Secretary of the Treasury). "They want the gold star, to get the A on the test. They want to be told they're doing a good job, and they want to get good feedback. We all do." Bob Steel agreed: "People here really care a lot about doing things right and doing them well. . . . It's just a characteristic of ours."

Once hired, analysts underwent a training regimen to align them with the firm and its standards. A rigorous Certified Financial Analyst (CFA) training program that focused on technical financial analysis and writing skills went hand-in-hand with unremitting socialization to Goldman's culture. A senior analyst then closely mentored each newcomer. Goldman managers described the unusual willingness of senior leaders to teach recent hires. "They treated me the right way, encouraged me the right way," one senior partner recalled. "It's a Socratic, collaborative style. Bouncing things off each other is fun, and you encourage that at every turn."

By the standards of Wall Street, where the sink-or-swim model prevailed, talent development and mentorship was atypically wholehearted at Goldman. "The best way to maintain [our] advantage is by recruiting, training, and mentoring people as we always have, one at a time, with great care," said Paulson. For him and others at the firm, developing analysts internally and augmenting their human capital—firm-specific and otherwise—was both a point of pride and a pillar of corporate strategy.

Best Practices

Two practices in particular embodied Goldman's commitment to collaboration (and thus to "soft" forms of nonportable, firm-specific human capital).

First, informal policy specified that the firm and its constituent departments be managed not by a lone chieftain but by "co-heads." Unique on Wall Street, the co-head strategy took advantage of co-leaders' complementary skill sets and also made for smooth transitions. If one co-head left the firm or received a promotion, the other—already well versed in running the department—would maintain continuity. "There's always this handoff, this apprenticeship, this kind of cordial approach to how we hand business over," a Goldman human-resources professional explained. "We take a lot of time, and we try to do it carefully."

Goldman's second noteworthy practice was its emphasis on a close connection between analysts and the firm's institutional sales force and its traders. As at other brokerage houses, salespeople were crucial to getting clients to accept and act on analysts' reports. At Goldman, however, they also helped analysts perform at a higher level. Analyst Abby Joseph Cohen remarked:

> Many of the people who serve in what would be described by many just as a sales function are in fact much more than that. Many of them are very capable investment thinkers in their own right. Sometimes the salespeople will ask the most thoughtful, perceptive questions. A good sales force really can improve the quality of what the analysts are doing, in part because they had their own thoughts and insights but also because they have a good sense of what clients are thinking about and might be looking for. Let's say an analyst recommends a particular stock for the first time. Salespeople will come back to that analyst and talk about some of the reactions clients have had. And a lot of those questions and insights are reflected in the additional work that's done.

The upshot of such practices was an environment that convinced analysts that they could not easily duplicate their high performance elsewhere. Lloyd Blankfein, current CEO and a member of Goldman Sachs's management committee, remarked that Goldman employees exhibited "an interesting blend of confidence and commitment to excellence, and an inbred insecurity that drives people to keep working and producing long after they need to."

Hard Nonportability

Not even the brightest star analysts can shine more dazzlingly than their data allow. At most investment banks, analysts used standard information-technology tools and drew their information from widely available databases. But some firms—Merrill Lynch in particular—invested in proprietary information systems that augmented analysts' skill sets in a very firm-specific way. Merrill analysts who joined rival firms had to contend with resources that were less sophisticated and less customized than those at Merrill. "It took a move to another firm to understand what I had," said one ex-Merrill analyst ruefully.

"The information systems are always populated with the best historic and trend information available on Wall Street," the same analyst said. "They play a key role in putting research together and subsequently delivering it to clients." Merrill began to invest heavily in information systems as early as the 1970s. The system in use in the 1980s was faster and more versatile, and more usefully formatted, than more generic systems. Proprietary software enabled analysts to sort information easily to suit their own preferences and the requirements of their financial models.

Bob Farrell, one of the best technical analysts on Wall Street, described the advantages an analyst enjoyed at Merrill Lynch:

> One of the things that's unique about Merrill Lynch is the accessibility of data. That's an awfully broad term, but take a look at what it means. A lot of data I work with is publicly available. But one of the big problems with this data is that there is so much of it. How can you filter it all—and make sure you see everything you want to see? First, because Merrill Lynch is such a big and well-capitalized firm, we've been able to invest in a computer operation that lets me get to and screen data in ways I don't think [are] available elsewhere. . . . Another advantage is Merrill Lynch's unique sample of activity in different kinds of accounts. We're big enough to have an accurate sample, and our diversity gives us a broad cross-section. And that's helpful in making judgments about market patterns and about what the market response might be to critical problems.[16]

Analysts could access data aggregated from clients' accounts and from the activities of the firm's retail brokers.

A later enhancement of the system was a unique and versatile global database called IQ, which allowed analysts to exchange information efficiently across regions, industries, and disciplines. A Merrill insider described the benefits of the database:

> Our retailing team did an analysis of return on invested capital. Before IQ existed, analysts in the United States would have had to contact

each of the analysts around the world that followed the retailing industry and ask them to either send their models or provide the information on a one-off basis. Here's the problem with that: as soon as that information is input into a spreadsheet, guess what? One of the companies may have announced earnings, so the numbers changed. Or somebody may have changed their estimates. So the information becomes outdated and stale just as quickly as it's input into the spreadsheet. The global database is a real-time repository for all the information that an analyst would need to do financial-metrics calculations.

The IQ database was also a boon to client relations. "We can deliver to clients a consolidated database that allows them to look at our financial metrics around any region, any industry, any company, and basically come to their own conclusions about where there are investment opportunities," said the same Merrill insider. "We can provide that to the client, essentially, at the click of a button."

Analysts themselves took part in populating the IQ database with information—a practice that entailed rigorous training in the use of this and other information systems. The resulting skills were applicable only at Merrill Lynch, as were the skills associated with using and incorporating data from these systems into analysts' reports.

Product-Based Nonportability

Sanford C. Bernstein built its research practice around a product called the "blackbook," a lengthy and comprehensive report on a particular industry or sector that took months to produce.[17] No other firm offered anything like it, so analysts who learned to compile blackbooks were acquiring firm-specific human capital whose value was applicable nowhere else. (The attentive reader may notice that Bernstein is not listed in figure 5.1. The firm is an outlier in terms of turnover—in the nine years of our study, only three analysts left, none to a brokerage of comparable quality. Thus we were not able to include it in our analysis. Bernstein's astonishingly low rate of exits speaks for itself, however, as to the power of product-based nonportability.)

Founded in 1967, Bernstein distinguished itself from its competitors by uncoupling research from investment banking. Other firms claimed to maintain "Chinese walls" between their research departments and their investment-banking operations, but conflicts of interest—real, potential, or perceived—plagued most of them. A few had even fired analysts for publishing negative opinions about investment-banking clients. Bernstein's founder, Sandy Bernstein, believed that most Wall Street firms were rendered incapable of producing sound research by their dependence on investment-banking fees. He forfeited that revenue source, but his firm gained a stellar reputation for the trustworthiness of its research. In a 1994 Morgan Stanley study, institutional investors named Bernstein's research group the purest in its class.[18] Its reputation also translated into a highly successful record of earning *II* rankings.

The blackbook, a trademark product recognized everywhere on Wall Street, was the cornerstone of the firm's differentiation strategy. Some clients described the 180-page reports as mini-dissertations. Written explicitly for sophisticated institutional investors, they offered deep industry analysis along with intensive reviews of companies, market-share forecasts, pricing forecasts, cost-structure forecasts, five-year earnings forecasts, and five-year cash-flow forecasts.

Director of research Lisa Shalett explained the rigor of the Bernstein method:

> You must have a defensible, quantitatively supported argument for everything that you say, and you have to attempt to lay out for investors the what-ifs of being wrong, because we know that 49 percent of the time you're going to be wrong. . . . You want to help them understand what your recommendation is really premised on: what are its sensitivities, what is the one thing that, if you are wrong, is going to blow the whole thing up. You also have to have the courage to identify for people exactly "Here is where I am different, here is what my model hinges on, and here is the implication if I am wrong."

Bernstein urged its analysts to steer clear of consensus views that offered clients no added value. "Almost by definition, if you're going to be right [in a] big [way]—if you're going to make your clients some money—you are going to be anti-consensus," said Sallie Krawcheck, Bernstein's director of research. "If you have a consensus opinion, then everybody else thinks the same thing and the money has already been made." Shalett summarized the Bernstein approach as focused on the big picture: "We're not trying to give you a weather forecast. We're trying to tell you if there's going to be a heat wave or an ice age. We spend a lot of time thinking about the really big issues for long-term investment."

Various aspects of the firm's operations supported its blackbook strategy.

Hiring and Development

"Most of the people who worked on Wall Street came with bad habits," said vice chairman Roger Hertog. "They had to unlearn so much. It would be hard to get people to change and do it our way." Instead of recruiting from the standard candidate pool, Bernstein aimed to hire people with deep backgrounds in specific industries; the in-depth nature of blackbook writing required no less. "The value proposition of every Wall Street firm is 'We have very smart people,'" Krawcheck said. "Our value proposition is 'Yes, we have smart people, but we have smart people from industry.'" Searches typically took more than a year, and the cost of hiring one new analyst was $500,000 to $1 million.

New analysts did not write reports for at least a year. They studied in solitude, gathered data for financial models and other blackbook components, and worked at finding a voice free from external influence. This emphasis on avoiding others' opinions attests to the firm's commitment to product differentiation. "I was *not* encouraged to read other [firms'] analysts' reports on my industry," said Michael Nathanson, a media analyst at Bernstein. "You don't want to be affected by anyone else's opinion. Even at this late date, I very rarely read what other people write about my companies." The result made an analyst's skill set more firm-specific and less portable.

Evaluation and Compensation

Among the firm-specific criteria used to measure and reward analysts was the degree to which they delivered proactive, rather than reactive, earnings forecasts. A typical reactive forecast took one of these forms: "The earnings came in and . . .", "There was an analyst meeting and . . .", "Management called me and . . ." By contrast, Bernstein analysts demonstrated proactivity by issuing stock calls that began "I did an analysis and . . ." or "We did a survey that . . ." This criterion helped perpetuate the unique outlook of Bernstein analysts.

Culture

By building its culture around a unique product, Bernstein bred in its analysts a sense that the firm itself was unique. "I've worked for four other firms," one Bernstein insider confided. "This is the only firm where I clearly understand who we are as a firm, where we are going, and what we stand for."

Those few analysts who left Bernstein to join other firms quickly discovered just how thoroughly the firm's differentiation strategy had differentiated them as well. They had to learn to write short, action-oriented reports for the first time. They also had to learn to handle investment-banking conflicts of interest and in some cases how to bring in investment-banking deals. "A lot of people who did leave Bernstein wound up unhappy, even though they were making more money," said Hertog. (Indeed, many analysts who left Bernstein later returned.)

Building Firm-Specific Human Capital: The Rise, Fall, and Rise of Lehman Brothers' Research Department

Perhaps more than any of its peers on Wall Street, the research department at Lehman Brothers excelled at generating firm-specific human capital.[19] During its heyday in the late 1980s and early 1990s, under the leadership of Jack Rivkin, Lehman essentially mounted a "triple-threat" department: in hard, soft, and product-based ways, it built a team of analysts whose skills were firm-specific. (As we will see, Lehman's fortunes rose and fell during the years of our study, which explains the firm's position in the middle of Figure 5.1. Lehman was a bimodal firm across time in terms of developing nonportability, characterized by strong nonportability investments during the Rivkin era and later under Steve Hash, and by weak nonportability between those two terms.) Rivkin encouraged analysts to work in teams, and to collaborate across sectors. Under Rivkin, Lehman also adopted proprietary information systems that were used nowhere else, and assigned idiosyncratic tasks and work products. Rivkin, in short, worked to build an integrated, value-adding department, instead of merely managing its components in the manner of an air-traffic controller. The result was a culture and a set of work practices that analysts knew they would find at no other firm.

Another result was stellar performance. In 1987, the first year of Rivkin's stewardship, Lehman jumped from fifteenth in *II*'s departmental rankings to seventh. "By the second year, our training program had been unbelievably successful," said Fred Fraenkel, Rivkin's second in command. "People who had been in last year's training program were getting onto the *Institutional Investor* All-America Research Team. Everybody in the firm said, 'A miracle is occurring. We have no idea what they're doing, but they're doing good.'" The following year, the department climbed to fourth in the *II* rankings. Then, in 1990, *II* ranked Lehman first in its annual departmental ranking.

"The research directors of other Wall Street firms were flabbergasted," Fraenkel recalled. "Our people . . . were better analysts than they would be somewhere else because of the people in their team helping them and giving them insights into their industry. Our competitors were offering them jobs with hundreds of thousands of dollars more salary, yet they didn't find it worthwhile to dislodge from what they had here."

Yet, viewed over a longer span of time, the Lehman story illustrates a profound truth about firm-specific human capital and hence about portability of performance: firms must work long and hard to create nonportable human capital, but they can lose it swiftly and with remarkable ease. It took Jack Rivkin three years to construct a department around a unique business strategy and organizational practices that generated firm-specific human capital. Then circumstances at Lehman and its parent company, American Express, changed: Rivkin left the firm and his achievement dissipated in his wake. Several years later, under new leaders inspired by Rivkin's achievement, the department again created a firm-specific, high-performance culture. At each stage, the Lehman story sheds light on the ramifications of encouraging top-quality knowledge workers to acquire capabilities that will render their performance less portable.

Creating a Vision

Rivkin, who had previously done wonders at Paine Webber's research department, signed on to head Shearson Lehman Brothers' global equity research department in 1987. Three years earlier Lehman had been acquired by Shearson American Express, and its research department still had not found its footing in the new corporate structure. "The research department was a mess," Rivkin recalled. "There were no systems in place, no use of electronics, no use of computers, no use of networks to capture and efficiently deliver information." Its culture, meanwhile, was undisciplined, defeatist, and lacking in unique qualities. And there was no strategy.

For Rivkin, a mere turnaround was not enough. "Our objective is to be the best in the business," he told the firm's analysts at the time. "When someone calls a corporation or an institution and asks the names of the best analysts, I want our analysts to be on top of those lists." Rivkin's vision also encompassed global expansion, collaboration among analysts, and innovative products.

To explain how the research group he envisioned would differ from its competitors, Rivkin invoked a sports analogy:

Merrill Lynch is like a baseball team; individual players fill positions and bat. Occasionally they throw a ball to one another, but that's about all the interaction they have with others on the team. If a position falls vacant, the team buys a good player from the free-agent market. Goldman Sachs is like a football team—with very good coaching, but the coaches call the plays. What I was trying to do was create a basketball team, where the players would be interacting and the coaches would be on the sidelines.

On the Soft Side: Building Strong Teams

A cohesive, collaborative culture was the centerpiece of Rivkin's strategy. Underlying his efforts was a commitment to improving analysts' performance by liberating equity research from its traditional silo model. Under Rivkin, Lehman was the first investment bank to organize analysts into sector teams.

Rivkin took numerous steps to foster team cohesion. He organized off-site departmental retreats, complete with team-building exercises. He named team leaders, delegated more and more responsibility to them, and gave them a 20 percent pay premium. And he and Fraenkel adopted a series of "soft" practices, all designed to encourage analysts to cooperate in developing firm-specific human capital.

Leadership and Culture

From the start, Rivkin demonstrated the seriousness of his intention to build a culture that was collaborative rather than individualistic. In a move that recalled a similar practice at Goldman Sachs, he ruled that analysts must refer to at least two colleagues during any presentation to clients. "I don't want to hear 'I . . . I . . . I' in the presentation," he declared. "I want to hear 'we,' and I want to hear other people's names. Believe me, that's going to come back to you in spades. Number one, other analysts will do that for you. Overall, your visibility will increase. Second, it's going to increase the sense among clients that we're a team."

The most important attribute of a research director, Rivkin believed, was "genuine respect for the people who are working for you. These are very capable professionals who are viewed as a cost center and pulled at by every constituency. You have to protect your people." Analyst Josie Esquivel testified to how stalwartly Rivkin championed his analysts: "Not only did Jack understand what we did, but also he loved, believed in, and stood up for what we did." Aware that analysts felt pressure to report favorably on client companies, Rivkin insisted that the department's mission was to produce research marked by integrity and objectivity. The research department, he asserted, was "the conscience of a company." Greg Nejmeh recalled an episode that attested to Rivkin's support of analysts:

> Lehman was the lead manager of a large equity offering for a
> company I covered. I had reservations about consensus earnings
> estimates following the offering, and so issued a neutral rating on
> the stock. It is unusual for a lead manager to not issue a buy rating,
> particularly immediately after a deal. Jack backed me completely,
> even though he took a lot of heat on my behalf. In the end, I was
> vindicated. But the extent to which Jack supported and protected me
> sent a powerful message of independence and autonomy to the rest
> of the department.

Thanks to leadership of this kind, analysts came to believe that Lehman's research department provided benefits that no other firm could offer. "I would wake up in the morning and just could not get there fast enough," Nejmeh said. "I really felt that I was a part of something special." Another analyst, Dean Eberling, said of Lehman research during the Rivkin era,

> We used to have an emotional bond, probably like what we see in a
> start-up firm: "We're kicking ass and we want to be number one." It
> was more than just a belief that we would all get rich together doing
> whatever Jack or Fred told us to do. There was also a strong emo-
> tional bond among the senior analysts, and we were having fun as a
> group. It wasn't a job. We didn't care at all whether we were Goldman
> Sachs or Wal-Mart Securities. What mattered were Jack and Fred.

Benefits ran in both directions. Under Rivkin and Fraenkel, Lehman's research department achieved high performance with a budget much smaller than those of Merrill Lynch or Goldman Sachs. (In 1992, Lehman's research budget was about $70 million, compared to Goldman's $105 million and Merrill's $125 million.) Star analysts stayed at Lehman despite less-than-prevailing compensation to be a part of a department headed by a charismatic leader—a phenomenon known in the department as "the Jack Rivkin discount."

Hiring

Rivkin built his team by hiring several "rate-busters," analysts who were better than their colleagues on at least one dimension of performance. Steve Balog, for example, had covered electronics for Prudential; he understood how to become an industry expert. "We didn't have to necessarily hire a number-one ranked analyst," said Fraenkel. "But the person we hired had to bring something that had not existed in the department. We would hire someone who really knew how to make phone calls or was truly an industry expert. Their practices, we hoped, would rub off on the others."

The goal, then, was to recruit analysts who would help other analysts by mentoring, collaborating, and training them, creating firm-specific human capital in the process. A good cultural fit was essential. For that reason, each job candidate met with several senior people. "Rivkin made sure everyone understood that we would have to live with this person every day," said Judy Sanders, departmental head of human resources. "The ten or twelve of us who had met the candidate decided by consensus."

When star hires failed to work out, Rivkin quickly negotiated their exits. He believed that retaining someone who was not a good fit could destroy his department's culture.

Rivkin was also emphatic about the people he would not hire. "I have a 'no-jerk' policy," he declared. "No matter how good an analyst may be, given the structure we are trying to create here, I am not going to bring a jerk into the department. To me, a jerk is someone difficult to manage, marching to his own drummer, not interested in what was going on within the department and within the firm."

Training

To supercharge the department's human capital, Rivkin and Fraenkel developed an intense thirteen-week training program for analysts. Each weekly session drew twelve to fifteen people, ranging from recent recruits to long-time veterans. "Fred gave lots of nuts-and-bolts lessons: how to conduct one-on-one meetings, how to conduct group meetings, how to deal effectively with different kinds of clients, how not to say stupid things to the press," biotechnology analyst Teena Lerner recalled. Top analysts also led training sessions. "We asked some of our rate-busters and top analysts to offer training sessions on subjects like making a marketing call, balance-sheet analysis, creating something special in your research, dealing with investment banking, and so forth," Rivkin explained.

At the level of content, the program trained analysts in skills that were general and highly portable. "Jack and I told our analysts to become the best industry experts, and we would show them how to become successful. We were going to help them with a training program to monetize that knowledge," Fraenkel explained. But Rivkin and Fraenkel also designed the program to solidify the department's unique teamwork-based culture. "We learned how to build our franchise molded to our strengths. And the camaraderie that the training sessions built was unbelievable," said Josie Esquivel, who became a ranked analyst shortly after joining Lehman. Steve Balog agreed: "People came to understand the importance of marketing, learned various techniques to become successful. But it was also an experience like hazing, like being initiated into a fraternity or a sorority, that strengthened people's bonds."

On the Hard Side: Systematizing Processes

Rivkin also initiated firm-specific processes and systems to further improve analysts' performance, most notably systems that tightened coordination between Lehman's analysts and its traders and salespeople. Among his early moves was rescheduling the morning meetings at which analysts reported new developments and new analyses to salespeople, who in turn conveyed them to clients. The meetings had begun at 8:45 A.M., too late for analysts' recommendations to affect clients' trades. So Rivkin rescheduled the morning meeting for 7:30 A.M. He also began requiring analysts to submit their recommendations to First Call, the system that distributed analysts' reports electronically, prior to the morning meeting; previously analysts had filed their notes to First Call as late as 2 P.M. With assistance from Michael Skutinsky, head of information technology, Rivkin installed a system to feed analysts' notes to traders and to First Call on an automated basis.

In a related move, Rivkin decided to move the morning meetings from the research department to the trading floor. The point, he explained, was to integrate research with trading: "I wanted our sales trader to immediately call up his counterpart and say, 'Wanted you to know that our analyst just raised her estimates on company X.' It would generate a chain reaction, since the institutional trader would go into his morning meeting and say: 'Lehman's analyst just raised her estimates on company X.' It was critical that our sales traders be able to use the information immediately." Another new system required analysts to record client contacts—calls and visits—and any significant information gleaned from those conversations, such as "XYZ mutual fund is about to buy ABC airline stock." Analysts' notes entered an information system, which generated reports distributed to people throughout the firm. Analysts and salespeople thus knew who called whom and how often. With these data in hand, salespeople pressured sluggish analysts to make more calls. Analysts in turn were better equipped to tailor their services to client needs. "From the correlations between calls made and analyst ranking," Skutinsky recalled, "it was obvious that analysts who were dialing the accounts were in fact dialing for success."

Performance Evaluation

Rivkin overhauled the department's performance-review process as well. "Jack knew that people were not going to have fun or succeed if they were continually asking themselves, 'How am I doing?'" Sanders explained. "He asked people to come to the performance-review sessions with their own sets of expectations. And then he engaged them in discussions, setting high yet achievable goals. . . . People understood what they needed to accomplish and what support was available to help them."

A highly firm-specific system of performance measurement complemented such support. "We counted everything: how many calls they made, how many pages they published, how their recommendations panned out," Fraenkel recalled. He and Rivkin charted analysts' recommendations against stock prices to identify missed upticks and downticks. They employed a confidential and highly sophisticated unique commission-tracking system to determine how much business each analyst brought in. Finally, Rivkin aligned these metrics with the most pivotal metric of all: *Institutional Investor* rankings. According to one ranked analyst,

> Noticing that the research department had a history of taking a lackadaisical attitude, Jack and Fred pulled sharply on the leash. Suddenly, there was pressure that shell-shocked some of us. There was a sense that if you didn't make *II* you would be out of the place. We began saying that Jack and Fred's approach was "*II* or die." A lot

of us worked twelve to fifteen hours a day, seven days a week, 365 days a year. But the great thing was that, in my class [in the training program], 95 percent of us made *II* within the first year and a half.

On the Product Side: Innovative Analysis

To differentiate Lehman research from competitors' work, Rivkin pushed analysts to deliver unique research products and to experiment with novel ways to generate analytic insight. "Jack would sit down with all the analysts," Teena Lerner recalled, "and try to help us figure out how to get recognized and ranked. He would preach to us to do something original and then broadcast it as loudly as we could."

Capitalizing on its strong sector-based teams, Lehman began to produce quarterly and annual reports that integrated research by several analysts in, say, the financial or technology industry. Steve Balog cited the example of an "annual report of all financials—banks, brokers, asset managers, insurance, life, property. You want to know how all that fits together, all the interest-rate-sensitive industries." A corresponding technology report would pull together analysis of an entire supply chain: semiconductors, personal computers, software. These hefty "toe-breaker reports," as Balog dubbed them, offered idiosyncratic analysis and contrarian views on evolving markets. Moreover, Balog said, "It's something that helps build our franchise, our teamwork franchise."

A remarkable instance of teamwork-driven product innovation occurred in 1988 when Teena Lerner suspected that Amgen and its marketing partner, Johnson & Johnson, were keeping mum about a potentially hot new drug. The drug, based on the hormone erythropoietin, was making its way through the FDA approval process. Lerner and Mimi Willard, a hospital-supply analyst, decided to assess the market for the drug. "We had two senior analysts—ourselves—and three junior analysts dividing up the fieldwork," Lerner recalled. "Some called oncologists, others called surgeons, others called Switzerland, because the product was already on the market there. The combined answer pointed us in one direction: this was going to be a blockbuster product with multiple secondary markets." Fraenkel described what happened next: "Once Teena described the potential of the drug, everyone in the health-care group set aside their careers for two weeks and began working on this project. . . . No research department could have possibly made this estimation with just one analyst and an assistant. That's basketball—people getting joy out of making the assist, not just the basket—giving up the spotlight for a teammate."

Reorganization and Decline

For three years in the early 1990s, Lehman had the best research department on Wall Street. But the triumph of the Rivkin strategy was relatively short-lived. During the same period, Lehman's position within the investment-banking industry slipped, leaving the firm with a weak balance sheet and hundreds of millions of dollars in bad loans. Its parent company underwent reorganization, and in 1990 research became part of a worldwide equity division reporting to Rivkin and a co-manager. In 1992, Lehman announced that Jack Rivkin would leave the firm. "I was fired," Rivkin later said, "and I could see it coming."

"Jack had always done a phenomenal job of protecting the analysts from firm politics and making them feel safe within their own world," one analyst recalled. "Jack's departure was probably the first indication to the analysts that the world around us wasn't as rosy and friendly as we had thought it was." Before long this series of shocks led to a decline in departmental performance. In 1993, the year after Rivkin's departure, Lehman dropped to second in the *II* rankings. The following year it plummeted to ninth and then fell to thirteenth in 1995.

At fault were management decisions that led the department's firm-specific human capital first to deteriorate and then to disappear. Senior managers at the reorganized firm failed to understand why Rivkin's group had to do things unconventionally. In an attempt to change the department's culture, they destroyed everything that was unique about it. They canceled training programs. They withdrew support from systems and incentives that promoted collaboration. They mandated the use of generic, nonproprietary information systems that were cheaper than those developed by Rivkin and Skutinsky. They undermined unique research products by bringing in new salespeople and traders who insisted on generic products. (To remain viable, firm-specific human capital must maintain alignment not just with other departmental and division functions but also with complementary functions across the entire firm. As we mentioned earlier, the culture and organizational practices of a given research department almost always reflected those of the parent firm. Lehman Brothers was an exception.)

Analysts complained that they felt unappreciated and underpaid, and many of them left the firm. Dean Eberling explained:

> Management cut the analysts' emotional ties by ejecting the nucleus of the department, Jack and Fred. Once the emotional thread was cut, people weren't going to stick. I don't believe for a minute that management planned on downsizing the way it occurred. Once all the common threads were cut, analysts started to leave in a domino effect. You could have thrown buckets of money at the analysts, but that wouldn't have stopped the turnover. Once rumors of disquiet in Lehman's research department reached other firms, it was like the sharks were hungry and looking for a feast. They knew that finally Lehman equity research people could be talked to.

Rebuilding the Department

By the mid-1990s, Lehman Brothers had learned that even something as hard-won as firm-specific human capital could be easily lost. After Rivkin's departure, years passed before Lehman's research department recaptured top-ranked status. Eventually, though, the department did so. Under two new leaders, Joe Amato and Steve Hash, it regained much of what Rivkin had built. By 2001, Lehman was again among the five firms ranked highest by *Institutional Investor*. The next year the department climbed to second place. Finally, in 2003, it ranked first once more. Lehman's comeback occurred after the period of our core study, but a brief description will offer worthwhile insights into the challenge of aligning a group of stars into a cohesive unit with firm-specific capabilities.

Joe Amato was appointed head of U.S. equity research at Lehman in 1996. In 1999 he was promoted to global head of equity research, and Steve Hash replaced him in the U.S. department. In the three intervening years, Amato had focused on replenishing the group's talent pool. "We had some real holes," he said, "that we needed to fill immediately." With fresh talent, Lehman's *II* ranking rose to ninth in 1997 and eighth in 1998. "We were firmly established in the second tier of fifth- to tenth-ranked firms," Amato said. "But being in the top five has a much greater impact. By the same token, it requires a very different level of commitment."

It fell to Hash to complete what Amato had begun. Hash, a star analyst, concluded that the way to improve Lehman's *II* ranking was to invest in a long-term plan to rebuild the research department. Amato had upgraded the department through the risky and expensive measure of hiring stars from outside. But he and Hash agreed that developing stars internally, and retaining them, was a far better way to build a department. "The secret to building a successful organization that can last over time is the talent bench," Hash explained. "The depth of our talent made our performance sustainable over time." He instituted practices reminiscent of the Rivkin era.

On the soft side, he held regular meetings to further departmental cohesion. Monthly meetings had remained in place since the Rivkin and Fraenkel era, but attendance had become optional. Hash made them mandatory. "I used these meetings the way Fred had used them: to institute, reiterate, and institutionalize discipline in the department," Hash explained. "We would discuss how we were going to run the department and what we expected of our people and what we were doing to support them. Once we forced them to begin attending, the analysts liked the meetings."

Hash also revived the marketing training program that his predecessors had created. "I had attended Fred's training program," he said, "and seen how powerful it was." The core group that Hash selected included both senior analysts and up-and-comers. The goal was ambitious: "I said, 'We're going to take these fifteen analysts and develop them into our first group of homegrown ranked analysts,'" Hash recalled. "'We're going to approach this project like a SWAT team. We're going to rebuild their marketing and selling strategies for them.'" Kim Santora, Hash's assistant, described the program's impact: "Analysts who started here as juniors, were promoted to their own sector, and participated in accelerated marketing training have gotten *II*-ranked within two years, which is amazing."

On the hard side, Hash reintroduced department-wide systems to track client interactions. Early in his tenure, he met with analysts and asked to see their contact lists and call sheets. "Most of them looked at me as if I had three heads," he recalled. "It dawned on me that there was no discipline in the department." While shaking up that dynamic, Hash worked to improve the information systems and supporting functions that he was asking analysts to rely on. For example, he hired an entire editorial team away from Deutsche Bank in order to upgrade the department's report-publishing process. (This team hire will be discussed in greater detail in chapter 7.) "We wanted them to know that we were serious about running the place more like a business, and to do that we needed to upgrade the infrastructure," Hash explained. "To be successful as analysts, you have to surround yourself with top-of-the-line complementary assets. Not only the analysts but the whole system must be upgraded if you want to go to the top."

By 2001, Lehman had turned a crucial corner. "Once we broke into the top five, we knew we had taken off," Hash said. "Not only did we have great people doing very well, but we were also building a powerful bench for the future." Of the firm's fifty ranked analysts in 2003, forty had been developed in-house.

Reflecting on how Lehman's research department had been rebuilt, Hash credited the influence of Rivkin and Fraenkel: "I had joined Lehman at the tail end of Fred's tenure as research director. But I had gotten a sense of the magic that he and Jack had wrought in the department." Hash consulted Fraenkel and even studied business-school cases on Lehman Brothers during its earlier heyday. "I took all of what Jack and Fred had done and did it again—and it worked," Hash said.

Culture and Commitment

Looking back on his years at Lehman Brothers, where he had been both an analyst and an executive, Steve Balog observed that building firm-specific human capital depended on sustained commitment by both analysts and their managers. The difficulty of achieving buy-in from analysts accounts, in Balog's view, for the long lapses before performance gains occurred—three years or so, during both the Rivkin/Fraenkel era and the Amato/Hash era. Balog explained the dynamic:

> It takes so long because you're starting with a gang that doesn't mesh and maybe starts out with [an attitude of] "I'm for myself, and I've got to watch out for myself, and I don't want to participate in team products, because life is too short. I have only a limited number of hours, and doing some kind of group project, or coming to these meetings, or helping train the juniors doesn't help my franchise." You have to make it a cultural value. You have to speak that language and have off-site meetings, and people have to understand that they are rewarded for that. It has to be something on their "goals and objectives."

Balog and other Lehman research executives pushed analysts to include collaborative work in their annual business plans. That way they came to understand that team-specific collaborative achievements would help determine their yearly bonus. "It takes a whole year before you can pay the person based on those items," Balog said. "You have to set it up in a business-planning environment. They have to commit to something. A year later, you have to 'ding' them or reward them. It takes a whole year."

And even once it has been meticulously established, that commitment can dissipate all too quickly. To explain how departmental morale can suddenly plummet, Balog used an analogy of soldiers in wartime: "No one wants to be the last dead soldier. . . : 'The regime has changed here at Lehman Brothers. Why should I do this stuff? They don't care about research. They're not supporting us. It's over. We're pulling out and shipping home. I'm shipping out—shipping out to Bear Stearns, to DLJ. The war's lost.' And it happens overnight, as everybody looks at each other and realizes that nobody's fighting anymore." The dynamic, in other words, is asymmetric: commitment to acquiring firm-specific human capital matures slowly; reversion to the norm—to investing only in general human capital—occurs at the first sign of trouble.

Nonetheless, leaders can reinforce analysts' resolve to acquire firm-specific human capital by making various displays of commitment at the firm level. Off-site team-building meetings and the all-important practice of requiring each employee to develop an individual business plan are two such measures. Less intensive measures can have comparable impact. Balog and other Lehman executives lavished praise and publicity on instances of outstanding performance, especially when it was collaborative in nature. "When a group came out with a big piece, if it was particularly good, one of us would introduce it at the morning meeting—which is huge," Balog explained. "I'd say, 'This is a project that's been going on for six months, we're revealing it this morning in this hundred-page report, everybody participated in it, and this is the kind of thing that we're trying to make happen. This is exactly the kind of world-class stuff that we want to be noted for.'"

To demonstrate the firm's commitment to collaborative work, Lehman executives also invested their own time in supporting group efforts. Balog described this practice and its rationale: "You get the schedules of the group meetings. If they're going to have a group lunch and talk about the project that they're doing, well, Fred or Steve or somebody is going to be there to hear it, to encourage them along: 'Uh-oh, so the boss is actually looking. It must be important enough that he's showing up. He's not just going to wait for the report.'"

Lehman Brothers' success in developing its analysts' firm-specific human capital flowed from a top-level commitment to aligning all of its human-resources systems—recruitment, training, evaluation, compensation, promotion, retention—with the goal of creating a collaborative high-performance culture. Nonmonetary awards such as plaques, jackets, pins, time off, gift certificates, flowers, free dinners, and more also helped with encouraging the right behaviors needed for the firm's success. These apparently modest steps also helped entice analysts to invest in skills that made their performance less portable. As Balog noted, "When you're making that much money, these kinds of things [nonmonetary rewards] mean a lot to people."

Firms of Origin, Retention, and Nonportability

The phenomenon of performance portability is closely linked to questions of retention and turnover. Firms' efforts to keep employees from leaving often go hand in hand with practices that lessen portability. Particularly in a fluid and opportunistic job market like equity research, in which stars receive constant overtures, nonportability and retention intersect when at least some analysts recognize that they are better off, and perform better, if they stay than if they leave. (Chapter 10 will discuss retention at greater length.) But a couple of points about firms of origin and their relationship to performance portability deserve note here.

In general, firms in our study whose analysts scored low on performance portability also had low turnover. Stars from portability-oriented firms like Montgomery, Credit Suisse First Boston, and Salomon Brothers opted for exit more frequently than stars from nonportability-oriented firms like Goldman Sachs, Lehman Brothers, and Merrill Lynch. The experience of nonportability companies suggests a powerful connection between keeping employees embedded in firm-specific human capital and processes, and limiting their ability to achieve star performance elsewhere. Both outcomes can result from essentially the same input: an idiosyncratic product, unique culture, system, or set of practices that yields firm-specific human capital.

These outcomes differ in one respect, however. As noted earlier, promoting nonportability of performance is rarely if ever an explicit corporate goal. Rather, firms that employ knowledge workers seek to make the most of those employees' valuable skills, and different approaches to doing so happen to promote or limit portability.

Fundamentally, portability depends on whether any other firm has an equivalent model. No other firms produced research reports the same way that analysts did at Sanford C. Bernstein. No other firm had Merrill Lynch's systems. No other firm had Goldman's teamwork and collaboration culture.

And how people are managed and developed reinforces these idiosyncratic products, processes, structures, systems, and cultures. Retention, by contrast, is an explicit goal at many firms. In a research department, for example, an analyst lost to a competitor becomes costly in several ways: the investment in training is lost; the analyst has to be replaced at high cost; the replacement must be trained; and the competing firm enjoys the fruits of the former employer's investment in training. Firms that depend on knowledge work would thus do well to link their retention efforts strategically to efforts to create nonportable (and valuable) firm-specific human capital.

Specifically, firms can benefit from understanding—and strategically communicating—how much value they add to their employees' performance. Employees' perceptions of whether or not their skills are portable vary from firm to firm and are not always in concert with the experiential record. Perceptions differed strikingly, for example, at Goldman Sachs and Merrill Lynch, although both firms contributed a great deal to their analysts' performance. Merrill employees believed in their own portability: "Superstars are free agents" was a typical comment there. Goldman Sachs employees, by contrast, tended to believe in their dependence on the firm: as one analyst said, "From their first day at the firm, employees are being told how much Goldman Sachs invests in their success."

At firms where the free-agency hypothesis is an article of faith, it appeared to be difficult for employees to recognize that they possessed and benefited from firm-specific human capital. The same goes for managers, as contrasting compensation practices at firms like Merrill Lynch and Goldman Sachs make evident: Merrill's annual budget for analysts' salaries in 2001 was much higher than Goldman's. In other words, Merrill Lynch paid its analysts at free-agent rates, while Goldman Sachs compensated its analysts more on the assumption that they were participants in a "firm-employee" partnership. Employees may have been more apt to recognize the firm-specificity of their skills when the firm communicated that message in a concrete way. When star analysts left Merrill Lynch, for example, they were typically surprised by their sharp decline in performance: they had not realized the degree to which their former firm's capabilities and relationships had complemented their own skills.

At Lehman Brothers under Jack Rivkin and later Steve Hash, analysts invested heavily in firm-specific skills. Because their work was valued and rewarded, and because they felt irreplaceable, they invested in firm-specific human capital even knowing that their portability was being compromised. As one after another attested, they loved working there; many passed up attractive offers to stay at a firm where their performance was supported in every conceivable way, and to be part of something they valued. Yet Rivkin and Hash had to devote three years of commitment to the research department before analysts were fully comfortable investing in soft, hard, and product-based nonportable human capital. In short, firms could only impart firm-specific human capital in the first place if their analysts were willing to invest in firm-specific training, skills, and relationships. And it invariably took a long time for management to persuade analysts to make such investments.

6 | Integrating Stars

The Hiring Firm and Portability of Performance

In chapter 5 we saw that investment banks impart different degrees of firm-specific human capital, and therefore portability, to their analysts.[1] Mobile analysts' post-move success depended, however, not only on the firm that they left but also on the firm they joined. It isn't easy to assimilate a star. A handful of the investment banks we looked at excelled at selecting star analysts and integrating them into their cultures and practices. But many did not, and their new analysts' performance deteriorated accordingly. Specifically, we found that most firms had hiring strategies of one sort or another—some remarkably painstaking and rigorous, most off-the-cuff or opportunistic—but few had put in place carefully considered strategies for assimilating incoming stars post-hire.[2] We also found that the role an analyst was hired to fill at the new firm had an impact on his or her ability to maintain high performance.

In addition to traditional regression analysis used in other chapters, an illustrative and intuitive way to measure destination firms' ability to hire and integrate is to calculate the probability that the star analysts hired by a given firm would achieve star performance again one year after joining. Overall, as we reported in chapter 3, ranked analysts' short-term performance declined quite precipitously after switching employers: only 69.4 percent of the ranked analysts who jumped from one investment bank to another succeeded in ranking again the next year. Of the star analysts who stayed put, by contrast, 84.9 percent ranked again the following year. This decline in performance persisted for mobile analysts. In fact, two years after moving, only 66.7 percent of mobile star analysts were ranked at their new employers, compared to 83.6 percent of ranked analysts who stayed put. Switching firms also increased the probability of losing ranking altogether. And analysts who did manage to rank after moving received consistently lower rankings than their counterparts who stayed put. Even after five years at a new firm, mobile star analysts, in the aggregate, consistently posted lower rankings than their counterparts who stayed put. We also found that there were significant differences in post-hire rankings among hiring firms.

Nine years' worth of data on the hiring of stars can reveal a good deal about the kinds of candidates different firms select and how those candidates perform after joining. Two hiring-firm factors appear to influence an analyst's performance: the firm's attention to hiring and integration, and the role that the analyst was hired to fill. But in exploring these phenomena, quantitative data can take us only so far. Insiders' accounts flesh out the picture by explaining the reasoning and practices of firms that handle integration well and the mechanisms that account for both success and mediocrity in individual performance.

This chapter will look first at hiring firms' selection and integration strategies as a predictor of performance portability. Then we will look at the lessons to be drawn from two firms' experiences with hiring, assimilating, and deploying stars. Next we will turn to the role that the newly hired analyst was hired to fill: was he or she hired to *explore* a sector that the firm had never covered before or to *exploit* the firm's existing capacities in a given sector? This distinction turns out to have implications for a mobile star's future success. Finally, we will take a fresh look at the stock market's reaction to acquisitions of star analysts, this time in light of the acquiring firms' relative abilities to integrate new stars and the roles assigned to incoming stars.

Maintaining Stardom: Hiring Firms' Records and Strategies

An interesting way to look at stars' post-move performance is at the level of individual destination firms. The likelihood that newly hired stars would be successful again within a year of moving differed dramatically from firm to firm. Fully 94 percent of ranked analysts who joined Goldman Sachs managed to rank again next year. DLJ performed almost as well, at 90 percent, thus demonstrating that promoting portability and excelling at selection and integration are not mutually exclusive. At the extreme lower end of the spectrum, Montgomery saw only 17 percent of the stars managed to rank again in the next year.

Interestingly enough, Merrill Lynch hired more ranked analysts than any other investment bank, but only 59 percent of Merrill Lynch's thirty-four new hires ranked again the year after moving—not an outstanding record compared to those of Goldman or DLJ but notably higher than those of Montgomery. Similarly, the efficacy of selection and integration efforts appears most conspicuous at Lehman Brothers, among the most successful firms at integrating new hires. When broken down by year, it becomes clear that Lehman's 81 percent stardom-recovery rate would have been higher were it not for the disruption caused by the departure of Jack Rivkin, as recounted in chapter 5.

Our findings suggest that hiring may be a more complicated matter than simply buying the best talent one can afford, and that post-hire integration efforts may have an impact on success. In the following sections, we will look at how different banks do—or do not—think strategically about hiring and integration, with special focus on the top performance protectors, DLJ and Goldman Sachs.

Picking and Integrating: How Research Departments Successfully Assimilate Stars

Most research on integrating new employees, a field known as *organizational socialization*, looks at inexperienced workers.[3] When we begin to examine the integration of experienced professionals, we are entering virtually uncharted territory. Very little is known about integrating experienced professionals into a new organization.[4] This section thus represents an initial attempt to examine the practices of firms that successfully integrated experienced professionals.

Many investment banks expect that they can simply "plug and play" a star. But the integration process is rarely that simple. Even stars need time to adjust to new settings, and successful integration has as much to do with the attitudes of veteran employees as it does with the newcomer.[5]

During our interviews, we learned that most research departments had no systematic strategies for integrating star newcomers into their firms.[6]

One research director spoke for many of his counterparts: "Obviously, you work to try to get them comfortable with your people and make them feel welcome in the firm, but we probably had about eighty research professionals and we had one research manager. So there just isn't a lot of time for a lot of team building."

It was striking, however, that the companies that assimilated stars most successfully were those that had thought deeply about both hiring and assimilation and had drawn up systematic plans to guide both processes. These companies took the time and effort to analyze and anatomize their own cultures and to pinpoint the desirable attributes of the stars they had developed in-house. They then set about very deliberately to replicate those attributes by seeking out stars with the same qualities from firms with similar cultures. Furthermore, the best recruiters didn't simply shop locally. They looked beyond best-known firms to identify up-and-comers and relatively less-known stars from regional firms and even from global markets (keeping an eye on cultural-compatibility issues all the while).

We found only a few companies among the twenty-four investment banks studied in-depth that had thought rigorously about hiring and integration; two of these firms were DLJ and Goldman Sachs, whose approaches we will look at in the next section. The other management—whose new analysts also had high rates of post-move success—was unwilling to fully discuss their integration strategies, which were guarded carefully as a vital source of competitive advantage.

Dissimilar Cultures, Similar Integration Styles:
How DLJ and Goldman Sachs Hired and Socialized Stars

DLJ and Goldman Sachs exemplified two distinctive manifestations of these general principles. DLJ's culture was frankly entrepreneurial, and the firm valued aggressive self-starters. Goldman Sachs, by contrast, was utterly team-oriented. Because star newcomers at both firms posted outstanding performance, the similarities and differences between the two research departments' selection and integration processes can be instructive.

DLJ explicitly sought stars with portable skills, passing up those with outstanding records who appeared unlikely to adjust readily to the firm's culture. Specifically, DLJ hired three star analysts from Credit Suisse First Boston, three from Paine Webber, two from Smith Barney, and one each from Salomon Brothers, Oppenheimer, and NatWest, all firms that relied on and reinforced portability in their analysts' skill sets. DLJ was reluctant to hire stars from Goldman Sachs and similarly team-oriented firms, however excellent their individual records and reputations, both because of cultural mismatch and because it was simply too difficult to sort out how much of a star's performance at such firms could be chalked up to the contribution of the firm itself. DLJ also adopted a rigorous interview process to make sure that the star analysts it hired would fit well in its entrepreneurial rainmaker-oriented culture. Candidates were told explicitly that they would be expected to build their own franchises.

Candidates at Goldman Sachs were urged with equivalent openness to look elsewhere if they expected to operate as free agents. Both the process and the content of Goldman's recruitment process emphasized the teamwork-based orientation of the firm's culture. "The challenge was trying to ensure that they fit culturally, intellectually, and analytically within a Goldman Sachs framework," recalled Steve Einhorn, head of Goldman's research department. "We spent an enormous amount of time interviewing folks to help ensure that they understood what it was we expected in terms of research, in terms of franchise creation, in terms of mentoring and nurturing younger, less experienced people, and interacting with the other divisions cooperatively."[7] Goldman preferred to hire stars from regional firms, believing that analysts who could succeed at a small firm despite its poorer resources would be powerhouses once they had Goldman's resources and reputation backing them up.

Strategic hiring does not preclude taking advantage of favorable labor-market conditions to build up a department. The key is to do so in a deliberate manner rather than reactively or impulsively. DLJ, for example, took advantage of Drexel Burnham Lambert's troubles to acquire staff as part of an ongoing strategic hiring buildup, as did Smith Barney. (Chapter 7 will discuss these large-scale hires—as well as two opportunistic group hires that did not succeed—in more detail.) As a matter of principle, strategic hires are far more likely to succeed than opportunistic "impulse buys."

Interviewing and Hiring

At both DLJ and Goldman, exhaustive informational binders were compiled on potential hires, assessing characteristics such as the clients' rankings and comments about analysts' support and the quality of the candidates' written research. Hiring decisions were also made in consultation with institutional salespeople and traders, who later helped new hires package their research reports and leveraged their ties to institutional investors to promote acceptance of star newcomers' recommendations. Upon learning that the research department had recruited a star analyst, other departments at Goldman would start to build a presence in the star's area of expertise by promoting and moving internal candidates or hiring new people.

The most distinctive aspect of Goldman's approach to hiring was the intensity of its interview process, which set it apart from most other research departments and even from DLJ.[8] "Their interview process is, perfectly frankly, from our point of view, almost insane," remarked Abram Claude, former managing director at the executive search firm Russell Reynolds Associates. Claude worked closely with Goldman and estimated that serious contenders at Goldman were subjected to twenty or so interviews.

"We did spend an enormous amount of time in the interview process," acknowledged Steve Einhorn. "People were interviewed not only by folks in research but by folks in sales, in equity trading, in fixed income, commodities, currencies, investment banking. So we had a broad range of input with respect to the person that we would be bringing in, in addition to talking to companies about the interview candidate. The interview would be the first thing that would help explain why we were able to bring in good people and keep them."

Investing staff time in interviewing job candidates has benefits that extend beyond the hiring decision itself. The involvement of many individuals in the recruitment and selection process promotes smooth transitions by eliciting buy-in from employees who might otherwise see the newcomer as competition or a roadblock. Because integration of a newcomer involves managing the reactions and interpretations of veteran employees as much as it does orienting the new employee, smart companies take pains to engage coworkers in the process in a proactive way. As Abram Claude pointed out, "They want total buy-in on this person. A firm like Goldman likes to bring people up within their own organization. When they go outside, they are taking away an opportunity for some of those people who have worked hard and well to earn that position internally. So this person better really be good and really be add-on value that people will buy into." Goldman management firmly believed that the interview process was significant from the point of view of departmental cohesiveness and morale.[9]

Compensation

Like the initial decision to hire an outsider, compensation of an incoming star is a question that touches many individuals besides the newcomer. Compensation rarely remains a secret, at least on Wall Street. It is thus of the utmost importance to manage compensation of the newcomer and of others as part of a single big picture and in such a way as to keep veteran employees from feeling undervalued and losing their motivation. Both Goldman Sachs and DLJ strategically managed the compensation of newcomers and existing stars in such a way as to minimize conflict and resentment.

The rule of thumb at both firms was that comparable homegrown stars and newcomers should be compensated similarly. The best integrators made sure that newly hired stars did not destroy the department's overall compensation strategy by becoming highly paid outliers. (We will examine compensation strategies more thoroughly in chapter 12.)

Integrating New Stars

Though the plug-and-play scenario is largely a fantasy, it is important to move fast on multiple fronts to orient the new star to the department and other parts of the firm. To put the point another way: hire with care but integrate *deliberately* and *fast*. It is less far-fetched than it may sound to draw an analogy between a mobile star analyst and the target firm in an acquisition.[10] Top analysts are often viewed and spoken of as franchises, and their compensation may even rival the revenues of small companies. And the success of both kinds of acquisitions depends heavily on integration. The more time is allowed to pass before a new employee is integrated, the more awkward and artificial overtures in the service of assimilation will appear.

Finally, we can say with some certainty that casual, ad hoc efforts at integrating a new employee are insufficient. Smart companies do a good deal of preliminary work to plan the integration of an incoming employee and plenty of hands-on orientation after the move. The firm needs to think through the role of the newcomer, the components of a thorough orientation to the firm's systems and procedures, and the relationships the new hire needs to establish. The models of DLJ and Goldman Sachs strongly suggest that it will pay off to initiate the process of integration extremely early, during hiring, by involving other employees in the process of interviewing and selecting new hires.

Rocky Transitions into New Firms

Once settled at a new company, top performers often find the transition to an unfamiliar workplace and an alien corporate culture a good deal rockier than they had anticipated. Peter Drucker's description of executives assigned to foreign posts applies all too often to newcomers at companies with unfamiliar cultures: "Brilliant executives who are being posted abroad often believe that business skill is sufficient, and dismiss learning about the history, the arts, the culture, the traditions of the country where they are now expected to perform—only to find that their brilliant business skills produce no results."[11]

We found that stars who changed employers overvalued their universally applicable general skills and underestimated the degree to which their intellectual tool kits were firm-specific. This unwelcome discovery parallels the surprise of the executives Drucker describes when they discovered the degree to which their brilliance was culture-specific.

Learning and Unlearning

The initial adjustment to a new job calls for learning new skills specific to the company while unlearning useless past routines and skills. Individuals who are prone to intellectual arrogance because of their past successes tend to resist this process of discarding and replacing useless knowledge and habit patterns. Stars who are slow to adapt to new practices may come around only when they realize that their performance is slipping. In the meantime, however, they may have developed reputations for high-handedness that are hard to overcome. And even those who are not temporarily disabled by arrogance will inevitably find the processes of transition time-consuming.

Strained Interpersonal Relationships

Even basic orientation to the roles and personalities of new colleagues, as well as to the firm's organizational structure, systems, and procedures—which any new employee must contend with—can be rough if the newcomer encounters resentment. Others in the department may avoid the star newcomer or offer only a grudging and chilly welcome, particularly if he or she has been brought onboard with a disproportionate salary or the promise of unusual perks. They withhold cooperation and information. As a result, the newcomer must contend with being simultaneously an insider and an outsider.[12]

Meanwhile the newcomer must find ways to forge working relationships outside the department with institutional salespeople, retail brokers, and traders. Such relationships typically take time because they are rarely promoted and streamlined by formal lines of communication.

Stars in New Roles: Exploitation versus Exploration

The specific roles that newly hired analysts were brought onboard to perform affected their performance. We found that newly hired stars' likelihood of success varied sharply with the demands of different positions. Broadly speaking, an analyst is hired into one of two situations—either to continue or improve coverage of a sector that the firm already covers or to initiate coverage of a sector in which the firm has no previous experience. Borrowing a distinction from organizational learning, we can characterize firms in the former situation as pursuing *exploitation*—the continuation or refinement of existing competencies—and the latter as *exploration* of new competencies.[13]

UBS and Deutsche were the biggest explorers, most likely to hire ranked analysts to expand the scope of their research departments by initiating new franchises. Other firms hired to exploit, in a variety of ways. Over half of all entries to Credit Suisse First Boston and Kidder were hired for exploitation. Merrill Lynch, a firm not known for its farm team, made aggressive use of the labor market to do both exploitation and exploration hires. How did these different roles affect performance?

We compared the performance of star analysts hired to exploit existing competencies to that of those hired to explore.[14] Of the stars hired in the period we studied, 61 percent were hired to cover industries already under coverage by the hiring bank, and 39 percent were hired to initiate new coverage. Table 6.1 compares the short- and long-term performance of two categories of mobile analysts (exploitation and exploration) to that of analysts who stayed put. To illustrate the impact on performance of joining firms in different roles, we again chose to spotlight one clear-cut outcome: the probability that a star analyst of any rank will rank first the year following arrival at a new firm. For purposes of comparison, the probability that a given star in a given year would rank first the next year if he or she stayed was about 10 percent. If the analyst changed employers to exploit, the probability of ranking first the next year was nearly halved, dropping to 5.8 percent. If the analyst changed employers to explore, the probability of ranking first the next year was 4 percent. These relationships are illustrated as bar graphs in figure 6.1.

These results are unsurprising. Firms hiring to exploit their existing capabilities have, by definition, capabilities and resources in place to support the newly hired worker, while firms hiring for exploration are creat-

Table 6.1

Effect of Switching Firms on Ranked Analysts' Short-Term and Long-Term Performance, by Exploitation and Exploration

Category	Independent variable	1988–96 Ordered probit regressions				
		Rank $(t+1)$	Rank $(t+2)$	Rank $(t+3)$	Rank $(t+4)$	Rank $(t+5)$
Hired for exploitation/exploration	**Hired for exploitation**					
	Coefficient	−0.280 ***	−0.117	−0.039	−0.014	−0.227
	Robust standard error	(0.085)	(0.102)	(0.113)	(0.131)	(0.153)
	N	225	203	166	133	104
	Hired for exploration					
	Coefficient	−0.451 ***	−0.547 ***	−0.609 ***	−0.615 ***	−0.337 *
	Robust standard error	(0.140)	(0.144)	(0.150)	(0.162)	(0.200)
	N	141	118	98	82	61
Coworker move for exploitation/exploration	**Hired solo for exploitation**					
	Coefficient	−0.309 ***	−0.079	−0.052	−0.010	−0.175
	Robust standard error	(0.097)	(0.114)	(0.122)	(0.145)	(0.177)
	N	167	149	125	98	80
	Hired as a team for exploitation					
	Coefficient	−0.174	−0.202	0.031	−0.046	−0.399
	Robust standard error	(0.160)	(0.192)	(0.229)	(0.242)	(0.248)
	N	58	54	41	35	24
	Hired solo for exploration					
	Coefficient	−0.705 ***	−0.668 ***	−0.710 ***	−0.534 ***	−0.381 *
	Robust standard error	(0.161)	(0.164)	(0.173)	(0.182)	(0.225)
	N	99	84	70	59	44
	Hired as a team for exploration					
	Coefficient	0.128	−0.263	−0.342	−0.853 ***	−0.215
	Robust standard error	(0.251)	(0.286)	(0.293)	(0.305)	(0.394)
	N	42	34	28	23	17

Source: Adapted from Boris Groysberg and Linda-Eling Lee, "Hiring Stars and Their Teams: Exploration and Exploitation in Professional Service Firms," *Organizational Science* 20, no. 4 (July–August 2009): 740–58, pp. 749, 751.

Notes: The marginal effect of the *Analyst move* variable is calculated as the discrete change in F(x) as this variable changes from 0 to 1: F(x = 1) − F(x = 0). N represents the number of mobile star analysts. The categorical and ordinal dependent variable (*Rank$_t$*) is represented by first rank, second rank, third rank, runner-up, and unranked. Models 1–5 examine the impact of switching firms on ranked analysts' short-term and long-term performance by whether they are hired for exploitation or exploration. Furthermore, we subdivide star hirings for exploitation and exploration activities into additional categories: (1) entries of solo analysts for exploitation; (2) entries of solo analysts for exploration; (3) entries of analysts with other employees, or team entries, for exploitation; and (4) entries of analysts with other employees, or team entries, for exploration. Each model is a robust cluster ordered probit specification with ranked analysts as clusters in which the dependent variable is analysts' *Institutional Investor* rankings. This table presents coefficients for the independent variables for ranked analysts, controlling for individual, firm, sector, and intertemporal variables (not reported). Only adjusted robust standard errors are reported.

*p < .10; **p < .05; ***p < .01

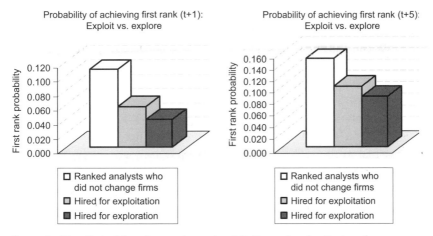

Probability of achieving first rank (t+1):
Exploit vs. explore

Probability of achieving first rank (t+5):
Exploit vs. explore

Figure 6.1. The effect of changing employers (exploitation and exploration) on the predicted probability of achieving the first rank, one and five years post-move.

ing capabilities in a new area. A company would also have a much clearer grasp of how to manage a worker hired for exploitation than one hired to do exploration. In the late 1990s, for example, Morgan Stanley floundered when dealing with new valuation models and new ways of analyzing Internet stocks. The investment committee even had difficulty approving analysts' recommendations because some Internet stocks were valued at very high price-earnings ratios. The firm was accustomed to valuing stocks with price-earning ratios that were much lower.

Fred Fraenkel explained the difference in the sales force's attitude toward accommodating a replacement versus creating demand for research on a new sector. A salesperson is excited to "sell" the newly hired star analyst to clients if he or she is a replacement:

As a salesman, I've done all that work already. I've made relationships; I've tried to make them dependent on me for that information. Now the biotechnology analyst leaves, and I have a void. I have to fill that void, or else I look like an idiot as a salesman, because I've been saying, "Depend on me for biotech, depend on me for biotech," and now I have nothing to say. So I want to believe the new person's better than the one we lost, and I want to go out and fill that void with this person. The trader has been trading the stocks; he knows them. The salesman has been selling the stock. He knows the sales traders. Everyone's all prepped for you when you make that replacement.

By contrast, Fraenkel explained, a salesperson who had never previously sold biotechnology research might well feel, upon news that a biotechnology analyst would be joining the firm,

> Now I have to start all over again and find out who are the people in this account that know biotechnology. I don't know them. I have to build relationships with them. It's a from-scratch start-up for the rest of the firm, too, not just the analyst. It's a huge difference. The only time that works well is when it's an unbelievably hot industry. Then those salesmen, the traders and the sales traders, they would want to learn it, find those people, because they're very, very important and helpful to their clients if they're bringing in something on a hot industry. But if it's not hot in the stock market right then, it's a lot of work for them that they're not going to want to do. They'll just blend it in when they get a chance.

Steve Balog offered a remarkably similar explanation of the hurdles facing an analyst who initiates coverage of a new sector: "A new guy has to do missionary work on a new group. You have to bring the entire sales force up to speed on what, say, pharmaceuticals are all about. Then you help them understand how your view of pharmaceuticals is different from other firms', and you have to teach them all the drug names and all the firm names. And then the sales force is going out there and making not-very-sophisticated calls, and the clients are thinking, 'Oh boy!' So all the leverage that you get from the sales force is not there, all the subtlety of your calls, your thought process, is lost until you get that group educated. And it can take a long time. It can take years."

Types of Exploitation and Exploration Hires

According to industry insiders, some stars who are hired to create something new for a company try to offset the new firm's lack of relevant capabilities by moving with colleagues. The movement of groups or teams from one company to another is known as a "liftout"; this type of movement is becoming more prevalent as team production becomes more common in corporations. Thus, we subdivide star hirings for exploitation and exploration activities into additional categories: (1) entries of solo star analysts for exploitation; (2) entries of sole star analysts for exploration; (3) entries of star analysts with other employees, or team entries, for exploitation; and (4) entries of star analysts with other employees, or team entries, for exploration.

Our findings suggest that solo stars hired to explore suffer the biggest drop in performance; they experienced both a short- and a long-term decline in performance. In contrast, stars who moved with colleagues to explore suffered no decline in performance. This group of stars was able to bring with them some knowledge and capabilities lacking in the new firm. The existing team-specific human capital served them well in entering challenging exploration roles. (Chapter 7 will look further at the effects of solo and team moves.)

The Stock Market's Response to Hiring Stars

Finally, we looked at firms' relative success at integrating the ranked analysts they brought onboard and at the market's reactions to hiring by firms that demonstrated themselves to be either skilled or inept at integration.[15] We categorized firms on the basis of these probabilities as either good or bad integrators, on the grounds that firms whose new analysts regained prominence must be providing useful support and vice versa.

The stock market appeared to value a research department's ability to integrate stars successfully but to view the acquisition of less able integrators as value-reducing.[16] Table 6.2 shows the aggregate reactions of the stock market to acquisitions of stars by the hiring firm's integration capability and by the roles analysts were hired to perform. As the table shows, the acquisition of a star analyst by a weaker integrator evoked a strong and statistically significant negative stock-market reaction (−1.25 percent) to the acquiring firm. A similar acquisition by a stronger integrator elicited a much smaller, nonsignificant negative reaction (−0.34 percent).

This finding is particularly provocative. It suggests that stock-market reaction was partly based on a set of observations or predictions about the internal operation and integration capabilities of different research departments. The discernment represented by the market reaction suggests that the market recognized certain research departments' ability to integrate talented new analysts and regarded comparable hires by bad integrators as value-reducing.

Table 6.2

Aggregate Abnormal Stock-Market Returns to Destination Firms
around Announcements of Acquisition of Star Analysts,
by Firm's Integration Capability and Nature of New Role, 1988–96

Category		Abnormal returns		
		Event window (−1, +1)	t-statistic	Sample size
Integration capability	Stronger	−0.34%	(−1.12)	57
	Weaker	−1.25%[a,c]	(−3.35)	44
Hired for exploitation/ exploration	Hired for exploitation	−0.56%[b]	(−1.93)	68
	Hired for exploration	−1.10%[a]	(−2.57)	33
Coworker move for exploitation/ exploration	Hired solo for exploitation	−0.44%	(−1.16)	46
	Hired as a team for exploitation	−0.81%[b]	(−1.89)	22
	Hired solo for exploration	−0.87%	(−1.71)	24
	Hired as a team for exploration	−1.72%[b]	(−2.14)	9

Source: Adapted from Boris Groysberg and Linda-Eling Lee, "Hiring Stars and Their Teams: Exploration and Exploitation in Professional Service Firms," *Organizational Science* 20, no. 4 (July–August 2009): 740–58, p. 752.

Notes: This table presents stock-market reactions to announcements of movements by the ranked analysts. A short window study of daily excess returns over the event window of −1 to +1 days (market model) was conducted. Stock returns data were provided by Center for Research in Security Prices (CRSP) of the University of Chicago.

[a] Different from 0 at 5% level of significance.

[b] Different from 0 at 10% level of significance.

[c] Abnormal returns for "stronger" integrators is different from abnormal returns for "weaker" integrators at 10% level of significance.

The magnitude of the abnormal returns also depended on whether firms were hiring stars for exploitation or exploration. The market reacted negatively and significantly to the news that ranked analysts had been hired to exploit existing capabilities (−0.56 percent). Announcements of acquisitions of star analysts to explore by establishing brand-new coverage of a sector generated a significant negative stock-market reaction (−1.10 percent). Investors might have been anticipating a drop in performance on the part of analysts who move to a firm that is exploring new areas. The market reactions to the news that ranked analysts had been hired to exploit were not significantly different from market reactions to news that ranked analysts had been hired to explore.

We also found that news of the hiring of an individual star analyst for exploitation was greeted with insignificant negative abnormal returns (−0.44 percent). News of the hiring of an analyst with a team for exploitation generated a significant negative stock-market reaction (−0.81 percent). News of the hiring of a solo star analyst when the firm is exploring was also met with negative abnormal returns (−0.87 percent). News of the hiring of a star analyst with a team when the firm is exploring generated a stronger significant negative reaction (−1.72 percent). Hiring a star along with his or her colleagues to explore appeared to destroy more value than hiring an individual star to exploit.

☆ ☆ ☆

These findings, along with those we reported in chapters 3 and 5, together make a strong case for the decisive role of context in performance, even among the very best performers. The performance of an outstanding performer is not owned by the individual alone, but is a property of the individual-team-firm combination.

Two findings in this chapter are of particular interest. The first is that the analysts who performed worst were those who were hired to explore. (Stars hired to exploit had much less to lose in terms of individual performance.) However, stars who moved with teammates into exploration roles suffered no performance decline. Bringing their colleagues with them and retaining some team-specific human capital seemed to mitigate the loss in firm capabilities.

As we will see in chapter 7, moving to a new firm with colleagues protected performance: star analysts who moved as a team (with junior analysts and/or colleagues from related functions such as sales or trading) were more likely to perform well after their move than were analysts who moved solo. Together, these results are compelling evidence for the powerful effect of team-specific human capital on performance: teams can truly make or break the individual.

In addition, we see that the firms that conducted the greatest due diligence on potential new hires and were strategic about integrating newcomers had the best rates of post-hire success. The lesson for firms is clear: do not assume that finding and buying the best and brightest will ensure success. An investigation into goodness of fit between the firm and the star is necessary to preserve performance. However, this investigation can be done from either the firm or the individual side. As we will see in chapter 8, performance can also be protected if the employee conducts due diligence on the firm. Female star analysts, aware that many investment banks are not advantageous places for women, tended to be very cautious when approaching new offers and investigated the culture of a research department thoroughly before deciding to make a move. Partly as a result of this caution, star women who changed employers did not experience the decline that star men did.

7 | **Liftouts** (Taking Some of It with You)

Moving in Teams

Among star analysts who changed employers between 1988 and 1996, those who moved in teams performed better than those who moved solo.[1] In fact, analysts who changed employers along with teammates suffered no significant decline in performance, in contrast to the decline of those who moved alone. (See table 7.1.) This finding suggests that team-specific human capital accounts for a significant portion of those analysts' performance.[2]

The effect on short-term performance of moving solo (0.061) was larger than that of changing firms with teammates (0.006). As figure 7.1 shows in graphic form, the probability of ranking first in year t + 1 was only .045 for analysts who changed investment banks solo, and .100 for ranked analysts who switched employers with their teammates. The probability of ranking first in the first full year after moving was almost twice as high for analysts who switched employers with teammates as for those who moved solo. This finding provides strong evidence for the effect of in-house relationships on performance. Stars do not develop in a vacuum; their performance depends heavily on the people with whom they work. If they can bring some of that firm-specific relational capital with them from one employer to another, their chances of maintaining their exceptional performance increase dramatically.[3]

Out of 366 ranked analysts' moves, 100 were with other ranked analysts, junior analysts, institutional salespeople, or traders. Paine Webber and Alex.

Table 7.1
Effect of Switching Firms on Ranked Analysts' Short-Term and Long-Term Performance by Type of Move

Category	Independent variable	1988–96 Ordered probit regressions				
		Rank $(t+1)$	Rank $(t+2)$	Rank $(t+3)$	Rank $(t+4)$	Rank $(t+5)$
Coworker move	Moving solo					
	Coefficient	−0.440 ***	−0.270 ***	−0.269 ***	−0.167	−0.242 *
	Robust std. err.	(0.086)	(0.097)	(0.103)	(0.118)	(0.146)
	N	266	233	195	157	124
	Moving in teams					
	Coefficient	−0.033	−0.149	−0.070	−0.267	−0.275
	Robust std. err.	(0.132)	(0.170)	(0.188)	(0.204)	(0.206)
	N	100	88	69	58	41

Source: Adapted from Boris Groysberg, Linda-Eling Lee, and Ashish Nanda, "Can They Take It with Them? The Portability of Star Knowledge Workers' Performance: Myth or Reality," *Management Science* 54, no. 7 (July 2008): 1213–30, p. 1224.

Notes: The marginal effect of the *Analyst move* variable is calculated as the discrete change in F(x) as this variable changes from 0 to 1: F(x = 1) − F(x = 0). N represents the number of mobile star analysts. The categorical and ordinal dependent variable ($Rank_t$) is represented by first rank, second rank, third rank, runner-up, and unranked. Models 1–5 examine the impact of switching firms on ranked analysts' short-term and long-term performance by whether they move solo or in teams. Each model is a robust cluster ordered probit specification with ranked analysts as clusters in which the dependent variable is analysts' *Institutional Investor* rankings. This table presents coefficients for the independent variables for ranked analysts, controlling for individual, firm, sector, and intertemporal variables (not reported). Only adjusted robust standard errors are reported.

$*p < .10; **p < .05; ***p < .01$

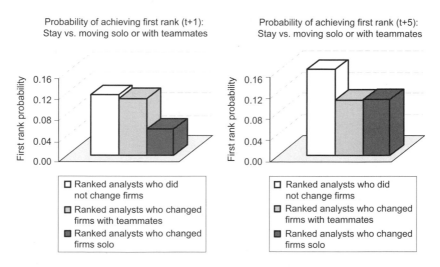

Probability of achieving first rank (t+1):
Stay vs. moving solo or with teammates

Probability of achieving first rank (t+5):
Stay vs. moving solo or with teammates

□ Ranked analysts who did not change firms
▨ Ranked analysts who changed firms with teammates
■ Ranked analysts who changed firms solo

Figure 7.1. The effect of changing firms solo or with a team on the predicted probability of ranking first, one and five years post-move.

Brown appeared to have built new franchises around superstars by simultaneously hiring complementary staff. Kidder and Deutsche Bank brought in star analysts only as opportunistic individual hires.[4]

Interestingly enough, the market reacted more negatively to team hires than to solo hires, suggesting that investors believe that firms overpay more to attract teams than they do to capture individuals. As table 7.2 shows, the news of the hiring of an individual analyst generated significant negative abnormal returns (−0.62 percent), and the news of hiring a star along with a team is more value-destroying, with a negative abnormal return of −0.99. Investors might believe that firms have to overpay more to attract teams than they do to capture individuals.

This chapter will look at team moves in the knowledge professions, with an emphasis on analysts, and will explore why team moves, also known as liftouts, are attractive both to acquiring organizations and to the teams themselves. We will use the stories of three team moves from Drexel Burnham Lambert (following that company's 1990 collapse) to illustrate the stages of a liftout. Finally, we will profile a liftout that was a success: the move of an entire editorial-production team from one investment bank to another.

This chapter also draws on supportive research from outside the analyst research sector: interviews with leaders of teams in multiple industries that have moved from one company to another; analysis of over thirty high-

Table 7.2

Aggregate Abnormal Stock-Market Returns to Destination Firms around Announcements of Acquisition of Star Analysts (Solo or with a Team), 1988–96

Category		Abnormal returns		
		Event window (−1, +1)	t-statistic	Sample size
Coworker move	Solo	−0.62%[a]	(−2.05)	70
	Team	−0.99%[a]	(−2.60)	31

Source: Adapted from Boris Groysberg, Linda-Eling Lee, and Ashish Nanda, "Can They Take It with Them? The Portability of Star Knowledge Workers' Performance: Myth or Reality," *Management Science* 54, no. 7 (July 2008): 1213–30, p. 1226.

Notes: This table presents stock-market reactions to announcements of movements by ranked analysts. A short window study of daily excess returns over the event window of −1 to +1 days (market model) was conducted. Stock returns data were provided by the Center for Research in Security Prices (CRSP) of the University of Chicago.

[a] Different from 0 at 5% level of significance.

profile team moves reported in the business press; interviews on practices with search consultants who facilitate liftouts; and three case studies of team moves. We believe that including this research offers greater insight into liftouts and enhances the generalizability of our arguments.[5]

The Phenomenon of Team Moves

Hiring teams, known colloquially on Wall Street as "block trading in people," has become a modest trend in investment banking—and other industries— over the last decade and a half.[6] Once rare, the practice of hiring teams has become more common.[7] *BusinessWeek* confirmed the emergence of liftouts as a new trend in numerous industries:

> While lift-outs have been common in such industries as financial services and law, the practice of snatching plug-and-play teams has been expanding into different fields. Professional services firms, such as management consulting and accounting shops, are seeing a rise in the hiring of teams, say some executive recruiters. And while it's rare so far, the practice has popped up among apparel manufacturers, software outfits, and medical firms, too. . . . Even in fields where they have long existed, lift-outs are growing. . . . When done well, lift-outs can pack a powerful punch. There's no denying the intangible value of team chem- istry that doesn't have to be developed from scratch. Such cohesive units can hit the ground running and quickly find scale in new business lines. And lift-outs can also prompt customers who had relationships with departing team members to eventually follow them, too.[8]

This chapter does not address the legal matters surrounding liftouts—ques- tions of noncompetition, nonsolicitation, confidentiality, and intellectual property. Both employees and firms *need* to understand the law; these is- sues are highly contested, vary by country, and reside within the domain of labor lawyers.

Team Moves among Equities Analysts

Among equities analysts in particular, Wall Street and its European and Asian counterparts have witnessed a steady trickle of liftouts over the past decade. Some notable examples include the following:

- In 1995, Morgan Stanley hired a six-member energy team from Credit Suisse First Boston (CSFB). The same day they started at Morgan Stanley, ranked oil-and-gas analysts Gordon Hall and James Clark returned to CSFB. Former CSFB colleagues had barraged them with phone calls asking them to return. "They realized they were in the wrong building and came right back home," said Charles Murphy, managing director of worldwide equities at CSFB. "There was a massive effort on the part of the firm to get them back."[9] CSFB did not even have to raise their pay to get them to return. "There was no overinflated Wall Street bribe, which makes it even more fun," Murphy reported.[10] Although one ranked analyst and three bankers stayed at Morgan Stanley, the event was an embarrassment for the firm. Morgan Stanley claimed that it valued each member of the team equally but had clearly been most interested in Hall and Clark.
- In 1996, County NatWest hired ranked chemicals analysts Andrew Cash and David Manlowe from Paine Webber and a team of two medical-technology analysts from Raymond James.
- In 1998, Salomon Smith Barney moved to expand its coverage in Asia by hiring five Union Bank of Switzerland analysts in Singapore and Malaysia and a team of two steel analysts from UBS Securities.
- In 2000, Deutsche Bank poached a team of two ranked energy analysts from DLJ.
- In 2000, Conseco Capital Management suffered a rash of poachings, losing sixteen or so members of its fixed-income management group to Delaware Investments (among other personnel losses), along with a number of clients. The loss of its fifteen-person equity-management team to Strong Capital Management even led Conseco to hire outside advisors to manage equity mutual funds.
- In 2000, CSFB hired two telecommunications analysts from Schroders. Salomon Smith Barney, which was merging with Schroders, retaliated by hiring seven telecom analysts away from CSFB two months later. "A jolly little spat between Credit Suisse First Boston and Schroder Salomon Smith Barney is bubbling away nicely," the *Financial Times* observed.[11]
- In 2002, J. P. Morgan's European equity research department poached HSBC's three-person metal-and-mining team and Morgan Stanley's first-ranked tobacco-sector team.
- In 2002, HSBC was left with only a trainee to analyze media equities when its entire media-analyst team decamped for ABN Amro.

- In 2002, Bank of America poached biotech analysts Karl Keegan and Michael Booth from UBS Warburg to bolster its new European equities group.
- In 2003, Bank of America Securities hired a four-person ranked health-care team away from CSFB.
- In 2004, Morgan Stanley poached a ranked team of UBS oil analysts.

Why the Rise in Liftouts?

Why have liftouts become increasingly prevalent? Does their popularity imply that despite the dominance of the free-agent ideology and the skeptical reaction of the stock market to team hires there exists nonetheless a recognition of the importance of team-specific human capital to individual success? Some anecdotal evidence and the analysis of executive recruiters and human resource professionals imply an awareness of contextual factors. But rather than reflecting a full-scale appreciation of the importance of firm- and team-specific human capital, the increasing popularity of liftouts appears to be attributable to structural aspects of the labor market, the particular goals of hiring firms, and the emotional comfort level of lifted-out teams.

The emergence of teams as organizational building blocks has become a noteworthy trend in corporate management practice throughout the industrialized world. By the mid-1990s, 68 percent of Fortune 500 companies were using self-managing teams to accelerate and improve development of products and services and thus shorten time to market.[12]

To some degree, firms may lift out teams because there are few other alternatives when seeking to move into a new terrain. Firms eager to establish a presence in a new sector or region were once far more likely to acquire a specialized boutique, as happened during the acquisition period of the 1970s. After the wave of mergers in the 1980s and 1990s, which shrank the ranks of smaller firms, however, acquiring specialty firms became a difficult proposition. Thus, there are more teams available for liftout than there are boutiques for acquisition.

Acquiring a team is also considered more efficient. Liftouts are more targeted than acquisitions; the hiring company is not burdened with excess baggage in the form of either unwanted employees or physical resources. Insiders argue that acquiring teams is faster, more efficient, and less expensive.

By enabling individuals to keep some of their firm-specific human capital intact, furthermore, the liftout can be a more reliable guarantor of success than an individual hire. Hiring a team can help avoid the problem of bringing in a new player who will fail to replicate his or her previous success.

As we noted in chapter 6, hiring even an individual analyst has certain similarities to a corporate acquisition. In strategic and operational terms, acquiring a team certainly resembles buying a small company far more than it does ordinary hiring. The process of integration can be similar, and similarly tricky. But though a large liftout can resemble a small acquisition, several fundamental dynamics differ. Since the lifted-out team has moved voluntarily, the resistance, sense of loss, and resentment that accompany mergers and acquisitions are not an issue. And the logistical issues that plague mergers and acquisitions (integrating physical and financial assets, coordinating production timelines) are less difficult in liftouts.

Hiring a team can also have a more dramatic impact on clients than bringing on a collection of individuals in ones and twos. "If you hire a team of people," pointed out Richard Lipstein of Boyden Global Executive Search, "you could have much more impact marketing that particular sector to the asset-management firms." And as one European headhunter noted, "Hiring a team raises your visibility; it's a great public-relations exercise."[13] (This exercise in public relations can turn into an exercise in humiliation, however, if the newly acquired stars underperform, return to their previous employer, or quickly defect to even greener pastures.)[14]

Lipstein also argued that a team can be more cost-effective: "If you make the assumption that $1 + 1 = 3$, hiring three people who have worked together is a lot more cost-effective than hiring three people who come from different firms and then putting them together." An experienced team can make an impact faster than a group of people brought together for the first time.[15] There is no need for the team members to get acquainted or to establish shared objectives, mutual accountability, or group norms.[16] "The hiring investment bank gets instant crucial mass," observed Maria Wallace, a consultant at a financial-services search firm.[17]

Companies also lift out teams to enter new markets. According to a financial-services executive-search consultant,

> In order to make a real impact in getting into a new market . . . you almost need to do an acquisition of sorts. If you want to be in the telecom space and you're not covering telecom right now . . . you

have the choice of either going out cherry-picking and getting a person and then hiring another person, then hiring another person, and all that can take several years before you have the team in place. And oh, by the way, the team may not be a great one, because they don't necessarily work well together. They're all from different places, and they may have been great where they were, but you put them together, it doesn't work. And so there's a higher probability that if you took a whole team away from a competitor and just repotted them they would be more successful.

Furthermore, a good liftout does not merely benefit the hiring company but also damages its rivals.[18] "If we lost a senior analyst, we would do everything we could to keep the team," said Sara Karlen, head of human resources in Merrill Lynch's research department. "It just cost too much institutionally to lose that entire team and bring a new team onboard after all the investment we had made in institutional knowledge." The unexpected departure of a team can prompt premature internal promotions or poaching from another institution, which can be the prelude to a tricky integration process and a financial hit if it is necessary to pay premiums to lure new recruits. And just as poaching a team of high-profile stars is a public-relations "win" for the poaching firm, it also damages the reputation of the poached firm.

Why Teams Move

Teams move for the same reasons individuals move: higher pay, a better work environment, more interesting challenges. But why do they move *as teams*? To a large extent, workers move as teams because they are organized as teams. Knowledge-based companies are increasingly organizing workplaces into teams and assigning the responsibility for hiring, socializing, managing, motivating, developing, and rewarding to team leaders. Team members in turn develop strong loyalties to their leaders and to each other—stronger, often, than their loyalties to the firm itself.[19] As one executive recruiter put it, "Increasingly, the new allegiance is to your group head or your mentor, not the firm."[20] In our interviews with junior analysts, for example, it was evident that many felt greater loyalty to a senior analyst than to the firm. "Your loyalty is with the person who hired and trained you," one junior analyst explained. "What exactly can my firm do for me that my boss can't?"

And the loyalty does not only flow upward; senior or star analysts are likely to recognize the importance of their juniors, especially when considering a move to a new environment. Steve Balog explained the contribution of junior analysts to a mobile team:

> Juniors are vital to the senior's success at the new place. They keep the wheels turning—models, reports, et cetera—and make the relaunch at the new firm quicker. Star analysts get a decent amount of pressure to launch quickly: the new sales force wants to run with the new toy. So that's why the senior wants to keep them. The junior typically goes because (a) they are comfortable with the devil they know, (b) the senior gets them a pay boost, (c) they can come into the new firm as conquering heroes, and (d) the old firm doesn't make an effort to keep them because they're reeling and are focused on replacing the senior, and they don't value the juniors and fail to take the longer view and don't see them as future seniors.

(Note that Balog contradicts Karlen's assertion, mentioned earlier, that firms would make a considerable effort to retain team members, reflecting differences in retention strategies between investment-banking firms that we will see in chapter 10.)

Most often, team members' motivation in moving together is to perpetuate relationships and networks that they value highly, especially with high-performing colleagues.[21] Ranked analysts and team leaders may want to take along members of their teams to ensure that they continue to have access to the resources that contributed to their exceptional performance. As Fred Fraenkel put it, "We preach to people. We preach giving up your individuality into this team, and the team makes you better than you would have otherwise been. And once that happened, people believed it, and they said, 'If I go without these two guys, I don't know if I'm going to be as good as I was.' And so I think the evolution that you are now seeing is the finishing of that cycle."

Headhunter Abram Claude made a similar observation but with a focus on moves to lesser firms: "If they're moving to a boutique, they want to take their team with them. They feel they will be more immediately successful and comfortable, and they don't have to rely on the firm they're going to. They bring a working unit with them. This happens a lot. . . . They want all those people around them because the firm they're going to doesn't have those people."

The Drexel Diaspora

In contrast to the vast literature on mergers and acquisitions on the one hand and strategic individual hiring on the other, the middle ground of the team move is largely unexplored.[22] Our research indicates that it is the role of the team leader that primarily distinguishes liftouts from acquisitions in a variety of industries. Nearly all the teams we studied had a leader or key player who orchestrated the move. The existence of a team leader, usually a ranked analyst, is the norm when analysts move in teams. If this leader is effective and credible, he or she can help the team recoup the firm-specific human capital that it has lost in the move and continue to perform well.

Although moving with a team helps preserve performance, not all team moves are successful. An examination of the fortunes of three groups that moved in the wake of the Drexel collapse—not only the performance of the analysts but the overall success of the new firm—can illustrate points of vulnerability.

When the high-profile and aggressive investment bank Drexel Burnham Lambert declared bankruptcy in 1990, a particularly dramatic rash of team moves followed.[23] Although the Drexel exodus was not voluntary, and therefore not representative of team moves in general, it remains an excellent case study of liftouts because so many variables are held constant. All of the teams shared the same corporate culture; all of the moves happened at the same time, controlling for shifting industry trends and the vicissitudes of the market; and the number of teams involved lends substance to any lessons we can extract from their comparative experiences.

Three teams of analysts left Drexel after the bankruptcy, along with other professionals—the largest group to County NatWest, another to Barclays de Zoete Wedd, and a team of two to DLJ.[24] (See table 7.3 for a list of Drexel's ranked analysts in 1989 and their post-move rankings.)[25] Many other ranked analysts moved alone, taking no complementary staff or junior analysts with them.

Two of the three moves we will look at—to County NatWest and Barclays de Zoete Wedd (BZW)—can be considered overall failures. The third, to DLJ, was a success. These findings demonstrate that though moving in groups is a performance protector for analysts, it is not a guarantee. Moving in groups promotes portability of performance by keeping intact some important relationships and hence some team-specific human capital. But unless an entire unit moves together, some firm- and even team-specific human capital will inevitably be lost. These losses need to be recouped in the

Table 7.3

Rankings of Former Drexel Stars in the Three-Year Period Following Drexel's Collapse

Name	Moved to	Rank in 1989 at Drexel	Rank in 1990	Rank in 1991	Rank in 1992
Chad Brown	BZW	Runner-up	N/R	N/A	N/A
Jeffrey Edelman	BZW	3	N/R	N/A	N/A
Joel Fischer	BZW	Runner-up	N/R	N/A	N/A
David Healy	BZW	3	N/R	N/A	N/A
Richard Hoey	BZW	3	N/R	N/A	N/A
Ernest Jacob	BZW	Runner-up	N/R	N/A	N/A
John Keefe	BZW	3	N/R	N/A	N/A
James McCann	BZW	2	Runner-up	N/A	Runner-up (at Merrill Lynch)
Terence York	BZW	2	Runner-up	N/A	N/A
Michael Derchin	County NatWest	2	1	3	N/R
Nicholas Heymann	County NatWest	Runner-up	N/R	N/R	N/R
John Kellenyi	County NatWest	1	3	N/R	N/R
Katharine Plourde	DLJ	1	1	1	1
William Young	DLJ	1	1	1	1
David Hawkins	Merrill Lynch	2	1	2	2
Terran Miller	Merrill Lynch	3	Runner-up	N/R	Runner-up
Joseph Kozloff	Smith Barney	3	2	1	1
John Reidy	Smith Barney	2	3	2	3
Andrew Wallach	Cumberland Associates	1	N/R	N/R	N/R
George Douglas	Dais Group	2	N/R	N/R	N/R
Daniel Lee	First Boston	Runner-up	N/R	N/R	N/R
Terence Quinn	Kidder Peabody	Runner-up	N/R	Runner-up	Runner-up
Kurt Feuerman	Morgan Stanley	2	3	2	2
Philip Friedman	Paine Webber (moved to Morgan Stanley by 1991)	3	Runner-up	3	3
Barry Bryant	Prudential-Bache	Runner-up	N/R	N/R	N/R
David Lippman	S. G. Warburg	Runner-up	N/R	N/R	N/R
Michael Gumport	Shearson Lehman	3	N/R	Runner-up	Runner-up
Kevin Simpson	Schroder Wertheim	3	3	Runner-up	2
Edith Barschi	Other	Runner-up	N/R	N/R	N/R
Laurence Lytton	Other	3	N/R	N/R	N/R
Deborah McNeill	Other	3	N/R	N/R	N/R
Nicholas Toufexis	Other (possibly Chicago Corp.)	3	N/R	N/R	N/R

Source: Compiled from published sources.

Notes: 1 = 1st team; 2 = 2nd team; 3 = 3rd team; N/R = not ranked. N/A = no longer listed as a research analyst. If an analyst was ranked in two industries in a given year, his or her highest rank was used for that year.

7 | Liftouts **151**

new organization. If the dynamics of the liftout prevent acquisition of firm- and team-specific capital at the new company, star analysts are at risk for declines in performance. (Even if the lifted-out team continues to perform well as a team, it may have been brought onboard to kick-start a venture that was itself ill conceived.) Though in the County NatWest and BZW cases large teams moved, it is clear from insider accounts that star analysts were the primary strategic assets the hiring firms were seeking.

County NatWest

By far the largest and most highly publicized group move in the wake of the Drexel collapse was that of equities head Arthur Kirsch and sixty members of his U.S.-based team.[26] Their move to County NatWest took place with dizzying speed. Drexel declared bankruptcy on Tuesday, February 13, 1990. Immediately, Kirsch started to look for a new firm. He initially attempted to take his entire six-hundred-person group—and then a smaller, three-hundred-person contingent—to a new bank. (See figure 7.2 for the ad Kirsch circulated informally to publicize his group's availability. It declared: "The Smartest People on Wall Street Can Be Had.") Wall Street responded to Kirsch's bold attempt with little more than a raised eyebrow; Kirsch knew he had to make something happen quickly before the best performers on his team got picked off. The best and quickest offer came from National Westminster, and one week after the declaration of bankruptcy, Kirsch struck a deal with the British bank to become president and CEO of its brokerage subsidiary, County NatWest Securities. Sixty U.S. professionals would accompany him, including three ranked analysts.

Kirsch was confident that those who followed him to a new firm would prosper and make money for their new employer. Some members stuck with Kirsch for the camaraderie. Some were loath to sacrifice the investment in teamwork that had made them successful. Steven Meehan, a member of Kirsch's management committee, stayed for career opportunities: "Arthur convinced me that, as opposed to a conventional firm of the kind that I had offers coming in from, such as Merrill Lynch and Morgan Stanley, I wouldn't fall into a lock-step promotion process. Rather, with Arthur and the group, I would be able to rapidly rise to senior partner. Working with Arthur was a chance to work with a group of proven winners."[27]

THE SMARTEST PEOPLE ON WALL STREET CAN BE HAD.

Over 300 of them. World-class research analysts. Outstanding sales representatives. Proven traders. All rated at the very pinnacle of their specialties by the industry's most authoritative poll.

In fact, the complete institutional equities department of a major investment bank can be yours. (You know whose it is.) A turnkey operation that can turn you into an equities powerhouse. Overnight.

What you get if you hire our department be some of the hardest working, most creative people in the business. Plus the business's best distribution network. With more than 800 domestic accounts controlling $XXXXXXX in investment capital. Professionals in New York, Chicago, Boston, Atlanta, Houston, and Los Angeles. And Europe's strongest equities distribution capability.

You'll also get some of the best corporate finance relationships around. Long-term relationships. The kinds of relationships money can't buy.

Except in this case, it can.

So call Arthur Kirsch at XXX-XXX-XXXX. But hurry. Because hiring some of the smartest people on Wall Street is just plain smart.

Figure 7.2. Display advertisement for Drexel's equity division, distributed February 16, 1990. *Source*: Arthur S. Kirsch.

Although the team needed to move quickly, Kirsch also attempted to move strategically. Meehan described the goals of the team as fivefold:

> One, to move to a global player, with a big asset base to afford the capital to succeed. Two, to do it with a large number of people to maintain our entrepreneurial spirit. Three, to do it quickly, and four, to do it at a pay level and compensation so that the people wouldn't feel that they had missed out on a better firm. Number five was the key component: Arthur had to convince the group that wherever we went to was devoted to making the business and all of us succeed. Making clear to the group that the resources, commitment, and focus were all dedicated to our effort was what Arthur did effectively.[28]

All five factors appeared to be in place at County NatWest. The bank had been in the American equities market for four years but still had only a small market share, with revenues of $7 million in 1989.[29] Kirsch's goal was to quickly establish NatWest as a midsized but effective U.S. equities business. "We won't be the biggest," he said. "That's not on my agenda. The trick will be to establish something that is profitable for the organization, attractive for the client and attractive to the people that work here—doable."[30] By late spring 1990 County NatWest was turning a profit, and Kirsch was appointed chief executive for the entire global brokerage operation. However, his relationships with the parent bank were troubled from the outset. Kirsch acknowledged "cultural barriers" and expressed his intent to "let [London] know that we don't want to change them, nor should they change us."[31] The culture clash may have been more profound than Kirsch realized: national differences were exacerbated by the differing skills and mind-sets of the investment-bank and commercial-banking industries.[32] After Kirsch's promotion, his authority and power were steadily eroded by reorganizations. The London office resented what it perceived as Kirsch's attempt to keep his team independent of, and segregated from, the larger company. Kirsch resigned from NatWest in 1992.

Kirsch "did not want to integrate the U.S. operation with the U.K. and the rest of the global network," the firm explained.[33] Within three years of Kirsch's resignation, his top deputies and many other ex-Drexelites left NatWest. Of the three ranked analysts who had accompanied him, two dropped in the rankings; one rose from second to first for a year and subsequently dropped.

Barclays de Zoete Wedd (BZW)

Barclays de Zoete Wedd (BZW) also lifted out forty salespeople and analysts (nine of whom were ranked) from Drexel.[34] BZW, owned by the Barclay's Group, was an investment-banking unit that had established a presence in New York in 1987 by offering non-U.S. institutional sales and research services. BZW had never participated in U.S. securities business and saw the Drexel liftout as a way to expand its U.S. operations. Like County NatWest, BZW was a subsidiary of a British banking giant looking to break into U.S. equities.

Initially, the differences between the aggressive, creative Drexel and conservative BZW seemed to generate creativity, not conflict.[35] Not long after joining, however, the ex-Drexelites questioned their decision. According to company insiders, the personality conflicts that soon surfaced between Drexel stars and the BZW team exacerbated the differences in corporate-cultural style. Strategic reorganizations at BZW had added internal layers, impeding communication and shrinking opportunities for the new stars to carve out niches.

Drexel's open-ended culture made it hard for many of its employees to accommodate to more structured and conservative environments. "It was difficult coming back into this bureaucracy. At Drexel, right up until the last year or so," one former Drexel professional said, there were "no layers, no bureaucracy, nobody was senior to anybody else. . . . The smallest guy on the rung could have a good idea, and that's what got used."[36]

The ex-Drexel analysts were unable to perform up to their previous standard in the BZW environment. Nine had been ranked by *Institutional Investor* in 1989. In 1990 only two of them made the cut, and both had dropped two notches from second place to runner-up.

Looking back on her stint at BZW, Abby Joseph Cohen called the U.S. venture's chances for success "an illusion. [BZW] lacked financial resources, didn't have the proper management in place, and was unable to handle basic problems."[37] She was apparently correct. In 1990 BZW lost between 40 million and 50 million pounds in its global securities operations.[38] A little over a year after BZW's Drexel hires, the company announced that it would close its U.S. equities business and lay off sixty staffers, the majority of them from Drexel.

Donaldson, Lufkin & Jenrette

DLJ also hired a number of Drexel teams, including two ranked analysts, twenty-three investment bankers from corporate finance and mergers and acquisitions, and teams from fixed-income, public finance, and institutional equities. DLJ was founded in 1959 with "a simple, but compelling and audacious, business model: Give institutional investors well-researched investment ideas, and you will attract their brokerage business."[39] *Investment Dealers' Digest* portrayed DLJ's corporate culture as "a collegial environment that's relatively free of political infighting."[40] Three years later the same magazine described DLJ's anomalous ability to be aggressive and competitive while maintaining a genteel reputation:

> DLJ likes to portray itself as almost white-shoe, cut from the same cloth as J.P. Morgan and Morgan Stanley. Yet the reality behind the image is a highly aggressive, roll-up-your-sleeves competitor. Its two big business lines—high yield and merchant banking—are on the gritty side for a white-shoe firm, but DLJ is still able to carry off the inconsistency. "You can be tough as nails and smile, or you can be tough as nails and grunt," a former DLJ official explains. "There's a classy way [to do it], and I would say Morgan Stanley and Goldman Sachs and DLJ know how to do that."[41]

A firm with Drexel's creativity, intellect, and aggression but without its pit-bull reputation would seem a perfect home for ex-Drexel professionals. Drexel, though portability-promoting, was also careful in its selection process and good at integrating new hires quickly, perhaps because of its relatively flexible corporate culture. Drexel's two chemical analysts, Katharine Plourde and William Young, made a seamless transition, as their undisturbed number-one *Institutional Investor* rankings testified. All in all, DLJ's Drexel hires were an exceptionally good fit. As the head of the restructuring team put it, "The one thing we did as a group was pick the right firm."[42]

The Stages of a Successful Liftout

As the foregoing examples illustrate, talent and a desire to succeed are necessary but insufficient for a liftout to be successful. In the course of research across a number of industries and nationalities, we identified four consecutive and mutually interdependent stages that must be worked through for a liftout to succeed.

- The *courtship stage*, before the move, when two series of conversations take place: one between the leader of the team and the leaders of the company interested in bringing the team onboard. During this phase the participants align business goals and expectations, ensure that the market opportunity the liftout is intended to exploit genuinely exists, discuss how they should be integrated with existing staff, and ensure that the leader will receive the resources necessary to succeed.[43]

- *Leadership integration*, post-move, in which the leader of the lifted-out team aligns expectations and begins to build relationships and firm-specific human capital in the new environment.
- *Operational integration*, when the leader of the team channels resources to the team, providing them the wherewithal to succeed on an observable level and to gain credibility.
- *Full cultural integration*, during which team members develop relationships with their new coworkers, exchange best practices, and are able to build sources of firm- and team-specific capital outside the liftout team in their new firm.

The Courtship Stage

A team in the process of moving can retain some of its team-specific human capital, but it will inevitably lose some relationships and other nonportable resources. One agenda of the courtship stage is to make sure that these losses can be recouped in the new environment.

The courtship stage is also the appropriate juncture for ensuring that the goals of the new team are clear and achievable. If the courtship stage is given short shrift, both parties are at risk of business failure and public humiliation.[44] This was clearly the case in the County NatWest and BZW moves. Neither bank had done adequate due diligence on the market opportunity, and the teams themselves, in their haste to find new employment, may have asked fewer hard questions than they should have.[45]

Conversations on these questions between the team leader and the hiring company are usually accompanied by a similar series of conversations between the leader and the team. If the entire team is not going to move, the overriding question becomes whom to approach to join the liftout. (Although team leaders are legally constrained from soliciting others to move with them, we found that doing so is a common practice. In some cases, the team leaders privately told their teams about moving and team members on their own proactively inquired about opportunities to accompany their leaders to new firms.) The hiring company may tend to focus only on the stars or the most visible professionals. But these client-facing professionals' success may well depend on the efforts of less visible individuals who should not be overlooked. When Kirsch realized that it would not be feasible to move his entire department (or even three hundred of them), "he whittled down the roster for his new staff using one character criterion: the desire to win."[46] This focus on individual excellence may have been too single-minded; bringing along a few less aggressive, more collaborative players might have helped the team's chances.

Leadership Integration

The leadership-integration phase begins once the team is in its new home.[47] The leader of the lifted-out team must have access to the new company's top leadership, both to communicate its business goals clearly to the team and to provide the team the resources to do their jobs. The literature on mergers and acquisitions is firm on the necessity of early, proactive planned integration.[48] Integration is important in team hires, too, but what is immediately crucial is not the cultural integration of the team but that of the team's leader with senior management of the hiring company—in other words, development of team-specific human capital at the very top. In the rare cases when there is no team leader, preexisting cultural compatibility and strong support from the new firm's leadership are imperative, as was the case in the successful DLJ moves. BZW, by contrast, lacked both cultural compatibility between the firm of origin and the new firm and a strong leader on the Drexel side who could shepherd the integration process.

Leadership integration promotes close relationships between the team leader and senior management, facilitating access and resources. The team leader uses his or her new firm- and team-specific human capital to channel resources to the team while structuring work and managing relationships to create the conditions for team success. These activities will not proceed smoothly if the leader is alienated from or resistant to the new company.[49]

Perhaps because of inadequate alignment during the courtship phase, as well as cultural differences, Arthur Kirsch found himself increasingly at odds with the firm he had joined. This misalignment forced his team to choose between the company that had hired them and the man who led them, and fostered a self-segregation that impaired the team's effectiveness. When this happens, the hiring company may force out the team leader, but this strategy often backfires: the team ends up no less isolated but also demoralized and directionless without its leader.[50]

Operational Integration

When the team leader and the new company's leaders are fully integrated—literate in each other's cultural backgrounds, aligned on business goals, practices, and values, and engaged in building team-specific human capital—the team is ready for operational integration. During this phase the team begins to acquire whatever aspects of hard or product nonportability are necessary for success, such as access to platforms, structures, systems, and instruction in technologies and procedures. If the hiring firm possesses proprietary technology and does business using product-specific human capital, this period can be lengthy. A team leader who has developed team-specific human capital in the form of a good working relationship with the leadership of the new company will be able to grease these transitional hurdles and facilitate acquisition of new firm-specific human capital. A leader who is isolated or marginalized will not.[51]

Continuity in the content of the team's work makes it easier to master new systems and procedures. Ideally, after joining a new firm, the team will at least initially draw on the same or similar relationships, clients, vendors, and industry standards. Severe disruption in work processes or relationships can derail a team. This can happen to teams lifted out to foreign-owned companies, such as County NatWest and Barclays de Zoete Wedd. A liftout that crosses national boundaries is almost certain to carry with it a higher level of cultural disconnect and to require a steeper learning curve than other moves.[52] The most successful transnational liftouts are those in which the team is hired for its regional expertise and—a key point—allowed to maintain its familiar business practices, as the County NatWest and BZW teams were not.[53]

Finally, these conditions for success must be sustained over time. A team characterized by talent and mutual trust also has momentum, and it is easy for such a team to move into a new environment and score a few quick business wins. Even in the case of team moves that ultimately failed, like the County NatWest venture, there appears to have been a honeymoon period.[54] Work is a dynamic process, and it is not sufficient to hire the right team, set up proper conditions, and let nature take its course. Cooperative work is inherently prone to some process losses, and ongoing commitment at the leadership level is necessary to prevent these inefficiencies.[55]

Full Cultural Integration

Once the team has begun to succeed operationally in its new environment, it will have the credibility to develop relationships beyond the confines of the team and begin to build soft firm-specific human capital.[56] At this point, the role of the leader may shift from ensuring that his or her team has adequate resources to convincing them that those resources and the relational capital of the team itself are not sufficient to preserve performance. An incoming team must realize that however impressive their previous accomplishments and however strenuously they were wooed, once in their new environment they must establish credibility and earn the trust of their new colleagues. Relying on their own existing relationships will not be sufficient for success; they must cultivate new sources of firm-specific human capital. Failure to do so undoubtedly accounts for some of the difficulties the Drexel teams encountered at County NatWest and BZW. The size of the groups that moved may have led team members to believe themselves more self-sufficient than they really were.

An Example of a Successful Liftout

Our research suggests that many similar dynamics are decisive in liftouts regardless of profession or nationality. Successful completion of each of the four stages is crucial to success. A final example from a behind-the-scenes function in investment banking will illustrate how a liftout can proceed when all four phases go well. In 2000 Cheryl Tortoriello and her entire editorial-production department—responsible for the design, copyediting, compliance review, and production of all of the equity research department's publications, including analysts' reports, marketing materials, and year-end stock reviews—moved from Deutsche Bank to Lehman Brothers.

The *courtship phase* of the Tortoriello liftout was facilitated by the fact that Tortoriello had worked at Lehman Brothers from 1982 until 1996, during the Jack Rivkin era. In 1996, unhappy with the changes in management that surrounded Rivkin's firing, she left for Deutsche with two other employees. When Steve Hash took over the underperforming research department (see chapter 5 for a more in-depth look at the changes in Lehman's fortunes), he thought that Tortoriello's team could help get it back on top. Even the most prescient stock predictions are of no use if they are not communicated to clients in an efficient and user-friendly way.

Tortoriello and Hash were already well acquainted and shared a clear vision of the corporate culture and specific accomplishment—a rise in Lehman's *Institutional Investor* ranking—they wanted to create. Because their familiarity with Rivkin-era culture was a shared point of reference, it was not difficult for them to align expectations. Tortoriello's team unanimously chose to follow her from Deutsche Bank. Tortoriello's exceptional *leadership integration* with Steve Hash assured her of continued access and support for her team. The solidity of this executive sponsorship was vividly demonstrated after September 11, 2001, when Hash's leadership and logistical support helped the editorial team continue production with almost no interruption.

Hash's support and the unusual autonomy and creative freedom the team enjoyed fostered effective *operational integration* and some striking successes. The events of September 11, wrenching as they were, represented a baptism by fire and knit together Tortoriello's original group and Lehman's existing editorial staff. Tortoriello's team also spearheaded a total redesign of all Lehman's printed materials, an immense task. Realistic about the challenges of coming together with the Lehman editorial team, Tortoriello planned integration in full awareness that some Lehman people would eventually drop out and that a new team dynamic would emerge as full *cultural integration* gradually and organically took hold.

The editorial department's liftout can be considered an unqualified success in terms of both team members' satisfaction and external metrics. Lehman's research department improved from eighth place in the *Institutional Investor* poll in 1999 to first place in 2003. In fact, in 2003 it achieved the largest margin of victory of any front-runner since 1983. The department maintained its first-place status in 2004 and 2005 as well. Given the importance of communications to the *Institutional Investor* poll results, Tortoriello's team was considered a key contributor to the department's rise.

☆ ☆ ☆

In sum, hiring away an entire team from a competitor is a high-risk, high-reward move. For both teams and hiring companies, liftouts represent a gamble on portability of performance and of human capital. If managed well throughout its four stages, though, a liftout can preserve team performance.

8 | Women and Portability

Why Is Women's Performance More Portable than Men's?

One group of analysts reliably maintained their star rankings even after changing employers: women. Unlike their male counterparts, female stars who changed employers performed just as well as those who stayed put.

In our interviews, we found two overarching explanations for women's portability. First, the best female analysts appeared to have built their franchises on external relationships with clients and the companies they covered, rather than on relationships within their firms. By contrast, male stars built up more firm- and team-specific human capital, investing more in the internal networks and unique resources of the firms where they worked.[1] Hence, in the course of becoming stars, female analysts' performance became portable in a way that their male colleagues' did not.

Second, although they relied less on firm-specific capabilities and relationships, women were more careful when assessing a prospective employer. They evaluated possible employers more cautiously and analyzed more factors than men did before deciding to uproot themselves from a company where they had already been successful. Female star analysts, it would appear, took their work environment more seriously yet relied on it less than male stars did. They looked for an employer that would allow them to continue building successful franchises their own way.[2]

The portability of women's performance thus appeared to be the result of strategic choices women analysts made in response to situations they faced at investment banks. Finding it difficult to build relationships with male colleagues, they instead built networks of external ties to clients and to the industries they covered and forged unconventional boundary-spanning in-house alliances. Aware of the sexism that pervaded investment-banking culture, they took care to ensure that a given bank would provide them the platform they needed to be successful and not hold them back on account of their gender.

As we analyze our quantitative and qualitative findings, we will also examine what they tell us about the status of women in male-dominated professions, the existence of multiple paths to stardom, and the overall phenomenon of portability of performance. It is important to note that we are not making attributions based on innate gender characteristics; building on the work of organizational researchers such as Rosabeth Moss Kanter and Robin Ely, we are looking at the behavior of female stars as a response to the workplace environments they face.[3] In Kanter's words, "Findings about the 'typical' behavior of women in organizations that have been assumed to reflect either biologically based psychological attributes or characteristics developed through a long socialization to a 'female sex role' turn out to reflect very reasonable—and very universal—responses to current organizational situations."[4] This approach is an effort to look more closely at how environmental constraints and opportunities differ for men and women and at the ways in which star female performers cope with and exploit these constraints and opportunities.

The 189 star women in our sample (18 percent of the star analysts we studied) were remarkably high achievers. During the period covered by our study, 1988–96, women accounted for 17 percent of all equity analysts. Female analysts achieved a higher average rank than men, and more women ranked first than any other rank. Women accounted for 21 percent of first-ranked analysts, 16 percent of second-teamers, 15 percent of third-teamers, and 17 percent of runners-up. It is possible that women, as a highly visible minority in the investment-banking arena, felt the need to overperform in order to be accepted. It could be that women's minority status in the profession called forth ambition, flexibility, resilience, intelligence, and/or single-mindedness—in short, that female analysts, in their efforts to survive, were simply better and tougher as a group than their male counterparts. One study of the industry suggested that being an average performer was not an option for women. As one insider asserted: "Around here at least, if you're liked you don't have to be a star performer to get ahead as a guy, whereas women, I think that category doesn't exist."[5]

Male stars who switched employers suffered an immediate decline in performance that persisted for at least five years, especially if they moved to a weaker firm. (Male stars who moved between comparable firms exhibited a three-year drop in performance, and those who moved to better firms showed no significant decline in short- or long-term performance.) When ranked analysts moved between roughly equivalent investment banks, 51 percent fewer women than men lost their star rankings altogether (37 percent of men and 18 percent of women became unranked). The majority of men (56 percent) suffered some loss of rank in the year following a lateral move, compared to only 32 percent of women—a 43 percent differential. These numbers attest to the role of firm- and team-specific skills, and firms' capabilities, in star male analysts' performance. Their female counterparts, by contrast, experienced little if any erosion in performance after moving. In other words, their franchises were portable. These findings suggest that women relied very little on firm-specific or team-specific human capital and that their performance was minimally affected by their firms' capabilities. Table 8.1 compares the short- and long-term performance of star male analysts who changed firms to comparable star male analysts who stayed put,

Table 8.1
The Effect of Switching Firms on Ranked Analysts' Short-Term and Long-Term Performance, by Gender, 1988–96

Independent variable	1988–96 Ordered probit regressions				
	Rank $(t+1)$	Rank $(t+2)$	Rank $(t+3)$	Rank $(t+4)$	Rank $(t+5)$
Male moving					
Coefficient	−0.413 ***	−0.379 ***	−0.315 ***	−0.283 **	−0.315 **
Robust standard error	(0.088)	(0.100)	(0.110)	(0.124)	(0.137)
N	292	254	211	170	135
Female moving					
Coefficient	−0.201	0.041	−0.153	−0.269	−0.385
Robust standard error	(0.151)	(0.206)	(0.220)	(0.252)	(0.242)
N	74	67	53	45	31

Notes: The marginal effect of the *Analyst move* variable is calculated as the discrete change in F(x) as this variable changes from 0 to 1: F(x = 1) − F(x = 0). N represents the number of mobile star analysts. The categorical and ordinal dependent variable (*Rank$_t$*) is represented by first rank, second rank, third rank, runner-up, and unranked. Models 1–5 examine the impact of switching firms on male and female ranked analysts' short-term and long-term performance. Each model is a robust cluster ordered probit specification with ranked analysts as clusters in which the dependent variable is analysts' *Institutional Investor* rankings. This table presents coefficients for the *Analyst Move* variables for ranked analysts, controlling for individual, firm, sector, and intertemporal variables (not reported). Only adjusted robust standard errors are reported.
$*p < .10; **p < .05; ***p < .01$

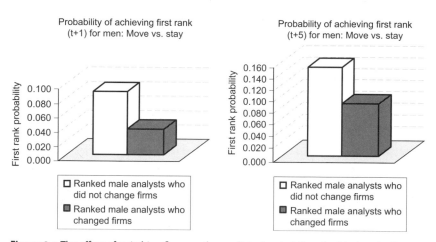

Probability of achieving first rank (t+1) for men: Move vs. stay

Probability of achieving first rank (t+5) for men: Move vs. stay

☐ Ranked male analysts who did not change firms

■ Ranked male analysts who changed firms

☐ Ranked male analysts who did not change firms

■ Ranked male analysts who changed firms

Figure 8.1. The effect of switching firms on the predicted probability of achieving the first rank for male analysts, one and five years post-move.

and mobile female analysts to their counterparts who did not change firms. Figure 8.1 presents these results in graphic form for star men.

After a brief look at Wall Street as a working environment for women, we will examine the two main explanations we found for female stars' portability—stronger external relationships and greater due diligence when approaching moves—with an eye to the structural conditions that led women to adopt these behaviors. Some observations about female analysts' career paths follow. The chapter will then offer recommendations for organizations that wish to retain their female stars—and to promote comparable skills in their male analysts—and some concluding thoughts about the generalizability of our findings.

Female Analysts on Wall Street: The Early Years

Research departments hired women earlier than most other Wall Street fields did. "I was one of six women hired as statisticians, as kind of an experiment," recalled Mary Wren, who joined Merrill Lynch in 1946. "Even when I became a full analyst, I couldn't go on trips. The research director didn't think he could send a young lady out to see company presidents alone."[6] Such views persisted. Muriel Siebert described job-hunting in the 1960s: "The New York Society of Security Analysts had a sort of clearinghouse for jobs. They sent my résumé out under my name, Muriel Siebert, and I got no inquiries. Then this wonderful guy there sent it out under my initials.

Apparently, this M.F. Siebert looked pretty good."[7] Siebert became the first female member of the New York Stock Exchange in 1967, having previously been rejected because there was no women's lavatory.

In the 1960s few female analysts had MBAs; most arrived on Wall Street by chance. "The answer for a woman is simple," wrote *Institutional Investor* in 1967. "Show them how to make money. . . . If your ideas are good, Wall Streeters couldn't care less what you look like. If you happen to be blonde and curvy, well, vive la différence." The same article quotes a man who commented, "We hire women because they do good work and they are cheap."[8]

Though the women who breached the bastions of Wall Street were not necessarily willing to identify as feminists, they were more than willing to piggyback on the gains of the women's movement. One analyst described herself as "an Uncle Tom woman—I'm prepared to let them [feminists] do the fighting."[9] According to some female analysts at that time, they were looking out for themselves and felt little solidarity with other women, content to be making a great deal of money—if not as much as their male colleagues. "People who have good jobs don't need to talk about it. It's the people who don't have good jobs who do all the shouting," said one woman described as an "ex-secretary who has gone on to better things."[10]

When *Institutional Investor* published its first All-America Research Team rankings in 1972, five women analysts made the cut: three in cosmetics, one in retailing, and one in textiles. Women remained concentrated in industries for which they were thought to have an affinity until the early 1980s.[11] "I had an unbelievable struggle to get people to take me seriously," recalled Elaine Garzarelli, who arrived on Wall Street in 1973 as a quantitative analyst with a Ph.D. in economics and finance. "I had to take my clients out one by one and explain to them what I was doing."[12]

By the mid-1980s, a few women had begun to show up in research management. But, as one analyst recalled, "Realistically, few of us believed we'd ever make managing director or partner. So we went as far as we could—and made as much money as we could—and most of us eventually left the Street when it wasn't fun anymore."[13]

An "Unparalleled Paradise for Ambitious Women"?
Perception and Reality on Wall Street

Media reports, as well as interviews with analysts and research directors, paint a complicated picture of the environment into which female analysts step. Wall Street has been hailed as a results-oriented labor marketplace that pays top dollar for talent and cannot afford to discriminate. But it is also known for its fraternity-style culture of "hegemonic masculinity."[14] Women eager to make a name for themselves on the Street have had to deal with a culture that simultaneously denied and embraced sexism.

In 1996, fifty years after female analysts began to enter investment banks, *Institutional Investor* declared Wall Street research departments "a veritable meritocracy and unparalleled paradise for ambitious women."[15] Few women on Wall Street would call it paradise, but many women who joined research departments in the 1980s and 1990s believed that the Street's focus on measurable performance and the bottom line made it a favorable venue for women eager to work hard and be judged on their merits.[16] "If someone can make you money," commented Michelle Galanter Applebaum, a former top-rated steel analyst at Salomon Brothers, "you don't care what they look like."[17] An executive search consultant concurred: "The quality of the research is the quality of the research. The Mary Meekers of the world [Meeker is a ranked analyst in the Internet sector] do what they do, and it could be Harry Meeker and nobody would know the difference. It's the work that's done. So it's a little bit unique that way—less opportunity for gender bias." Helane Becker, a ranked airline analyst, described investment banking as "the kind of business where it's gender- and color-blind, because as long as you've got information, people will talk to you for what you know. It's definitely a user game. If you can use me, you will."

These assertions were seconded by research directors who claimed that analyst recruitment was gender-blind.[18] "I never thought of it in terms of gender at all. We were looking for the best athletes. And the evidence is supportive of that," said Steve Einhorn, who headed Goldman Sachs's research department in the 1990s. "Whoever can perform should be given the opportunity to perform, and I think we succeeded in providing that opportunity to women. But we never focused on it. We focused on finding the best person, the best fit." Search consultant Abram Claude agreed: "Research searches are totally neutral. . . . I don't know of anyone who would lean a search toward a man or a woman. They're looking for talent."[19]

Fred Fraenkel, director of research at Lehman Brothers in the 1990s, elaborated: "We figured very early on that a woman can be just as good an analyst as a man. So we had totally gender-blind recruitment and evaluation processes. In recruiting, if we thought a woman was a better candidate than a man, we hired her. Period, end of story. As the department evolved, if I were asked who were better analysts, the women or the men, on average, I would say it was the women. I have no idea why, but that's my observation."[20]

In an industry that once hired women because they did good work cheaply, salary discrimination had virtually disappeared by the end of the 1980s, according to industry insiders. Frank Pedone of Pedone Associates, which performed an annual survey of analysts' pay, reported in 1989 that "at the request of a women's group, I looked particularly at disparities in pay between men and women on the same level and found none."[21] Many analysts and headhunters believe that salary discrimination would be a near impossibility in a market where analysts receive regular offers from competitors and where compensation rates and abilities are common knowledge. "I get calls from headhunters all the time," Barbara Allen, a Kidder Peabody analyst, told a reporter in 1989. "The market determines what you're worth."[22] (This is not the case elsewhere in investment banking, where women systematically earn less than comparable men.)[23]

But an absence of overt discrimination in recruitment, compensation, and ranking does not mean that women and men encountered identical circumstances in the workplace.[24] For one thing, women remained a minority, a status that is often problematic for professionals trying to navigate workplace politics and relationships.[25] As recently as 1984, women accounted for fewer than 5 percent of equity analysts. Women's representation in the profession began to rise rapidly in the mid-1980s, eventually leveling off in the neighborhood of 20 percent, where it has remained ever since—fluctuating from a low of 15 percent to a high of 25 percent.

How Star Women Build Research Franchises

Our interviews revealed that women often adopted different career strategies than men because of obstacles they faced at work. Their stated reasons for emphasizing external relationships and for exercising extreme care when making a job change reflected awareness of sexism on a cultural and institutional level. Helane Becker, for example, who claimed that the industry was gender-blind, also pointed out that a research director with daughters would be apt to favor the advancement of women. If the industry were genuinely gender-blind, such observations would not be necessary.[26]

Across a wide swath of firms, female stars adopted a number of strategies to enhance their careers on the uneven playing field of equity research. These strategies made them stars—and made their skills highly portable.

Some of their actions were designed to help them advance within their firms and only incidentally increased their portability; others were deliberately adopted to ensure that they would be able to succeed elsewhere in the event of layoffs.

Building an External Network

Our interviews elicited consensus that female analysts tend to concentrate their efforts on building relationships outside their firms with their clients, contacts at the companies they cover, and even with the media.[27]

Airline analyst Helane Becker spelled out in detail the particulars of her campaign to achieve *II* ranking by developing direct relationships with clients and with the sources that clients looked to for guidance:

> I called, I wrote, I visited. I wrote at least one report a day. I called at least ten to twelve people a day. And I visited them. I was on the road at least one week a month visiting clients. I was Miss American [Airlines] for awhile, because that's the only stock I talked about for days on end. Then I became Miss United. I would just focus on those names and make sure that people associated me with those names. And then I cultivated the IR [investor relations] people, so that if you were a new analyst at Fidelity and you called United and said, "Who really knows your stock?" [they would answer] "Helane knows our stock. Call Helane." And then I cultivated reporters: the *Wall Street Journal, USA Today,* the *New York Times.* I responded to their phone calls. I did it because if people in Wichita or Omaha or Seattle saw me quoted in the *Wall Street Journal,* they might think I was really smart and they would call me, too. And then I would build a relationship with them, get to talk to them, and build my clients that way.

According to Lisa Shalett, research director at Sanford C. Bernstein, Becker was not an isolated case:

> Women are building their franchises not based on stock-picking prowess, not based on their ability to walk onto the trading floor and make something happen. They're building their franchises based on: Am I of value to the portfolio manager at Wellington? Does the person at Fidelity think I'm a really trustworthy, important person

to dialogue with? I think female stars on Wall Street tend to be much more marketing-intensive, much more externally intensive, much more relationship-intensive.

Josie Esquivel, who personified the approach that Shalett described, pointed out that "this is still a service industry, and calling that client, being receptive to whatever questions they have, visiting with them one-on-one, and following up with questions and issues and spreadsheets, or whatever it is they're looking for, is very, very crucial to the success of an analyst."

A small minority of our interviewees suggested that women's focus on client relationships was grounded in gender-specific characteristics. Shalett, for example, said that "Women see themselves as people-pleasers, as service-oriented, as relationship-focused—as a generalization." But most described the decision as a strategic and adaptive one driven by situational factors. Morgan Stanley star Carol Muratore explained women's orientation toward external service-based relationships in structural terms. "For a woman in any business, it's easier to focus outward, where you can define and deliver the services required to succeed," Muratore said, "than to navigate the internal affiliations and power structure within a male-dominant firm." Another star woman analyst observed,

> If you can't build relationships inside the firm, you go outside the firm. It's not that you sit in your car and you say, "I don't want to build relationships with salespeople, traders, or investment bankers." They just don't spend as much time with me as with other men. So I will spend my time on clients and companies. It's not that men don't spend time with clients. It's just that outside relationships are more important for women. Also, for women, it's easier to build relationships outside because there are more women in the companies. And even in companies that have few women, at least they have more receptive corporate cultures, not the macho-men cultures found at most investment banks.

It is also noteworthy that the rubric for this kind of external orientation is *client service*, but that, as many of the women interviewed made clear, the relationship is a two-way street: external relationships often generated information and other direct benefits for the analyst.[28]

Four main reasons emerged for women's decisions to maintain an external focus: uneasy in-house relationships, poor mentorship, neglect by colleagues (notably the sales force and traders), and a desire to protect their portability.

Uneasy In-House Relationships

As a conspicuous minority entering an entrenched culture, female newcomers lacked natural alliances. "The power structure, communication techniques, bonding activities, and language at Wall Street firms remain male-dominant," said Carol Muratore. "Women are not easily assimilated into the culture." Outright malice and deliberate exclusion were rare but less-than-wholehearted acceptance was not. Men who viewed an influx of women skeptically made few accommodations—either because of entrenched sexism or simply because it never occurred to them that the corporate culture ought to change. "Because, for the most part, men don't have to work that hard at it, they resort to—it's a comfort thing, it's convenience—'I'm just going to develop relationships with those who I feel most comfortable with,'" said Sara Karlen, human-resources head in Merrill Lynch's equity research department.[29]

And women, in turn, felt less than comfortable. "Working in a male-dominant environment is like being a non-native speaker in a foreign country," said Muratore. "You can't assume that you are understood or that you comprehend the nuance of the culture around you." Even good intentions can backfire; as Kanter astutely pointed out, "It is a dilemma of all cross-cultural interaction that the very act of attempting to learn what to do in the presence of a different kind of person so as to integrate him can reinforce differentiation."[30]

Many women analysts said that in-house relationships with male colleagues continued to present a handful of subtle hurdles, hazards, and dilemmas—adapting to or resisting group norms, avoiding gossip, discussing or avoiding discussion of their personal lives, capturing the right tone—that militate against high expectations from those relationships. Star analyst Bonita Austin explained her thinking:

It's not just that men can build relationships with other men more easily, but it's also that women cannot build those relationships—because you never want to have someone say, "She got the top vote from that salesman because she's sleeping with him." You have to be very careful with your reputation and how you interact with people on the buy side and within your firm as well. I think that you're better served as a woman analyst maintaining a cordial but very professional relationship with all the men in your firm, especially sales force and trading—anybody who can have an impact on your compensation. I always felt I could be friendly, and if I needed to go out with clients or with a salesman, no problem. But I kept a very big distance between me and them because I never wanted to jeopardize my reputation.

Female analysts thus faced a double bind. In an industry largely based on relationships and networks, they could not afford to get close to men for fear of having their relationships misconstrued. Several of the problems women encountered are faced by any outsider group (Kanter notes, for example, that semi-social workplace events intended to be fun and relaxing are often the most stressful for individuals in a token position), but the problem of sex is unique to women in male-dominated professions.

Poor Mentorship

Most female analysts who become stars have had mentors; in fact, the most conspicuous difference between star and non-star women in equity research is access to a supportive mentor. But star women reported more difficulty forging mentor-protégé relationships, less support from their mentors, and fewer mentors than their male counterparts.[31]

Mentoring is a complex function. Studies of mentorship in organizations have defined two mechanisms whereby mentoring enhances the career and personal development of protégés: career-related support in the form of coaching, protection, exposure, and sponsorship; and psychosocial support in the form of acceptance, confirmation, counseling, and friendship.[32] A third function, role modeling, has also been identified.[33] The career-related and psychosocial functions can only be pursued in a relationship, but the role-model function does not require direct contact. A junior analyst could adopt a female star as her role model, for example, and derive benefits from the star's success (as evidence that women can reach professional heights), as well as career-development benefits from learning about the star's career and adopting the star's strategies as her own.

While role modeling is important, an ongoing relationship with a mentor, or several mentors, clearly provides greater benefits. And forging these relationships can be particularly difficult for women. Female analysts reported that early in their careers, when a mentor is most useful, they tended to be treated as more probationary than their male counterparts.[34] As *Institutional Investor* reported in 1996, "most of the men's sexist and patronizing behavior is aimed at young women who have not yet proved themselves."[35] Renowned strategist Abby Joseph Cohen attributed delays in her career to lack of a mentor early in her career:

I had no mentor at Goldman Sachs. There was nobody looking out or blocking-and-tackling for me. . . . There was not much awareness or concern at the time that this was missing. Men weren't very receptive, and there were very few women in the industry ahead of me, so there was no one to whom I could reach out along the way. I have obviously succeeded in my career, but the exception does not prove the rule. My career progress has been a function of hard work and persistence. Had I had a mentor, or had I been given appropriate resources along the way, who knows what I would have accomplished and at what pace?[36]

In general, it appears, promising women had less success than men at finding experienced analysts willing to show them the ropes. "The men—I hate to put it this way, but the white males who were successful, they didn't have to look for a mentor," said Karlen. "People just naturally took them under their wing and would guide them along."

One male star ascribed his reluctance to mentor women to their higher rate of turnover (a subject we will return to): "I want to mentor people, and the satisfaction comes from seeing them succeed. But so many female analysts that I mentored are no longer with the firm, so it feels that the mentorship was for nothing. Many female analysts leave because it is just hard to succeed in this business; many leave for personal reasons. I still mentor, but I can understand people that prefer mentoring men. They tend to stay around longer, so the fruit of your mentoring is around." Men who mentor other men also appear to provide more multilayered support than men who mentor women. A male analyst can provide little in the way of role modeling for a woman.[37] She cannot look to his successes for reassurance that people like her can be successful or for guidance on how to balance work and family in a culture that expects women to be primary caregivers.[38] Men who mentor women often provide little by way of psychosocial support, though they do offer such mentoring to other men.[39] Male mentors can provide a woman with valuable career-development advice, but the effects of the two types of mentoring are multiplicative more than additive: career help without psychosocial support is by no means as beneficial as career help in the presence of psychosocial support.

When men do provide psychosocial support to their female protégées, the effect is powerful, as Karlen noted:

If you look at [three successful female analysts at Merrill Lynch], they all worked for men who made it very clear through the mentoring that "here are the key things that you need to do to ensure that you're getting the credit you deserve, that you're being included in what you need to be included in," and to not be afraid to push for things. And while they have the natural inclination, I think it was really developed and drawn out through a very strong mentor.

While mentors are usually envisioned as helping their protégés develop skills and learn the unspoken rules of the business, one of the most valuable services that a mentor provides is access to the mentor's own network of relationships. Rosanna Durruthy, a former human-resources executive at Merrill Lynch and now at ÆQUUS Group, which specializes in career advice to women, emphasized integration into the network of relationships as an important outcome of mentorship. "The guy who doesn't have a mentor is likely to already have access to those relationships. It's the relationship with the other guys that starts to make a difference. And a mentor is instrumental in introducing that woman to the other guys." Durruthy called the relationship-building aspect of mentorship "a mitigation of vulnerability," in that collegial in-house relationships can strengthen an analyst in his or her areas of weakness.[40]

"I took her around to meet with my clients," said one man who was mentoring a female analyst. "I also told salespeople to pay attention to what she is going to say. Finally, I advised her on how to build relationships. For example, I told her to first win these people over before going and speaking with everyone else. You can't win all salespeople at the same time. Several called me to find out more about her. 'Is she that smart?' "[41]

The importance of network access presented women with another double bind: a female mentor, who can provide a better role model and psychosocial support, may not be in a position to facilitate her protégée's integration into the firm's culture.[42] Karlen also noted that the assumption that women want to be mentored by other women can be a trap. "Women many times don't want to be mentored by a woman, because it's not integrating them into the larger fabric of the organization," she explained. "It doesn't necessarily help, in terms of further integrating that high-potential woman into the organization. You've got to get somebody who is respected and held in high regard to mentor the high-potential women and minorities. Otherwise you might as well not waste your effort."[43]

Not all women agree. "I was lucky that I had a great mentor early on in my career," volunteered Jill Krutick, a star media analyst at Salomon Smith Barney. "She showed me how to succeed as a female analyst on Wall

Street. Just being able to observe her made a big impact on me as an analyst." For women, a mentor can facilitate both mastering the job and coping with a setting dominated by male styles of interaction and self-presentation. As Krutick put it, "My advice to up-and-coming female analysts: If you're lucky, find a mentor who can show you how to navigate the minefields."

Perhaps the ideal for an up-and-coming female analyst would be to have mentors of both sexes. Male analysts often had several mentors who jointly constituted a sort of advisory board that could be relied on to dispense advice, support, access, and diverse perspectives.[44] But women often had a hard time finding one good mentor, let alone several.[45]

Neglectful Colleagues: The Case of the Sales Force

Analysts depend on the sales force to promote their work to clients: their reports and investment ideas are customarily disseminated to buy-side clients by the investment bank's sales force. The sales force does not usually specialize by industrial sector: a given salesperson sells the research reports of analysts in all sectors to clients in a particular geographic area. Thus the sales force is a crucial cog in the mechanism that generates competitive advantage, which in turn translates into stardom.

Unlike research departments, Wall Street sales forces are virtually all male. (There are even fewer female traders.) Their cultures, though not necessarily hostile to women analysts, partake enough of the attitudes and assumptions of the locker room and the sports bar to make it difficult for female analysts to forge strong bonds with the sales force.

One salesman described a point of disconnection between women analysts and the sales force charged with promoting their franchises:

> When you sell an analyst, you're selling both the product and the person. For example, an analyst is recommending IBM. That's only part of the story. The same analyst worked at Dell for ten years in business development; you sell his background, because clients are more likely to trust someone with an industry background. And if you spend time with a person, you can also tell a client that she or he is very smart, has dinners with computer executives all the time, and so on. You have this information from traveling to clients together and having drinks at the bar. Many female analysts travel less, especially if they have families. Those who do most likely will not meet up with you at the bar after having met the client. But even those who do are not going to share anything personal with you. And as I

said, you sell both the product and the person. Overall, there are just more opportunities to establish relationships with men.

This salesman may sound disingenuous or merely lazy—a glance at an analyst's résumé or a ten-minute conversation would reveal the particulars of her background—but he is clearly talking less about sheer information than about a lack of easygoing fellowship.

Another salesman expressed his own skepticism about female analysts with unalloyed frankness:

> If there are two analysts, John and Joanna—equally smart, equally hardworking, equally good analysts, both in their late twenties/early thirties, single, both spend fourteen hours a day at work—I have to understand both of their products to be a successful salesman. The day is only twenty-four hours, so I have to allocate my time intelligently. I ask myself: Who is a better analyst? Well, they're equal. Who is most likely to stay at the firm? Here, based on my experience, I have to say John. Joanne is going to get married: her husband might transfer to a West Coast firm; she might decide to have children and take some time off. She might also discover that she can't travel as much because of extra personal responsibilities outside work, and it's essential that analysts travel to see clients and companies. Is this not rational? It's just the way the business is. After all, I have to invest a lot in learning their industry and their backgrounds. Over time I understand John's product better, so I can sell him better to the clients. I spend more time talking about his stock picks and probably making more calls.

Clearly, it has been problematic for women analysts to rely heavily on the sales force for energetic advocacy of their work to clients. Thus it is probably no accident that many successful female analysts have built their franchises essentially by doing end runs around the analyst-salesperson relationship.

Josie Esquivel spelled out the connection between reluctance to rely on the sales force and her own strategic decision to focus on direct service to clients:

> A lot of the male analysts I knew went drinking with the traders, went drinking with the sales force. Some of them would go down to the trading floor and talk about women. I didn't care that they did that. I just said, "I can't do that, so what can I do?" And I could just provide services to the client directly. It wasn't like I was going

to go to Fred [Fraenkel, head of equity research] and say, "This is sexist, this is a sexist environment." That's bullshit. I said: This is the way the world is, and how can I get around it? You get around it by providing services to the client directly. Of course, now all this stuff is supposed to be gone. But the reality is that men are sitting there and building an internal relationship. And in the B School they say, "Why can't the women do that? Why can't they build those male relationships?" Well, because it doesn't always work that way. They've got different conversations and different interests. And so, at the end of the day, it's still a service industry. A lot of women succeeded. We just found a different route to do it.

Krutick concurred: "Building strong relationships is the key to being a successful analyst," she said. "Because the sales forces on Wall Street are so male dominant, and indeed often hostile to women analysts, I found it far easier to build strong relationships with my clients and the managements I covered. Thus many of my best relationships were outside the firm."

Building relationships with other investment-banking functions can also be difficult. "Corporate finance is a difficult world. I've really had to stand my ground with those guys," said First Boston's Joyce Albers-Schronberg, a former top analyst in hospital management. "If you're a woman, they don't really respect you. It's taken me ten years to get that respect."[46]

Strategic Protection of Portability

Female analysts clearly made choices with an eye toward advancing their careers, but some decisions represented a strategic effort to protect their portability in the event of a layoff. Even firms friendly to women laid off more women than men during economic contractions. In 1986 women accounted for 21 percent of Wall Street analysts. A year later, following the 1987 market crash, that percentage had declined to 15 percent. At a time when the total population of equity analysts was reduced by 13 percent, that of female analysts dropped 38 percent. Women represented a significant percent of those who were let go.

The industry's consistent record of laying off far more women than men during bad times makes it a matter of simple self-interest for women to pursue and protect portability. Uncertainty of success in a male-dominated profession is apt to promote the same self-protective strategy. Interviews suggest that female analysts protect their portability in the belief that the culture of many investment-banking firms makes their probability of success quite low. (The ironic paradox is thus that women are more portable but that there may be fewer destinations for them to take their portable franchises to.) Other women are simply concerned that they will be the first to get fired.

Whether a female analyst focuses on external relationships to counterbalance the vexations of a male-dominated workplace or for reasons of psychological comfort and good fit, doing so is clearly highly adaptive and strategically shrewd. An external orientation has the consequence, intended or not, of making performance maximally portable. It has other advantages as well. Helane Becker emphasized that clients are sources of information: "Sometimes you might talk to a client not because they're paying you but because they have access to information you don't have. I mean, I have clients all the time who go to conferences. It helps to have clients who are in conferences who are Blackberrying you, e-mailing you information as it's happening."

And women who managed to prove themselves by achieving *II* ranking on the strength of their client relationships subsequently found themselves taken more seriously in-house. "When I became ranked for the first time, I got many congratulatory phone calls from people I hadn't heard from before," one female star recalled. "Many wanted to take me out for lunch to talk about what I do. It's like you need the client recognition to get people at your own firm to notice that you exist." One salesman unapologetically confirmed the reality of this phenomenon from the other side: "Things change when someone becomes a star. Actually, clients now ask me, 'What did you think about her research?' and they force me to learn more. So first, I want to learn myself, but in the second place, it's like this famous push-versus-pull theory. I'm being pulled into learning her product." As Kanter has noted, "Power wipes out sex"[47] and "a preference for men is a preference for power,"[48] rather than sexism plain and simple. Once an individual has made it into the winner's circle, gender and other delegitimizing factors may become less relevant.[49]

A final note about women's tendency to focus on external rather than in-house relationships: women changed employers as members of teams less often than men did. We found that only 20 percent of female stars who changed employers moved as part of a team, in contrast to 29 percent of male stars. Furthermore, the star women who did leave in teams usually took only one or two colleagues with them, typically a junior analyst or an unranked senior analyst. When star male analysts moved in teams, they tended to bring a larger and more cross-functional group with them, often including salespeople or traders. This pattern may attest both to men's more robust in-house relationships and to the tendency toward self-reliance manifested in women's portability rates.

"Women understand the need to be a part of a team, but I have seen it is very rare that they actually become a part of the team or a franchise in that way," said Rosanna Durruthy, who observed numerous group moves during her tenure at Merrill Lynch. "Part of it could very well be the elements of homogeneity. Much like the construct of social networks, those teams typically become fairly inbred. These individuals not only work very closely together but their personal lives become very intertwined as well. Outside of work, their families are socializing together. It becomes more like a family than like a team of people that work together. I don't know if there is just kind of an innate fear that women and perhaps even minorities have to rely on anyone for their success that greatly."

Scrutinizing Prospective Employers

Women and men overwhelmingly agree that women approach changing employers differently than men do.[50] Women, they say, are more deliberate and careful, probably because experience has taught them the importance of environment and culture in both performance and job satisfaction.[51] This orientation is not at odds with the emphasis women place on developing external, portable franchises; women analysts tend to see organizational factors as necessary but not sufficient for success. Essentially, they look for a firm that will allow them to keep building their successful franchises and not get in their way.

Weighing Multiple Considerations
Sara Karlen expressed the virtually universal consensus we found in interviews: "When women are looking at opportunities, they are weighing many more variables than men are."[52] Recruiter Debra Brown elaborated: "In our experience, women consider many more factors than their male counterparts when looking at a new professional opportunity, such as the working environment, the reputation of the research director, the quality of their colleagues, whether there are other female analysts at the firm, and if those female colleagues are successful. Women also want to know whether the firm is political, whether the firm pays attention to hard measures of performance, and whether it emphasizes objective as opposed to subjective measures in evaluating analysts' performance and determining compensation."

Josie Esquivel speculated that women plan carefully when contemplating a move: "Women tend to think out their move much more, perhaps have—whether it's written or in their heads—a well thought out plan on how to make the entire transition, whereas men (I'm guessing) just aren't putting that much attention to it, and perhaps haven't thought out all the issues that it takes to move."

Carol Muratore, a star at Morgan Stanley, offered an explanatory hypothesis: "Women may be more careful, more apt to consider the downside, before moving, because if they fail there may not be a safety net of strong [in-house] affiliations to support them."

Treating Compensation as One Factor among Many

Numerous observers agreed that male stars are inclined to concentrate single-mindedly on compensation. "Men were much more focused on 'What's my salary, what's my bonus, what's my cut of the investment-banking fees going to be?'" said Fred Fraenkel. "And women were much more focused on 'Am I going to step into quicksand here, where they hate women, there's a glass ceiling, where they don't make any accommodations for the things I need?' There's a real hard-and-soft kind of difference on that."

Recruiter Debra Brown agreed that "compensation is not as significant a factor for women as it is for men when making decisions on job changes." As Esquivel said of her former male colleagues, "Maybe benefits are somewhat important, but in the overall package the compensation's the most important thing: 'I was a star here; I can be a star there. I just want to make more money.' They're only thinking about the money. They want to bring more money home." Esquivel noted that many male analysts stayed in touch with search consultants to keep track of how much they were worth on the market, especially if a big-name analyst in their sector had recently changed jobs. Women, she claimed, did not use search consultants for this kind of compensation scorekeeping. Abby Joseph Cohen made the same observation: "Many of the men who are leaving are leaving because of the financial package. . . . Very often the men star analysts will engage in a bidding war, and they'll basically shop themselves around. We don't see that with the women."

Bonita Austin described the role of compensation in her decision to move from Schroder Wertheim to Lehman Brothers this way: "The arguments that Fred put forth for why I should join Lehman were very appealing. He had a lot of young analysts, and he had a lot of young women analysts as well, and I found that very appealing. And he also, frankly, doubled my compensation. But had he just offered to double my compensation and I hadn't liked the other things, I wouldn't have gone. I had actually interviewed in a couple of other places, just because they called me, and I didn't like the culture in the other firms and I just said no."

Scrutinizing the Culture

The array of factors that women considered when contemplating a move largely involved the culture of the department, in terms of how women fit in and its values, atmosphere, and tone.[53]

Receptivity to Women. "They look for things like how are women treated here, and are there any female role models?" said Lisa Shalett, head of research at Sanford C. Bernstein. "When a guy decides he's going to move from CSFB to Goldman Sachs, does he say, 'Oh, I wonder if there's going to be any male role models for me'? I think when a woman moves, that's one of the first things she says. 'Can I interview with any of the women who work here? And what are they like? And what has it taken for them to survive?' And that puts the whole dialogue around the culture. I think for a lot of guys it just never even comes up."[54]

"They are much more inquisitive about the culture of the firm," concurred Fred Fraenkel. "Because you hear over and over and over again that, say, Goldman Sachs had this great culture—but it was a great culture for men. And so it wasn't enough to know if a firm had a good culture. You have to know, how does a woman actually stack up? And, you know, 'Here's our big-name women'—does that mean anything? Or does that mean that they're just showing you some big-name women? What does it mean for *all* women? It varies quite a bit."

Abby Joseph Cohen observed that star women of her acquaintance who contemplated moving did so to pursue more support or greater opportunity to advance:

> In many cases women are leaving because they feel that they're not getting the proper internal support. In instances that I'm familiar with, women have moved on to other firms because they think that the management of that other firm will be more receptive. Obviously, if you're being recruited someplace, your new manager has a commitment to you. And so in many cases women have left firms because their star ranking may be due more to their own contribution as opposed to getting the support from the organization that they're

leaving. . . . They will look at not necessarily the number of female analysts but whether female analysts have been allowed to rise to the top. There are quite a few firms that have increased the percentage of women at the bottom end of the pyramid. So the question is how many of those women actually rise, and do they rise in the same proportion that men do.[55]

Miriam Cutler Willard, who left Goldman Sachs to join Shearson Lehman in 1988, commented a year later: "Shearson impressed me as an unusually good place for a woman; it had an unusually high percentage of women analysts. It had a unique ability to make women welcome in the department and make us feel in the mainstream socially. I never felt I had to pretend to be male to fit in here."[56]

Other Features of a Departmental Culture: Latitude and Flexibility. Women look for departments that will be receptive to their individual styles and personalities and their methods of distinguishing their franchises. In past decades, particularly at certain firms, both women and men had to contend with very narrow definitions of acceptable style. (Recall from chapter 1 that Josie Esquivel was advised that long red fingernails were not considered appropriate for investment banking.) "Most of Wall Street had a powerful culture that allowed only a particular type of person to succeed," recalled Judy Sanders, former head of human resources for capital markets at Shearson Lehman Brothers, describing Lehman in the 1980s (prior to Jack Rivkin's appointment as research director). "It was as if they all came from the same dorm. Everything from the clothes you wore to the jokes you told telegraphed whether you were in the in-group or not."

These clubby enclaves have become more diverse, but women still find themselves walking tightropes. Female analysts are urged by their mentors and research directors to stand up for and promote themselves; at the same time, aggressive women are frowned on. "Strong, aggressive women are still seen as bitchy and irrational and emotional. Even the senior research analyst—a lot of the male managers will go, 'Uh, she's such a bitch. If she would just shut up for a minute,'" said Sara Karlen. "Men for the most part, with women, don't want an aggressive interaction. It's, I guess, the maternal aspect that men seek. There were times where I had to be really careful as to who I was aggressive with, because they would look at me like I was the biggest bitch walking on the face of the earth. Yet if a guy walked in and did the exact same thing, he respected that person."[57] Similarly, mentioning one's personal life can seem unprofessional, especially for a single woman, but refraining from doing so can look standoffish. Women who have chafed at restrictive conventions and conflicting unspoken rules, as well as those who have enjoyed more latitude at woman-friendly firms, look for new workplaces where they can let down their guard and be fully themselves—or at least put less energy into consciously crafting a self-presentation style.[58]

Durruthy cast the dilemma in more abstract terms: "White men don't have one identity at work and another one outside of work. . . . Their social network and social systems will intertwine with the work environment. Women and people of color struggle more with that, and that creates kind of a wall, a firewall, in their relationships. And it makes it harder for them to build relationships."

Female analysts contemplating moves also take a hard look at more general aspects of departmental culture. "The things that were important to me were about the culture," said Helane Becker, who maintained her star status at several firms. "When you walk around the office, are the people smiling? Are they happy? Are they on the phone? Are they moping around? Is there griping? Anywhere you go, you're going to get a lot of griping, but I tried to get a sense of what the gripes were like." As one female analyst explained, "Growing up as a minority, you realize how important a good and friendly environment is to your success. You never take it for granted."[59]

Sizing up the Research Director. Female stars readily admit that they scrutinize the research director, who sets the tone for the department, for supportiveness to women.[60] "Women want to make sure that their director of research, and the people on their team, are people that they like, people that they trust, people who have resonant values," said Lisa Shalett. Describing her reasons for joining Drexel, Cohen said, "I noticed in Burt Siegel's office a prominently displayed picture of his three daughters in basketball uniforms with Burt, who was the coach of the girls' team. I thought just as he had provided opportunities for his daughters, he would create opportunities for me. While chatting with him during the interview process, I felt that Burt understood that young women wanted a fair shake. I was further reassured when I looked around the department and saw that he had hired some high-quality women who seemed to be doing well at the firm."

Independently, Helane Becker had made the same observation and drawn the same inference: "Burt [Siegel] had daughters, Arthur Kirsch [research director at Drexel Burnham Lambert] had at least one daughter, or maybe two. These people were raising children who were obviously a generation behind me but were women. And I think from their perspective, they wanted the opportunities that were available to men of my generation to be available to their own daughters."

Management could also shape how women analysts are treated by the sales force and by investment bankers. One analyst recollected a meeting with Jack Rivkin and some senior sales executives that she attended with another female analyst. "Midway through the discussion," she said, "a salesman turned to us and asked, 'So what do the girls think of—?' Jack turned to us and said that we didn't have to answer that question."[61]

Seeking Objective Measurement Criteria. Several women spoke of an impartial departmental measurement system as a bulwark against politics and favoritism.[62] "The expectation of an impartial performance measurement system is quite simply necessary for survival," said Muratore. "The same for confidence that someone, most likely the director of research, can be relied on for constructive support. So women may naturally select firms where there has already been management effort to enhance analyst efficacy and objective performance standards."

Teena Lerner, recalling Lehman Brothers under Jack Rivkin and Fred Fraenkel's leadership, said, "You felt that management was on your side, trying to improve you. They were giving you these measurements and telling you how you stacked up for your own benefit." Recruiter Debra Brown spelled out the protective function of objective performance measures: "Women like positions that are transparent—i.e., have measurable results—so that their abilities can be validated by objective measures. Women tend to prefer market-facing roles instead of internal or support functions. Positions requiring direct contact with the marketplace provide validation of their credibility, thereby minimizing politics."

Further Observations on Gender

The Turnover/Portability Cycle

As noted earlier, some men on Wall Street suspected that women were not invested in their careers for the long haul and that it therefore made little sense to mentor promising women or to work at retaining experienced women. Our research suggests that a cycle of linked expectations and behavior may have evolved: male counterparts do not invest in collegial relationships with women, which leads women to develop highly portable skills, facilitating their turnover, which in turn leads to the perception that women are more likely to leave, causing male colleagues and management to be less willing to invest in women.

A look at the numbers shows that women analysts do have higher rates of turnover than men do. Annual turnover rates for male and female stars are 10.8 percent and 14.3 percent, respectively; women's turnover is thus 32 percent higher than men's. Moves to competitors are 24 percent higher for star women than for star men (8.7 percent for men and 10.8 percent for women). And 5 percent of ranked women and 3.3 percent of ranked men left the profession annually to take positions with buy-side companies, hedge funds, or the industries they had previously covered, or to exit the job market entirely.

For purposes of comparison, annual turnover rates at the top twenty-four firms for *all* analysts—both stars and non-stars—were 21.2 percent for men and 29 percent for women, a 37 percent differential.[63] Moves to competitors occurred at annual rates of 13.5 percent for men and 14.5 percent for women. Departures from the profession occurred at rates of 7.6 percent for men and 14.5 percent for women, a 91 percent differential. Women's rates of turnover were consistently higher than those of comparable men, though star women's turnover rates were lower than those of the general population of men.[64]

The struggles that female analysts experienced might prompt suspicion that these turnover rates, and particularly departures from the profession, reflect defeat or failure or even dismissal. As we have seen, women are often the first to be laid off in hard times and may strategically pursue portability as a result. But stars are not downsized; their moves reflect success, not failure. If we take female stars at their word, those who changed employers or left the profession did so essentially out of strategic opportunism: a decision to make the most of their star status by finding a more compatible setting where they could build on their success.

Their high turnover, however, combined with a high profile as a minority group made it difficult for women to convince their male colleagues that they were indeed committed to their jobs. "Two of my predecessors, both women, stayed for eighteen months and three years [respectively], so I felt that I needed to show that I am here to stay," said a ranked woman analyst describing her arrival at a new firm. "There are various ways in which you signal to people that you're here to stay. I threw a party in my house once to show that I had purchased this house and put a lot of thought and effort into it—basically to say that I am not going anywhere. I invited all the key people from research, sales, and trading. I wanted everyone to know that they weren't wasting their time dealing with me."

This analyst designed her strategic overture to overcome a prevalent impression that female analysts, particularly young unranked ones, are unlikely to stick with their jobs for long—an assumption reinforced by the short tenures of her two predecessors. A salesman quoted earlier was disinclined to bother acquainting himself with the franchises of female analysts until they had demonstrated staying power. And a senior analyst also quoted earlier described his frustration and sense of futility when women he had mentored left the department.

With regard to the assertion that high female turnover makes it rational to invest less in female analysts, a phenomenon that scholars of prejudice call *the mote-beam mechanism* may be pertinent here: the faults of individual members of minority groups are used to justify preexisting biases even as the same faults on the part of mainstream individuals are interpreted more benignly.[65] In Wall Street research departments, for instance, a woman's decision to move over to the buy side might be dismissed as a defection for personal reasons, while a man's identical decision is admired as an understandable pursuit of an irresistible offer.[66]

Divergence from Male Career Paths

Female analysts' careers—both their entrance into the profession and the methods they use to become successful—tended to be more individualistic than the typical male analyst's career. Rosanna Durruthy hypothesized that the scarcity of role models for women promoted inventive approaches. "It's easier for men to, as it were, imitate other guys, go along with other guys, do what other guys are doing that has made them successful than it is for a woman to do that," said Durruthy. "She almost has to apply her own style. Again, the idea here is if you do what others have done that's made them successful, you'll be OK, but it won't necessarily make you a superstar."[67]

Lisa Shalett characterized female analysts as unusually adaptable, a characteristic she traced to women's minority status in the industry: "Their mere survival in the industry has forced them to adapt. When it comes to them being able to make a change and make their franchise portable, they can rest on those skills of adaptability because they've been adapting to 'get by' in what has ostensibly been kind of a man's world."[68] Women appear to bring more diverse backgrounds to the field, to do better covering less-established industries, and to make a point of forging unconventional in-house alliances.

The adaptability of female analysts was apparent in their varied routes of entry into the profession and in how they capitalized on prior experience. A number of women who chose to become analysts in the 1960s–1980s came to Wall Street from industries they later covered and relied on an insider's mastery of the industry to distinguish themselves from their competitors. "Forget understanding the numbers of the company first. Understand the mechanics of the industry first," said Esquivel. "I think a lot of analysts, when they don't have an industry background, tend to focus on these great spreadsheets, and that's all well and great, but there's fifteen people covering the textile industry. Why do they need to call me? I was a new analyst. I think the reason they started to call me was because I *did* understand the industry."

Others had technical credentials that gave them access to areas closed off to other analysts. Like the legendary strategist Abby Joseph Cohen, star biotech analyst Teena Lerner counted on her formidable technical expertise (she earned her Ph.D. in biology at Rockefeller University) to help her move into a field too new to have developed an exclusionary culture:

> The first generation of biotech analysts to hit Wall Street was well represented by women, maybe fifty-fifty. Because the field was so new, there was no preexisting old-boys' network that could fill positions with a friend of a friend or a son of a friend. Because of the highly technical nature of the sector, finding people with both the right education and skills to do the job was hard. That technical knowledge put me in an unusual position. . . . There were definitely times when I got beaten up by older male portfolio managers in terms of stock picking or the stock market, but they certainly couldn't beat up on me in my area of expertise.

Forging Unconventional In-House Alliances

Within their banks, women analysts often developed productive relationships with a group typically ignored by male analysts: retail brokers (stockbrokers who serve individual clients, as opposed to institutional investors). Because male analysts typically disdained the retail sales force as unsophisticated, and even ignored their phone calls, female analysts found retail brokers to be both receptive and forthcoming.[69] Bonita Austin noted that it was a retail broker who had arranged an important telephone call for her with the CEO of Toys "R" Us. Helane Becker pointed out the informational value of retail brokers: "I had a very large retail network. And, you know, when you're dealing with retail brokers, . . . somebody has a client or brother-in-law, friend, sister, whatever, who works for an airline company. And they would call me with information. And I would listen to what they had to say. Some of my peer group would never talk to retail brokers. And I would always endeavor to return their calls and get to them in a timely fashion, because you never know."

As a beginning analyst, biotech star Teena Lerner valued the retail network for a different reason:

> The retail brokers loved me . . . and it was a huge advantage to me that their network could move stocks whenever I said something. They'd put me on the squawk box and I'd explain to all the traders what was really going on. I had no idea that analysts typically don't like to deal with retail that way, but I was new to the business so I did what seemed to make the most sense. . . . They loved it because they can't stand it when the analysts leave them in the lurch. I never did.

Female analysts' pursuit of affiliations with retail brokers (many of whom work at regional offices rather than the investment bank's headquarters) was decidedly unconventional.[70] This willingness to swim against the current of departmental culture sheds further light on the attitudes and strategies that contribute to female stars' portability. It appears that women who later became stars entered the profession expecting that the mainstream ways of doing the job wouldn't necessarily work for them or be available to them. They then looked around for ways to turn their apartness, or lack of embeddedness in the culture of the department, to advantage by forming useful relationships with clients, executives at the companies they covered, and retail brokers.

Difficulties with Internal Career Progression

A focus on external relationships serves women well in terms of portability and building a successful franchise, but it can cause problems for a woman who wants to move up in her organization. The in-house career path for an analyst usually progresses from junior to senior analyst, then to manager of a sector with multiple senior analysts, later to associate research director, research director, and possibly head of equities. A star analyst progresses from being a producer to becoming a producing manager, who will spend a significant amount of time managing and directing the work of others.[71]

This transition was difficult for women. A successful producing manager needs a deep and broad understanding of the in-house culture and a solid set of relationships within the firm. Lisa Shalett, research director at Sanford C. Bernstein, explained:

> Your life changes when you become a manager. . . . You really have to start developing peer relationships at the firm. That's how things get done: through relationships. If you are an analyst who built your franchise on your clients and on your companies, you have to refocus and start building in-house relationships. When I got promoted, I was very proactive. I just went and started introducing myself to everyone I had to work with, in other departments and functions. . . . It really helped that I had credibility by being a successful analyst, so my colleagues would meet with me. In reality, you do not have a choice when you get promoted to be a manager; you have to become more and more internally focused. Relationships and trust are what gets things done in organizations. If you don't have relationships, you have no trust, and you will soon not have a job.

Women analysts typically found it difficult to develop this kind of team-specific and firm-specific capital and strategically opted to build up outside relationships. But relationships outside the organization may not facilitate managing within the organization.[72] While women who moved to new jobs continued to perform well, some of those who were promoted within their firms fared poorly.

The Stock Market's Response to Hiring of Male and Female Analysts

Table 8.2 shows the aggregate stock-market reactions to firms' acquisitions of male and female stars. Firms acquiring male stars experienced a significant share-price loss of 0.93 percent, but the acquisitions of female stars generated a nonsignificant share-price increase of 0.07 percent. This finding suggests that the stock market did not view the acquisition of female stars as value-reducing. Furthermore, investors appeared to believe that firms over-

Table 8.2

Aggregate Abnormal Stock-Market Returns to Destination Firms
around Announcements of Acquisition of Star Analysts, by Gender, 1988–96

	Abnormal returns		
	Event window (−1, +1)	t-statistic	Sample size
Female	0.07%	(0.12)	20
Male	−0.93%[a, b]	(−3.54)	81

Notes: This table presents stock-market reactions to announcements of movements by ranked analysts. A short window study of daily excess returns over the event window of −1 to +1 days (market model) was conducted. Stock returns data were provided by the Center for Research in Security Prices (CRSP) of the University of Chicago.

[a] Different from 0 at 1% level of significance.

[b] Abnormal returns for female analysts is different from abnormal returns for male analysts at 10% level of significance.

pay more to attract male stars than they do to capture female stars. Finally, investors might be anticipating a drop in performance on the part of male analysts.

Implications for Organizations: Retaining Women, Developing Men

Female stars appeared to opt for the career strategies they do because of structural factors—legitimate concern about protecting their portability and a focus on external relationships to compensate for difficulties forging in-house alliances. As our data show, however, women's strategies were not a second-best alternative but a powerful skill set from which men would do well to learn. By paying closer attention to the careers of star women, firms could do a better job of retaining women and developing men.

Developing women's firm-specific human capital could lessen turnover of high-performing women and facilitate their in-house career paths. (One way to promote retention of female stars would be to hire more women across the board, particularly outside of research.) Inventorying the skill sets that male and female stars have used to build their franchises and cultivating a culture that helps both genders can also benefit firms. Some individuals will still favor one or the other approach, but the choice need not be dictated by gender. Our work shows that there are multiple paths to success in equity research.[73] It would benefit female analysts to have access to male pathways, and it would benefit male analysts to recognize the female pathways as an option.

There is no reason that male analysts could not benefit from adopting the external focus characteristic of high-performing women (or women adopting the internal focus of men). "The job of an analyst is necessarily focused outward, on industry, companies, and clients. This is where your reputation is made and any clout you may wish to have is developed," Carol Muratore observed. "I would think this would be true for male analysts as well, although they may have more affinity for the internal politics." Male analysts, whose career paths have long been seen as the norm, may not be leveraging all the strengths they have.[74]

Lehman Brothers was an example of a firm that gained competitive advantage by creating a fair and woman-friendly environment. Under Jack Rivkin and Fred Fraenkel, Lehman Brothers' research department encouraged female analysts to participate in the recruiting process and rigorously pursued gender-blind policies in every facet of the department's operation. Meanwhile the department jumped from fifteenth in the *II* rankings in 1987 to seventh in 1988 and fourth in 1989. That year a higher percentage of female analysts were ranked at Lehman than at any other firm. "Jack and Fred had a blind eye toward hiring," said Esquivel. "That is, they just wanted to hire the best analysts across industries. The best didn't necessarily mean male." Rivkin explained his recruiting strategy:

> Many of our competitors had recruiting committees that were almost exclusively composed of men. . . . Many of these firms failed to realize that they were sending a signal to the prospective candidates: there was only one way to succeed. At Lehman, our recruiting process was set up to evaluate talent and to send a signal that no matter what strengths or weaknesses you have, we know how to make you successful. That's why I wanted to expose the candidate to the full diversity of our department. After meeting with ten very different people, the candidate was bound to find someone with whom he or she could associate. Several candidates, even ones that didn't receive an offer from us, commended us for showing them that there was more than one path to success. The recruiting process, however, did keep some analysts from joining our group: some male analysts opted out because they were uncomfortable being interviewed by so many female analysts, who were actually evaluating them and could possibly have become their team leaders.

Lehman's recruiting process helped female analysts in two ways: by signaling during interviews the kind of culture they could expect and by screening out men uncomfortable in a culture in which women could thrive and men could learn from them.[75]

Generalizability to Other Knowledge Professions

The portability of women's performance can be traced to behavior patterns that are both adaptive and strategically shrewd given the structure of the profession, its incentive system, and the constraints women encountered. First, they relied heavily on external relationships—particularly relationships with clients, whose votes are the mechanism that create stardom. In chapter 5 we noted that analysts from certain banks were more portable than others, regardless of gender. Firms that fostered high portability (intentionally or unintentionally) created a work environment in which analysts did not develop strong relationships with the sales force or traders, had few opportunities to work in teams, and forged their closest relationships with external sources in the industries they covered. The environments at these banks replicated the environments that female analysts encountered to some degree at almost all banks. Their response—building a strong external network and developing portable skills—makes sense, given these environments. Women's career-management strategies, therefore, seem to have more to do with structural constraints than with innate or socialized gender traits.

Where portable women differed from portable men was in their careful scrutiny of potential job changes. Given the difficulties that underrepresented groups face in the workplace, this kind of due diligence also makes strategic sense.

The fact that unacknowledged sexism continues to exist even in a profession as externally benchmarked as equity research suggests that women may face an even steeper uphill climb in more subjective knowledge professions, like consulting.[76] Also, women in equity research have the option of building an external franchise by focusing on clients and the companies they cover. In some professions, such an external orientation is not an option.[77]

These findings point to a couple of relationships pertinent to portability of performance in general. First, in this population there appears to be a strong relationship between individual portability and the likelihood of changing employers. Female analysts move more frequently, and their performance is portable. Among star research analysts as a whole, however, there appeared to be very little correspondence between actual individual portability and one's *perception* of one's portability. Consistent interview evidence suggests that those whose skills were most portable—star women—were unusually painstaking about avoiding ill-advised moves that would degrade their performance. Those whose skills were least portable—star men—were more likely to be lured away by higher compensation and often paid a price in diminished performance. Individuals' decisions to move or stay put seem to operate independently of realistic assessments of their own portability.[78]

Second, we would misconstrue the portability of female stars' performance if we concluded too hastily that they simply transported their general skills and portable resources to a new workplace and continued to flourish independently of their new environments. On the contrary, female analysts' careful assessment of the cultures of their destination firms was critical to their success. It is possible, in fact, that careful moves alone account for a significant portion of the portability of women's performance. But it is clearly more than careful moves. These accomplished women made certain that their new firms would provide the resources that experience had taught them they would need to overcome the drag on performance that a job change entails.

Part Three | Implications for Talent Management: Developing, Retaining, and Rewarding Stars

9 | Star Formation

Developmental Cultures at Work

If portability of star-quality performance is more often a myth than a reality, it is crucial for knowledge-based firms to figure out how to cultivate and retain their own stars. On Wall Street it was uncommon to do so. Research departments rarely provided formal training or mentoring to supplement the traditional apprenticeship method (assigning a junior analyst to assist a senior analyst, who may or may not have seen fit to oversee the junior's development). Even less common was a concerted internal effort to develop analysts into stars; the most popular means of acquiring star analysts was to lure them from other firms.[1] Only a handful of Wall Street research departments successfully developed their own stars. This chapter will look at the strategic advantage of doing so, at how these firms differed from their competitors with regard to talent development, and at the methods these developmentally minded departments use.

Over the course of our study, only nine firms developed more than 8 percent of their analysts into stars.[2] The percentages of unranked analysts who eventually became stars at a given firm varied from 15.4 percent at DLJ and 14.9 percent at Sanford C. Bernstein to only 3 percent at Merrill Lynch and 0.6 percent at UBS. As this chapter will show, firms with what we call *developmental cultures*[3] were far more successful at both producing and retaining stars.[4] Such firms enjoyed a star-formation rate of 11 percent, compared to 5.4 percent at other firms. (See table 9.1 for star-development and turnover rates at the firms with developmental cultures and at other firms among the top twenty-four research departments.) The seven firms with developmental cultures[5] invested significant funding and effort over a considerable period of time in systematic training and mentoring.[6] The other firms had virtually no consistent mentoring or training programs, formal or informal.

Firms with successful track records for turning analysts into stars were also better at keeping them: overall annual turnover of stars was 9.2 percent at the firms with developmental cultures and 12.9 percent at the other firms. Turnover to competitors (as opposed to departures from the profession) was 6 percent at the firms with developmental cultures and 9.8 percent at the other firms. Finally, turnover of stars and non-stars was 14.4 percent at the firms with developmental cultures and 20.6 percent at the other firms. Apparently employee development has a strong effect not only on star formation but also on retention.[7]

Despite these favorable outcomes, there was no consensus on the Street about the efficacy of initiatives to promote star-quality performance in-house. Firms that subscribed to the nature theory remained skeptical, attributing the differences in productivity between stars and solid middling performers to differences in innate traits or general education. Smith Barney and NatWest, for example, both active players in the labor market for ranked analysts, were skeptical that star performers could be developed. As Smith Barney's director of global research, John Hoffmann, put it, "I could find CFAs who have some understanding of financial statements, and we could develop them, but they aren't substitutes for established analysts. Sure, they may have the skill sets, the background, the motivation that with a little time will make them decent analysts. But making it to excellent-analyst status is harder, and the people who do so are few."[8]

Table 9.1
Rates of Star Development and Turnover at Research Departments, 1988–96

Type	Analysts developed into stars (%)	Stars' turnover rate (%)	Stars' rate of turnover to competitors (%)	Overall turnover rate (stars and nonstars) (%)
Firms with developmental cultures	11.0[a]	9.2[a]	6.0[a]	14.4[a]
Other firms	5.4	12.9	9.8	20.6

[a] Different from other firms' mean at 1% significance level.

There was much overlap but not perfect correspondence between developmental firms and nonportability-promoting firms or between nondevelopmental and portability-promoting firms. Some portability-promoting firms, for instance, actively developed their analysts' general human capital. DLJ did so by training its analysts to analyze companies, write research reports, and service clients. These are generic skills that would be applicable at any Wall Street research department—yet DLJ enjoyed low overall turnover. At the other extreme, Merrill Lynch was a nonportability-oriented firm that did not offer its analysts developmental opportunities. Its nonportability resided in its proprietary information-technology systems.

Developmental Cultures

Research directors who opted to develop stars in-house tended to share an interventionist, can-do outlook. As Steve Hash, global head of research at Lehman Brothers, explained: "We have focused very much on developing all of our own star analysts, under the observation that . . . a star analyst certainly wasn't born that way. . . . If you take a good—I want to say young, but they're not always young—and you give them an opportunity, and you teach them—that's the key, you have to show them how to be successful. You have to teach them."

Techniques for developing knowledge-based talent vary, and this chapter will look at a handful of successful approaches and cultural differences between firms that pursued such efforts and those that did not. It is striking that many of the developmental approaches we will look at turned out to share certain identifiable features. These shared characteristics were (1) individualized developmental agendas; (2) cross-fertilization via peer mentoring, mutual critiquing of work products, sharing best practices across analysts and sectors, and adopting varied developmental practices and processes rather than affiliating exclusively with one method; (3) the research director's energetic involvement and support of in-house development; and (4) ongoing, open-ended development of mid-career analysts as well as beginners.

Individualized Developmental Agendas

Analysts prize their individuality. Furthermore, no two analysts at a given firm do exactly the same work—there is scant overlap, for instance, between the analytical approaches of a biotechnology analyst and an airline analyst. The work of analysts in different industries can be synergistic, though, if the overlapping areas of knowledge and expertise are exploited strategically (for example, those of a biotechnology analyst and a medical-supplies analyst). Similarly, the differing skill sets and strategies that analysts bring to the job can make for disjunction or for harmony. As Lisa Shalett, director of research at Sanford C. Bernstein, commented, "[Analysts are] not a group of people who lend themselves to traditional management science."[9]

The goal of successful in-house development efforts is thus not to nudge participants toward a formulaic model but to help them better pursue their individual strategies and creative impulses. A cookie-cutter approach would be alien to the culture of equities research, a waste of analysts' time, and an inevitable failure. Acknowledging analysts' individuality, Mayree Clark, research director at Morgan Stanley, emphasized the importance of respecting different intellectual styles and strengths:

> We had some people who were great stock pickers, some people who were great at writing these tomes of incredibly helpful thematic work. . . . There were other people who took a very short-term view of stock picking because they were in a sector that had a lot of volatility or because that was their style. Rich Bilotti covered highly leveraged companies, so he would do these elaborate models, really tearing apart the balance sheets. . . . Chuck Philips, who covered technology stocks, didn't do that much in the way of models, but he was the guy who always understood better than anyone else what was happening at the customer level with his companies. . . . So the important thing was that the analysts' style matched the sector they were in to be able to really meet the needs of people who were buying and selling the stocks that the analysts covered.

Describing the training program at Lehman Brothers, Josie Esquivel said, "In each session, we were learning how to build a franchise that was molded to our strengths. Jack and Fred believed that you could develop a franchise in a number of different ways; there was no 'right' way to do it."[10]

Cross-Fertilization and Flexible Developmental Processes

Individualized agendas spawned a diverse and flexible set of developmental practices. Some analysts were mentored and others attended individually designed training programs. Individualized development practices often went hand in hand with both deliberate and spontaneous intellectual cross-fertilization between analysts. Among the practices that many developmental departments encouraged were peer mentoring, critiquing of colleagues' work products, and sharing best practices across sectors. Such approaches were feasible, noted Michael Blumstein, director of U.S. equity research at Morgan Stanley, because analysts are not their colleagues' competitors: "I used to say to people, 'Remember, your competitor is the analyst at the firm next door; your competitor is not the person in the office next door.' So the culture at Morgan Stanley was really to try to learn best practices from the guy next door."

Firms that offered systematic skill development, of whatever kind, tended to encourage such collaboration by building it into their developmental practices. Up-and-comers may have achieved stardom more quickly at developmental firms than at firms with more go-it-alone cultures in part because best practices spread more rapidly.

Intense Support from the Research Director

Jack Rivkin, research director at Lehman Brothers, was brought in from Paine Webber with the mission of improving the department's performance and reputation. He was appalled by what he found—"When I got to Lehman, the research department was a mess," Rivkin recalled—and ambitious for distinction on behalf of the department and its analysts.[11] Relative to Merrill Lynch and Goldman Sachs, Lehman's research department was not well financed. Rivkin's determination to grow his own stars, however, seemed to be motivated less by the impossibility of buying stars from other firms than by his conviction that it was possible to build a first-rate department by supercharging the performance of its existing analysts.

In interviews, directors of developmental departments expressed intense, even impassioned, belief in nurture. Evidence from observation and interviews with analysts also indicated that research directors were typically involved in a hands-on way with developmental initiatives. Both observations strongly suggest that committed leadership is a sine qua non of effective in-house development of star-quality performance. For one thing, the director's efforts and high expectations had a profound motivating effect. As Steve Hash put it, "When you commit your own time and the firm's resources to helping train and develop these people, I think they feel a sense of obligation to do the absolute best that they can and succeed. . . . You take someone who would be performing at X and you get X + 30 percent out of them. . . . If you just give them an office and send them over in a corner and say, 'Gee, I hope you're successful,' you get a different result." Furthermore, intense involvement from the research director was necessary in order to push developmental programs through the culture and keep the practices ongoing. As we saw in chapter 5, consistent sponsorship from the research director at Lehman Brothers was necessary to keep a strong developmental culture going. When the department's training processes were dropped and its culture started to disappear, analysts' performance began to suffer.

Ongoing Development of Experienced Analysts

The feature of Wall Street developmental cultures that was directly pertinent to stars' performance was the conviction, embodied in practice, that training and mentorship are appropriate for experienced practitioners as well as beginners. This is a belief well grounded in practicality, in that it has implications for retention of outstanding performers, for individual and departmental morale, and for the departmental budget. If it is a departmental goal to outperform the competition, furthermore, it seems only logical to provide maximum support to those on the threshold of stardom.[12]

But practical advantages alone were apparently insufficient to bring developmental cultures into being. Belief systems came into play as well, and the belief that stars are born, not made, appeared to be deeply ingrained at nondevelopmental firms. To believers in development, this point of view seemed senseless. "Hiring a senior analyst takes a lot of time and a lot of money," said Steve Hash. "And you just can't constantly hire, and have turnover, and expect a department to get anywhere. You're paying above-market rates, you're not engendering any type of loyalty, and it eats up so much management time trying to recruit stars that you just—you don't succeed." By contrast, Hash continued, "By training your own up-and-coming stars, you end up having very low turnover in the overall department, which is extraordinary—I can't stress how important that is to department success. . . . Once you create this program where we're using up-and-comers, training them, and they start succeeding, then all the other up-and-comers say, 'Aha, look! I see how it works!' And then you create a culture of success, which is like a snowball going downhill. It breeds on itself." In a developmental culture, by extension, the same individual could be both a recipient and a provider of suggestions, guidance, and feedback.

The bedrock concept underlying such training was that it is possible to teach the skills necessary to ratchet up performance in the same way that it is possible and necessary to teach basic skills and concepts. A brief survey of conventional methods of training and mentoring analysts will serve as a baseline for assessing the innovations that developmental departments have adopted.

Mentorship in Wall Street Research Departments

Neither a first-rate education nor experience in the industry they cover guarantees that analysts know what they are doing at the beginning of their careers.[13] "Most of the MBA programs teach you how to analyze numbers and how to read a balance sheet and how to build an income statement," pointed out Helane Becker, a star airlines analyst. "You know how to take a balance sheet apart and reconstruct it, but you don't know the nuances." Not even the ideal candidate—a top graduate of a top business school with industry experience—will be adept at the job right away.[14] "Having a mentor or putting someone through a training program is a much better way to go than just throwing someone to the wolves and saying, 'Here, go be an analyst,'" Becker asserted. "You have no idea how."

Orientation to the Profession: The Junior-Analyst System

The conventional mechanism for orientation and training of beginning analysts was the position of junior analyst. Most research departments offered very little further organized training or mentoring, relying nearly exclusively on junior-senior interaction to teach the basic intellectual and marketing skills. But the junior-analyst system made inexperienced analysts subject to the luck of the draw: some senior analysts were generous, encouraging, and challenging mentors; others restricted their juniors to routine tasks. Ideally, the position of junior analyst would provide the skills—number crunching, writing, presenting ideas to clients, interacting with the sales force and traders—that the analyst would need when covering his or her own sector as a senior analyst.[15] Chris Kotowski, a star research analyst covering the banking industry who named "good apprenticeship, good mentors, and native talent" as the three crucial factors in an analyst's development,[16] described his own apprenticeship with ranked banking analyst Mark Biderman in the early 1980s:

Generally you work with a senior analyst, and they start you out by just crunching numbers: "Here are fifty press releases. Put all those numbers into a spreadsheet." After you've mastered what the numbers mean and it's accurate and reliable, maybe you can do some writing: "Here's some company; they reported earnings. . . . Here, Chris, you write that one up." Then they'd have you start speaking at the morning meeting: "I'm busy, I'm traveling. Chris, you go talk about thus-and-such a company." Or go to company meetings. . . . And then hopefully the senior analyst is more busy all the time. And at some point you get the salespeople making the call, saying, "Mark's on the road. Let me get Chris Kotowski, who's been doing most of the writing and work anyway." You get introduced to clients that way. At some point, after you've built a franchise with your institutional sales force, they start taking you out on the road visiting clients. That, to my mind, is the way it should work.

Other analysts described comparably systematic processes of learning the ropes and gradually being granted responsibility.

But some juniors were trained merely to become proficient juniors. Self-protectiveness on the part of senior analysts could discourage openhanded mentorship of juniors.[17] "The last thing you want to do is give somebody all your earnings models," said Helane Becker. "And they go across the street and they become the airline analyst or the energy analyst or whatever with your model." Bonita Austin, a ranked household-goods analyst, agreed: "Many people really don't want their junior analysts to go on and pick up the groups that they are already following. So it can be quite difficult to move from a junior-analyst position to a senior-analyst position."

Research directors who were serious about talent development could and did encourage senior analysts to function as full-fledged mentors for their juniors, both by promoting institution building as a value and by making substantive mentoring of juniors a criterion for assessing seniors' performance and for determining their compensation.

Informal Mentoring of Young Senior Analysts

Some beneficiaries of mentorship were junior analysts, but mentoring was common between senior analysts, one older and more experienced than the other. In contrast to the junior-senior analyst mentoring relationship, two senior analysts rarely saw each other as potential competitors because they covered different sectors. Informal one-on-one mentoring seemed, in fact, to have been instrumental in the development of many star analysts.

Informal mentoring could occur spontaneously in any research department if the two participants were willing.[18] A mentoring relationship was likely to develop, in other words, only if the inexperienced individual was persuasive enough and the experienced individual was generous enough to devote time to it. But prevailing values shaped behavior: at firms that operated on the nature theory, mentoring was often viewed as a waste of time. At firms that did not explicitly encourage mentoring, doing so may even have been viewed as a sign of poor time management.

Developmental firms valued mentoring as a contribution to the collaborative enterprise of building a strong department and found ways to explicitly encourage it.[19] Some firms codified their support by making mentoring a criterion for measuring analysts' performance. "Great research departments that perpetuate themselves through internal development, as opposed to external recruitment, have much in common with the medieval guild," said Barry Tarasoff, research director at Schroder Wertheim. (Although not statistically one of our top firms in creating stars—it was number fifteen in percentage of analysts developed—Schroder Wertheim represents a special case to be discussed later in the chapter.) Tarasoff described this guild mentality as "the practice of passing on the craft from one generation to the next. At Wertheim, our senior people understood this obligation very well, and our developing people appreciated the value of the apprenticeship."

Skillful mentors were careful to preserve and promote their protégés' autonomy. When Bonita Austin arrived at Schroder Wertheim from industry as a beginning senior analyst, her mentor was Emma Hill, an older ranked analyst in advertising, cosmetics, and household products.[20] Austin described the firm's culture and the care with which Hill respected Austin's autonomy.

> The environment at Wertheim was very nurturing. They had just embarked on a program of starting their own analysts from scratch, and they gave me a lot of time to get to know the companies that I followed. Emma Hill was a good mentor. She would never second-guess me, and she refused to ever discuss my stocks with the sales force. . . . I would brainstorm with her, but her style was "It's your group now. You do what you want. If you want to ask me anything and I can help you, great, but if you don't, you're on your own."

Hill passed on to Austin both technical skills and less tangible habits of mind. "From a nuts-and-bolts standpoint, I had access to her earnings models, and I saw how to build earnings models. From reading her basic reports on companies, I learned how to break the companies into pieces and cover the significant pieces," Austin recalled. "And one thing that Emma encouraged was that it's good to be skeptical. I always keep in the back of my mind . . . that more often than not the CEO was the most successful salesperson in the company, and that's how that person got to be CEO. . . . You need to remember that you're dealing with an organization that's full of salespeople. She definitely encouraged me to remain skeptical." Hill also introduced Austin one by one to key salespeople and traders. A mentor could accelerate a protégé's development by efficiently passing on qualitative tips and technical know-how that could otherwise take years to acquire.

Mentoring could be highly untraditional in its particulars, depending on the preferences and creativity of the participants. Helane Becker's experience was probably the most unusual: she was trained in part by an analyst at a competing firm. Becker moved to Prudential Securities with her mentor, Craig Kloner, initially as his junior analyst. Six months later she became Prudential's airline analyst. "So I needed to learn the airline industry," Becker recalled, "and Craig said, 'I don't know anything about the airline industry, but Michael Armellino knows everything about the airlines. I'm going to put you in touch with Michael.'" Armellino, the number-one-ranked airline-and-railroad analyst, was at Goldman Sachs, where Kloner had worked for him as a junior analyst. Becker explained:

> Michael taught me what about the airline industry is important and what drives the stocks. From his perspective, he was looking at it as: "I'm better off having a strong competitor than I am having a weak competitor who flounders all over the place with a big sales force." Remember, I was at Prudential at the time, and not only did I have an institutional sales force but I had a retail network. I think his view was, if I'm a half-assed analyst and I go off and say, "Short American Airlines!" for whatever reason and everybody does it, the risk is that it moves stock for the wrong reasons. Mike made introductory phone calls [to airlines] for me. He called them and said, "There's this new analyst at Pru. She's been on Wall Street for a couple of years; she knows how stocks trade, but she doesn't know anything about the business. So help her out where you can."

Meanwhile Kloner advised Becker on internal matters. This scenario was probably unique in its particulars, but not in its results.

Helane Becker's mentorship experience highlights another consequence of the convergence of a profession in a particular locale. In most fields, experts are scattered around the country, if not the world, but the best equity research was clustered in Manhattan. Such concentration didn't just shrink the opportunity costs of switching firms; it also facilitated developmental clusters in which best practices were occasionally shared across firms, as we will see in the section on formal training.

Fostering Stardom In-House: Training Experienced Analysts and Institutionalized Mentoring

It is noteworthy that research departments with developmental cultures did not see a need to affiliate themselves with a particular developmental practice. The firms that offered formal training for mid-career analysts tended to be the same firms that actively encouraged mentorship and other forms of collegial interaction like sharing best practices, peer review of publications, and collaborative projects. This nonexclusive and multidimensional approach probably reflected some combination of a wholehearted desire to make the development ethos pervasive, a flexible whatever-works mindset, and recognition of analysts' individuality and aversion to lockstep thinking.

Furthermore, training and mentorship are hardly mutually exclusive. Training programs are organized events, typically intensive, though some last for weeks while others are one-shot off-site meetings.[21] Mentorship is continuous and embedded in the daily execution of the job.[22] Steve Einhorn described how the two approaches operated under his aegis at Goldman Sachs:

> We did have formal training programs, where we would have the analysts go through courses selected for them: accounting, security valuation, the impact of macroeconomics on industry and stock performance, things like that. So one element of it was a formal training program where they actually spent time in class.
>
> The second element was to work under a senior analyst, and that analyst could mentor, nurture, train that person in real time, so they had someone they could go to and learn from. That element of the

training program was probably the most intense, because you're working one-on-one with a person. And the senior analysts knew from me that part of their success in the department would be how well they mentored and nurtured these younger folks.

At DLJ, too, newly hired analysts were immediately enrolled in a formal program that concentrated on financial analysis and writing skills, and were mentored by a senior analyst for one year. "They had a mentoring program at DLJ where they'd have junior analysts sit with senior analysts and talk about stuff," recalled Ed Comeau, a star analyst at DLJ. "Sales was always included, trading and all that." Some firms viewed development as so important that they created a formal executive position responsible for training. At Prudential, Michael Culp, head of research, made Deborah Bronston formally responsible for analytical training to signal and reinforce the importance of research to the firm.

Formal Training of Experienced Analysts

A remarkable number of the most intensive in-house training programs for experienced analysts on Wall Street traced their origins to a single program, originally developed at Prudential Securities in the 1980s when Fred Fraenkel was its research director.[23] Versions of this program were still in use at a spectrum of firms at the time this book was written, which attests both to its effectiveness and to the interfirm cross-fertilization that is one of the outcomes of analysts' mobility. Even its earliest form was a hybrid. "We stole First Boston's idea of calling institutions on the phone to get their votes to improve our analysts' ranking," Fraenkel cheerfully admitted. "We stole the written-product delivery processes of Goldman Sachs and Merrill Lynch. We were totally shameless."[24]

Accelerated Marketing Training

The original program, known at Prudential as the Accelerated Course, was adopted and modified at several of the firms that were most energetic in their efforts to develop in-house talent. When Fraenkel moved to Lehman Brothers to work with Jack Rivkin, he and Rivkin introduced a thirteen-week version of the program that they called Accelerated Marketing Training. It became near legendary for its extraordinary success at transforming experienced analysts into stars.

Program Design and Content. At Lehman, Rivkin and Fraenkel conceived of the training program as a central component of their campaign to supercharge the performance of high-potential analysts, with the goal of systematically improving Lehman's standing in the *II* rankings. The success of this effort has been described in chapter 5.

Enrollment was limited to twelve to fifteen people, both to give the training program the cachet of a reward and to promote the kind of camaraderie and collegiality that can only develop in a small group. Participants ranged from recent MBA graduates to fifty-year-olds who had worked as analysts for twenty-five years. Classes met for thirteen weeks, once a week, for three hours during the regular workday. The content of the course was an eclectic, down-to-earth patchwork of technical analytic skills, know-how, and salesmanship that replicated the mix of skills that equity research calls for. (See exhibit 9.1 for excerpts from the materials used in the Lehman version of the course.) The technical component was designed to convert industry expertise into high-quality analysis and to be immediately applicable to an analyst's own work: each analyst used his or her own sector as the content of exercises. "It was like being tutored in your own work," said airline analyst Helane Becker about Prudential's precursor program. "When they said, 'Go build a dividend discount model,' they didn't ask me to do it on XYZ Corp. They said, 'Go do a dividend discount model for airlines.' So you learned a lot of different ways of doing things, and you did it within your own group so that you could determine what works best: discount model, EVA when it became popular, cash flow, EBITDA, EBIT, net income—what definition of cash flow works for the group and how does that affect your industry?"[25]

"We told our analysts to become the best industry experts and we would show them how to become successful," Fraenkel explained. "We were not going to teach the semiconductor analyst how to differentiate between Pentium and the 386. We were going to help him with a training program to monetize that knowledge. As a result, an industry expert entering our training program could be accelerated fairly dramatically into a recognized analyst."[26]

Josie Esquivel, who became ranked in one of the fastest ascents in Wall Street history, attributed her success in part to Lehman's training program: "We covered every aspect of our job, from stock picking to dealing with the press, salespeople, retail brokers, clients, and company management. We also discussed how to make our reports interesting and different so that clients would read them before reading any other analysts' reports."[27]

Exhibit 9.1

Excerpts from Materials Used in Accelerated Marketing Training at Lehman Brothers

---

MEMORANDUM

Date:	April 14, 1988
To:	Accelerated Mktg Class 1988
From:	Fred S. Fraenkel
Subject:	Syllabus

May 6, 1988	Videotaped Initial Presentation. Each participant presents exactly 3 minutes on an overview of factors affecting his group and his two favorite stocks. This session is later used as a benchmark for what we accomplish in the course.
May 12, 1988 (Thursday)	Utilizing Department Assets. Review of the Department's resources including Economics, Strategy, Sector and Technical and how to put them to work in marketing without compromising your investment prerogatives or appearing to be constrained to a top down view. Systems support current and prospective.
May 20, 1988	Group Presentation Skills. The Kiss, Kiss, Kiss system. The mental map. Top Gun. Ringing the Cash Register.
May 27, 1988	One on One Presentation Skills. Knowing your audience. The art of handout design. The library of tailored approaches.
June 13, 1988 (Monday)	What the buy side wants. Portfolio managers' approaches to utilizing research product. Doing your counterparts' job for profit and greater glory. The value and methodology of succinct contact.
June 30, 1988	What the sales force needs. The Salesman's day. Selling the sales force. The sales force's bitch list of Research don'ts. The do list that expands your impact.
June 30, 1988	Media Magic. How to make a big splash without drowning in the pool of yellow journalism. How to be the user instead of the use-ee. Proactive press tactics. Defensive moves that protect your franchise.

June 24, 1988 (Thursday)	Company Phone Calling. The interactive research process. Last in is lucky philosophy of call scheduling. Looking for an edge in company calling.
July 8, 1988	The Client Calling System. Concepts in client calling: Multiplicity of contact, QOS, Time management, Systems are solutions, Script and delivery plan, Record keeping and transaction orientation.
July 15, 1988	Video Wrap-Up and peer critique session.
July 20, 1988 (Wednesday Evening)	Maximizing Social Interaction Techniques: Field Trip to an Ethnic Restaurant of the group's choice. Good Bar is a must! Submit recommendations for locations no later than July 1. Anyone who misses the next day's morning meeting receives the Andrew Shore honorary award.

Each class begins promptly at 9:05 of the day scheduled. All participants are subjected to impromptu interrogations on the previous week's subject material. If you miss a week, ask me for the lesson plan in advance or following the meeting. Three strikes and you're out, anyone who misses three classes in a row is scratched from the roster no ifs, ands or buts. Distribution: Coury, Curro, Diverio, Esquivel, Exstein, Lerner, Levy, McCarthy, Plodwick, Rosenberg, Savage, Shoemaker, Spielberg, Ubelhart, VanLeeuwen

---

May 20, 1988

Marketing Strategies for a Group Lunch Presentation

KISS—<u>K</u>eep <u>I</u>t <u>S</u>imple <u>S</u>tupid!
KISS—<u>K</u>eep <u>I</u>t <u>S</u>hort <u>S</u>tupid!
KISS—<u>K</u>eep <u>I</u>t <u>S</u>tock (Oriented) <u>S</u>tupid!

Take Control of the Luncheon Situation

☠ Death to the Hecklers—(don't take shit from nasty hecklers)
🔔 Ring the Middle of the Bell (shaped curve)—(focus on trying to get most of the people paying attention)
☺ Levity, Brevity, Novelty—(try to have attention getting opening line—humor)

(continued)

Exhibit 9.1 *(continued)*

How to Prove You're Smart:

Don't Tell Them All You Know—(intentionally leave out something important which requires data &/or thought process—leave it as an obvious question for them to ask—then you can show off as being smart at extemporaneous answers)

Eye Contact Is Key to Attention

Target two smart guys or friends

Ask the audience a question or two

Audio, Video, Props or Charts—(naturally refocuses people's attention—keep them from refocusing—gimmicks are good)

Ringing the Cash Register

You have to ask for the ticket—(gotta tell them to buy or sell something) Something must be compelling—(time related, . . .)

You can't sell unmarked merchandise—(gotta give them prices—relative multiples/EB something to make it look compelling on prices basis)

Make the Salesman give you a Mental Map of the Guest List

Research the Researchable, Let the Economists Handle the Rest

June 30, 1988	Fred Fraenkel

What the Sales Force Needs: Potential Points of Impact

1. AM Meeting	The more clear and compelling your comment the better chance it will be used.
	A summary or easily excerpted text will allow more calls to be made.
2. Phone Calls	Rather than waiting to see what paths are crossed a first call to a salesperson to see who he can call can allow you to split up accounts to be covered.
3. Meeting Clients	If you hit it off particularly well with a client a request by you to see that client on a trip or in New York for a one on one is in order.

| Trading Info | Whenever you receive transaction oriented information make sure it is relayed to your salesman as quickly as possible. We should all focus on creating this type of information by probing regarding prices that a client would buy at or sell at whenever such questions can be smoothly inserted into discussions. (be price conscious on stock) |
| Selling Deals | When a deal is being sold in your area of expertise it is perfectly appropriate to mention it to your counterparts when you are making regular phone calls and when the client sounds interested this should be immediately fed back to the salesman. |

Proactive Interaction

Acting in a timely fashion	immediate access to SSI/SSA calling in from the road/meetings anticipatory comments immediate response to call requests
Supporting clients	responding to requests for custom information providing clients with graphics and tables direct calls pre-AM mtg to counterparts re news
Create differentiation	unique style or subject matter unique supported industry stance specific differentiated strength, i.e., models
Go out on a limb	ease of understanding position is key one handed analysts are used most change should be identified
Repetition is important	key stands or points over and over again writing, verbal, writing, verbal group context, individual contact

Negatively Perceived Interaction

Presentations that are too long
3,3 mentality
Many small estimate changes on a stock
Major changes in ratings or estimates when you're not there
Trips that are canceled when itineraries are in place
Recommendations that aren't followed up
Key investment banking clients that aren't covered

Recognition of In-House Experts. Star analysts taught others the skills that they themselves were best at.[28] "The training sessions served two purposes," Rivkin explained. "One was bringing people up to speed so they understood how to do their jobs effectively. The second part was recognition of our experts. We asked some of our rate busters[29] and top analysts to offer training sessions on subjects like making a marketing call, balance-sheet analysis, creating something special in your research, dealing with investment banking, and so forth."[30]

According to Teena Lerner, a Lehman biotechnology analyst, "We were very systematic at a time when Wall Street was not systematic. Fred gave lots of nuts-and-bolts lessons on how to conduct one-on-one meetings, how to conduct group meetings, how to deal effectively with different kinds of clients within a group-meeting context, how not to say stupid things to the press."[31]

Helane Becker, a participant in the Prudential program who later helped Fred Fraenkel and Jack Rivkin implement it at Lehman Brothers, described the lessons of experience that she passed on to fellow analysts. Her account illustrates well the pull-no-punches flavor of the program and its emphasis on the interplay between analytic ability and interpersonal adroitness.

> One of the things I enjoy doing for the new analyst is saying, "My first three rules of being an analyst are: Management lies. Management lies all the time. Management lies. Never believe what management tells you. Take the information, but figure out a way to double-check it. Play the devil's advocate. . . . Ask different people in the company. Cultivate your contacts. . . . When you truly listen, sometimes you pick up something that you wouldn't necessarily pick up if you were just waiting for them to finish so you could ask your question or hear yourself talk." It's very hard to train analysts to do that, because analysts have to talk. That's their job, to stay on the phone. They're supposed to cultivate this company, cultivate these clients, cultivate the sales force, cultivate the trading desk, cultivate the press, have everybody know who you are so they call you all the time. And all the while keeping your mouth shut and listening to what everybody's telling you. If you can do that, you'll be really successful, because you have to be able to hear the new piece of information.

Collegiality and Camaraderie. The conviviality of the course also generated a camaraderie and collegiality that promoted teamwork and had a positive effect on retention. "People came to understand the importance of marketing, learned techniques to become successful, and at the end of the course had a great party," said Josie Esquivel. "It was like being initiated into a fraternity or a sorority. That strengthened people's bonds. Fred [Fraenkel] would act like an idiot and people would just love it. The entire class would go out some evenings, come in the next morning absolutely hungover, and the people that had been through the class would see the new participants come in all hungover and remember their times together. It strengthened the feeling that this was a fun place to be."[32] The final class, listed in the syllabus as "Maximizing Social Interaction Techniques," was described as "Field trip to an ethnic restaurant of the group's choice. Good bar is a must!"

An unforeseen outcome of the training program was that analysts initiated collaborative projects with little or no prodding from management after the course had come to a close. Repeatedly, analysts who had gone through the training program together spontaneously undertook joint research projects. Thus the trust and familiarity that developed during training outlasted the class, generating spontaneous idea sharing.

Transferability. Among the participants in the Lehman program were analysts Steve Balog and Steve Hash. Balog later used the same program to teach analysts at Furman Selz, where it was rechristened the Furman Selz Hi-Impact Analyst Training Program. When Steve Hash became head of U.S. equity research at Lehman in 1999, he reintroduced Accelerated Marketing Training and even recycled the same syllabus, binder, and handouts he had used as a participant. In 2005 Leerink Swann asked Steve Balog, then working as a hedge-fund manager, to teach its analysts using the same program.

When Steve Hash joined Lehman Brothers in 1999 as research director, the department had been in decline since Rivkin's firing seven years earlier. Hash "shocked the system," as he put it, with an initial hiring spree and then promptly reintroduced Fraenkel and Rivkin's accelerated program. Hash described how the program was conducted.

> A forty-year-old analyst who's been ranked for eight years might be sitting next to a twenty-nine-year-old who launched just a year ago. They help each other; they learn from each other. I learned from Fred [Fraenkel] to use a particular exercise in the very first module: Every participant presents their best idea in front of a television recorder for five minutes and then we all review the tapes. What this exercise does is break down all the walls. Everyone laughs at one an-

other. It's culture building. I do a mock presentation too and they can laugh at me. But beyond that exercise, it's a very focused class. Each session focuses on specific topics such as: here's how you're going to deal with the sales force, here's how you're going to do your structured marketing, here's how you're going to do your calling, here's what the marketing handouts are going to look like, here's what the buy side wants.[33]

Hash's associate Kim Santora described the program's impact: "Steve covers ways to convey an effective message. It seems rather simple, but such training has generated some amazing results with some of our up-and-comers. Analysts who started here as juniors, were promoted to their own sector, and participated in Accelerated Marketing Training have gotten *II*-ranked within two years."[34]

General Training and Development of Firm-Specific Human Capital. It would be tempting to call this training program unique had it not proven otherwise by spreading almost virally from one firm to another. Certainly its longevity and the enthusiasm and gratitude of its participants over the course of thirty years were unusual. Participants singled out different aspects of its content as noteworthy, but certain of its characteristics are particularly so in a discussion of training programs. It was utterly practical, focused on detailed, down-to-earth, how-to advice. There was no overt cheerleading for the firm, no indoctrination or exhortation; the meta-message of the program was that it is all about the participants and whatever will help them do their jobs better. The tone of the written materials and the presentations was informal, collegial, irreverent, and straight-talking. The topics covered were of immediate practical value and were presented by fellow analysts; there were no external speakers. Participation was treated as a privilege, and teamwork and camaraderie were encouraged.

At least in its early Lehman Brothers incarnation, one session was devoted to utilizing departmental assets. More broadly, though, the content of the course was not firm-specific; its portability attests to that. What appears to be firm-specific, or specific to the few firms that adopted it, was the developmental culture it promoted and embodied. Though its content would probably be useful to any analyst at any firm, a course of this kind is apt to be unpackageable because so much of its value resides in the workings of the department. Marketing tips may be portable, but much of the worth of such training resided in the relationships and collaboration it sparked. Because such benefits were embedded in the firm, they tended to embed the analysts who were exposed to them.

Institutionalized Mentoring

Mentoring appears to be particularly effective when it is woven into normal day-to-day operations and thus acquires the institution's imprimatur. This primarily happens when mentoring is a routine and conspicuous component of the job responsibilities of influential participants in the department's operation. At several Wall Street firms, mentoring by the research director,[34] by an investment committee, and by the sales force acquired this kind of institutionalized status.

Goldman Sachs

Under Steve Einhorn in the 1990s, the culture of Goldman Sachs emphasized intellectual rigor and cross-fertilization. "What I tried to do was to establish an environment where the analysts felt intellectually secure and excited about what they were doing," explained Einhorn. "And by that I mean they had the freedom and the resources—people-wise, database-wise—to pursue research as deeply and as broadly as they needed to do. There would be no constraints on them in terms of how they approached the research effort. There was no 'do it this way or no way.'" Einhorn took a hands-on role in mentoring analysts.

> I made it a practice to read virtually every major report that an analyst would put out. I would comment on those reports face-to-face, in a written memo, or via voicemail. So they understood that I was reading the work, I understood why they had the positions they did, and if I disagreed or wanted to be devil's advocate, I could provide that perspective as well. Analysts, I think, appreciate it when folks they're working with show a sustained interest in what they're doing and how they're approaching their research universe. I cared about the quality; I cared about what they were saying. I think that provided a particular bond between me and the various analysts within the department.

Goldman also maintained a careful balance between developing and hiring stars. Steve Einhorn considered it crucial to the culture, to morale, and to retention for the department to nurture and develop its own stars.

A lot of firms in that period hired only stars. We didn't do that. We had a good mix of prominent people who we brought in from the outside, and people who started with us as junior analysts and who we had confidence could grow into substantive, respected analysts. Amy Low Chasen, she's number-one-rated in household products; Lori Applebaum is number-one-rated in banks: two of the most prominent analysts on Wall Street started with us at very junior levels. We gave them the opportunity to take on more responsibility rather than hire over them. So the department never got overloaded with strangers to Goldman Sachs. These people knew each other. I think that show of commitment to people, that show of loyalty, benefits the department. Even the All-Stars see that and understand they're working in a decent, embracing environment.

Sanford C. Bernstein

Chapter 5 described Sanford C. Bernstein's unique approach to hiring and training new analysts: hiring from industry and letting new analysts immerse themselves in study and preparation for a year under rigorous guidance from senior analysts and the research director before beginning to write one of the firm's trademark "blackbooks."

Mentoring was only slightly less intensive after a new analyst had begun producing. It was a fundamental principle of Bernstein's culture that when a beginning analyst identified a senior analyst he or she would like to work with, the senior analyst could not say no. In fact, Bernstein expected its veteran analysts to devote fully 20 percent of their time to mentoring, hiring, and other institution-building activities.

Bernstein had originally hired experienced analysts from outside the firm, but dissatisfaction with their performance and attitudes prompted a decision to train its own analysts. "I consider staff-development skills one of our key assets," said Lewis Sanders, former CEO of both Sanford C. Bernstein and Alliance Capital Management. "There are not too many firms that actually have any track record at all of building research talent."[35] As research director Lisa Shalett put it, "We grow people who are successful at our model, which is very narrowly defined and perhaps even idiosyncratically so." The research director actively mentored inexperienced analysts, meeting with each regularly to help strengthen their arguments, fill in gaps in their training, and hone their strategies. "I do not think I manage them in the sense of saying, 'Here is an objective, or here are the ten approaches that you have to get to that goal, and there's the best way to go,' said Shalett. "I say, 'Choose the way that is right for you.'"[36]

Inexperienced analysts also had mentors within the sales force. At investment banks, the sales force sells other products besides research; because Bernstein was a pure research firm, its sales force sold only research. Thus its salespeople became thoroughly familiar with analysts' products and ideas and could participate fully in training analysts in best practices. As Lisa Shalett put it, "In many ways Bernstein analysts are spoiled, in the sense that they have been supported by this dedicated 100-percent-commission sales force who's completely undistracted by anything else other than selling research." This configuration was unique to Bernstein. "Our analysts sit in a room for nearly twelve months and develop their thesis. Our mentor-mentee program tries to make that process feel less like a black hole," said Brian Raab, a domestic large-market salesperson. "I help new analysts appreciate what the client voting system is all about, what the infrastructure of a mutual fund is all about, how particular analysts' messages resonate with the portfolio managers and analysts."[37]

Bernstein built a culture that emphasized and rewarded continuous learning. Even veteran analysts continued to receive feedback on their written products from the research director. According to international salesperson Elise Lelon, "Ralph Waldo Emerson said, 'Knowledge is the antidote to fear.' There are many people at Bernstein who never want to *not* know the answer, and that drives them to be far better than your average institutional salesperson or research analyst. It also makes all of us a little on the obsessive side, but it's a corporate character trait that serves our clients really well."[38] (See exhibit 9.2.)

Exhibit 9.2

Excerpts from Sanford C. Bernstein's *Guide for New Analysts*

Gary Black's Eight Simple Rules to Success as an Analyst

1. Be first
2. Be proactive
3. Be value-added
4. Be visible
5. Be decisive
6. Be opportunistic
7. Be clear
8. Be humble

Objective: Dominate your category

Exhibit 9.2 *(continued)*

The Research

A. Determine the key industry controversies
    1. What are the primary drivers of company earnings?
    2. What are the primary drivers of company earnings volatility?
    3. What are the emerging/declining drivers of company earnings?
    4. What are the investors not yet focusing on that they should be?
    5. Ask the sales force and clients what the controversies are.

B. Determine and forecast key industry variables
    1. Develop long history (lag, coincident and leading indicators)
    2. Sources for forecasting (publications, companies, industry groups, government agencies, FactSet)
    3. Primary research is high value-added, when appropriate (polls, focus groups)
    4. Forecast more than one scenario and give probabilities
    5. Backtest if appropriate
    6. Statistical work that can demonstrate leading or coincident indicators is analyst nirvana

C. Company research
    1. Forecasting
        a. Company help (publicly available documents, investor relations, management, other competing companies)
        b. Visiting the company
            i. The IR department's job is to convince you to recommend the stock
            ii. Respect management's opinion, but recognize that their point of view is biased and that you may have more information and a broader viewpoint than they do
        c. Developing contacts . . .
        d. For your earnings model, break out long history, through a couple of cycles
        e. Robustness of the model (ease of updating, getting information again, clients using, too many links to other models and inordinate complexity are cited by many analysts as their biggest mistake)
        f. Quarterly earnings and importance of near-term estimates

g. Forecasting is more than just extrapolating a trend (which is generally what consensus is); the most valuable forecasts are those that correctly incorporate inflection points, meaningful changes in growth rates

h. Go through a few iterations
  i. Revisit the thesis during the initial launch period, putting it through several iterations
  ii. Know when to stop, for the time being (time, experiencing the industry, possible recasting later) . . .

3. Top-down and bottom-up forecast must meet (i.e., someone must lose share)

4. Balance sheets and cash flow statements
  a. Are typically (but by no means always) less meaningful for investors than income statements
  b. However, can be crucial in highlighting inflection points (bloated inventories/declining cash flows, for example), accounting issues or in illuminating earnings quality
  c. Watch the bond market—when it is "saying" something different about a company than the equity markets are, this is worth investigating
  d. Cash flows generally the most important for consolidating industries

D. Factors Affecting Stock Price Performance
  1. Fair value for a stock . . .
  2. What makes the stock trade to (and above and below) its fair value . . .
  3. Consensus
    a. Keep up on where consensus is, as this will tell you a good deal about the expectations resident in the stock
    b. Don't be afraid of being different from consensus: it is the stuff of great recommendations
  4. Investment recommendations should be based on 15% relative performance over 6–12 months (see section on Stock Picking), adjusted for the risk profile of the company . . .

F. Special Tips
  1. Flexibility to change (you are allowed to change your mind and you should)
  2. Keep up on stock news
  3. "Practice" following the stocks during your pre-launch period

Exhibit 9.2 *(continued)*

The Product Line

A. Research what will work
  1. Launch on more stocks, rather than fewer, as the extra month it will take you before you launch will translate into several after you launch—and greater critical mass at the beginning will get you more, and better, client meetings
  2. Ask the clients what they want (sales force and external)
  3. What does the competition do (strengths and weaknesses)

B. Determine what product you want to supply
  1. The single greatest leading indicator of success in the business is *number of proactive* research publications
  2. In all cases, aim the product at the PM, with the ability to talk to the analyst contact as well (it is easier for Bergdorf to put products on sale than it is for K-Mart to price products up)
  3. Key industry variables and trends
  4. *Major* companies
    a. Regular (e.g., forecasts, analysis of a division)
    b. Irregular (e.g., analysis of a special event)
  5. Stock valuation . . .
  6. Proprietary studies . . .
  7. Keep the quality of the product uniformly high
    a. Make the Bernstein call the first thing the client pulls up to read
    b. Do not dilute the value of the brand through "filler" or too much "maintenance" research; happily cede this low-margin ground to our competition

C. Remember what you do <u>not</u> want your product to be
  1. A means for disseminating the IR message or company guidance
  2. A mirror of consensus thinking
  3. Comments on what is in the newspaper (stay ahead of the reporters)
  4. Comments on earnings ("The company came in a few pennies ahead of my estimate . . .")
  5. Even if clients say they like what you're doing, constantly assess its value—how much will they pay for it? (e.g., they like *People Magazine*, too, but won't pay a lot for it) . . .

Stock Picking

A. One of a number of routes to success
   1. Better to be right than wrong
   2. But stock picking without strong research is not enough
B. Rules of thumb (to be taken as guidelines, not as hard and fast rules—know your stocks)
   1. Above consensus is good
   2. An increasing consensus is good
   3. A higher than perceived quality (often translated into a lower volatility) of earnings is good
   4. An increasing ROE or profit margin is good
   5. Easy annual (in some cases, quarterly) sales or earnings comparisons are good, even if they are forecasted by consensus
   6. Accelerating earnings are good
   7. Accelerating earnings growth is good
   8. Cheap is good (but not always: it depends on the sector)
   9. The first time you cut estimates on a growth stock, downgrade it
   10. It takes about four months for a stock to get over an estimate miss, even if all else goes well from there
   11. Always go through the analysis of what the stock is discounting/ telling you; the stuff you see may already be priced into the stock
   12. Keep an eye on the macro environment, but be judicious in making stock calls primarily on this basis
   13. Keep in mind that rules of thumb can change, so be open to it
   14. In setting recommendations, the ultimate question to ask yourself is "What would I do with my own money?"
C. The recommendation committee
   1. A review meeting of DoR, analyst peers and salespeople
   2. Must be held before initiating coverage of new stocks or changing ratings
   3. The purpose is to discuss and challenge the research, much as the client base will
D. What to do when you are wrong
   1. Remember that it happens to everyone
   2. Admit it (everyone knows it anyway, so disarm them with your honesty)
   3. Don't fight the tape (getting shriller and shriller as you get wronger and wronger)

Exhibit 9.2 *(continued)*

      4. On the other hand, don't hide—revisit your research and continue to state your case

      5. The best new idea is often an old idea that hasn't worked

      6. Be sensitive to the clients that are wrong along with you; part of their commission dollars is for the right to fuss at you

      7. No-one is smarter than the market

F. Underperforms

      1. A differentiator for SCB due to absence of an investment banking arm and a potential means to analyst super-stardom

      2. Be prepared for anger from the company and controversy in the investment community

G. Other

      1. If you have all market-performs, the message to clients is that there are no ideas you have for making them money, and that all your research is already incorporated by the market into the prices of the stocks

      2. Don't whipsaw clients with your recommendations (i.e., pound the table one day and downgrade the next)

      3. Provide clients with a roadmap as to what you would look for in changing a recommendation on a stock

Marketing

A. Goals

      1. Clients and companies view you as the best service in understanding, explaining and predicting key variables

      2. A key way your product can be highly successful is through delivering it in a value-added way to clients—know your audience, with the message tailored appropriately for the sales force trading desk, PMs and analysts

      3. Set the agenda

      4. Own the stocks/be the ax

      5. Create controversy; wade into controversy; enjoy it (the best calls are most often controversial, while the best-received calls often mean that the information you are relaying is already discounted by the stocks)

      6. Sell the benefits, not the features (clients are not interested in how complicated your model is or how hard you worked to get the

analysis done, nor are they impressed with how many spreadsheets feed into the output page)

7. Make competitors respond to your work, rather than vice versa
   Tip: Servicing clients is as important to the job as the research

B. Marketing to the sales force and trading desk

1. They are your client
2. The 7:45 meeting . . .
   a. For trading, boil down the conclusions to 90 seconds or less;
      for sales, give more color, but don't be repetitive
   b. Don't make the sales force and traders guess what you want
      them to do
   c. Trading format: Conclusions/quick restatement of thesis/new
      information/impact on thesis/action to be taken
   d. Own the room while you are at the mike
   e. If the traders/sales force quits writing what you are saying or
      listening to you, put down the mike and walk away
   f. Don't try to out-talk the other analysts (two wrongs—of talk-
      ing too much—don't make a right, and the more laser-sharp
      presentation garners outsized attention) . . .
5. Regularity of calls
   a. Be visible to the sales force with a good flow of research (a
      couple of calls a week)
   b. But don't "make up" research in order to be talking
   c. You don't get full credit for good ideas if you only highlight
      them once
6. You don't expect the sales force to do your research for you, so
   don't expect them to market for you—only you get the votes
7. Treat the sales force with respect, as their jobs are hard too

C. Marketing to the client

1. The tier list
   a. Super tier 1—you should call at least two times a month
   b. Tier 1—a minimum of one call a month
   c. Tier 1 PM—calls made initially "on request"
   d. Tier 2—call every other month
   e. Tier 3—when requested
   f. Tier 4—no outgoing calls
   g. But remember, be courteous and helpful to all clients, as they
      talk to each other and can change accounts
2. The phone call/voicemail

Exhibit 9.2 *(continued)*

    a. Make a number of client phone calls after publishing a significant piece of research

    b. Schedule phone calls into your day (one morning a week free for phoning clients, for example)

    c. Use blast voicemail and e-mail discriminately (clients almost uniformly complain about them)

    d. Keep message simple, actionable and to the point

    e. A two-way conversation—one size does not fit all here

    f. <u>Listen</u> (this is a rare thing among sell-side analysts)

    g. Keep a log of when you have last talked to a client/what stocks they like/what information and thoughts they want from you

    h. Don't barge in/be respectful of the client's time

    i. It's always showtime, so be upbeat, have fun—but don't just call your friends

    j. Do not leave the office at the end of the day without returning all client phone calls

    k. When returning a phone call and getting voicemail instead, do not place the burden on the client's shoulder of returning your call; leave a message and call back later

3. Marketing trips

    a. Can't have a relationship without meeting the client face-to-face

    b. Preparation

        i. Find out from the salesperson the client's investing style/what they own/their biases

        ii. Don't make the research fit every client—adjust presentations for growth and value clients, for example

    c. The meeting

        i. Don't talk <u>at</u> the client

        ii. Be respectful of covering the ground the client wants to during the meeting; this is their hour, not yours

        iii. The goal is to give clients new information and analyses/help them think about issues that they have not yet explored ("cut a swath across Texas")

        iv. The best marketers fall into their clients' rhythm

        v. If you and a client disagree, strive to make the interaction friendly rather than confrontational

  vi. Present yourself as the client's partner in thinking about the industry and the stocks

  vii. Can be useful to try to leave the meeting with a "task" from the client, so that there is a tangible reason for follow-up . . .

 d. If the salesperson doesn't ask you to go, ask him or her

 e. If the salesperson won't go with you, go anyway

 f. Follow up on the meeting quickly by phone to cement the relationship/be sure to end the meeting by asking how you can service the account or follow up on the meeting—and then do it

 g. Follow up every meeting (particularly in the beginning) by asking the salesperson how it went and how you can improve . . .

6. Getting clients and managements together

 a. When asked, this is <u>the</u> thing most requested by clients

 b. Can be done in small groups (of important clients), in larger groups or via conference calls (particularly terrific, because you don't have to do a lot of work)

 c. Done in combination with new research can be effective

 d. Additionally serves to elevate the analyst's profile

 e. Travel time and "war stories" are great relationship cementers . . .

10. Collaborative work

 a. Hard to coordinate (analysts are natural entrepreneurs)

 b. But gets twice the client interest, particularly among PMs

 c. Differentiates us from competition, as this is enormously rare . . .

12. Additional Tips

 a. Stay up all night the two times a year it will make the big difference (i.e., the night after a merger announcement, when clients are really looking for help—they will appreciate it)

 b. Special service and favors win very big points (or, "why I like calling from airports, hospital beds, exotic vacations or with a crying child in the background")

 c. Make the client your friend—there are a number of times when you are wrong, and you want clients pulling <u>for</u> you, not smirking <u>at</u> you

Exhibit 9.2 (continued)

        d. Be nice to all your clients; they talk to each other, and a tier 4 client could end up at Fidelity someday

        e. If you don't have anything to say, don't say anything at all—<u>much</u> better to not answer sales force's and clients' questions on breaking news/mergers until you have the needed information and have done your analysis than to go out wrong—better a day late and right than fast and wrong

        f. As a rule of thumb, two-thirds of what you say and write should be forward-looking

D. Company contacts

    1. Have the companies you cover review your research before publication

        a. To catch your mistakes

        b. As a courtesy so that you won't "blindside" them

        c. But stand firm in your opinions

    2. Put the companies on your mailing list, as clients often ask them who the best analysts are

    3. This does not mean, however, to pull punches on research

E. Press

    1. Has benefits for both your franchise and the buy side

    2. Use the press intelligently

    3. Put the quality publications on your distribution list

    4. Goal is to have your name (spelled correctly) and/or picture (posed powerfully) in a quality publication with generally innocuous remarks attributed to you ("Management has clearly thought hard about its strategy.")

    5. Do not give the press any research that has not yet been published/presented to clients—regardless of any promises made to embargo it

    6. Do not comment on anything in the press before you have communicated to the sales force (i.e., don't comment after-hours on breaking news)

    7. Quotes can be taken out of context, so watch carefully what you say; each sentence should be able to stand on its own

    8. Assume everything you are saying is for attribution . . .

    9. Do not comment on rumors, particularly merger rumors

   10. Do not malign management

11. Never talk about underwritings in which SCB may be involved
12. Avoid being quoted in articles that are about your competitors' work or in which they otherwise set the agenda
13. Avoid being quoted in articles on the topic of how wrong or stupid sell-side analysts are, or what their compensation is
14. If you don't have anything to say, don't say anything at all . . .

Morgan Stanley

Morgan Stanley's approach to enhancing analysts' performance mixed routine teamwork, idea sharing, and feedback with formal conferences and teleconferences. Michael Blumstein, director of U.S. equity research, described a culture in which the sharing of ideas and best practices could be said to represent a kind of mutual mentoring. "We really tried to have people realize that you could get a competitive edge by not working as a one-man band but by talking and working with the folks next to you and putting your heads together," Blumstein said. "And remember, the world is not in the neat little boxes that analysts think they're in. If you're the life-insurance guy but you talk to the bank guy, collectively the two of you should be able to come up with some insight that you wouldn't get working alone."

Blumstein had experienced the value of collaboration when he worked as an insurance analyst:

I would look at the reports that all our best analysts were doing because you would get ideas, for example, for valuation techniques. Or sometimes there would be analytical ideas in terms of how to model something out. And you would look at what the best analysts were doing, in terms of how they were handling their client relationships. How often are you talking to clients? What kind of reports do they seem to want and appreciate? Are you going to see them in person, or are you talking to them on the phone? Are you doing small conferences or big conferences? One of my insurance colleagues, Alan Zimmermann, came up with an idea we called CEOs Unplugged: to put a CEO in front of a group of clients and not let the CEO make a presentation but just fire away at the CEO and ask all the burning, pressing questions. We did this in the insurance group, and we then made sure that everybody else in the department knew about it, and CEOs Unplugged became a Morgan Stanley hallmark. It was a Morgan Stanley event that the airline analyst could do and the life-insurance analyst could do. So there are ideas—everything from how can I look at evaluation of stocks to how do I present the most value-added content to my clients—that you absolutely can share from industry to industry regardless of how unrelated they might be.

Morgan Stanley also put in place more formalized and systematic institutional practices to provide feedback and support. As Blumstein pointed out:

> We had a stock-selection committee that focused on new analysts and younger analysts; it didn't spend a lot of time with very senior established analysts but spent time with junior up-and-coming people to really help them through their ideas. . . . We had a marketing person who helped people market their material. We always had very good people running the morning meeting, so when you had to talk in front of the morning meeting, you could run it by the guy who was going to be running the meeting and get some feedback as to how it was going to play. Morgan Stanley has always had a monthly department meeting, and part of what would be done would be sharing of best practices. And a research manager could send out an e-mail to the department saying, "Here's what one group did. This has been a success. Think about it."

Mayree Clark offered a further portrayal of development at Morgan Stanley, touching on training, traditional mentoring, and institutional mentoring:

> We encouraged the senior analysts to help the junior analysts. Historically, we were taking MBAs right out of school and randomly assigning them to an industry. We shifted to a system where people would apprentice as research assistants and then get their own industry. We also had a stock committee for younger people. We didn't allow them to make any recommendations without this group helping them formulate those recommendations.
>
> The sales force were very good teachers, and we definitely had a culture in our sales force to help the younger analysts get better. Our morning-meeting coordinators, who screened all the material for the morning meeting, did a lot of coaching of analysts. They were very senior sales people who not only understood the investment dynamics and what the market was looking for on any given day

but understood how an analyst should position it. They were very important teachers.

Byron [Wien] was a portfolio manager's portfolio manager, and as a strategist he was very interested in the analysts. He would . . . attend the meeting every morning. So in addition to this very professionally run event, with the salesman up at the front running the meeting as though it was the *Today Show*, you'd have Byron out in the audience asking tough questions. And Byron was very inspirational. He felt it was important that people be committed to the values of Morgan Stanley, that they value integrity, that they love their jobs and love stock picking, and he was very vocal about it and very unambivalent about it. . . . He and Barton Biggs were both deeply experienced, mature, wise men who were committed to having a great research department. The associate research directors were also seasoned analysts who equally served in a teaching role for the younger analysts and spent a lot of time helping them get ready for the stock committee and with their rollouts and so forth.

Morgan Stanley also hosted an annual off-site "Equity Research Conference of the Americas" for its senior equity analysts. Clark inaugurated the conference series, which Blumstein described as focused on best practices: "We covered all sorts of aspects of being an analyst: everything from effective analysis to effective stock picking to effective client relationships. And even effective use of your time and building a strategy for being able to be an analyst over the long haul." Though comprehensive, the content of the conference was also flexible. As Blumstein comments, "Morgan Stanley tended to do what felt right at the moment, as opposed to locking into some formula. It was: what topic do we need to cover when?"

Organized around panel discussions and breakout sessions led by facilitators, the format of the conference was expository; the atmosphere was corporate but casual. Considerable attention was paid to celebrating and reinforcing the firm's culture, values, history, and reputation. In 1999, one of the topics at the conference was "The Life Cycle of an Analyst." Panelists representing different points on the career continuum discussed matters like establishing bonds with the sales force, team building, effective use of research associates, hiring decisions, stress, and strategies for sustaining the energy, drive, and competitive fervor to "run a marathon and not just a sprint." At other sessions, star analysts discussed relationships with traders, the retail sales force, and portfolio managers (with ample attention to practical matters like returning phone calls, the resonance of a handwritten thank-you note, and the value of cultivating relationships with "loudmouth" clients who will spread the word about analysts), as well as the question of whether one-hundred-page reports build credibility.

In sum, developmental cultures in Wall Street research departments clearly did not limit themselves to one particular developmental practice. They adopted idiosyncratic configurations of practices designed to embody an embedded, firm-congruent, institutional commitment to learning and collaboration.

Further Outcomes of In-House Development

Developmental Relationships, High Performance, and Retention

The research on mentoring and development can help us generalize from our findings and the foregoing portraits of developmental departments. When we undertake to explain how firms with developmental cultures succeed at producing and retaining stars, research shows that organizations can either facilitate or discourage developmental interactions and that many developmental cultures constrain portability by promoting firm-specific capital, two of whose forms are strong localized developmental networks[39] and strong working relationships.[40] Our findings lend further support to the evidence for the value of numerous mentors[41] and establish a relationship between development and retention.

Various researchers have found that developmental networks foster commitment to the organization, a hypothesis consistent with our findings that the presence of multiple strong developmental relationships within a firm discourages turnover. More precisely, specific practices promote the systematic construction of a developmental network that tends to elicit loyalty in those who benefit from it. Mentoring by the research director alone, if plotted graphically as a network, would look like spokes on a wheel. But the camaraderie and collegiality that grew out of training programs like Lehman Brothers' resulted in relationships that could be represented as an overlay of interconnecting triangles and polygons. Each link between individuals acted as a buttress, thickening and strengthening the firm's overall network. The support, interaction, and access to resources afforded by a dense network thus added value for all those in the network, making it, in the words of Larry Fraser of Management & Capital Partners, "harder for homegrown talent to leave." One may lose more than one bargains for, in other words, in departing a firm with a strong and densely populated developmental network.

Steve Hash explained the link he perceived between Lehman's development program and lower turnover:

> One of the most important aspects of success for the whole research
> department is low turnover, because hiring stars who leave two
> or three years later is not a very good long-term strategy. . . . It's
> extremely expensive, and it's like running in sand. You're not really
> getting anywhere. . . . So if you select good people and you spend the
> time to show them the way to be successful, give them the resources,
> let them know that you care about their career, that you're rooting
> for them, that you're helping them, and that you're committing your
> own time to developing them, you create two things: one, a level of
> intensity. Because these are, by definition, people that want to suc-
> ceed. They wouldn't have gone to business school and put in all the
> hours if they didn't. . . . Then if they succeed and you do all the right
> things in terms of compensating them fairly and promoting them
> along the right progression, . . . you create a person and an entire
> army—a hundred of these people that are extraordinarily loyal to the
> firm so they don't quit.

According to Hash, the key to sustaining the developmental culture was putting in time and effort to institutionalize it. In fact, lack of institutionalization and integration of a department into the overall firm can be a significant threat to a developmental culture. For example, after Rivkin's firing, the parent firm became less committed to sustaining a developmental culture at Lehman Brothers' research department. Years of turnover and underperformance followed.

Integration in Developmental Cultures

Departments that developed their own stars were also better at incorporating stars from outside the firm.[42] Such departments tended to understand very well what made their best analysts great, and were therefore adept at identifying good fits for their firm. And the same kind of franchise-building assistance that helped younger analysts grow into the job could also help an established star through the integration necessitated by a move. Some newly hired stars were even asked to participate in formal training programs to facilitate their acquisition of firm-specific human capital and to jump-start their integration. Finally, the flexibility that most developmental firms embraced ensured that a newly hired star would still be able to apply his or her most well-honed skills to the fullest. At Goldman Sachs and DLJ, for example, stars were not only developed more readily but also hired and integrated with more success. All of these observations are consistent with our finding, discussed in earlier chapters, that portability of talent is a characteristic not just of an individual star but also of the firms that the star departs and joins.

Economic Rewards and Developmental Cultures

Firms with developmental cultures reaped economic rewards: all else being equal, the average research budget of a developmental firm was smaller than that of a comparable nondevelopmental firm. As many research directors were aware, and as we will explore further in chapter 12 on compensation, internally developed talent can often be retained at lower costs.

Some departments with thriving developmental cultures initially decided to concentrate on fostering talent in-house for economic reasons. Lewis Sanders of Sanford C. Bernstein explained the origins of that firm's develop-your-own strategy. When the firm initiated its mentorship approach to developing analysts in 1973, "we were not a particularly good firm. We were financially challenged, and our image on Wall Street was mixed, probably negative," Sanders recalled. "So we weren't in a position to attract an interesting talent pool. Instead we had to speculate on the untapped potential of people who couldn't easily get in the business." As the firm's reputation improved, however, its strategy did not change. "Later we did [development]," Sanders said, "because it was clearly superior."[43]

The Case of Schroder Wertheim

Perhaps the most dramatic example of the benefits of a developmental culture is the case of Schroder Wertheim. As a second-tier, underfunded bank, Wertheim did not have the option of poaching stars—and was in turn vulnerable to having its own stars poached. "We didn't have the kind of platform that allowed us to staff our effort with stars that were created somewhere else," said Barry Tarasoff, research director from 1989 to 2000. "We were very dependent on perpetuating our ability to create our own stars. . . . Retention required that we invest only in those who shared our distinctive values, so our recruiting focused on ensuring this buy-in."

Bonita Austin, whom Tarasoff hired from industry and trained as an analyst, elaborated on the firm's reasoning: "It was pretty much straight economics. It's very expensive to hire an analyst who's already very well established. There's a lot less risk to hire somebody that had some industry experience and, hopefully, get the benefit of that. If you give them a little leeway, maybe you get a really super-high-producing analyst at a very low cost. It did work for them."

During Tarasoff's tenure as research director, Schroder Wertheim utilized a handful of developmental techniques. One such technique was critique: irrespective of seniority, all members of the department mentored one another by reviewing upcoming publications. Tarasoff explained the process:

> On Friday afternoon we would give out copies [of manuscripts] to
> the entire research department. Everybody was expected to read
> it over the weekend, and we would assemble on Monday morn-
> ing to critique the work. This accomplished three things. First, the
> Monday-morning meetings supplemented my work: it made the
> product better than it would have been if I were the only outside
> contributor. Second, the fact that we took several hours out of every-
> one's time to critique a report spoke volumes about our values. It was
> the single most important thing that reinforced with great regularity
> that we were focused on high-quality investment thought more than
> any of the other trappings of Wall Street research. Third, the discus-
> sions in those meetings provided me another window into each
> analyst's stage of development. It was a very useful management tool.

John Casesa, a star U.S. automotive analyst who spent ten years at Schroder Wertheim, described the review process from an analyst's point of view:

> When an analyst would write a draft of a report, we'd take it home
> over the weekend, and then we'd come in and be prepared to make
> comments and constructive criticism on Monday. I don't think I'd be
> able to tell [a pharmaceutical analyst] much about the drug pipe-
> line, but there might be a similar accounting issue, there might be a

similar competitive issue. And people in other industries had lots to say on accounting or labor or government policy, and of course valuation. Most analysts were very open to learning about other analysts' valuation techniques—you could steal the best ideas. That was a big part of it: how did somebody determine whether stocks were overvalued or undervalued?

Analysts also taught each other informally. "I had an MBA, so I knew how to do financial-statement analysis and build models," said Casesa. "But getting that to a practical level I learned from the other analysts there. We had a very collaborative environment. We sat close to one another and there were lots of forums to talk to people. A lot of it was going into other analysts' offices and asking if they've had a [particular] situation. . . . So I learned from the other people there."

Tarasoff also acted as a mentor for individual analysts. Bonita Austin described his formal one-on-one mentoring of novice analysts: "I would do a report on a company and turn it in to Barry. These were sixty-page reports. I would get those reports back, and there would just be red ink everywhere. Barry would question all of my assumptions. And then I would go in and argue with Barry about whatever the assumptions were, and he would tell me where I was missing something."

Tarasoff explained the broader purpose of his close attention to analysts' written work: "We were sufficiently compact that I could read most of the work before it was published. In the case of our developing staff, I read all the work and spent hours discussing it with the authors. That practice communicated pretty loudly our respect for high-quality investment thought."

Steve Haggerty, a research manager at Merrill Lynch, who was at Schroder Wertheim during the same era, gave an example of Tarasoff's mentoring style:

> When I first got there, I was learning the stuff and I had a question about the capital structure. Barry was grilling me. He was saying, 'Why do you care how a company acquires capital? Why do you care whether they do it through debt or if they do it through equity?' He was asking all these questions, trying to help me understand the capital structure. Barry used to say, 'What we want is to have the correct non-consensus view.' It was the most concise summary of what an analyst could do that I ever heard. Now other people use it, but

the first guy I heard say this was Barry. He had a thoughtfulness and a rigor—he was a math major at Duke—that permeated the place. There was definitely a culture there, absolutely a culture there.

John Casesa pointed out that the benefits of Tarasoff's mentoring were not limited to inexperienced analysts.[44]

> He was as effective at mentoring analysts that were older and more experienced as he was at mentoring younger analysts like me. He made it very collegial; he encouraged discussion, reminded us what we were in business for, which was to find moneymaking ideas for our clients, and was a zealot in defending the independence of the analyst. We celebrated anything that was out-of-the-ordinary and value-added. I knew a lot about the product pipeline, so I started to publish this color chart that showed the product pipeline by automaker, looking out four years at a time. It had data that clients could use to forecast market share. That was the kind of thing that we were encouraged to do. We celebrated creativity.

Tarasoff also located his office in the midst of the analysts; other research directors typically preferred a corner office on a top floor. He wanted to structurally reinforce his hands-on role in the department and to be available to analysts when they needed him.[45]

As a result of this intensive development culture, Schroder Wertheim enjoyed the lowest turnover rate (2.3 percent) in the industry during the years covered by our study. The firm's star-formation rate was 5.8 percent during that time, which is not outstanding compared to powerhouses like DLJ or Sanford C. Bernstein but nonetheless remarkable given the firm's limited resources. Clearly, Schroder Wertheim had found a way to turn developmental culture into a remarkable strategic advantage, one that allowed it to compete with firms far richer in resources.

☆ ☆ ☆

Whether introducing a promising young analyst to the fundamentals of research or integrating an established star, developmental cultures work at maximizing their human capital. Such firms' development networks create feedback cycles that thicken like the snowball of success that Steve Hash described earlier. The collaborations that ensue from cross-fertilization diffuse best practices throughout the firm, as the "CEOs Unplugged" program did at Morgan Stanley. Methodological flexibility promotes excellence in multiple arenas via both cross-fertilization and effective specialization.

Conventional wisdom holds that homogeneity promotes camaraderie; we would counter that heterogeneity can promote learning and interdependence. For example, two analysts, one expert at valuation models and the other adept at marketing, can forge a symbiotic relationship in which they promote each other's development. Dense developmental networks embed employees, both stars and non-stars, retaining skill and knowledge within the firm. In sum, developmental cultures do not merely promote star formation and retention. They contribute to the overall strength of the firm.

10 | Turnover

Who Leaves and Why

The effort a company makes to develop stars is, clearly, not a wise investment if the stars then depart to shine in some other firm's constellation.[1] What factors influence whether or not stars stay in their organization? Understanding the patterns and drivers of turnover among the best and brightest is crucial for knowledge-based firms, whose star employees constitute their primary strategic assets.

Turnover is expensive. Researchers have estimated the cost of losing a seasoned professional as 75–150 percent of that person's annual salary.[2] Turnover also imposes hardship on the departments that mobile employees leave. Positions may remain open for months or even years. Other analysts take up the slack, at the expense of their own work and possibly their rankings. When Lehman Brothers lost thirty of its seventy-eight analysts within a single year, including seventeen stars, the firm dropped four places in stock-underwriting rankings, lost IPO business, and even suffered from a lowered credit rating.[3]

By the same token, our findings suggest that long-established organizations can gain competitive advantage by retaining and leveraging their human assets more effectively than new competitors do. In knowledge-based industries, competitive advantage of this kind can represent a formidable barrier to entry: even large and powerful commercial banks like Deutsche

Bank and UBS Securities have had trouble breaking into the investment-banking and securities-brokerage business for exactly this reason.

Human-capital theory predicts that turnover will be higher than average at firms that reinforce their employees' general skills and lower than average at firms that promote firm-specific human capital. Human-capital theory also generates predictions about the effects of job tenure on turnover: as an employee's tenure at a firm lengthens, his or her firm-specific human capital inevitably advances, and the accumulation of such human capital discourages turnover. Long-tenured employees should therefore exhibit low turnover. If stars possess more firm-specific human capital than non-stars, furthermore, they should experience lower turnover. However, an alternative hypothesis can also be made: stars' greater visibility in the labor market may act as a countervailing force to increase turnover.[4]

Again, we studied the top twenty-four investment banks. Our focus on the top twenty-four firms thus biased our data in favor of ranked analysts: 36 percent of the analysts in our sample were ranked, though fewer than 3 percent of all analysts were ranked by *II* nationwide.[5] Focusing on the top twenty-four firms made it possible to control for multiple variables, since such information is readily available for those firms but spotty for smaller organizations. We thus made a trade-off, gaining richer information in exchange for limiting our sample to a smaller set of analysts. We also looked at the broadest possible spectrum of influences on individuals' decisions to stay put or move: individual characteristics, both demographic and performance related; numerous features of departments and firms, including the quality of colleagues; and sector-specific and macroeconomic factors. We then explored how different turnover destinations—a competitor, or departure from the industry—related to these variables and to turnover rates.

No prior study has simultaneously examined all these variables on individual turnover. Employing five levels of analysis enabled us to examine a wide range of possible drivers of turnover, and controlling for multiple variables made our findings both more thorough and more reliable.

We found a number of influences on turnover, ranging from individual characteristics to the performance of the organizational factors. The complexity of these findings should not be surprising, in that we are studying the aggregate life-changing decisions of a population of ambitious and intelligent individuals. Analysts receive frequent inducements to change jobs, both from competing firms and from search consultants.

Patterns of Turnover

Turnover among Star and Non-Star Analysts

The most arresting of our findings about turnover is that star research analysts were only half as likely as non-stars to change employers: annual turnover rates in the population we studied were 11.3 percent for stars and 22.7 percent for non-stars (for the top twenty-four firms that comprised our sample).[6] The low turnover of ranked analysts contradicts the popular view that star analysts function as constantly mobile free agents with highly portable skills. This finding is particularly striking in that stars are apt to receive more frequent and more attractive job offers. It seems that firm-specific investments are in play even in a highly efficient labor market in which performance is measured regularly and publicly.

Star analysts who left their firms offered several rationales for moving. The two most common reasons, which are not mutually exclusive, were increased compensation, cited in announcements by 25 percent of the analysts, and the desire to join a better firm or team, cited by 24 percent. A "better" firm presumably meant one with more resources, including money, so these two reasons may overlap significantly. (In addition, some analysts might feel that citing the desire to move to a better company is a more socially desirable, strategic-sounding reason for a move that was primarily about increased salary.) Personal reasons, including lifestyle change, drove 20 percent of analysts to leave their jobs.

Turnover at Portability-Promoting and Nonportability-Promoting Firms

The twenty-four firms in our sample differed to an extreme degree in their ability to retain high performers. Nonportability-promoting firms like Schroder Wertheim, Sanford C. Bernstein, and Merrill Lynch enjoyed very low turnover rates, while many portability-promoting firms like NatWest and Salomon Brothers experienced very high turnover.

Differences in Turnover between Portability- and Nonportability-Promoting Firms
Firms that fostered firm-specific human capital enjoyed a lower aggregate star turnover rate than did firms that promoted general human capital. Overall turnover (of both stars and non-stars) at all twenty-four firms was

18.6 percent; at portable firms it was 20.4 percent and at nonportable firms 17.1 percent. Turnover among stars at all twenty-four firms was 11.3 percent; at portable firms it was about 13 percent and at nonportable firms 10.1 percent. (See table 10.1 for differences in turnover between portability- and nonportability-promoting firms.)

Differences in Turnover between Intentional and Circumstantial Portability-Promoting Firms

Among the portability-promoting firms, turnover of ranked analysts again varied widely, from a high of 33.3 percent at NatWest Securities to only 7.1 percent at DLJ. DLJ also enjoyed low turnover among its unranked analysts, only 11.9 percent of whom left the firm. Portable firms retained fewer of their stars than did nonportable firms, but a noteworthy difference emerged when we distinguished between firms that intentionally instilled portability and those where portability was the circumstantial result of internal problems or shortcomings. Overall turnover was 18.3 percent at intentionally portable firms and 22.7 percent at circumstantially portable firms. Among stars, turnover was 9.6 percent at intentionally portable firms and about 17.4 percent at circumstantially portable firms—a striking difference. In other words, intentionally portability-promoting firms enjoyed a turnover rate

Table 10.1

Differences in Turnover between Portability- and Nonportability-Promoting Firms among the Top Twenty-Four Research Departments, 1988–96

Type	Overall turnover rate (stars and nonstars) (%)	Stars' turnover rate (%)	Stars' rate of turnover to competitors (%)
Nonportability-oriented firms	17.1	10.1	7.3
Portability-oriented firms	20.4[a]	13.0[a]	9.4[e]
Intentional portability firms	18.3	9.6	5.5[c]
Circumstantial portability firms	22.7[b,d]	17.4[b,d]	14.4[b,d]
All 24 firms	18.6	11.3	8.2

[a] Different from nonportability-oriented firms' mean at 1% significance level.

[b] Different from intentional portability-oriented firms' mean at 1% significance level.

[c] Different from nonportability-oriented firms' mean at 10% significance level.

[d] Different from nonportability-oriented firms' mean at 1% significance level.

[e] Different from nonportability-oriented firms' mean at 5% significance level.

among stars roughly comparable to that of nonportability-promoting firms. Among stars moving to competitors, turnover was 5.5 percent at intentionally portable firms and about 14.4 percent at circumstantially portable firms (see table 10.1). In firms where portability was circumstantial, turnover might also be affected by these firms' internal problems in addition to analysts' general human capital.

Ed Comeau, a star analyst at DLJ, gave voice to the kind of thinking that may underlie stars' inclination to stay put at an intentional portability-promoting firm:

> For a number of years, Merrill Lynch was trying to get me over, and they were dangling money in front of me that was almost too hard to resist. And I stayed at DLJ, and I never . . . went to them and said, "You know, I'm getting offered this over here, so you'd better match." . . . I felt like I couldn't do that to them, because they treated me so good. So I stayed there, even though . . . I probably could have made more money if I went over to Merrill Lynch. It was a different philosophy. And so it wasn't like you eat what you kill. It was that you can be sure that if you work your ass off, and you do well, you'll be compensated.

The case of Lehman Brothers, discussed in chapter 5, demonstrates the fluid and volatile relationship between portability and turnover. During the golden years (1988–92) when Lehman's research department embodied triple-threat soft, hard, and product nonportability, its star turnover rate was 8.9 percent and hardly any stars chose to move to competitors. During the subsequent era of turmoil and the abandonment of firm-specific investments and resources (1993–96), Lehman's turnover rate was 24.1 percent and stars jumped to competitors regularly.

The Drivers of Turnover

We can draw more fine-grained conclusions about turnover by controlling for a number of factors that affect turnover rates. To this end, we examined individual performance, length of tenure, and the role of gender. We also looked at departmental performance, strength, size, and leadership tenure. At the firm level, we examined firm performance and governance structure. We also considered the number of analysts in a given sector and sector performance, and the performance of the investment-banking industry as a whole.

In an effort to pin down the effect on turnover of access to high-quality colleagues, we looked at the quality of colleagues at the team, department, and firm levels. Our hypothesis was that high-performing colleagues enhance the desirability of an individual's current job by improving his or her performance (and thus compensation) and by increasing work satisfaction. Ties

Table 10.2

Findings from Regression Analyses on Turnover

Drivers	Moved	Moved to a competitor	Leaving the profession
Individual			
Individual performance (being a star)	–	–	–
New star		+	
Analyst gender (being a man)	–	n.s.	–
Analyst industry experience	–	–	–
Analyst firm experience	–	–	–
Number of jobs	+	+	n.s.
Departmental			
Quality of teammates	–	–	n.s.
Departmental performance	–	–	n.s.
Departmental strengths	–	–	n.s.
Departmental size	+	+	n.s.
Departmental leadership tenure	–	–	n.s.
Firm			
Quality of firm professionals	–	–	n.s.
Firm governance (being a private firm)	–	–	n.s.
Firm performance	n.s.	–	n.s.
Sector			
Sector size	n.s.	n.s.	n.s.
Sector performance	n.s.	n.s.	n.s.
Macroeconomic			
Investment-banking industry performance	n.s.	n.s.	–

Source: Adapted from Boris Groysberg and Linda-Eling Lee, "Star Power: Colleague Quality and Turnover," *Industrial and Corporate Change,* forthcoming; Boris Groysberg, "The Portability of Star Knowledge Workers: Evidence from the Analyst Market" (Ph.D. diss., Harvard Business School, 2002); Boris Groysberg and Ashish Nanda, "Does Stardom Affect Job Mobility? Evidence from Analyst Turnover in Investment Banks" (HBS working paper).

Note: Symbols indicate positive (+), negative (-), and insignificant (n.s.) associations at traditional levels of significance (5%).

to colleagues promote "firm embeddedness" when employees conclude that they have a lot to lose by leaving a firm where they have invested time in productive work relationships.[7] For a far more detailed description of the study's methodology, statistical findings, control variables, robustness check, and analysis relating to turnover models, see the sources in the note.[8] (See table 10.2 for summary of findings on the factors that drive turnover based on the research articles mentioned in the first endnote to this chapter.)

Individual Drivers of Turnover

Performance
We found that star analysts were more likely than their non-star colleagues to remain at their firms. With all other variables held at their means, the predicted probability of exit for all analysts was 15.2 percent at the mean. Having been ranked by *Institutional Investor* in the previous year reduced an analyst's probability of leaving to 10.9 percent. Stardom thus lowered the probability of exit by about 30 percent at the mean.

Experience and Tenure
Like other researchers, we found experience or tenure at a given firm to be negatively associated with turnover.[9] Each additional year of experience (or tenure) reduced the probability of turnover.

Gender
Women's turnover was higher than men's. Being female increased the probability of turnover by 3.6 percentage points, or 23.7 percent, at the mean. A primary explanation for this difference is that women were more likely than men to quit the profession entirely—whether because of the competing responsibilities of parenthood or because of the institutional factors discussed in chapter 8.[10]

Departmental Drivers of Turnover

Departmental Performance and Strength
Drawing on Greenwich Associates' annual ranking of research departments, which aggregates the opinions of institutional clients, we used as a measure

of departmental performance the percentage of clients who rated a particular research department among their ten primary sources of equity research in a given year. This measure incorporates reputation and overall quality of colleagues, as well as departmental capabilities. Departmental performance varied dramatically: UBS Securities scored 6.5 percent, for example, versus 37.5 percent for DLJ and 53.5 percent for Goldman Sachs, the top-rated firm in Greenwich Associates' surveys.

High-performing departments tended to experience lower turnover. But departmental performance had a decreasing marginal effect on turnover: beyond a certain point, further improvement in a department's performance did not affect its turnover rate. We also found, significantly, that departmental performance had a particularly strong effect on retention of high performers. Apparently stars placed a high value on continuing to work in high-performing departments.

To gauge departmental strength, we borrowed *Institutional Investor*'s use of the ratio of ranked analysts to all analysts as a proxy for the strength of a given department. Stronger research departments also experienced lower turnover, further confirming the thesis that stars value the presence of other stars.

Departmental Size

We designated the size of each research department as its total number of equity analysts. The relationship between departmental size and probability of exit was nonlinear: the smallest and largest departments both experienced relatively low turnover. Smaller firms, presumably, create a greater sense of camaraderie and the possibility of creating team-specific human capital; larger firms provide greater resources, which a savvy star is unlikely to give up lightly. Midsized research departments had higher turnover. The probability of exit was greatest at a department with seventy-six analysts.[11]

Departmental Leadership

Examining whether the stability of departmental leadership ignited turnover, we found that for each additional year of a research director's tenure, the probability of turnover declined. As we saw in chapter 7, established team and departmental leaders develop stable cultures that promote retention. Talented professionals exit more frequently in the wake of their manager's departure.[12] When leaders leave, furthermore, they frequently take their teams with them, as we also saw in chapter 7.

Departments with new research directors also experienced relatively high turnover. One explanation may be that new managers introduce new organizational practices that existing employees dislike.

Quality of Teammates

Analysts who work in the same sector might regard themselves as a team and draw on each other's expertise and knowledge. For instance, analysts who research international oil, domestic oil, oil exploration, and gas all look at energy markets, and their knowledge and insights are mutually relevant. Colleagues also function as sounding boards and sources of feedback for each other.

We assigned each analyst in our sample to one of twelve sectors, such as basic industries, capital goods, consumer services, or technology. We then calculated the percentage of ranked analysts in each analyst's department and sector each year.

We found consistently lower turnover at firms that provided higher-quality colleagues. Overall, analysts appeared to be reluctant to leave high-quality colleagues within a team.

Firm Drivers of Turnover

Firm Performance

Individuals are more likely to stay at a firm if they are well compensated.[13] In the investment-banking industry, compensation consists largely of year-end bonuses. The main driver of the size of bonuses is individual performance, but the firm's profitability also enters in. Because high-performing firms—those with large profits—might have more money to pour into their bonus pool, we can hypothesize that such firms will experience lower turnover than less-profitable firms.[14]

We defined firm performance as the proportional change in the ratio of its profits from equity and debt underwriting and merger-and-acquisition advisory fees to total industry profits in the preceding year.[15] We found that firm performance has a negative but insignificant effect on overall turnover.

Firm Governance

Several theorists have predicted that a firm's governance structure will influence turnover. In particular, partnership firms might inculcate a stronger sense of ownership than publicly traded firms and might therefore experience lower turnover.[16] Our study bore out this theory. We found that analysts employed by investment banks that were private were less likely to leave than those at public investment banks. Specifically, the probability of analyst turnover decreased by 3.1 percent for the partnership firms.

Quality of Firm Professionals

As a proxy for the quality of a firm's resources, we used the quality of the firm's institutional sales force (client-interface resource).

We again used Greenwich Associates' annual ratings, which surveyed investment clients about which sales representatives provided the best support in a given year. Specifically, we used the percentage of investment clients who rated a given firm as having the best sales force in a given year. We found that a higher-quality sales force significantly reduced analyst turnover.

Sector-Specific Drivers of Turnover

Sector Size

As the size of an industrial sector increases (that is, as more and more investment banks cover the industry), so will opportunities for analysts who study that sector, making it easier for them to switch firms. Thus, in theory, turnover in a growing sector might increase. And when only a few investment banks specialize in a given sector, the resulting small labor market would presumably lead to low turnover. However, we found that turnover did not increase with sector size.

Sector Performance

Industry insiders insist that turnover varies by sector: some sectors are "hot" and others are not. As *Institutional Investor* asserted in 1997:

> Debra Brown of Russell Reynolds has noticed a continued hiring "frenzy"—especially in the telecom, technology and health care arenas and, recently, in energy, real estate investment trusts and financial services—as firms scramble to fill existing holes. "If a sector is hot, every shop feels it had better be there," she says. "If an analyst is recruited away or a competitor is establishing a stronger foothold

in that sector, no firm can afford the opportunity cost of not filling the position. Everyone has to be in the game."[17]

As demand for research in a hot sector increased, the reasoning went, the number of opportunities for analysts in that sector would also increase.[18] Consequently, turnover would increase as well. However, we found no evidence to support this theory: turnover among ranked analysts in a given sector did not correlate with sectoral performance or with the rate of increase in the number of analysts covering it.

Macroeconomic Drivers of Turnover

The broad macroeconomic environment will theoretically affect turnover rates by enlarging or shrinking opportunities for potential job changers. An expanding industry, in other words, will exhibit higher turnover than a contracting industry. Some studies have found that when an entire industry performs well, turnover is indeed high: as an industry expands, employees seek out higher satisfaction, higher compensation, or improved benefits.[19]

We found the opposite to be true. As an indicator of the performance of the investment-banking industry, we used proportional change in the Dow Jones Securities Brokers' index, as deflated by the S&P 500 index.

We found industry performance to be negatively but weakly related to turnover. When the securities-brokerage industry expanded in a given year, turnover rates declined the following year. A possible explanation for this unexpected finding is that firms that depend on high-performing knowledge workers make special efforts to retain them during periods of expansion.

Types of Turnover

Certain studies have found that good performers are more likely to leave because of their attractiveness to the market. Others have found that poor performers are more likely to depart because turnover is for them a defensive maneuver. Still others have found no relationship at all between individual performance and turnover.[20] Failure to differentiate between types of turnover may help explain these inconsistent findings, and our findings on different kinds of turnover may suggest promising directions for further research.

We examined three types of turnover: joining a competitor, exiting the profession, and pursuing entrepreneurship. Of all the departures in our study, 59.9 percent were moves to a competitor and 40.1 were exits from the profession. Entrepreneurial ventures are a subset of professional exits (to be discussed in chapter 11). Among star analysts, 69.9 percent went to a competitor and 30.1 percent exited the profession. Among non-stars, 57.2 percent went to a competitor and 42.8 percent exited the profession. These data enable us to draw some conclusions about the nature of turnover among analysts.

Moving to a Competitor

Many factors that drove overall turnover also drove turnover to competitors. To recap: midsize departments and those with relatively few stars suffered higher turnover to competitors than did more star-studded departments. Analysts also did not want to leave high-quality colleagues within a team and a firm. Investment banks that were public experienced higher turnover to competitors than did partnership investment banks. And the most significant finding of all is that stars were less likely than non-stars to move to competing firms. However, few drivers of turnover changed. Analyst gender was not correlated with the probability of analyst turnover to competitors. We also found a firm's performance relative to that of the rest of the investment-banking industry to affect turnover to competitors among its analysts. Specifically, strong firm performance in the preceding year reduced the probability of turnover. Analysts whose firms had underperformed the previous year departed far more readily than those whose firms had met or exceeded the industry average. In other words, analysts were far more likely to jump ship if the ship was sinking.

Stars were less likely to join a competitor but newly ranked analysts departed from this pattern. New stardom *increased* the probability of turnover to competitors by 7.5 percent at the mean. In short, established stars tended to stay with their firms, but newly anointed stars had a greater propensity to jump ship; presumably these new stars were seeking to capitalize on their increased visibility right away. Industry insiders have speculated that new stars are more likely than established stars to join competitors because they are eager to capitalize on their new rankings; other banks, for their part, are just as attracted by the prospect of snapping up new talent with a long and promising future ahead.[21]

Leaving the Profession

Unlike turnover to competitors, exits from the profession were not positively associated with department size, department strength, leader tenure, firm governance structure, firm performance, or sector size. The only situational factor that affected industry exit was macroeconomic performance. Among individual factors, only gender, experience, and stardom influenced industry exits: women were more likely than men to exit the industry, and stardom and experience decreased the probability of industry exit.

The lack of significance of other variables raises the suspicion that "exit from the profession" is too broad a concept. It conflates retirement, layoff, leaving for family reasons, founding a new firm, joining a money-management firm, and joining a firm in the industry the analyst had covered, each of which might have a different set of drivers. (Again, we call on researchers to distinguish among different types of turnover.)

Leaving for Entrepreneurship

As we will see in chapter 11, stars were more likely than non-stars to become entrepreneurs. Turnover to entrepreneurship thus differs from turnover to competitors and other forms of exit from the profession, both of which are more commonplace among non-stars. Situational factors like departmental and firm performance did not drive turnover to entrepreneurship; in this respect it resembled other kinds of exit from the profession but not turnover to competitors. For managers of knowledge-intensive firms eager to find ways to retain their most capable employees, these findings suggest that efforts to minimize turnover to competitors may have little effect on entrepreneurial turnover.

Turnover Dynamics in Summary

Turnover is a complex phenomenon. We found, first of all, that multiple factors—individual, departmental, firm related, sectoral, and macroeconomic—influenced turnover. Second, we found that stars were less likely than non-star analysts to leave their employers. Certain organizational dynamics were also noteworthy: analysts at firms boasting higher-quality personnel at various levels of the organization were less likely to move. This is an argument for enriching the environment for stars in order to increase retention. Also, our findings about differences in turnover among nonportability-promoting departments, departments that deliberately promote portability, and departments with circumstantial portability suggest that firms' internal strategies affect turnover.

One implication of these findings is that managers' ability to retain employees depends in part on factors outside their control. Managers rarely have much influence, for example, over the quality of employees in related departments whose performance affects people under their supervision. They exercise no sway over the performance of an entire sector or of the broader economy.

Stars might enjoy greater firm-specific skills than non-stars because they have received more training, mentoring, or firm resources. Another explanation is that stardom in itself might make an individual more cautious about upsetting the applecart (tinkering with a "good thing") even without specifically crediting any particular features of the existing situation. And, by the same token, the cumulative experience of aiming at a goal and missing it (and thus earning less and enjoying less status) might tend to make non-stars more globally dissatisfied and/or restless.

Individual idiosyncrasies also affect turnover. Fundamentally, turnover is an aggregate measure of numerous decisions that individuals make in the expectation that they can do better elsewhere. Those decisions can be strategic: individuals may move because they see roadblocks in their path, because they want to do something else entirely, because they dislike the research director, or because they receive an offer that is too good to refuse. Such decisions can also be shortsighted and mistaken. Quite often, as we have seen, stars who left a firm failed to grasp how much they had relied on its resources. Our findings also shed light both on the actual limits of managerial efforts to increase retention, and on the power of first-rate colleagues and other resources to keep excellent employees within the firm.

11 | A Special Case of Turnover

Stars as Entrepreneurs

Instances in which star analysts quit their jobs to become entrepreneurs represent a special case of turnover, an alternative to joining a competitor that offers intriguing insights into portability: in a departure for entrepreneurship, the individual has only his or her own human capital to rely on and no organizational resources to draw upon.[1] The allure of entrepreneurship is usually the prospect of creating a company in one's own image. Accordingly, some star analysts expected it to be easier to succeed as an entrepreneur than at a new firm, which would require a period of adjustment to learn a new corporate culture. By starting a firm, they believed, they would be able to tailor its environment to their own skills and values.

The reality they encountered was quite different. Analysts who founded their own businesses faced the double burden of losing their team- and firm-specific human capital and their access to investment bank capabilities, while simultaneously experiencing intense pressure to build up new human capital and firm capabilities quickly. Unlike analysts who moved to competitors, entrepreneurs could not immediately begin to recoup these losses by forming relationships and learning to navigate in a new environment. Instead, even the majority whose new enterprises built on their expertise in a particular industry had to create new relationships and capabilities from scratch. This process almost always entailed acquiring new forms of general human capital as well—that is, learning the skills of a manager and a business generator. A colloquial way of describing the most basic roles in professional services is the "minder-finder-grinder" distinction: the minder handles the administrative end, the finder drums up business, and the grinder produces the work. Many analysts are essentially grinders, but successful entrepreneurs need to be able to play all three roles, at least until the business takes off.

The idea of heading off to become an entrepreneur is likely to arise repeatedly in the careers of successful Wall Street research analysts. The financial press frequently spotlights talented former Wall Streeters who have chosen to go it alone.[2] Stories about legendary analyst-cum-entrepreneurs like Benjamin Rosen, who left Morgan Stanley and founded Compaq Computers, tend to emphasize sheer ability, inventiveness, and a risk-taking mentality as the driving forces in analysts' mid-life entrepreneurial career changes. "Take a culture that puts a high premium on entrepreneurship. Make it a people business, in which contacts and relationships are a prime asset. Add to it the probability of making enough money to be financially independent at an early age," wrote *Investment Dealers' Digest* in 1990. "Throw in some big egos for good measure. What you have is a surprising number of people leaving established careers on Wall Street to start their own firms."[3]

Such stories imply that the star is a wholly portable free agent. Thus they also represent a heads-up to managers that their most talented players may eventually fly the coop. Some managerial literature makes the same argument. "It is sometimes impossible to keep valuable employees by means of incentives. It is the most able who have ideas of their own, and do not want to work for a large organization forever," one trio of managerial researchers has written. "At some point, they will leave to set up an independent company, in spite of the risks."[4]

Ultimately, though, few analysts turn their backs on the relative security of a research career to start a venture whose likelihood of success is slim. The characteristics of their labor market explain why only a small percentage of analysts become entrepreneurs and why stars are more likely than non-stars to take the entrepreneurial plunge. It is typically reported that new entrepreneurs are strongly driven by the aspiration to build equity.[5] Wall Street analysts, however, are unusually well positioned to extract the value of their human capital because of the transparency and visibility of their performance, as we saw in chapter 2. To put the point more plainly, Wall Street analysts already make a great deal of money, perhaps blunting the entrepreneurial urge. In an effort to satisfy stars' entrepreneurial urges, furthermore, many brokerage houses allow their star analysts to operate as independent franchises under the protective aegis of the firm.

The level of independence enjoyed by analysts satisfies some—but may whet the appetite of others for even more autonomy. And stardom has its privileges. Ranked analysts are more likely than non-stars to pursue entrepreneurship because their star status tends to exempt them from the discouraging effects of certain barriers. First, stars can leverage their professional relationships and reputations to attract capital, clients, and employees to their new ventures. They are also likely to enjoy greater tolerance of risk taking than non-stars because they are wealthier. And they are apt to have less to lose because their reputations make reentry into the industry an attractive option if the entrepreneurial venture proves disappointing.

What are the realities of analysts as entrepreneurs? Which analysts leave for entrepreneurship, and when, and why? And are stars more likely than their non-star colleagues to succeed as entrepreneurs?[6]

In an effort to answer these questions and to portray the entrepreneurial option fully, we compiled data on star analysts who became entrepreneurs over the course of nine years, 1988 to 1996, and compared them to two other groups: non-star entrepreneurs, and star and non-star analysts who switched from one investment bank to another.[7] We also conducted extensive interviews with star and non-star analysts who became entrepreneurs.

This chapter will explore how analysts have fared as entrepreneurs and the differences between entrepreneurial and other types of turnover. Using archival and qualitative data, it profiles entrepreneurial analysts, their reasons for becoming entrepreneurs, and the challenges they face.

Former Analysts' Survival Rates as Entrepreneurs

There are no directly equivalent ways to measure success as an entrepreneur and success as an analyst, but we can do a very rough comparison by looking at the three-year survival rate of analysts' new businesses in the light of the probability of remaining a star for three years. The probability of remaining ranked (at any rank) for three years was 80.5 percent for ranked analysts who did not change firms and 65.9 percent for ranked analysts who left to join competitors. By contrast, the rate of three-year survival for ranked analysts' entrepreneurial ventures was 57 percent. Given what we have already seen about the contribution to performance of general, firm-, and team-specific human capital and firm capabilities, this ordering is what we might expect. Analysts who remain at their firms lose no firm capabilities or firm-specific capital; those who move to other firms lose one or both but encounter immediate opportunities to rebuild. Those who start their own firms lose the most and have to equip themselves with entirely new forms of human capital at the same time.

We can also compare this 57 percent survival rate to the survival rates of new businesses reported in other studies, especially studies of other labor markets. The probability that a star analyst's new enterprise would survive for three years was lower than the survival rates of new firms in other settings. Perhaps the most apt comparison is to former employees of financial institutions who founded their own investment-management firms. Fully 88 percent (44 out of 50) of new investment-management firms started by 111 individuals in 1980–81 were still successful and in business five years later. By contrast, the survival rate for the ventures of analysts—even star analysts—was low. Other studies support the observation that analysts' success rate was comparatively low.[8]

Thus, using the available metrics, entrepreneurial analysts' success rates did not stack up favorably against comparable rates of entrepreneurial success or the success rates of analysts who did not become entrepreneurs. The modest success rate of entrepreneurial analysts suggests that their simultaneous loss of firm-specific human capital and need to build new general and firm-specific human capital came at a high price.

Stars fared considerably better as entrepreneurs than non-stars: their three-year survival rate of 57 percent compared favorably to the 29 percent survival rate of unranked analysts.[9] Having been ranked by *Institutional Investor* thus increased the probability that a former analyst's venture would survive for three years with a marginal effect of 40.5 percent over the mean (45.9 percent). This suggests both a role for innate ability in entrepreneurial success and the extent to which some aspects of star status, if not permanently portable, can at least smooth the transition to running one's own business.

Counterbalancing this evidence of individual factors in success, however, we found evidence of macroeconomic effects on success as well: the probability that a star analyst's new enterprise would survive increased with the growth of the U.S. economy. Specifically, a 10 percent increase in the S&P 500 index during a three-year period increased the probability of an analyst's entrepreneurial success by 7 percent over the mean.[10] (See table 11.1 for a summary of findings on the factors that drive the probability of new venture survival for three years based on the research articles mentioned in the first endnote to this chapter.)

Table 11.1

Findings from Regression Analyses on the Probability of Firm Survival

Drivers	Moved to entrepreneurship
Individual	
Individual performance (being a star)	+
Analyst gender (being a man)	n.s.
Analyst industry experience	n.s.
Macroeconomic	
S&P 500 performance (three years)	+

Source: Boris Groysberg, Ashish Nanda, and M. Julia Prats, "Does Individual Performance Affect Entrepreneurial Mobility? Empirical Evidence from the Financial Analysis Market," *Journal of Financial Transformation* 25 (March 2009): 95–106, p. 105.

Notes: Symbols indicate positive (+), negative (–), and insignificant (n.s.) associations at traditional levels of significance (5%).

Entrepreneurial Exits versus Ordinary Job Changes

Many studies of individual turnover look at all exits in aggregate. We found, however, that the dynamics of turnover to entrepreneurship differed fundamentally from those of turnover to competitors. We expected, on the strength of earlier studies, to find that entrepreneurial exits were driven by the same situational variables as other turnover, such as the quality of the department, the firm's performance, and activity in the analyst's sector. To our surprise, we found that star analysts who departed to pursue entrepreneurship did so independently of developments within their departments, firms, sectors, or the broader economy. The decision to start a new enterprise appeared to be idiosyncratic—undertaken because an individual wants to do something new—and independent of the factors that influenced more conventional job turnover. Theoretical models and empirical studies of turnover should thus subdivide turnover by destination.

Two factors do consistently influence which analysts leave to become entrepreneurs: stardom[11] and gender. Star analysts were more likely to choose entrepreneurship than non-star analysts, and men were more likely to do so than women. Being ranked by *Institutional Investor* generated a marginal effect of 0.7 percent over the mean (0.5 percent) in the probability of becoming an entrepreneur.

Contrary to industry insiders' beliefs, "hot" sector performance did not correlate with entrepreneurial exits. At the macroeconomic level, the prob-

Table 11.2

Findings from Regression Analyses on the Probability of Moving to Entrepreneurship

Drivers	Moved to entrepreneurship
Individual	
Individual performance (being a star)	+
All-star (ranked five years)	+
Analyst gender (being a man)	+
Analyst industry experience	n.s.
Number of jobs	n.s.
Departmental	
Departmental performance	n.s.
Firm	
Firm performance	n.s.
Sector	
Sector size	n.s.
Macroeconomic	
S&P 500 performance	n.s.

Source: Adapted from Boris Groysberg, Ashish Nanda, and M. Julia Prats, "Does Individual Performance Affect Entrepreneurial Mobility? Empirical Evidence from the Financial Analysis Market," *Journal of Financial Transformation* 25 (March 2009): 95–106, p. 101.

Note: Symbols indicate positive (+), negative (–), and insignificant (n.s.) associations at traditional levels of significance (5%).

ability of entrepreneurial turnover was not affected by changes in the S&P 500 index.[12] Nor did the quality of the department (measured by the ratio of stars to all analysts) or the performance of the analyst's firm correlate with departures for entrepreneurship.[13] (See table 11.2 for a summary of findings on the factors that drive turnover to entrepreneurship based on the research articles mentioned in the first endnote to this chapter.)

When we looked for differences in entrepreneurial activity between departments of differing quality, we found none. We did find, however, that analysts from nonportability-oriented firms like Goldman Sachs, Lehman Brothers and Sanford C. Bernstein opted for entrepreneurship less frequently than did analysts from portability-oriented firms like Montgomery, Credit Suisse First Boston, and Dean Witter Reynolds. Many portability-oriented firms treated their analysts as semi-entrepreneurs who managed their own franchises. Such firms' structure may thus have attracted analysts with independent tendencies and made it even more tempting for them to leave to start their own ventures by developing their entrepreneurial skills. In fact, among the top twenty-four firms, the annual entrepreneurial turnover rate at nonportability-oriented firms was about 0.3 percent, compared to 0.6 percent at portability-oriented firms. This ratio is similar to the direction for overall turnover, 17.1 percent at nonportability-oriented firms and 20.4 percent at portability firms, as we saw in chapter 10.

Entrepreneurial Stars: A Profile

Analyzing turnover at the top twenty-four firms, we found that star analysts were far more likely than their non-star colleagues to leave their jobs to become entrepreneurs. Overall, entrepreneurial turnover was 0.5 percent yearly: 0.8 percent among ranked analysts (28 out of 3,408) and 0.3 percent among non-ranked analysts (17 out of 6,123). Approximately 7.3 percent of ranked analysts who left their jobs between 1988 and 1996 became entrepreneurs (28 out of 385), compared to only about 1.2 percent of non-ranked analysts (17 out of 1,392). These percentages are very small. More than half of the major sectors that research departments cover produced no entrepreneurial analysts between 1988 and 1996. But even these modest numbers represent a striking increase over the 1970s in the frequency with which analysts quit to become entrepreneurs.[14] Far higher rates of entrepreneurial activity have been reported in the general population. One study, for instance, found that 4 percent of U.S. adults are starting new firms.[15]

The thirty star entrepreneurs[16] we studied collectively founded fifteen money-management firms and hedge funds, eight research and advisory companies, four new ventures that provided both services, two investment-banking firms, and an airline.

Personal Characteristics of Entrepreneurial Stars

Star analysts who quit to start new ventures did so, on average, at the age of forty-four. They had worked as analysts for an average of 11.5 years and had been with their most recent employer for nearly eight years; the typical star analyst had held only 1.5 jobs in the profession before quitting to become an entrepreneur. These numbers make entrepreneurial analysts slightly older and more experienced than their counterparts who departed for competitors or decided to stay put, though the differences are not statistically significant.

Interestingly enough, entrepreneurial star analysts had moved around somewhat less than either other stars or non-stars before making the leap to entrepreneurship, having built their reputations and contacts primarily at their most recent employer. This pattern and our interviews suggest careful preparation and a long incubation period for their entrepreneurial ventures. In keeping with this finding, star analysts who left their former employers for entrepreneurship reported having contemplated doing so for three to five years.

Motives for Pursuing Entrepreneurship

People who undertake major life changes typically have multiple, intertwined motives, and in our interviews several ex-analyst entrepreneurs articulated visions that combined a handful of agendas. Still, it would not be an oversimplification to say that four overriding motivations convinced star research analysts to make the leap to a start-up: intellectual independence, money, the chance to create an organization, and personal growth.

Intellectual Independence

Garo Armen, a biotechnology analyst at E. F. Hutton and Dean Witter who became CEO of Antigenics, expressed the urge toward freedom of thought and action with particular eloquence.

> The reason I went to Wall Street in the first place and became an analyst was because of my fascination that you could have an idea which was basically seeing the future develop in front of your eyes. And there was a means in America of capitalizing on your vision and turning that idea into profit. When I had the opportunity, because I was financially more secure, to set up my own shop and do this full-time, instead of servicing other clients—to take my ideas and turn them into a profitable business for myself and for my own partnership clients—I jumped on it. When you're driven with ideas and when that becomes so compelling to you, a secret of entrepreneurship is that you really don't want to have any roadblocks, any barriers.

Sano Shimoda, a chemical analyst with First Boston who cofounded a research banking firm focused on the chemical industry, put it more succinctly: "I'm independent. Wall Street basically thrives on independent people."

Building Wealth and Equity

Others expressed a desire to capitalize on their talents to make more money. Several used almost identical turns of phrase to express their urge to "put my money where my mouth is." A number of new entrepreneurs said that they wanted to build equity.

Star analysts know their own market value because their performance is regularly evaluated against a standardized and visible measurement system and because compensation is reported in the financial press and by word of mouth; some stars said that they took the entrepreneurial route because they were no longer willing to let anyone else trade on their equity even if their firms took a modest share.

A number readily acknowledged that they had not put much at risk financially by pursuing entrepreneurship. Several claimed they were putting relatively little money on the line—at most one year's pay—in establishing their new firms. Given their stellar records and the shortage of qualified professionals, furthermore, the worst-case scenario they envisioned was to return to their former employer. This assessment was accurate: we found that some ranked analysts who failed or were unhappy as entrepreneurs were able to reenter the industry, usually at their former employer.

Creating an Organization

A number of new entrepreneurs admitted that despite confidence in their own abilities, they had experienced sleepless nights debating the pros and cons of starting a new business. Even for an individual who is cushioned against the worst consequences of financial failure, it is daunting to rely entirely on one's own resources. For this reason, the desire to make more money can be an adequate reason to change employers but not to start a new business. What appears to distinguish entrepreneurial stars from their counterparts who merely change jobs is their deep convictions about how their businesses ought to operate. A number of new entrepreneurs were fed up with or disillusioned by the bureaucracy and politics at their old firms. Most asserted a desire to create an organization founded on their own values, and a number volunteered that ethics and integrity were of prime importance to them.

Others mentioned the burnout factor in research: long hours, marketing demands, and travel. "I left because I was working all the time and there was no joy in it for me," said Carol Muratore, who left Morgan Stanley to found a consulting firm. "What I wasn't so good at was being on an airplane all the time, functioning with no sleep."

Personal Growth

A number of entrepreneurial ex-analysts said they had evaluated their accomplishments and realized that the time had come to make a break if they were ever going to; otherwise they would reach retirement with a sharp sense of regret. As Michael Sorell, a pharmaceutical analyst (and former physician) who quit to become the CEO of a pharmaceutical start-up, observed:

> I'm in my mid-fifties. I really think the best way I could add value out there is, number one, stick to what I know best. Number two is find an opportunity where I can add value based on judgment, wisdom, experience, people skills, and patience, not just by being the smartest kid on the block. That's fine when you're thirty. But by the time you're fifty, you should develop another set of skills. The underlying attitude you need is still the same; you need boundless physical energy and you need optimism. But there's another set of skills that just don't happen early in life. . . . It's [research is] probably still a fun job for somebody who is just starting out, but . . . it's a confining role, ultimately. It's just too confined a world. I want to do something that's a lot more substantial at this point.

Some former analysts said that because star status represented the highest possible achievement in the research business, their *II* ranking had left them no further room to grow in the profession.

What Kinds of Businesses Do Entrepreneurial Analysts Found?

The former analyst who founded an airline is highly unusual. Ordinarily, entrepreneurial analysts built on their well-honed skills, reputations, and contacts, which meant that most opted for one or another of three types of enterprises: a research advisory boutique, a hedge fund, or a consulting firm.

Research Advisory Boutiques

A research boutique can be a new lease on life for analysts who love their work but not the obligation to conform to the demands of an investment bank. In order to survive, a boutique must find a niche—often a sector not yet large enough to attract the attention of large investment banks—and foster and tend personal relationships.

This is how Thomas Petrie, an oil analyst at Credit Suisse First Boston, approached the challenge of establishing his boutique, Petrie Parkman. Petrie focused on independent energy firms and, in particular, on helping these firms sell stock in thin markets. Over time Petrie Parkman became a trusted source for many independent firms, and the boutique grew with the sector. This once-obscure sector eventually attracted the attention of large investment banks, but by that time Petrie Parkman had established longstanding personal relationships built on loyalty and trust. "When we formed the firm in 1989, people asked if we could have a viable practice focusing on the independent sector. . . . But that was the beauty—nobody was paying attention," Petrie said. "Now that the majors are working on it, not everybody is going to stay loyal to us. But where it exists, that loyalty is very deep."[17]

The entrance of large banks into the sector turned out, in fact, to generate new opportunities. Merrill Lynch invited Petrie Parkman into a $60 million IPO in 1994, and Petrie found its way into large-scale mergers and acquisitions. By 2000, Petrie Parkman was advising on multibillion-dollar mergers and had grown sufficiently to become an underwriter in large IPOs. By concentrating on a market in which it could demonstrate its deep knowledge, the company has managed to become a major player in the oil-and-gas sector. For a boutique, winning a piece of a merger or an acquisition can bring in a lot of money.

Hedge Funds

One of the most common entrepreneurial options chosen by former analysts was to found a hedge fund. A successful hedge fund will typically have $100 million or more under management; the largest manage billions of dollars. A standard 1 percent management fee plus 10–20 percent of the gains positions a successful hedge-fund manager to earn far more than he or she could hope to as an analyst.

Analysts who started hedge funds had confidence that their deep knowledge of their industries would make them good stock pickers. They also relied on their reputations as analysts to facilitate raising capital. Most were convinced that as analysts they brought in far more value than they were paid and were thus willing to forgo steady income in the expectation of reaping far larger and more direct rewards.

Several health care analysts created firms in the sectors they had covered as analysts. R. Brandon Fradd, a ranked analyst with Montgomery Securities until 1995, was becoming frustrated with the job of sell-side analyst. "I found that a lot of what plays in biotech stock prices is sentiment," Fradd said. "If sentiment is negative, the fundamentals don't seem to matter much. As a sell-side analyst, you do a lot of fundamental work and have little or no impact on price." Fradd left to start a hedge fund, Apollo Medical Partners. He had a knack for trading stocks, and the fund got off to a fast start. The firm produced relatively well in rougher times.[18]

A pharmaceutical-analyst-turned-entrepreneur who took a more unusual path was Garo Armen, who left Dean Witter Reynolds in 1989 to launch a hedge fund. The fund, Armen Partners, was an immediate success, attracting over $100 million in capital and making Armen wealthy. Equally valuable were the investment ideas that others brought him. One in particular, Pramod Srivastava, had an idea for a cancer vaccine using heat shock proteins. Armen, who had been a physician before becoming an analyst, saw the potential in Srivastava's research. In 1994 the two founded Antigenics; Armen invested his own money but, on ethical grounds, none of Armen Partners'. Almost a decade later, Antigenics' vaccine was in phase-three trials and had proven promising in treating kidney cancer.

But health care analysts are not the exclusive source of hedge-fund stories. Some analysts were simply good stock pickers, and some were lucky in their timing, entering the market when their sectors were on the cusp of a period of high growth. Others overcame the risk inherent in starting a specialized hedge fund by broadening their focus. R. Gamble Baldwin, a ranked analyst with Credit Suisse First Boston, left in 1988 to start Natural Gas Partners. His reputation and his partner's contacts brought in around $200 million at the outset. Though Baldwin had been a natural-gas analyst and the name of his firm indicated a specialized focus, Baldwin invested more broadly. By 2000 the firm had over $1 billion under management.[19]

Consulting Firms

The third popular option for entrepreneurial analysts was to start a consulting firm. The potential financial rewards were perceived to be less lavish than those offered by either research boutiques or hedge funds, but the risks were also considered less extreme. The reputation of a ranked analyst typically attracted clients readily. Consulting firms were also frequently hired by firms in the analyst's sector and by investment banks. Consultants thus enjoyed far more freedom than they had as analysts while continuing to capitalize on their Wall Street reputations. The cost of start-up is minimal and the risk of failure was far lower than in other entrepreneurial ventures.

Carol Muratore was a highly ranked computer analyst with Morgan Stanley before leaving in 1990 to found a consulting firm, Green Tree Research. She began with the well-defined goal of helping Silicon Valley entrepreneurs negotiate the challenges a young company faces, particularly IPOs. Though her skills as an analyst and her Wall Street savvy proved invaluable, Muratore's plan explicitly did not involve continuing to work as an analyst under the guise of an independent consultant. The result was a consulting firm that has found a niche on the West Coast.

The Challenges of Entrepreneurship

If a new entrepreneur does a good job of leveraging industry contacts, the new firm will have clients before its doors open for business. Most try to sign up their former employer's clients as clients of their new ventures. "The principal revenue source was purely my relationships that I acquired at DLJ," said Robert Gay, an analyst who founded a financial data and software firm and later moved to managing assets. When Andrew Zunser, a top-rated insurance analyst, became unhappy at his firm and decided to set up his own operation, he made overtures to his major accounts; 90 percent agreed to follow him if he went out on his own, and the remaining 10 percent were noncommittal but open to the idea. John Maxwell claimed that he retained about 125 of his 600 clients upon departing from Oppenheimer to found the Maxwell Company.[20] As several management theorists have pointed out, the cost of changing employers can be quite low for star knowledge workers because they own their clients.[21]

Identifying a Competitive Edge and Honing a Business Strategy

The long lead times that entrepreneurial analysts allowed themselves before taking the plunge to entrepreneurship were in many cases a matter of taking time to hone the original concept and position the new enterprise appropriately. "I very deliberately took the parts of the job that I enjoyed the most and that I thought I was best at and took them into my consulting practice," said Carol Muratore.

"You'd better figure out something where you have a competitive edge," said Sano Shimoda. "Where you can differentiate yourself as a small company is to create a knowledge franchise. . . . You have to say, 'Where can I create competitive advantage?' At the forefront in terms of expertise, that's where you want to be. When you're on the treadmill, you want to be at the top of the treadmill, because lots of people are running after you. Lots of good people. My view always was you have to create a personality for the company so people would know what you are and what you are not."

High Performance Expectations

Stars sometimes discovered that they were prisoners of their own reputations. Clients expected star performance from stars' new ventures, and those who were quick to follow trusted analysts to their new firms may have been even quicker to leave the new venture at the first signs of underperformance. Many star entrepreneurs learned to their chagrin that their customers' loyalty lasted only as long as the new firm exhibited strong performance.

Star analysts who established investment-management firms found that the pressures of managing money and clients' focus on short-term performance made for an environment very different from the longer-term perspective of writing research reports. Stars whose skills were more firm-specific than they realized and who experienced a decline in performance as a result could find the going especially tough. "In the first year and a half," Garo Armen reported, "these [skeptical] people were right, because my performance suffered. I went from being a major moneymaker to losing money for me and my clients. . . . Some years later, one of the limited partners called me and said, 'After that first eighteen months of miserable performance, I thought your business would go under, because I've never seen anybody come back from that level of financial damage before.' And then, in the subsequent eighteen months, I recovered all of that and made more money."

Narrowness of Skills and Focus

A more substantive problem that plagued many former analysts who started up hedge funds and investment-management firms was that a good analyst is not necessarily a good stock picker. Analysts who enjoyed longstanding relationships with people at the firms they followed might assess those firms more positively than was merited. More critically, individual analysts were narrowly focused on a single sector. They developed an encyclopedic knowledge of a handful of companies, but such knowledge was likely to prove inadequate in a less specialized investment-management environment unless one of those companies was an unqualified winner.

Charles Rose, who left Oppenheimer as a top-ranked chemical analyst in 1991 to start a hedge fund, was one of those who found stock picking more difficult than it seemed. "You can't have someone who follows five or six companies," he acknowledged.[22] Sometimes experience as an analyst can even turn out to be a handicap rather than an advantage. After a year on his own, Rose took his $30 million fund to an investment-management company, Weiss Peck & Greer, where he would receive a salary and a bonus and would have the financial and administrative resources of the firm at his disposal. "It's very easy to say, 'Well, I want to go start something on my own,' Sano Shimoda observed. "Starting your own company and making a company run are two entirely different things. To be successful, you've got to be able to do a lot of things other than be a good Wall Street analyst."

Raising Capital and Finding New Clients

When Edward S. Hyman, a star economist for more than a decade, left the brokerage house C. J. Lawrence (where he had singlehandedly accounted for 14 percent of annual revenues) to set up his own firm, $400 million of the $640 million he had managed for C. J. Lawrence immediately followed him. Much of the remainder followed within a few months. This capital allowed Hyman's new firm, the International Strategy and Investment Group, to count on $2 million in fees at the outset.[23]

But raising capital and finding clients could be hard even for stars. A new firm without a track record may have difficulty soliciting new business or new capital from potential clients who are unfamiliar with the entrepreneur's reputation. And it could even be hard to raise money from those who did know the founder's credentials. The coveted *Institutional Investor* ranking could only take former stars so far. "It wasn't as easy as I thought it would be," recalled Garo Armen. "People were not willing to part with their money to give it to me, because I was starting on my own. I was not part of a bigger organization. So it wasn't as straightforward as I thought it would be. . . . People out there are intuitively smart, and intuitively . . . a lot of them will not want to take a chance with that change, because they don't know how your performance and behavior will change within a changed environment."

Competing with Giants

Entrepreneurial analysts lose the resources formerly available to them at investment banks and then find themselves in competition for clients with their deep-pocketed former employers. "You're competing against monster firms with tremendous talent, with tremendous distribution capability, tremendous marketing capability," said Sano Shimoda. "Who am I . . . to start a firm and compete with those kinds of expertise and resources?" Analyst Robert Gay pointed out a particularly problematic dilemma for research boutiques: "It's just a tremendously difficult environment for anybody who is not basically subsidized by another part of the organization. . . . In all of the big brokers, all of these services are provided to institutions for free, effectively, and as a result to try to compete with a zero-priced product is tremendously difficult."

Organizational Challenges

Growth can be highly problematic for a new enterprise. Systems appropriate to a larger organization must be put in place under time pressure, and new employees need to be hired and trained. Star entrepreneurs naturally sought to use their reputations and industry relationships to attract talented employees, but some found it hard to compete with large Wall Street firms. "You have to compete against firms that can pay for all kinds of resources that you as a small company can't pay," said Sano Shimoda. "In small firms, it's a function of the attitude of people, and people who roll up their sleeves—understand what you're trying to do, roll up their sleeves, and we work together. The key is: how do you keep those people? Part of it is compensation, but part is opportunity. For a lot of teams on Wall Street, it's the senior analyst who takes all the credit. With people who work for me, if they produce a report and it was truly their work, their name goes first."

Entrepreneurs also found that though they themselves were risk takers, many of the kinds of employees they sought to attract were too risk averse to sign on with an untested enterprise. "There are challenges in attracting people in the beginning," Garo Armen recalled. "But you tend to attract an entrepreneurial crowd, which is better for you. . . . Being able to bring in superstars and develop superstars is probably the number-one challenge of a good company on its way to greatness."

As former employees of large organizations, new entrepreneurs often found marketing particularly difficult. "On Wall Street, the firms I worked for marketed me as a brand," Carol Muratore said. "I had never done that myself."

Adjustment to a New Role: From Producer to Manager

Finally, some former analysts who started consulting firms and research boutiques found, to their surprise, that they missed Wall Street. Entrepreneurship turned out to be less enjoyable and more difficult than they had anticipated. Garo Armen admitted that "at Dean Witter, I was the king. I had a staff of twelve people. When I wanted something, it got done. . . . So I started my own firm. Well, things were different. I was the guy, and I had two people working with me, but I had to do a lot of the menial things myself."

Others missed the camaraderie and the spotlight; they disliked feeling alone on a desert island. There were no more upscale dinners at the company's expense, no first-class seats on planes or other perks. On the other hand, Carol Muratore, who did not miss Wall Street, pointed out that analysts have plenty of practice at self-reliance: "You feel pretty much by yourself as an analyst anyway," she said, "particularly if you've said something and the market goes against you."

For many analysts, the transition from producer to manager was a complicated one. Managing others is a skill that new entrepreneurs must acquire quickly while running their firms. Most former analysts who became CEOs had previously managed only an assistant and one or two junior analysts. Former analysts also had to learn general management skills—the skills needed to gather, cultivate, and deploy financial, technical, and human resources, as well as leadership, decision making, and functional expertise. In most cases these general skills had to be self-taught from scratch, since few former analysts already possessed them. To complicate matters, time was of the essence and the process of becoming a capable manager required more of it than new entrepreneurs could afford.[24]

A comparable challenge for analysts who became consultants was accustoming themselves to a consulting role. "It's a real surprise to give up control," Carol Muratore said. "One of the attributes that most successful analysts have in common is, to a greater or lesser degree, a sense of perfectionism in their work. And as a consultant, you advise. You do not control the outcome."

Reassessing Entrepreneurship

It was not at all unusual for former analysts to abandon entrepreneurship and rejoin their former firms. Edward Greenberg, a ranked telecommunications analyst with Morgan Stanley, quit in 1991 to start a firm in the expectation that he would find it more interesting to advise individual companies. But Wall Street never lost its allure for Greenberg, and Morgan Stanley never fully recovered from the loss of his talents. Two years later Morgan Stanley created a new position for him.

Consultants were particularly prone to being lured back because their new enterprises had less structure and required less commitment than a research boutique or hedge fund. A small consulting firm, in particular, presents minimal barriers to exit. Some consultants returned to investment banks due to failure and others by choice, but only a determined few remained with their firms. For others, as they argued, an interval as an entrepreneur represented a needed break from a grueling lifestyle and a fresh vantage point that they believed ultimately makes them better analysts.

☆ ☆ ☆

Highly capable star analysts quit their jobs to become entrepreneurs at a higher rate than did more run-of-the-mill analysts. Then, having established their new enterprises, more stars than ordinary performers survived as entrepreneurs, and still more survived when the economy was healthy.

More surprising is the actual rate of three-year survival for ranked analysts' entrepreneurial ventures: 57 percent (as compared to 29 percent for unranked analysts). It is difficult to know how to interpret this finding. For one thing, discontinuing a business does not always signify failure, particularly in the case of entrepreneurs who have a highly attractive fallback option. As our interviews confirmed, some analyst-entrepreneurs discovered that they preferred Wall Street and chose to return; not all were forced to do so by the poor performance of their enterprises. Furthermore, the survival rates that other researchers have reported for entrepreneurial start-ups are so wildly disparate that there is no reliable norm against which to measure a 57 percent survival rate. In relative terms, however, this number seems low especially compared to other professional labor markets. Further research might be warranted to pinpoint which professions move into entrepreneurship most easily and which fare less well.

What does this survival rate tell us about talent and its portability? The least arguable conclusions may merely confirm some unsurprising truths. Talent matters, for instance—hence the superior performance of stars—but it doesn't conquer all. Even the prodigiously talented need a sound idea, capital, good timing, dedicated employees, a platform, systems, energy, confidence, and self-knowledge to go it alone. Talent that has been narrowly focused can only sometimes be transformed into a service that the market is willing to pay for separately. And talent might also be best leveraged when market conditions are optimal.

Our findings do suggest, at a minimum, that many analysts' franchises were not portable to entrepreneurial endeavors. As we saw in chapter 3, some analysts' skills are so firm-specific that they are not portable at all. Analysts who became entrepreneurs had to learn new skills. Most had to become managers as well as producers, and they had to master general management skills very quickly. And those who started non-research firms or firms in industries that they were not familiar with had the added pressure of learning their way around a new industry context.

12 | Measuring and Rewarding Stars' Performance

Institutional Investor's rankings were by no means the only rating of analysts' skills. The *Wall Street Journal*, Reuters, Greenwich Associates, and several other firms regularly assessed analysts' performance.[1] And both client firms and analysts' own departments compiled data about analysts' track records and activities. Much of this information sought to measure, in various ways, prevailing opinions at client firms about the relative value of individual analysts' output. Analysts themselves tended to prefer highly objective external measures because such measures kept them marketable outside their firms.

How research directors used the vast amount of information available on analyst performance depended on whether their firms were developmental or not and whether they tended to impart portable or nonportable skills. The most avid consumers of information on analysts' performance were undoubtedly hands-on research directors. These were the same research directors, by and large, who paid close attention to developing talent and often to promoting teamwork and distinctive nonportable ways of working. In an effort to pinpoint and correct individual analysts' performance shortcomings, they pored over and compared the various external assessments, and looked for correlations with their own data on analysts' daily activities. Compensation was linked to performance in all research departments, but many hands-on research directors also tended to use performance data separately for development.

More hands-off research directors viewed this cornucopia of information as undeniably interesting but fundamentally beside the point. In their view, the *II* rankings made it evident who was succeeding with clients and who was not. Performance evaluation and compensation decisions tended to be essentially one and the same process at these firms: the *II* rankings represented objective performance evaluation, and compensation was in turn pegged to analysts' standing in the poll (occasionally supplemented by other data).[2]

The literature on compensation, rewards, and incentives, though diverse, is virtually unanimous that an assessment-and-compensation policy needs to be congruent with the firm's overall culture and strategy.[3] This chapter will first describe some basic mechanisms of compensation and trends in the equities research industry and will then look at the challenges faced by research directors and how they are handled at different banks.[4]

Financing Research and Compensating Analysts

Investment banks' research departments were largely considered to be a sort of cost center. Because clients did not pay directly for research, funding for research departments at full-service brokerage houses typically flowed from institutional trading commissions, fees on investment banking, and retail brokerage. (The mix differed at firms that lack investment-banking or retail-brokerage arms.) A survey by the executive-search firm Management & Capital Partners[5] found that in the aggregate, the contributions of investment banking and institutional equities trading were roughly comparable at 42 percent and 45 percent, respectively, supplemented by 12 percent from retail brokerage.[6] At firms with very large networks of retail brokers, the contributions of the three sources were roughly equal.

The only component of this mix that was directly affected by the work of the research department was institutional trading commissions. Generally speaking, the more highly clients valued the work of a bank's equities analysts, the more they traded with that bank, and the more revenue from trade commissions the bank enjoyed. Thus research directors' attention was trained on clients' opinions not only because usefulness to clients was the raison d'être of the research enterprise but also because client satisfaction translated directly into a larger departmental budget and a larger bonus pool.

The Mechanics of Compensation

Research analysts were paid a fixed salary and a much more lavish and variable bonus based on performance. At one firm, for example, analysts' salaries tended in 2005 to cluster within a narrow range around $175,000. The bulk of their compensation took the form of cash bonuses and long-term compensation consisting of options and unvested stock. This pay structure was the industry standard and did not vary significantly from bank to bank. It was also standard practice on Wall Street as a whole.

As a rule of thumb, incentive and compensation systems tended to become embedded and to change very little over time.[7] Once specific goals had been put in place, the compensation system built around those goals operated like an informal contract. Changing the goals and the metrics could alienate veteran employees and prompt them to seek another employer who still rewarded the behaviors they had worked hard to perfect.[8]

Trends and Determinants of Compensation

Compensation at a Top-Ten Investment Bank, Part 1

We analyzed data on compensation at a single top-ten investment bank over the seventeen-year period 1988–2005, and observed the following trends.[9]

- Million-dollar analysts were rare until the mid-1990s. After that, there were consistently a sizable number. Compensation rose steadily until around 2002 and then fell and kept falling. Both effects were most pronounced at the top: the rich got much richer but were also the most acutely affected by the decline of the market. (Figure 12.1 shows total compensation of senior analysts from 1988 through 2005, and figure 12.2 shows a breakdown of bonus and salary during the same period.)
- Salary accounted for only 27.3 percent of analysts' compensation; 72.7 percent of total pay took the form of bonuses. Base salaries also exhibited little variation from individual to individual or over time; bonuses accounted for most of the significant compensation dispersion and change over time. The compensation ratio between an analyst at the 90th percentile and the analyst at the 10th percentile more than doubled from 255 percent in 1990 to 610 percent in 2000.

- Being ranked by *Institutional Investor* was a very strong predictor of compensation. Ranked analysts earned 68 percent higher compensation than unranked counterparts.
- Surprisingly, stock-picking profitability did not affect compensation. The industry rankings of sell-side analysts' activities frequently placed stock picking outside the top ten activities valued by their clients.
- The aggregate market capitalization of the industries followed by analysts rose from 1988 to 2005. We found a positive relationship between the aggregate value of the companies a given analyst covered and his or her compensation. Analysts who shifted to covering bigger companies were also paid more. Possible explanations are that these stocks generated more trading and thus more commissions, and/or that better analysts were assigned to cover bigger stocks.
- The investment-banking contributions affected analysts' compensation.

Compensation at a Top-Ten Investment Bank, Part 2
We also found strong relationships between *II* ranking, commissions, and compensation at a different top-ten investment bank in 1992 and 1993.

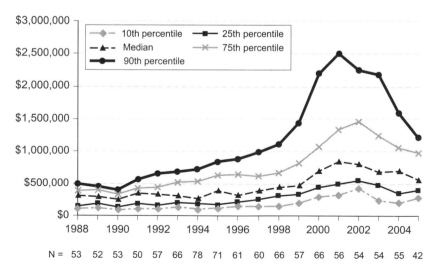

Figure 12.1. Total compensation of senior analysts at a top-ten investment firm, 1988–2005. Boris Groysberg, Paul M. Healy, and David Maber, "What Drives Sell-Side Analyst Compensation at High-Status Banks?" (Harvard Business School working paper).

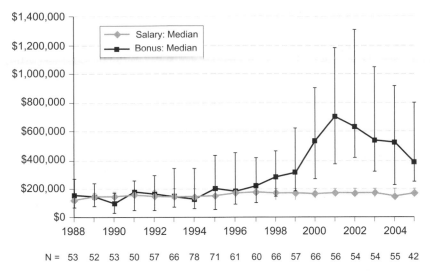

Figure 12.2. Salary and bonus compensation of senior analysts at a top-ten investment firm, 1988–2005. The vertical bars represent the inter-quartile range (i.e., the first and third quartiles). *Source*: Boris Groysberg, Paul M. Healy, and David Maber, "What Drives Sell-Side Analyst Compensation at High-Status Banks?" (Harvard Business School working paper).

- Again, ranking in *Institutional Investor* was a very strong predictor of compensation. On average, ranked analysts were paid $519,138 and non-ranked analysts were paid $296,065. Average compensation for analysts was $389,135, with standard deviation of $212,574. The highest-paid analyst took home $1,691,208.
- A given analyst's compensation was positively associated with the total amount he or she generated in commissions. The average analyst was attributed $8,559,506 in commissions, with a standard deviation of $8,006,262. One ranked analyst generated $32.9 million in commissions in 1993. Even though full-service investment banks understood that there was no direct link between analysts' impact and commissions, some firms tracked that activity by recording commissions in analysts' stocks.
- A ranked analyst generated more in commissions, on average, than an unranked analyst ($10,871,545 vs. $6,209,565).

Budget Analysis
Budget and compensation data are hard to come by, but we examined an aggregate budget data of ten research departments at mostly large invest-

ment banks. These data allowed us to examine the differences between developmental and nondevelopmental firms, and between portability- and nonportability-oriented firms (using the definition offered in chapters 5 and 9).[10] Given the very limited and small budget data set, we are very cautious in making any generalization. Data (1997–2001) suggested the following trends:

- Departmental budgets grew every year. The average research department budget increased from 1997 to 2001 by 92 percent.
- The average number of analysts in a department increased by 55 percent during the same period.
- Budgets were higher in departments with more analysts and more *II*-ranked analysts.
- The developmental firms enjoyed a 6 percent budget "discount" compared to nondevelopmental firms.
- The average "budget per analyst" at nonportability firms was not significantly different from the average at portability firms.

Making Choices in Compensation

Within the financial landscape outlined in the preceding section, research directors had multiple options for assessing and compensating analysts.[11] These choices can be characterized by three decision points.[12] According to the research directors, these choices and the corresponding questions can be characterized by three decision points.

Input
What criteria should be taken into account when determining pay? Should compensation be based primarily on performance or seniority? On individual results or team results?[13] Should performance be evaluated on quantitative or qualitative criteria, or by a mix of the two?

Process
Whatever the inputs, should the process of determining compensation be entirely formula driven or should there be room for adjustments? How transparent should the compensation process be? Should employees be fully informed about the elements in compensation decisions?

Output

What should the ultimate amount of compensation be? How high should total compensation be relative to the market? What proportion of compensation should be fixed and what proportion variable? What proportion of compensation should be short term (salary and bonus) and long term (pension, equity)? How much disparity should be allowed in compensation, between employees at the same level and vertically throughout the department or firm? How public should compensation outcomes be?

Along with promotion, compensation is one of the most influential ways a firm has at its disposal to shape behavior, reward results, and attract and retain employees.[14] What is crucial is that compensation practices support the kind of culture—entrepreneurial or hierarchical, competitive or cooperative, portable or nonportable—that the firm wants to foster. Some of the questions articulated above have, through long tradition, simply become part of the culture of the profession. A prime example is that investment banks have chosen a highly variable form of pay for analysts, awarding most of it as a bonus. And analysts' high profile in the media has meant that even if compensation was confidential, analysts were better placed than most workers to know their own market value. The investment-banking culture as a whole also rewarded performance over seniority, partially because of the highly public nature of the *Institutional Investor* polls.

Where departmental cultures differed most was in the information they used to manage performance and the extent to which they used that information to develop analysts, rather than in the details of their compensation schemes. Quantitative data are hard to come by, but firms appeared to differ in the amount of compensation disparity they tolerated. The rest of this chapter will discuss these differences.

Focusing on Client Impact

For some firms, the only measure of excellence that mattered was the favorable opinions of buy-side clients—and the corresponding commissions. Some of these firms used only one metric (*Institutional Investor* rankings); others used a combination of *II* rankings, client votes (also known as broker votes), and internal polling of the sales force.[15] Research directors at these firms believed that focusing on a single criterion of excellence helped analysts maintain clarity and perceive the compensation system as objective and fair. "We manage toward one and only one metric," said a research director who focused exclusively on client impact. "If you try to get really dedicated professionals to aim toward five disparate targets at the same time, they'll probably miss them all."[16]

The *Institutional Investor* Rankings

The results of the *Institutional Investor* poll became highly influential on Wall Street soon after their introduction in 1972. Research departments welcomed thorough and systematic information on how their own analysts stacked up against competitors in the eyes of their clients and promptly adopted the *II* rankings as a primary metric for evaluation. "The shorthand for figuring out who had the expertise pretty quickly became the *Institutional Investor* poll," recalled Jack Rivkin.

Some firms were explicit about their orientation toward *II*. "A lot of the behaviors that [research directors] would want an analyst to engage in, all those things could also be associated with being a number-one-ranked analyst," explained Larry Fraser of Management & Capital Partners. "They saw it as a proxy for a whole series of other behaviors." Making *II* was the exclusive goal, as one analyst said of his former firm: "There was one business plan: it was be an All-Star, *II*-ranked."

Top analysts in turn used their rankings to negotiate high salaries: once the *II* rankings became the industry standard, the formerly modest salary differential between top-ranked stars and the rest of the pack widened massively. It is no surprise that many more analysts then gave their undivided attention to getting ranked as soon as possible. (Exhibit 12.1 shows a typical analyst's answers to a departmental questionnaire, repeatedly expressing his single-minded focus on attaining *II* ranking.) As Fred Fraenkel explained:

> After *II*, the divergence from the mean was extraordinary. In the mid-1970s an *II* analyst was getting paid $100,000. There were lots of average analysts who were getting $60,000. The dollar spread was only $40,000. The percentages were starting to pull apart, but it wasn't a lot of money. It eventually got to the point where instead of a 50 percent or 60 percent premium, it was many hundreds of percents. Plus the dollars were bigger. It got outlandish.

In a manner of speaking, the price that the industry as a whole paid for the transparency provided by the *II* poll and other sources of comparative data was a massive increase in the market value of the most coveted talent.[17]

Exhibit 12.1

Excerpts from an Analyst's Answers

to a Departmental Questionnaire, 1986

EQUITY RESEARCH DEPARTMENT

Analyst Questionnaire

March 1986

Introduction

This questionnaire has been designed to help identify your strengths and weaknesses as an analyst and marketer, which in turn will allow us to develop an individualized game plan that will maximize your effectiveness, your enjoyment of your job, and your net worth. It will help me to better understand who you are, where you are, where you want to go, and how best to get there.

There are no right or wrong answers! But there are more honest and less honest answers. And the more honest you can be with me, the more helpful I can be to you. Period.

As soon as you return the questionnaire to me (and I want every one back by Friday, March 14), I'll make a date to sit down with you, one-on-one, to discuss it and to lay some plans for the future.

While it should go without saying, I'll say it. All answers are completely confidential. Nonetheless, feel free to skip any questions that you're uncomfortable answering.

Do you think you can be a #1-rated analyst without necessarily being a good stock picker? Why?

> *ABSOLUTELY—Because we are in a <u>service</u> & <u>information</u> <u>business</u>. (Also they forget some of the disasters)*

In a general sense, how do you feel about the marketing demands of your job?

> *I like people and getting to know them. But I find most of the marketing superficial and tiring . . . but it gets better as you get closer to these people. However, I want the goal so badly I'll do it.*

Exhibit 12.1 *(continued)*

Do you ever call clients when you really have nothing to say? Why or why not?

> *YES, to introduce myself and my services. Also to keep my name on their mental shelf space.*

Do you call clients who clearly have no interest in your group? Why or why not?

> *YES, to get II votes.*

How many days each month do you typically spend marketing? Would you like to spend more time or less time on the road?

> *Since I got the Connectors Group under coverage—4–5 days/month. I'd like to spend as much time as it takes to get on the cover of the magazine. . . .*

How much of your time are you now spending on Corporate Finance? How much, ideally, would you like to spend?

> *Less than 5% now. 0% would be ideal (until I get on the II list).*

On Research Dept. Management

What are your three biggest concerns about what's been going on in this department?

> *1. Loss of momentum—We lose so many people that it becomes very difficult/impossible (?) to make the II at this firm.*
>
> *2. That you get frustrated and chewed up and spit out before getting to do what you want to do.*
>
> *3. That the cynicism returns after a brief flurry of optimism—and we fail. . . .*

What would you like to tell me that I didn't ask you about?

> *I'd like you to know the struggle it has been for me working here. I was hired to follow software—an industry I worked in. About one year later I was told to stop adding software names and follow micro-computer stocks. Three months later I was told to follow Semi-conductor equipment. On July 5, 1985 I was assigned Connectors—a real live II group! I busted my ass to get coverage up—20-page industry piece plus five 12-page company pieces in 4 months. I think I actually have an outside shot at the II list this year, given the weak group . . .*

Source: An analyst.

// Data Packaged as a Research Product

In 1995 *Institutional Investor* decided to sell a far more comprehensive set of rankings than those that appeared in the magazine. The magazine published only a small fraction of the information it collected; firms wanted to know how the rest of the analyst population, the non-stars, stacked up. "What people were interested in was who were the next fifteen, because they were the up-and-comers," explained Peter Derow, *II*'s CEO at the time. The magazine capitalized on this demand by selling customized versions of the data it collected to sell-side research departments, along with interpretive services. "They didn't want to just buy the data," said Derow. "They wanted to buy our time explaining the data to them."

These customized reports, known as *Institutional Investor Summary Profiles*, provided raw scores for all analysts, ranked and unranked. The scores revealed the degrees of difference between analysts' standings all the way up the chain, showing firms how their own up-and-comers stacked up against promising competitors at other firms. David Wachtel, former publisher of *II*, viewed this data point as the most valuable feature of the research package: "Once they got the full data, it meant a lot more. If they were a number three, were they within striking position of being number one, or was that number three really just an also-ran?"

The *Summary Profiles* also broke down the vote geographically and by the asset size of the respondents' companies, revealing which regions and types of institutions analysts needed to pay greater attention to. "The report was really legitimate research," Wachtel commented. "And by going out and selling it, and explaining all the background that we were collecting, it increased the value that firms placed on the research. I don't think the firms realized how much we were measuring. Once we showed the Street what level of research we were doing, it was a no-brainer that they would want access to it." The magazine charged thousands of dollars for each *Summary Profile*, and research departments could commission nonstandard customized versions to answer specialized questions. The popularity and influence of the *Profiles* has only increased since then.

Before the *Summary Profiles*, firms had to rely on what was published in the magazine. During those years, analysts and research directors tried other methods to pinpoint the qualities that would lead an analyst to become a star. Table 12.1 is a research director's effort to specify the attributes of ranked analysts; table 12.2 is another research director's compilation of quotes from clients, extracted from *Institutional Investor*, explaining why particular analysts were ranked in 1991. Exhibits 12.2 and 12.3 are internal documents compiled by research directors during the period of our study that illustrate the prevailing degree of preoccupation with *Institutional Investor* rankings. At one investment bank, it was desirable but not obligatory to be *II*-ranked to become a director; to reach the next level, first vice president, an analyst was *required* to be *II*-ranked, as exhibit 12.2 shows. At least one research head strategically reviewed his analysts' chances of being ranked and compared his firm's expected number of winners to those of other firms, as exhibit 12.3 shows.

Exhibit 12.2

Promotion Criteria for Analysts at a Leading Investment Bank

Global Securities Research & Economics

Recommended Criteria for Promotion

Overview

Recognition titles can be broadly defined as follows.

Assistant Vice President: an analyst who still needs to develop expertise and credibility, but who has demonstrated good analytical skills, good judgment, a level of expertise in his/her industry or specialty, and who has exhibited the potential, and ambition, to become a senior analyst.

Vice President: an analyst who has demonstrated in-depth knowledge of his/her specialty/industry, who has earned the confidence of the market, demonstrated excellent analytical skills and earned the recognition of clients as a result of the analyst's contributions and recommendations.

Director: an analyst who has become a recognized expert in his/her field, *may be II ranked,* has become a spokesperson for the firm, has greatest exposure to top-tier clients, generates revenue for the firm and is relied upon by internal client groups. This individual may also supervise a team of analysts. [emphasis added]

First Vice President: an analyst who has achieved the highest level of recognition, is well-known to both internal and external clients, as well as the media, *is II ranked*, and making significant contributions to the firm. This person has managerial responsibility for a team, a sector, or a region. [emphasis added]

Source: A research director.

Exhibit 12.3

Lehman Brothers' Competitive Analysis of Likely Numbers of Ranked Analysts at Each Firm

Confidential—For Internal Use Only

MEMORANDUM

Date:	July 17, 1991
To:	Jack Rivkin
From:	Fred Fraenkel
Subject:	*II* Projections

	Slb	Gs	Mer
Start #	48	46	44
Lost	5	2	1
Gains	3	2	3
Subtot	46	46	46
Probable	+2	?	?
Total	48		

Source: Shearson Lehman Brothers; Slb = Shearson Lehman Brothers; Gs = Goldman Sachs; Mer = Merrill Lynch.

Attitudes toward the *II* Poll

Given the poll's stature as a contest, a public-relations tool, and a performance and compensation metric, it is unsurprising that the *II* rankings and supporting data elicited a spectrum of opinions on Wall Street. Steve Hash of Lehman Brothers argued that taking the poll seriously promoted behavior that firms wanted to encourage. "If you don't make the *II* polls an important priority for the department and for the individual analyst, you cater to mediocrity," Hash asserted. "You're playing to mediocrity by not caring about the polls."[18]

Other research directors expressed skepticism about ceding evaluation to an outside entity. Barry Tarasoff of Schroder Wertheim went even further: "I don't think that I, as a manager, can abandon my responsibility to evaluate my own people's contribution to our success."

Table 12.1

Attributes of *Institutional Investor* Ranked Analysts

		Positive commentary			
	Number of comments	Stock picks	Industry knowledge	Analysis	Stock focus
Advertising agencies	3	1	1	1	
Aerospace	4	2	3		
Airlines	4	2	2	1	
Autos and auto parts	5	1	3	2	2
Banks – money center	5	2	1	2	
Banks – regional	5	2	1	3	1
Beverages	5		1	2	
Biotechnology	3	1	1		
Broadcasting	5	4	1	2	
Building	5	2	2	3	1
Cellular	4	1	1	3	
Chemicals	3	1		2	
Chemicals – fertilizers	4	2	2	3	1
Chemicals – specialty	5	3		2	1
Coal	3	1	1	2	
Cosmetics	6	1	1	3	
Defense electronics	4	1	1	1	1
Electrical – consumer	5	3	2	1	
Electrical – equipment	5	4	1	3	
Electronics	4	3		1	
Electronics – connectors	3	2			2
Engineering and construction	3	1		2	1
Financial services	5	5		1	1
Food	3	1		2	1
Games and lodging	3	1		2	
Gold mining	3	2	1	1	
Govt. sponsored enterprises	3	3	1		
Healthcare services	5	3	1	2	1
Household products	4	2		2	2
Inf. Tech. – mainframe	5	2		3	2
Inf. Tech. – midrange syst.	5	4		2	
Inf. Tech. – pers. comp.	4	2		1	1
Inf. Tech – software	4	3	2	1	
Insurance – life	3	3	1	2	
Insurance – nonlife	5	3	1	1	

				Negative commentary			
Industry focus	Non-consensus	Reports	Service	Late/wrong	Estimates	Service	Invest. banking
	1	1					
			1	1			
	1	1		1	1		
	1	1		2			
	2				1		1
	2			1			
1	1	1	3	1			1
	1	1	1				
	1	1		1		1	
1		1	3	3	1		
1		1	2				1
2		1	2	1			
4		2	5				
1	1	1	2	1			
2	1	1		1			
	1		2	2			
1			1				
1	1	1	2	4		1	1
				1		1	
2	1	1	1	2			
1			2	1			1
	2		2				
2	1	2		2			1
			1	1			
1		1					
	1						
1							
	1		1				
	1		1	1		1	
1	1	2	3	2		1	
2		1	1	1	1	1	
2			1	1			
1		1	1	2			
			2				1
2	3						2

(continued)

Table 12.1

Attributes of *Institutional Investor* Ranked Analysts *(continued)*

	Number of comments	Positive commentary			
		Stock picks	Industry knowledge	Analysis	Stock focus
Leisure time	5	2		1	
Machinery	3	3	2	1	1
Medical supplies and Tech.	5	1	2	3	2
Natural gas	5	1		1	
Nonferrous metals	4	2			
Oil – domestic	5	4		1	
Oil – exploration	3	1	1	3	1
Oil – international	5	3		1	1
Oil services and equipment	5	3	1	2	3
Packaging	3	3		2	
Paper and forest products	4	2	2	1	
Pharmaceuticals	4	1			1
Photography and elect. imaging	3	3		1	
Pollution control	5	1	1	1	1
Publishing	4	2		3	
Railroads	5	1	1	3	1
Restaurants	3	3		1	2
Retailing	5	2		2	1
Retailing – food and drug	5	1	1	3	1
Retailing – specialty	3	1	1		1
Savings and loan	4	1	1		1
Steel	4	2	3		1
Telecommunications equipment	5	5		1	
Telecommunications Service	4	2			2
Textiles and apparel	4	4	1	2	
Tires and rubber	4	2	1		2
Tobacco	5	2	2	2	
Trucking	5	2	3	1	1
Utilities	4	3	1	1	1
Multi-industry	4	2	2	2	1
Small growth companies	4	3		2	
Total	276	142	58	100	43
		25.2%	10.3%	17.8%	7.6%

Source: Compiled by a research director by analyzing clients' quoted rationales for voting for individual analysts, extracted from *Institutional Investor*, October 1991.

Industry focus	Non-consensus	Reports	Service	Negative commentary			
				Late/ wrong	Estimates	Service	Invest. banking
	1		1	1			
			2	2	1		
2		1	1				
2	1	1	1	2			
	1	1	1	1			
2	1		1	3			
2	1			2			
1	2			2			
	1	1				1	1
2		1	2				
1			1	1			
2	1	2	1	1			
		1		1		1	
2				2			
1		1				1	
2				1	1		
1		1		2			
1		2	1	1		1	
2	1	2	2	2		1	
		1		2			
	1						
			1	1			
1			1	3			
1			2				
2	1	2	1	1	1	1	1
	1	1	2	1			
1			3			1	
1	1	3		2		1	
3		3		2	1	1	
2		2	1	2			
1		2	2	2			
64	39	50	67	73	8	15	11
11.4%	6.9%	8.9%	11.9%	68.2%	7.5%	14.0%	2.0%

Table 12.2

**A Research Director's Summary of Clients' Quoted Rationales
for Voting for Individual Analysts**

Research

　　Very detailed research

　　Being right about stocks

　　Adds something to what is common knowledge

　　Constant flow of written and oral work

　　Knows companies inside and out

　　Good and accurate numbers

　　Knows lots of management and insiders so gives objective evaluation of company

　　Talks to companies weekly

　　Not afraid to change mind

　　Excellent knowledge of numbers and cash flow—does not take numbers at face value

　　Carefully documents reasons for changing ratings and monitors trends

　　Covering stocks that nobody else covers

　　Level-headness (relating to valuation)

　　Does tons of research

　　Impacts of macro factors on companies

　　Quick to find new information and make rating changes

　　Keeps crunching numbers to get estimates within $0.05

　　Sounding board for management

　　Uncovers hidden gems

　　Reads management like a book

Marketing

　　Aware of client needs

　　Accessible

　　Conference calls after Quarterly Releases and company trips

　　Persistently calls clients

　　Returns calls quickly

　　Conferences

　　One-stop shopping

　　Writes the best, in-depth, thoughtful pieces regularly

　　Writing makes company sound interesting

　　Works harder and talks to more people than anyone

　　Keeps clients current on stock all of the time

　　Sends faxes received from companies out to clients

　　Sends personalized letters to clients every few weeks with rundown of recent events

　　Monthly dinners that bring management and investors together

　　Makes trading calls

　　Smothers clients with service—in-depth and frequent company reports

　　Is THE one to call on a particular company

Source: Compiled by a research director by analyzing clients' quoted rationales for individual analysts, extracted from *Institutional Investor*, October 1991.

The Client-Vote System

Most research departments received client votes—the results of periodic polls at buy-side firms about sell-side analysts' work, used to allocate trading commissions—from the buy-side clients that disseminated votes, but not all research directors scrutinized them. Firms that used client feedback as the performance metric relied heavily on the *II* rankings as the easiest and most encyclopedic measure. Some firms used *II* and client votes as complementary measures of clients' satisfaction; they processed direct client votes in such a way as to make them usable as a management tool.

As we saw in chapter 2, much of the influence of the *II* rankings arose from their position as a proxy for client voting and thus an indicator of how a bank's buy-side clients would distribute their commissions. The *II* polls, however, bypassed a number of methodological flaws in the client-vote metric. Though client voting was "a fairly accurate indicator of how clients distribute commission dollars around the Street," according to Management & Capital Partners,[19] it was less effective as a measure of individual analysts' performance. As a means of supporting research, the client-vote/commission system worked quite smoothly,[20] but trades themselves were not an accurate indicator of endorsement of a given analyst's work. A client firm did not necessarily pay for, say, a biotechnology analyst's research by trading biotechnology stocks with the analyst's firm; it was just as likely to trade in automotive or insurance stock. "We don't just measure trading activity," said Lisa Shalett of Sanford C. Bernstein, "because on a day-to-day basis there isn't a direct match. After all, we only cover 150 of the S&P 500's stocks. And so even if, let's say, Fidelity wants to direct commissions to us on a given day, they may not happen to be trading any stocks we cover on that day." Barry Tarasoff elaborated: "You do good work in IBM, [the client] doesn't necessarily pay you in IBM currency. He may pay you in Exxon currency." That is why correlating trading commissions in analysts' stocks with analysts' impact had limitations.

As a feedback system, furthermore, the client-vote system did not accurately represent the client base and did not standardize information. Until the late 1990s, only about fifty buy-side clients shared their votes with sell-side research departments, a number too small to be representative and reliable. Also, as Steve Balog pointed out, hedge funds rarely submitted votes: "With the increase of hedge funds, the percentage of money under management and commissions being generated by firms that don't do a broker poll is rising. And if hedge funds are more and more of the commissions, more and more of the commission flow is coming out of a dark space. It's only the traditional institutions—the Fidelities, the Alliances—that did this. Even then, you have tremendous variation. There are big institutions that didn't do a poll."

Institutional Investor surveyed far more institutions—more than three hundred in 1996 and over nine hundred in 2002—and thus captured more thoroughly, though less directly, the thinking of buy-side clients. Its more complete representation of the client base explains how *II* established itself so quickly as an arbiter of analyst talent.

Another feature of client votes that limited their utility was unstandardized information. Some buy-side firms compiled rankings quarterly, some semiannually, others annually. "Nobody gives information in the same form or fashion," said one insider. "While one firm might provide us with the number of votes for each analyst, another might just provide us with a list of analysts that have done a good job." Steve Buell elaborated: "Some are binary. They just say, 'This analyst was or was not recognized.' More and more of them are quantitative, giving a range of size of votes proportional to the impact the analysts had on the clients' investment process." As Mayree Clark of Morgan Stanley pointed out, "The problem with the client votes is that they look from the lens of that institution, and typically what they say is 'The following twelve analysts helped us.' But what they don't say is which twenty-four analysts *might* have helped us. And they don't say which twelve analysts *didn't* help us. So interpreting that data is very difficult."

Votes were only occasionally accompanied by explanations and commentary, and they never included direct comparisons to analysts at competing firms. Many clients voted on investment banks' equity operations as a whole without distinguishing analysts from sales and trading. Thus, the use of these periodic report cards to assess analysts' performance was problematic for research management. "What I'd really like is to see clients rank the drug analyst against all the other drug analysts, and rank the retail analyst against all the other retail analysts," said Steve Buell. "Hey, if they all did that, we wouldn't need *II*. Two very large mutual fund firms do this now. I'd love to see it become a standard practice."

Despite all these shortcomings, however, some research directors went to the trouble of standardizing and compiling client votes and used them to evaluate analysts' performance on the grounds that the votes represented the most direct feedback on what matters most: client impact and revenue generation. To correct for differences in metrics from client to client, research managements typically translated votes into tiers or quintiles. Mayree Clark of Morgan Stanley explained:

> We spent a lot of time developing [a system for standardizing client votes]. And it gave us a lot of strength in managing our people because we could tell them, "Yes, you're being effective," or "No, you're not." The difficulty in dealing with these very talented people is that typically, if they're good, they have a very high opinion of their ability, and they're often given feedback that helps them have a high opinion of themselves, but sometimes it's not the right feedback. It's the feedback from the actual accounts that matters, with all the positives and negatives factored into the equation in a balanced way. So we found it was really important to have an independent tool that would allow us to measure success.

Research directors who performed such comparisons reported high correlations between *II* rankings and client votes. "I find that our *II*-ranked analysts are highly concentrated among our best performers in client vote," said Steve Buell of Prudential. "It isn't that the clients are paying us because they're ranked. It's that they're ranked because the behaviors that get you paid are the behaviors that get you ranked."

Firms that paid attention to client votes could sometimes help analysts manage their time more strategically, such as by targeting the institutional investors where they had been receiving few votes. Though client votes rarely included detailed feedback on analysts, they did disclose the identity of the client firm. (The *Institutional Investor* rankings, by contrast, concealed clients' names, identifying them only by region and type; thus they offered less guidance about how to allocate analysts' time and effort.) Some research heads used this information to help analysts develop better business plans. Some analysts even used brokers' votes to initiate conversations with their buy-side counterparts about how to improve their performance. Finally, some client votes were solicited more frequently than *Institutional Investor*'s annual rankings.

Polling the Sales Force

To correct for the shortcomings of the client-vote system, some firms also periodically polled their sales forces about the impact of analysts' work on the clients that the salespeople knew best. (See exhibit 12.4 for an example of sales-force poll results.) This practice was most common at nonportability firms and those that emphasized in-house development.

Exhibit 12.4

Summary Sheet from Sales Questionnaire about an Analyst, Sanford C. Bernstein & Company

Sales Results

Rank out of:	21
Is client-focused	11
Research is useful in addressing issues that my PM clients are interested in	7
Research is useful in addressing issues that my analyst clients are interested in	9
Is responsive to short-term investment issues (i.e., "trading calls")	11
Provides clients with a longer-term roadmap for the sector	8
Written research is clear	11
Publishes primarily proactive research	5
Morning meeting presentations are clear	15
Afternoon meeting presentations are useful	7
Is responsive to my requests to contact my clients	11
Proactively contacts my clients	15
Is responsive to my requests for travel	9
Has strong relationships with my clients	10
Hosts useful conference calls	12
Is "visible" to the sales force (i.e., has enough research flow)	20
Handles PM client meetings well	4
Handles analyst client meetings well	3
Has a clear and useable marketing package	8
Is receptive to my feedback	10
Is receptive to clients' feedback	8
Uses the media effectively	16

Comments

Strengths

Smart; hard working; proactive; knowledge of sector; very nice guy
Background, industry knowledge, product knowledge
Right on money on his stocks; knows the medical aspects as well as
    anyone
Good thinker with well developed viewpoints

Industry experience helps him assure "expert/insider" role. Great Guy—
wants to help

Original research really appreciated by clients

Has a great presence, looks and sounds authoritative

Great with client meetings and calls

Suggested Improvements

Accelerate response time to news/events

Speaks too fast, not clear enough

Cover more companies

Needs to be "out there" more

Needs to be more client focused, has developed relationships better to
capitalize on his reputation for excellent work

Expand coverage, try to be more visible

More media exposure

Needs to be way more visible, more calls, more stocks more client service (voice blast?)

More calls and more product

Additional Comments

Underachiever due to poor task management and apparent lack of strategy to be #1, needs to get focused and could be great.

He goes in and out of visibility with the sales force—weeks go by and we
never hear from him.

"In an ideal world," said Barry Tarasoff, "I would ask all of our clients, hundreds and hundreds of clients, with some regularity—let's call it every six months—to tell me how much of the business they've done with us over the last six months was for the credit of each analyst. In our business that's not practical. So I've always believed in doing the next best thing, which is to ask the sales force to pretend for a minute every six months that they're the client and to give me the same information."

Sales-force surveys were thus intended as one more proxy for client votes, accompanied by more systematic feedback. Mayree Clark emphasized the competitive intelligence that sales-force polls can capture: "You have to know what kind of landscape your analysts are operating in, so you have to have good intelligence on how they're doing relative to their own competition. Because the sales force is out there competing with other sales forces, they tend to have quite a good sense of what all the competitive analysts were like."

Each research director who performed sales-force polls appeared to have come up with the idea and the mechanism independently; they tended to proudly describe the polls as a good solution to the problem of spotty client-vote data. Mayree Clark pointed out that the sales force could focus more specifically than *II* did on the clients whose effect on revenues was most decisive. Chris Kotowski of Oppenheimer described its sales poll similarly: "If the sales force thought an analyst was making a major contribution at an account, we would capture that. We had a fairly well-developed methodology."

Steve Buell of Prudential explained the mechanics of the process: "We go through an exercise every six months where all salespeople are asked, with respect to each of the large accounts they cover, to rank an analyst as a large, small, or unpaid resource. We do it for 250 to 300 accounts. We ask the salespeople, 'Is that analyst a major, minor, or unpaid resource for the last six months?' We weight that by size of account and rank the analyst. I think the best that we can hope for is the salesman who has covered the account for years says, 'He's big; he's small; he's not on the radar screen. Counterpart doesn't know him; knows him, doesn't like him; used to pay him but doesn't anymore; never paid him up 'til this year, but now he's a paid resource.'"

But star analyst Bonita Austin, who left Schroder Wertheim for Lehman Brothers, found gathering input from sales distinctly unfair and demotivating. Austin cited the sales-force evaluations as a key reason for her dissatisfaction.

> The institutional salesmen would rank each analyst on all their major accounts, and I think overall as well, and then the director of research would get back the surveys, and they would rank each analyst based upon the surveys that the salesmen sent back in. . . . Whatever the sales force wanted, you pretty much had to do, as an analyst at Wertheim, and there were a couple of salespeople that I had problems with. I didn't feel that they appreciated my product, and I didn't feel that they respected me as a person, and I didn't like working with them.

Use of Multiple Criteria

Some research directors incorporated an element of subjectivity in how they managed analysts.[21] As Lisa Shalett of Sanford C. Bernstein put it:

I think 80 percent of [bonus calculation] is very formulaic. . . . Here's the *II* rank; there's this, here's that, boom. Here's the regression line, and you're number seven, so you're seventh highest paid. I think that's 80 percent of it. I think that there's 20 percent where we say, "So-and-so, they're a key role model, they're a key cultural carrier. They represent everything that's going on." Yes, the guy has been here fifteen years; yes, maybe he's not the most aggressive. Maybe it's not as sharp as it was in some other year, but [to penalize him] would be a blow to the brand, to who we are in the marketplace, to the new junior people coming in.

Research directors at developmental and/or nonportability-oriented firms wanted to encourage collegiality.[22] Thus, they tried to collect information on teamwork and other institution-building activities. They were also unwilling to exclude sources of information that presented a rounder and more nuanced picture. While client impact was by far the most important factor in analyst compensation, the research directors, by and large, rejected what they considered a formulaic approach to compensation. Michael Blumstein of Morgan Stanley touched on all these arguments.

Morgan Stanley never paid formulaically, never had any formulas that if you make this rank in *II*, we're going to pay you this amount. The compensation philosophy . . . was a combination of quantitative and qualitative metrics, everything from "Did you make good stock calls?"—which is something that you can try to measure on a quantitative basis—to "What did you do for the greater good? Did you help with recruiting? Did you help with best practices? Did you help with training?" If you do things on a formulaic basis, people just watch the formula. As one of my colleagues used to say, you get what you measure. So if you're just measuring a few quantitative items, that's all people are going to focus on. Versus if you try to get people to do what's right in building the business, everyone together, I think you get better results. And so people knew that they were going to be measured and compensated based on a whole broad variety of metrics.

A flexible compensation process also allowed for reward of non-revenue-producing activities important to the future of the department, including recruiting, training, and management responsibilities. Mayree Clark described the three metrics Morgan Stanley used under her leadership.

The most important thing was investor impact, and the second most important thing was translating that into the commercial results of the firm. The third thing was contributing to the department in a broader way that led to the department becoming stronger. So when we were evaluating people for compensation purposes, we also looked at whether they're helping teach younger people, if they're taking on leadership responsibilities in the department of various kinds, if they were working well with other divisions, and so forth. And we developed a lot of different ways to measure those contributions across all those dimensions.

Steve Hash of Lehman Brothers used a culinary metaphor to describe his compensation approach.

All of that goes into what I call the lasagna, and compensation for an individual analyst at the end of the day is as much art as it is science. I can't tell you how many times research directors have tried to put a formulaic approach to it, and it fails more often than not. There's a lot of quantitative information that goes into the mix, but you've got to take into consideration how the sector is performing, how an individual is performing, what their expectations are, what's happening out in the market, et cetera, and being able to benchmark someone to the financial results of Lehman Brothers. The bottom line is: I could take you through a thousand different iterations, but if you try to put a quantitative calculation or formulaic approach to equity-research compensation, you'll be reasonably unsuccessful because it spits out results that are not accurate.

A flexible bonus-determination process also took into account competitive considerations such as what happened to analysts' compensation in hot sectors at other firms. A single instance of unusually high compensation at one firm might thus affect compensation at many firms.

Internal Tracking Data, Diagnosis, and Development of Analysts

The amount of data that research directors could have at their fingertips to help assess analysts' performance was remarkable. Many developmental firms used this information to manage and develop their analysts. Research departments' computerized control systems automatically recorded multiple features of analysts' activities and decisions: appearances at morning meetings, rate of publication, client contacts, ratings changes, buy and sell recommendations, and much more. Many hands-on research directors compiled and tracked—and sometimes disseminated throughout the department—comparative data on particular measures of input that they had pinpointed as significantly related to favorable outcomes.

"I have a report which I call the monthly activity report, which I circulate every month," said Barry Tarasoff. "So all the analysts can see what their levels of activity are relative to all the other analysts." Tarasoff echoed other research directors in his catalogue of all the data he captured.

> We measure the number of morning-meeting appearances. We measure the number of client conference calls, the number of reports, the number of pages, the number of First Call notes. We measure the number of times they change their opinions, the number of times they do squawks—a break-in during the day in which they talk over a microphone system to the entire organization about some breaking news event. We measure the number of blast voicemails that they do, outgoing phone calls that they make, the number of incoming phone calls they receive. We measure the number of days they spend on the road seeing clients, the number of non-deal road shows they cover, and the number of companies they follow. I use the activity figures as a diagnostic. If an analyst is not doing as well as he or I would like, the activity data help me understand where the problem might be. But they play no role in my measurement of an analyst's effectiveness—i.e., revenue generation. My two overarching principles are, one, reward results, not activity, and two, employ a system that is clear, fair, and objective to measure results.

Mayree Clark explained Morgan Stanley's method of tracking analysts' stock picking.

> We had a sophisticated system that looked at a passive portfolio for the analysts, which was just a collection of all the stocks they covered, equal weighted. The second basket, the active basket, was weighted by the stock ratings. We measured the performance of the passive portfolio versus the active portfolio, and we also measured the active portfolio versus the index. This was one of the elements in measuring investor impact.

Steve Einhorn, research director at Goldman Sachs, described a painstaking and transparent approach to measuring analysts' progress that took into account multiple metrics.

The analysts knew the items we were looking at, so there was no surprise, and they should know what they were, and we shared with them as much information as we could about the various metrics we used. For example, one would be their score by the equity sales force. Then we had various categories: frequency of research, quality of research, quality of conference calls, visits and trips, telephones. Each one of these had subcategories. Then we would have a kind of survey of the traders that the various analysts interacted with, in which we would ask about the analyst's flow of information, consistency of information, timeliness of information, et cetera. We would do the same thing for investment banking. We weren't interested in specific deals. We were interested in how the analyst aided investment bankers in understanding strategically the opportunities and risks surrounding the various industries they covered, and under that we'd have various categories as well. Then we had the outside surveys, we had *II*, we had Greenwich, we had Extel, we had *Financial World*—there were about eight different surveys that all ranked analysts, globally. We would look at those. Then we would look at client surveys directly and aggregate all of that. Then we had measures of productivity within the department: number of pages written, which by itself means nothing because it could all be junk, but then we would have a group that would read it for quality, and we would have how many industry pieces they did, how many global pieces they did with their counterparts, how many days marketing did they go domestically, how many days marketing did they go internationally, how many global marketing endeavors did they go on, what was the performance of their recommended stocks versus their universe and versus the market and versus the peer group? And I'm sure there were some others as well, but that's the bulk of them— and we would have, rightly or wrongly, scores for each one of these, recognizing you can't quantify everything, but to give the analysts an understanding and a sense of where they were doing well and where they weren't, and within the various dozen or so criteria what needed improvement. And that's how we reviewed them.

Clearly, research directors with an appetite for measurement could find themselves swimming in information. Some research directors went so far as to make these records public. Jack Rivkin, when he was head of research at Lehman Brothers, disseminated many of the analysts' statistics. He expected analysts to initiate at least 125 client calls per month, for example, and asked analysts to record their client contacts—outgoing calls, incoming calls, and visits—and anything significant they discussed. Copies of client-contact records were also entered into the departmental control system, which generated a report detailing analyst contacts. Everyone who accessed the system—analysts and salespeople alike—knew who was making calls to whom and how often. Salespeople began to use the report to pressure certain analysts to make more calls. "Once the report card on analyst contacts was electronically pinned up on a board," recalled Michael Skutinsky, head of information technology at Lehman Brothers' research department,

> all the analysts began trying to get to the front section of the rankings; no one wanted to be near the end. From the correlations between calls made and analyst ranking, it was obvious that analysts who were dialing the accounts were in fact dialing for success. People realized that, in trying to become a top analyst, you sell some steak and you sell some sizzle. You had to have good research to get client support, but talking to clients also helped. The analysts started asking one another: "How do you make so many calls? Where do you find the time?"[23]

One danger of collecting information on multiple criteria was overvaluing, even fetishizing, the data itself. Most research directors were aware of this risk and bent over backward to treat data as *indicators* of performance, not as proxies for performance itself. In Steve Balog's words: "What you're looking for is impact. Did you get on client-vote lists? Did you get on the *II* vote list? How is our commission market share? You look at all those other things—the calls, the reports, the travel, all that stuff—as the inputs that get you the impact. You could have an analyst with great stock picking and lousy sales-force votes. We had one of those; he walked on water. Lazy, lazy, but a good stock picker."

Despite this caveat, research directors who embraced the nature hypothesis—the view that you've either got what it takes or you don't—tended to see limited value in diagnosis and data mining. They relied heavily on *II* rankings, or a combination of *II* and sales-force polls, as performance evaluation. They were essentially content, in other words, to let the industry's reward system shape behavior, and not to invest a lot of time and effort in developing analysts, letting them figure it out for themselves on their own.

Steve Buell invoked a popular joke to illustrate a hazard of excessive dependence on data. "When I was a scientist, we often cited to each other the story about the drunk who is out at night looking for his keys under a lamppost," Buell recalled. "And somebody came along and said, 'Why are you looking here?' And he says, 'Because it's light here.' I think there is a tendency in science and in academia to measure what is readily measurable, and if it's the only thing you could measure readily, to place all possible importance on it. You're looking where there's light, not necessarily where there is valuable information that can help with the evaluation process."

This fable could be invoked by either side in the debate on the genesis of talent—nature or nurture—enacted by competing Wall Street research departments. Advocates of a hands-on nurturing style of management could fault their hands-off counterparts for looking only where the *II* spotlight was already pointed. Their hands-off counterparts could retort that it was foolhardy to make too much of some obscure correlation that your own flashlight happened to illuminate.[24]

Using Performance Data to Shape Behavior

Fundamentally different schools of thought about management of research were also manifested in research directors' interpretations of the fact that, as Management & Capital Partners' 2001 study put it, "the industry's reward system shapes analyst behavior."[25] Some portability-oriented departments were content to leave the shaping of behavior to market forces, but most hands-on research directors were not. They wanted to shape behavior themselves, in the interests of developing talent in-house, retaining that talent, and building particular kinds of departmental cultures. Internal tracking data in particular could equip the research director to align analysts' activities with the department's goals, and open dissemination of comparative data introduced an element of competition among noncompeting employees that served as a goad to performance. No one wanted to appear at the bottom of such lists. (These initiatives must be carefully managed. A spirit of healthy and good-natured competition can increase productivity, but it should not be allowed to undermine teamwork and collaboration.)

This outlook encompassed both compensation and measurement: what is rewarded undeniably shapes behavior, but so does what is measured. In other words, departments that asked their analysts to expend time and effort on idiosyncratic firm-specific activities had to use performance measures that gave weight to those activities; otherwise analysts would not invest in them. Nonportability firms like Schroder Wertheim, Sanford C. Bernstein, Bear Stearns, and Lehman Brothers used such internal criteria as whether an analyst participated in institution-building activities like hiring, mentoring, or leading a team. At Leerink Swann, a boutique firm that specialized in the health-care and biomedical industry, analysts were measured on their ties to the medical profession, such as the number of client calls they made accompanied by doctors and how well they leveraged MEDAcorp, the biomedical consulting branch of Leerink Swann that contracted with doctors.

Research directors at nonportability-oriented and developmental firms, by and large, methodically analyzed client votes and used their findings for performance enhancement. At some firms managers even convened analysts, salespeople, and traders to review the votes and discuss how to focus more attention on neglected clients. Analysts paired up with other analysts and their counterparts in sales and trading to discuss how to tackle difficult clients. Development-oriented firms also used client votes to give analysts feedback on their performance in the middle of the year. This was not easy to do, however, because the comments that accompanied client votes were typically less than explicit, and some were aggregated at the firm level.

The few portability-oriented but developmental firms tended not to collect internal data so assiduously for purposes of evaluating performance. But some did closely examine external data like client votes and *Institutional Investor* rankings to evaluate their analysts, identify trends, and respond nimbly to the market forces that those external data represented. In the late 1990s, for example, initiatives like visiting companies and organizing conferences at which clients could interact with CEOs became more decisive in winning client votes. This trend first became apparent to research directors who looked closely at client votes, identified the pattern, and fed it into the business model. DLJ was the prime example of a portability-oriented firm that worked at developing its analysts' general skills in this fashion: the skills that it promoted in its analysts were general, not firm-specific, but the firm was proactive about recognizing the skills that were important to the market and promoting and rewarding them. Many portability-oriented and nondevelopmental firms, by contrast, also received client votes but did not actively mine them for market intelligence.

The Performance-Review Process

Research directors who compiled and scrutinized multiple sources and types of data emphasized that the purpose of doing so was to identify winning strategies and to diagnose and tweak lackluster performance. Those who distinguished between compensation decisions and evaluation for purposes of development underlined the distinction by approaching the two processes separately. In their departments, evaluations were typically performed in June and December; decisions about the size of analysts' bonuses were also made at the end of the year, but the mid-year evaluations focused exclusively on development of the individual analyst's skills and on promoting behaviors that would create a better product. Barry Tarasoff explained how he used one survey to give analysts rich feedback about how the organization viewed various aspects of their performance.

> This survey asks for feedback from the salesmen on some areas of performance: diligence, effort, consistency, morning-meeting effectiveness, communication and marketing skill, quality of written product, investment judgment. I tally all those points and show the analysts what their rank is in the department. On, let's say, investment judgment, every six months the analyst gets a piece of paper from me that shows whether he was number 1 or number 30 in investment judgment over the last six months. That's valuable feedback for the analyst.

In essence, sales-force feedback and internal tracking data were used to *interpret* the analyst's standing in client votes and external polls: what the analyst was doing right and what was falling through the cracks. "What client votes do not specify," according to Management & Capital Partners' 2001 study, "are the particular behaviors and technical skills that result in receiving votes from clients. How can management guide analysts towards acquiring client votes if the reasons for obtaining them remain vague?"[26] The point of all the data was, in short, to pinpoint those reasons. Figure 12.3 shows data on one analyst compiled for purposes of a periodic performance review.

Steve Balog described the performance-review process as exploratory: "You have to go through the whole thing and try to make some guesses as to what the data mean." Steve Buell put it similarly: "We just look through for a signal. What do you do well?" Buell gave a couple of examples:

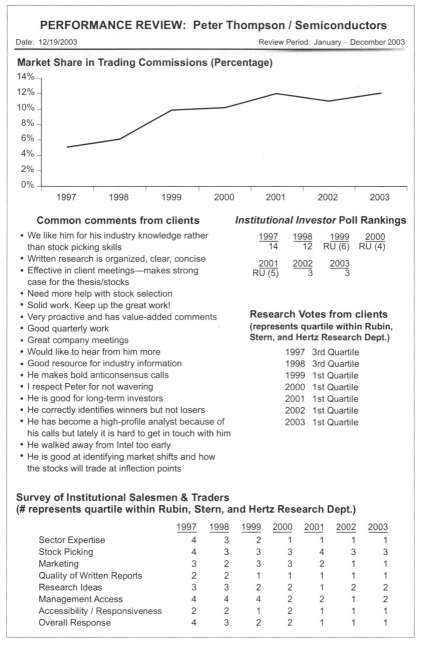

PERFORMANCE REVIEW: Peter Thompson / Semiconductors

Date: 12/19/2003   Review Period: January – December 2003

Market Share in Trading Commissions (Percentage)

(chart with y-axis from 0% to 14%, x-axis years 1997 through 2003)

Common comments from clients

- We like him for his industry knowledge rather than stock picking skills
- Written research is organized, clear, concise
- Effective in client meetings—makes strong case for the thesis/stocks
- Need more help with stock selection
- Solid work. Keep up the great work!
- Very proactive and has value-added comments
- Good quarterly work
- Great company meetings
- Would like to hear from him more
- Good resource for industry information
- He makes bold anticonsensus calls
- I respect Peter for not wavering
- He is good for long-term investors
- He correctly identifies winners but not losers
- He has become a high-profile analyst because of his calls but lately it is hard to get in touch with him
- He walked away from Intel too early
- He is good at identifying market shifts and how the stocks will trade at inflection points

***Institutional Investor* Poll Rankings**

1997	1998	1999	2000
14	12	RU (6)	RU (4)

2001	2002	2003
RU (5)	3	3

Research Votes from clients (represents quartile within Rubin, Stern, and Hertz Research Dept.)

1997	3rd Quartile
1998	3rd Quartile
1999	1st Quartile
2000	1st Quartile
2001	1st Quartile
2002	1st Quartile
2003	1st Quartile

Survey of Institutional Salesmen & Traders
(# represents quartile within Rubin, Stern, and Hertz Research Dept.)

	1997	1998	1999	2000	2001	2002	2003
Sector Expertise	4	3	2	1	1	1	1
Stock Picking	4	3	3	3	4	3	3
Marketing	3	2	3	3	2	1	1
Quality of Written Reports	2	2	1	1	1	1	1
Research Ideas	3	3	2	2	1	2	2
Management Access	4	4	4	2	2	1	2
Accessibility / Responsiveness	2	2	1	2	1	1	1
Overall Response	4	3	2	2	1	1	1

Figure 12.3. Performance review for Peter Thompson, 2003. *Source*: Research director. (Some information has been disguised.)

We share a wide range of information with analysts, including both where they stand in performance metrics and where they stand in productivity metrics. They come in: "I get excellent votes at key accounts but my overall ranking according to your metrics is low." "Well, yes, you do well at the ten accounts you talk to. But you're not talking to nearly enough accounts." And then an analyst comes and says, "I'm covering a lot of small companies. Why do they say I'm not covering enough small companies?" "Because you don't talk about them. You only talk about your two big stocks, and they don't think you do the little ones. You have to start to talk about those more, get more focus, write about those." So you have to go through the whole thing and try to make some guesses as to what the data mean and how to use the data to improve the overall penetration in the account base.

Steve Balog distinguished different kinds of mistakes on the analyst's part: "'You had a buy on this one but it was up 2 percent. This stock was up 50 percent and you were neutral on it.' That's an error of omission. 'A hot stock—you missed it.' . . . Or 'Your top pick was a disaster.' That's the worst thing—that's an error of commission: 'You picked the stock and it went down—you actually lost people money.' The next-worst thing is you're in a group that's hot and you're sitting on the sidelines going, 'I don't believe it.'"

Research directors also used data derived from client votes to pinpoint an analyst's strengths. There is more than one way to be a successful analyst: a research director might use industry knowledge as a guide with one analyst and stock-picking strength with another, depending on their individual strengths. Such data equipped research directors to initiate searching and forward-looking conversations with analysts. One research director explained:

> You tell him about his scores on all these different dimensions and try to explain that clients value him for industry knowledge and that is his competitive advantage. The data give you confidence to help someone to reposition his franchise. And continued data allow you to monitor their progress. If it's industry knowledge, "Let's figure out how many industry pieces you need to write, how many conferences you need to have, how many investor trips you need to make, how many CFOs you should take to investors. Let's come up with a short-

term and long-term plan and then measure its progress. Let's take a look at your ratings in six months, a year. What do we have to drop? What do we have to add?" The data make it more like a science. "You've made this many marketing trips. What is your impact?" If it's stock picking, "Here are the data. You have a tendency to give up on stocks that you recommended as buys. You take off your buys too early. Why? Here are the data saying that over the last three years, six out of seven stocks have increased in value 50 percent the month after you gave up on them. Let's figure out why. Let's put [together] a business plan that works just for you!"

Business Plans

The ultimate product of data-based performance management at several firms was an individual business plan for the subsequent period, devised jointly by the analyst and the research director using the analyst's responses to a questionnaire or template. The plan typically specified activity levels to correct shortcomings in the analyst's immediate past performance. (See exhibit 12.5 for a memo soliciting analysts' draft business plans.) Steve Buell described the thinking behind individual business plans:

> We provide a ton of data, and we use those to develop hypotheses
> as to what would be the best thing to do in the next six months
> to improve an analyst's performance on the client vote next time
> around. My approach to the semiannual review is generally to devote
> about 20 percent of the time to past performance and 80 percent to
> specific future plans to enhance future performance. It isn't enough
> to say, "I think you're underperforming in the client vote. You better
> do better next time." We go through all those metrics and, basically,
> I take the risk. I say, "I think these are the two things you need to do
> to improve your standing. If you do those two things and you don't
> improve, I'll take the hit. But that's what we're going to focus on for
> the next six months." The analysts, by and large—both those who are
> starting out and those who have been at it fifteen to twenty years—
> are quite responsive to that sort of focused business plan, as opposed
> to a general "You better do better next time."

Exhibit 12.5
Memo on Business Plans, Sanford C. Bernstein, 2001

BERNSTEIN INSTITUTIONAL SERVICES—MEMORANDUM

To: U.S. Analysts

From: Lisa Shalett

Date: November 20

re: Business Plans for Next Year

Each year we endeavor to measure the progress of our respective franchises and set/reset our goals for the following year in written business plans to ensure that we remain focused. Like the companies we follow, our competitive strategies for success are often only as good as the analysis that has gone into formulating them. In that spirit, this year, we have collected a series of metrics that we hope may give you insight into your franchise.

These "Franchise Progress" books include data on the following dimensions:
- 2001 Product/Business Plan goals: Coverage and any outstanding product commitments
- Research Productivity and Proactivity (through Oct.)
- Stock Picking and Recommendations
- Sales force/Trading survey feedback (Trading feedback will be available on Wed. Nov. 21)
- Marketing Trips/Services Productivity
- Client Research Vote Penetration (Top 60 domestic accounts, Middle Market and Int'l to follow)
- External Poll showings (*II*, Greenwich, Reuters)

Although there is no single recipe for success—and the most critical element of any strategy is the degree to which it fits your own personal predilections and strengths and weaknesses—we believe that thinking through your approach on these dimensions is broadly helpful.

After you have had a chance to digest this, please begin to prepare your 2002 business plans and have them to me by Wednesday, December 12. While I am available any time to work with you on them, we will have official one-on-one meetings to discuss them the week of December 17. As in prior years, the plans should include the following:

1. *Franchise positioning.* What franchise positioning do you have, and what are you driving for?

2. *Franchise goals.* What are your goals for your franchise this year? How will you measure your success?

3. *Commitments for new company launches and blackbooks.* Blackbooks are the single best product we produce, one that sets us notably apart from our competition. You should aim for at least two blackbooks a year; in addition to the launch tomes that they historically have been, they should also take the form of issue-oriented pieces of no more than 30 pages.

4. *Ideas for Long Views.* Each analyst will be asked to produce at least two Long View notes a year. These notes are unique in that they should have a longer-term perspective than most of our work and allow you play with issues that will be/may be important over time but which are just surfacing as investable issues.

5. *Use of proprietary research.* The proprietary research we do is strongly in demand by our clients and can be highly value-added to their investment process. In your plans, please propose at least one major proprietary project, such as a survey, a focus group or market research, that will work to illuminate one of the key controversies in your sector.

6. *Targeted marketing objectives.* Where can you strengthen your client relationships? Please target a few of our most important accounts, where your relationship is not as strong as it could be, and work to establish or improve the relationship. Strategies can include calling much more often, inviting the client(s) to management meetings and field trips, establishing more of a personal relationship, etc.

7. *Other marketing events.* According to data from the *Institutional Investor* vote, the second most important factor in voting for an analyst (after Industry Knowledge), is Special Services, which includes setting up management meetings, conference calls, etc. In general, this is an area in which we have lagged. Please lay out plans for at least one client/management trip or conference call during the year.

8. *A monthly calendar.* Please (realistically) map your research and marketing priorities against a monthly calendar, allowing for marketing weeks and earnings periods.

Michael Blumstein of Morgan Stanley emphasized a specific component of business-planning sessions: "When I was research director, we would specifically ask people in their business-planning sessions, 'What kind of proprietary content [reports] do you plan to develop this year?' And so we would have something at the end of the year where we could look back and see what people said at the beginning of the year they were going to do."

Steve Hash described hammering out the business plan as an opportunity to tweak analysts' work habits and to encourage and energize them:

> It allows you to influence the way you think they should be behaving without having to be really aggressive. It becomes "Here's your business plan. I might tweak it these two or three different ways: move these numbers up, do a few more non-deal road shows, cover some more of the big-cap names. And why don't you launch an industry conference?" It's a tool that allows you to work with this person to help them build a franchise. You sit down in the middle of the year for an hour and a half and go through it, and you sit down at the end of the year and go through it again. And that gives you the opportunity to say, "You've done a really good job here, here, and here. You still need to work on this or that."

Hash pointed out that meetings constructed around business plans are also an opportunity for the research director to do one-on-one "internal marketing."

> You're also doing a little bit of selling. Some of the analysts used to say, "I'd go to my year-end review and I'd come out all pumped up about Lehman," because I'd be selling what we're going to do and how we're going to win. It gets them excited to achieve. Stress the positive, make people feel good about what they're doing, and then say, "If you really want to get to the next level—and we need you to cover more companies or need you to be top-ranked or interact with the trading floor more—I need to see this happen over the next six to twelve months. But you've done a great job on these other things, so let's go get 'em." When you're dealing with star performers, who are overeducated, overachieving, approval-seeking people, a negative and harsh response generally just does not get you the great results.

Steve Balog emphasized that business plans should be mutually negotiated by the research director and the analyst, and that their effect on compensation should be direct and fair:

It's not fair to say to somebody at the end of the day, "Well, I'm not paying you as much as I would have" or "I'm cutting your compensation because you didn't do a group project." "Where does it say group project on my business plan? It doesn't say group project on there." You have to agree to it at the beginning of the year. Otherwise you can't compensate on something that's not there. It's like changing the rules on the guy. So it has to be in there, and they have to sign off on it. But they don't get to just freelance their business plan. The business plan is the most important tool to guide someone, so you say, "There's a form. Fill out these questions and answer this stuff: What stocks are you going to pick up? What industry piece are you going to do? What group project are you going to do?" And anything else. They get to say, "I'm not doing that." You review that business plan at the beginning of the year. You look at them all, talk about them, the person walks you through it all, and then say, "I'm not accepting your business plan, because you don't have anything for the group. Forget it. Go back and rewrite this. Give me something, because this is important."

Challenges for Firms

Trade-offs between Incentives and Perceptions of Fairness

All the research directors we interviewed reported very high ratios in their departments between the extremes of total compensation (salary plus bonus) and between top and average compensation.[27] High disparity might pose a threat to the perception of equity if the process of determining compensation is perceived as opaque, unfair, or subjective. Such perceptions can sap motivation and play havoc with a sense of teamwork and shared enterprise.[28] Research directors were acutely aware that compensation is a delicate balancing act. "When you get someone that far outside, relative to the averages, it's a demotivator for others," Steve Hash commented. "But that said, you also want to skew, as we call it, to incentivize. You want to skew because you want people to be hungry and do a great job. I want [an up-and-comer] to say, 'I'm going to be the next [big star]' right? 'I'm working hard, and I want to make as much money as he does.' So you want to incentivize people. . . . You also have to be careful, because it can be a demotivator if people don't view that they have enough opportunity to get to the higher levels of compensation."

Research directors at nonportability-oriented firms appeared to be particularly sensitive to questions of fairness and distribution, fearing that too extreme a compensation spread would hurt collaboration and teamwork: analysts would feel that they were in competition with one another to get to the top, rather than working together for the good of the company.[29]

Quantitative data bore out this apparent relationship between salary compression and nonportability for senior analysts. The maximum-to-minimum and maximum-to-average compensation ratios were 86 percent and 62 percent higher at the portability-oriented firms than at the nonportability oriented firms.

Developing and Retaining Talent in the Face of External Offers

The *Wall Street Journal* reported in 1991 that three factors largely determined analysts' pay: the *II* rankings, the results of the sales-force survey, and job offers from competitors.[30] Larry Fraser of Management & Capital Partners, discussing his firm's survey of compensation practices, asserted his belief that competing job offers still heavily influenced compensation:

> Up until very, very recently, demand was the number-one driver of compensation. The way prices, in my opinion, have been set is the market. Most research directors, among the first things they would do, if not the first thing, upon learning that they had to fill a chair, would be to open the magazine [*Institutional Investor*]. Literally. So an analyst is making $1 million at Firm A. Our client comes along: "We love you, we love you. We will pay you $1.5 million." "Oh, that's great. That sounds wonderful. I'd love to come. Let me go resign. . . . Oh, guess what? My firm now wants to pay me $1.5 million also." Did that person really change in value to Firm A? That rate of acceleration is unnatural to the economics because the economics obviously are deteriorating—certainly not increasing—at those levels. Same analyst, same chair, same work, same everything, except the price went up. . . . My whole thesis is that lateral demand—meaning one firm coveting another firm's analyst—is the single biggest driver of compensation. Not something that's intrinsic, but external demand, and supply being exceeded by demand. Because there's only one per-

son, you know—Joe Smith, at whatever firm—and if someone else wants him, then there's two buyers.

Steve Balog, describing an earlier era when compensation was lower, spelled out the effect of an overheated market for analysts on in-house development of talent:

> People's value in the open market rose faster than the organization could monetize. Let's say we brought a person earning $100,000 at a little regional firm into our firm at $220,000. A year later, if he panned out, he'd be an All-Star runner-up and he'd be earning $350,000. By then, the market knew he was an up-and-comer and offered him, say, $550,000. We were faced with a tough choice: should we pay to keep him, or should we go through the whole cycle again and grow another All-Star?[31]

Larry Fraser pointed out that, according to his firm's studies, "There are clearly certain firms that systematically acquire and keep labor at a below-median price and are more efficient than others. That's where the culture of the business comes in. The firms that have to do more lateral recruiting and are more likely to have to go to the outside actually are more likely to have higher labor prices. Firms that hold onto their players longer don't have to pay as much per head because you get a home-field advantage."

Steve Einhorn from Goldman Sachs explained how his firm was able to retain star analysts even in the face of competitive job offers. First, he explained, a good performer stood an excellent chance of making partner at Goldman Sachs.

> Second, a lot of people at Goldman Sachs understood that their achievement to some extent rested on the platform Goldman Sachs provided and that Goldman Sachs was committed to them and to research. So while we may not have been the absolute top payers, there was more of a sustained commitment to the various research people, more of a security, if you will, in the good sense. And I think that explains part of the reason why analysts were willing to take compensation somewhat below the very top of the competition. The third reason, I think, is the department could see other firms operate, where there would be an analyst there, and all of a sudden a top-ranked *II* person would become available, and bingo, the first person would be fired, and the firm would hire the top-rated *II* person. So there wasn't a commitment. If someone came along better, many firms just

said, "Well, fine. This person's better. You're gone." We didn't do that at Goldman Sachs. And I think the Goldman Sachs franchise helped. Analysts truly enjoyed and enjoy working with other bright people in trading, in investment banking, in sales. And Goldman Sachs was prominent and dominant, for example, in investment banking, IPOs, and mergers and acquisitions. The analysts had an opportunity to work on very interesting transactions within the banking context or the trading context that they wouldn't have had at other places, and that also encouraged them to remain. So I think all of those go into why we didn't need to be the absolute top payer, though we were very competitive in terms of compensation.

Steve Balog described the home-field advantage as real but also as under enormous pressure from competing offers: "We were able to kind of hold it together by waving our arms and saying, 'Look at the good fun we have here,' and all this stuff, and the loyalty that was created, because you did help them, you did bring them from nowhere to your big platform and you did make an investment in them. But at some point that wears out."[32]

Still, the cost of labor was higher to firms that bought talent developed elsewhere. In Steve Hash's words:

> We tend to believe the margin is about 20–25 percent—meaning that if the market rate for what we believe is the fair value of an analyst covering semiconductors is $1 million and you develop your own, you'll get to a point where you're paying them $1 million. If you have to go hire that person, you might have to pay $1.2–1.3 million to get him. We call it the premium to get someone to leave another firm. You're always paying your own people a little bit less, something less than what it would cost to hire that same person on the open market.

Hash's estimate appeared to be accurate. Using compensation data from one top-ten investment bank, we matched the twelve stars hired over the nine years of our study, 1988–96, with similar stars already employed by the firm. (The two groups were matched by year of hire, rank, and number of years ranked.) On average, we found, outside hires were acquired at a premium of 23.3 percent over the compensation of existing stars.

Larry Fraser made a point similar to Hash's from a different angle: "What firms rely on for comfort is knowing that they will get what I'll call the last look—that even if they think they're under the market slightly, that it's OK, the guy won't just come in and walk out. He'll tell us what's going on, and we can always fix it then. So why proactively fix it now?" Fraser then approached the question more abstractly: "The pricing of labor is not homogeneous across firms. It begins with its point of acquisition, and certain firms are more inclined to grow their own, as opposed to those firms that are more active in the external labor market on Wall Street. The starting point of labor obviously affects the overall prices of labor in the department."

Steve Balog spoke vividly of the tendency at some banks to overvalue analysts, underplay the bank's own role in making that analyst successful, and worry excessively about losing a star:

> Back when we had Shearson Lehman Hutton—the biggest, huge retail force—electric-utilities analyst Ed Terello would say, "Look at all these commissions we're doing on my stocks! We're huge in these stocks. I should get paid a lot of money." And when Ed Terello quit, he said Fred [Fraenkel] had told him, "We could put a monkey in your chair and we would do big commissions in this. We have fifteen thousand retail stockbrokers. They're going to do commissions in retail. You've got to look at what your market share is above our natural market share." So, when Ed quit, everyone said, "Why are you quitting, Ed?" "Well, Fred called me a monkey." And Fred had to talk around that so many times: "I didn't call him a monkey. I told you, Ed, a monkey in the electric-utility analyst chair makes a lot of commission, you know. They do a lot of commission in stocks."

Profitability Analysis

Differences in Value by Sector

Two analysts at the same firm with identical *II* rankings might not have been compensated equally. Analysts who covered industries with large market capitalization favored by the market and thus covered by many other firms would be paid more. This was a matter partly of the magnitude of the business that covered stocks in the sector generated for the firm and partly of enhanced competition for skilled analysts in the sector.

"In addition to paying according to a fair internal performance-based economic metric, we need to superimpose on that the market price for that analyst," said Steve Buell of Prudential. "There are certain sectors where analysts command a much higher level of pay than others. I would cite biotech and medtech as sectors where pay scales are generally on the high side; industrials and utilities are often at the lower end of the market pay scale."

"Groups have different values to the business," Steve Balog agreed. "Coal is worth a lot less than pharmaceuticals or semiconductors or banks." According to Balog, this was a fact of life that analysts understood and accepted: "They know that some industries are worth more to a firm than others. They know that quarterbacks make more money than linemen in football."

At times "linemen" suffered cuts so that the "quarterbacks" could be retained and compensated according to their market value. Steve Hash spelled out the point by referring to two Lehman Brothers stars, one in financial institutions and the other in autos:

> Those are two monster sectors. They're both number-one-ranked in multiple categories. They both manage teams which are ten people, and their franchises are identified with Lehman Brothers. They generated a lot of business in many different ways to Lehman Brothers. So for me to go to [the financial analyst] and say, "Well, things have gotten tough on Wall Street, et cetera, and, you know, equity business is down 20 percent, so you're getting paid down 20 percent," that's probably not fair relative to the value that he contributes. Whereas in the same year, an auto analyst—who may be successful, but the sector just has no comparable value, and that person isn't adding a lot to the value—you may take them down more so that [the financial analyst] doesn't need to get paid down.

Such practices could of course be demoralizing to analysts in smaller industries, requiring research directors to motivate them in other ways. Hash went on to describe how he maintained the motivation of analysts in out-of-favor industries by offering them opportunities to enlarge the scope of their franchises:

> Will you ever be able to pay an auto analyst as much as you can pay a semiconductor analyst? Probably not, right? So to make sure you're not demotivating that person, you have to go to the auto analyst and say, "OK, well, this obviously isn't a sector that's going to be as dynamic as the [financial institutions] group." Say, "Well, why don't we try to build out a franchise where you'll have autos and auto parts and machinery. Then maybe you'll have an opportunity." So you

want to be giving them the chance to win. When people feel like they can't win, that's a huge demotivator.

Linking Individual Compensation with Value to the Firm in the Twenty-First Century

By 2005 firms were beginning to look more strategically at which sectors add value and where they should build up or downsize coverage. They were also developing new ways of assessing the actual value generated by individual analysts. It became increasingly possible, at least conceptually, to calculate compensation based on an analyst's actual value to the company rather than the most recent offer for his or her services from a competing firm. Larry Fraser reported that some research departments had begun using new analytic tools to rationalize compensation by linking it to revenues:

> In most research departments, while they had many metrics to evaluate performance, the understanding of how much each firm wants to pay for an analyst was not particularly linked to any market base—meaning their customers, meaning the revenue opportunity. There was very limited profitability analysis being done. In a world of supply and demand, most of the brokerage firms did not have the capacity to measure the analyst's contribution. They didn't say, "We've got to pay Joe $2 million because his work is worth $2.5 million and we want to get a 25 percent return on our analyst." They didn't have any of that information. They just now, in the last year or two [2004 and 2005], have been developing all these tools to try to do that and to attribute the time and effort and output of an analyst and create some sort of monetary equation. It never is going to be that precise. But what they are doing is figuring out "If Fidelity is going to pay us $7 million, how do we make sure that it doesn't cost us more than $7 million?"

Fraser acknowledged the greater difficulty of assigning precise value to analysts' work at firms with more irons in the fire but observed that such firms were nonetheless making efforts to do so: "Firms in general are getting better at this, are more able to set an intrinsic valuation and stick within reason. Most of the big firms are rapidly evolving methodologies to measure the cost of analysts' time. They have to decide how many visits, and where this person spends their time, and on what kind of accounts, and so on, on the costing side. And on the pricing side, they're starting to have a better idea—it may not be to the penny, but I think they have a better idea of what this person is worth, and what's it worth to keep the person in their chair."

☆ ☆ ☆

Assessment practices at nonportability and portability firms differed considerably. Nonportability firms used more metrics to measure a wider variety of behavior. They did not ignore external metrics like client votes or *II* ratings, but they often used internal assessments and measures of activity as well, on the grounds that the market could not be expected to understand their particular needs and idiosyncratic products. These metrics were used for both skill development and performance management. Inevitably, the internal metrics were more subjective than external metrics, and in most cases nonportability firms' compensation policies were less formulaic and allowed for more managerial discretion.

Because of the more subjective nature of nonportability firms' assessment processes, it was essential that their analysts trust the inputs to be accurate and the process to be transparent and fair.[33] The assessment practices typical of nonportability firms might have helped maintain culture and retain good performers, but they were more labor-intensive. Research directors at such firms spent far more time administering management systems: one research director who had worked at both types of firms estimated that a director at a nonportability firm would spend as much as 75–80 percent more time on compensation than a counterpart at a portability firm. This additional time was spent not just administering the process but also defending and explaining it to analysts. Nonportability firms were under constant pressure, from other firms and from their own analysts, to base compensation solely on market measures away from firm-specific ones. Firm-specific compensation processes carried a much higher risk of provoking discontent if analysts lost faith in their fairness.[34] Even at the best-managed nonportability firms, some analysts were unhappy with the more subjective, firm-specific aspects of the compensation process.

Research director Barry Tarasoff explained the importance of maintaining fair and objective standards of compensation:

> I believe that compensation systems have to have three characteristics to be effective. They have to be clear—and what I mean by clear is there can be no ambiguity about what people get paid for. They have to be fair, which is self-explanatory. And they have to be objec-

tive. What I mean by objective is that no matter who is sitting in my chair, the director of research's chair, the outcome of the process ought to be largely the same. There ought to be enough objective input so that the guy who is sitting in the chair doesn't have a huge influence over the outcome.

Analysts watched compensation decisions carefully. Ultimately, the amount of the bonus might have been an incentive to stay as well as the belief that the contributory inputs and process were fair and nonpolitical and that the firm was committed to its analysts' success over the long term.

13 | Lessons from Wall Street and Elsewhere

We began twelve chapters ago by asking what a systematic look at the career moves of a group of star knowledge workers could tell us about the concept of high-performing free agents with perceived portable talent, and about human-capital theory's thesis that general human capital is portable from one employer to another while firm-specific human capital is not.

Researchers look at portability for two reasons, one descriptive and one prescriptive. The descriptive goal is to use portability of performance as a way of examining the nature and sources of exceptional performance. The degree to which individual performance is portable and the circumstances in which it is portable hold the promise of telling us something fundamental about that performance. The prescriptive goal is to offer applicable insight to firms about how to acquire, motivate, retain, and compensate talented employees, and to individuals about how to manage their capabilities, resources, and opportunities. In both instances, mobility is a phenomenon that offers a window into the nature of knowledge-based work, and portability is the applicable metric.

We found that exceptional performance was more context-dependent than is explicitly recognized by star performers or their employers. The overall decline in performance that accompanied star analysts' career moves demonstrates that the loss of firm-specific resources and relationships has a

detrimental effect. But it is the nuances in our findings that are most revealing and suggestive. The picture is not murky, but it cannot be condensed to a
simple formula: it is insufficient merely to assert that general human capital
is portable or that firm-specific human capital is not portable. There is far
more to be said about both points. Our findings are still a work in progress,
and they raise some intriguing new questions to pursue. But the insight they
offer into the factors that govern portability of job performance can potentially contribute to sound strategizing about competitive advantage and
priorities on the part of organizations and to clearer thinking about career
choices on the part of individuals.

Chapter 2 enumerated several reasons why Wall Street equity analysts
represented a near ideal population among whom to study portability. Another reason, which did not become apparent until we had analyzed our
data, is that the profession of equity analysts was one in which successful
individuals could acquire extensive firm-specific human capital—or virtually none. The route an individual took depended on the orientation and
offerings of his or her employer and on the interaction between the employer's characteristics and the employee's personal inclinations and career
strategies.

Wall Street research departments' strategies of hiring, development, retention, and compensation clustered into two broad categories: portability-
oriented firms that emphasized reliance on general skills and nonportability-
oriented firms that invested in their employees' firm-specific human capital
and encouraged them in turn to invest in the firm.

For both firms and individuals, there is more than one path to superior performance. But it is important to keep in mind as well that
firm-specific human capital, of whatever kind—unique systems, specialized training, collaboration, interaction with colleagues—is highly
likely to have performance-promoting value for those who possess it
(and who remain with the same employer). Firm-specific undertakings
require effort and investment on the part of the individual employee
and thus would not be pursued except in anticipation of a payoff in enhanced performance, compensation, and/or tenure. Firms that provide
these sources of firm-specificity, and hold forth the credible promise
of enhanced performance, compensation, and/or tenure for engaging in
them, can reap a powerful benefit: they can keep their star performers
imperfectly mobile and thus create a potential source of sustained competitive advantage.

Determinants of Portability

We identified a handful of factors that have a decisive impact on portability of performance. Let us review these findings as succinctly as possible in order to keep them all in mind simultaneously.

The relative quality of the two firms matters. Stars who moved to superior firms experienced no decline in short- or long-term performance relative to their counterparts who stayed put. Those who moved to weaker (less resource-rich) firms experienced the sharpest declines in performance.

The orientation of the employee's firm of origin matters. Stars who left portability-oriented firms that promoted general human capital performed just as well after moving as stars who stayed put. Those who departed from nonportability-oriented firms that offered their analysts customized resources, idiosyncratic processes, firm-specific training, unique culture, opportunities to work on special products, and encouragement to collaborate with colleagues saw their performance decline after moving.

The hiring and integration capacities of the new firm matter. The rate at which newly hired stars maintained their ranking or regained it within a year ranged from over 94 percent at the companies most adept at integration to a low of 17 percent.

The function an analyst is hired to perform matters. Stars hired to support existing capabilities (exploitation) performed far better than those hired to initiate coverage of a new sector (exploration).

Leaving solo or with a team matters. Analysts who changed employers along with teammates suffered no significant decline in short- or long-term performance relative to comparable star analysts who did not move. Those who moved solo performed less well.

Gender matters. Women's post-move performance surpassed men's.

Finally, it merits repeating that, portability aside, outstanding performance owes a good deal to the quality and culture of the firm.

These findings do not readily lend themselves to further reduction, but the interactions among them remain to be further explored. We can safely say that institutional factors—the orientation, resources, relative quality, and managerial adeptness of both the firm of origin and the destination firm—play a highly influential role in the achievement of superior performance in the first place and in the subsequent portability of that performance. But these findings are not deterministic. First of all, they do not account for why some individuals at high-quality, resource-rich firms become stars while others do not. And our finding about the portability of women's performance, above all, sheds light on how individual strategies and choices can interact with institutional factors, offsetting negative realities and leveraging institutional flexibilities.

Our findings reveal that there is in fact such a thing as high-performance free agency in this profession, one in which individuals who change employers perform precisely the same job equally well at the new employer. Free agency of this kind is not a characteristic shared by all knowledge workers or by a particular generation of such professionals. Other investigators' findings, which we will review shortly, have shown that firm-specific human capital matters in some professions and not in others and that within certain professions it matters in some jobs but not in others.

In the aggregate, these findings suggest that it is time to move on from debate about whether performance is portable to more fine-grained examination of *under what circumstances* performance is portable, *in which jobs* it is portable, and, in some cases, *at what cost* it is portable. There is clearly a continuum, and it appears to depend on exactly what job an individual performs and at what employer.

General Management Skills and Portability

Our finding that an array of institutional factors conditions and modifies portability suggests that, though free agency is a reality among some equity analysts whose human capital is not firm-specific, even their performance is influenced by institutional characteristics. In an effort to characterize general managerial skills, which are widely viewed as portable, we studied a different population: twenty former General Electric executives who were hired as chairman, CEO, or CEO-designate by other companies between 1989 and 2001.[1] We chose GE executives because GE is renowned as a source of managerial talent. Its top executives can be expected to have first-rate general management skills, and the company's executives are frequently recruited into unrelated industries; GE alumni are disproportionately represented, year after year, among sitting CEOs in the S&P 500.

When we looked closely at the past experience of the twenty GE alumni, we identified three types of skills and experience that can be seen either as subcategories of general managerial skills or as intermediate points on a continuum between general and firm-specific skills: strategic human capital, industry-specific human capital, and relationship human capital. This finding is noteworthy in itself: these three types of human capital are neither portable across industries nor firm-specific.[2] We also looked at the importance of company-specific human capital.

Strategic human capital takes the form of expertise at cost-cutting, growth, or managing cyclical markets; a given executive is highly likely to have accumulated more experience in one of these contexts than in the other two. We categorized these individuals as cost controllers, growers, or cycle managers on the basis of their line-management experience at GE. Using research reports, we also categorized the prevailing strategic needs of the companies that hired them. We then compared the performance of the nine executives who joined companies whose strategic needs matched their experience with that of the eleven whose new companies' needs represented mismatches with their strengths. Companies whose strategic need matched the strategic experience of the former GE executive enjoyed annualized abnormal returns of 14.1 percent, while mismatched pairings saw returns of -39.8 percent.[3]

Industry human capital consists of technical and regulatory knowledge unique to a particular industry. Most managers operate under constraints and parameters specific to a given industry, such as the regulatory environment, the nature of the competition, relationships with suppliers, the distribution system, and the like. Entering a new industry imposes a steep learning curve. We compared the performance of managers who moved to a company within the same industry with that of executives who entered a new industry. When former GE executives moved within the same or a related industry, their new companies generated annualized abnormal returns of 8.8 percent; those who moved into a dissimilar industry saw abnormal returns of −29.1 percent.

Relationship human capital is a measure of a manager's past experience working with a team of colleagues. We looked at the effect on the executive's performance of bringing in former GE colleagues. Companies that hired three or more former other GE executives enjoyed annualized abnormal returns of 15.7 percent, while those that hired a single executive (or only one or two subordinates) had annualized abnormal returns of -16.6 percent.

Company-specific skills are those that are nonportable—familiarity with routines and procedures, corporate culture and informal norms, and specific management systems and processes. CEOs, of course, are in a position to impose the systems they prefer over time. We found that the former GE executives who took over, built, or implemented management systems that resembled GE's were more successful than those who entered firms with less familiar systems and did not impose changes. The ten companies that most resembled GE enjoyed annualized abnormal returns of 17.5 percent, while the other ten experienced annualized abnormal returns of −37.7 percent.

In sum, the GE executives who moved to industries they knew did well, as did those who brought other GE people with them. So did cost-cutters and revenue growers who joined companies that needed those skills. Those who went to different industries, those who moved solo, and those who joined companies whose needs called for different skills performed poorly. These findings suggest that general managers specialize in particular context-specific skills and that such general human capital can be valuable at more than one firm but only within the same context.

The records of ex-GE CEOs demonstrate that even skills that are widely considered general are constrained by context and imperfectly portable. This finding suggests that human capital is more accurately and usefully formulated as a portfolio consisting of multiple skills and assets, rather than a binary phenomenon with only two categories. Even general managerial skill sets become more context specific and specialized than is widely recognized by hiring firms or by the possessors of such skills.

Directions for Future Research

Extending Our Line of Inquiry

We have identified a potent combination of variables that contribute significantly to the portability or nonportability of performance, but as yet we are unable to specify which factors matter most. Is the quality of the destination firm more decisive, for instance, than the orientation of the firm of origin? There is also more to learn about the relationships among variables. For instance, what is the relationship between the quality of a department or firm and its orientation toward developing its own stars or hiring them on the labor market? Organizations with developmental cultures are well represented among those named by clients as the highest-quality organizations in the industry, but we have not yet quantified the nature of the relationship. And what is the relationship between the quality of a firm and its adeptness at integrating new hires? Can firm quality quickly overcome the loss of a new hire's firm-specific human capital? How? Is there a relationship between a firm's orientation toward portability or nonportability and its skill at integration? Or, to put the question another way, is unsuccessful integration more of a problem at portability-oriented or nonportability-oriented firms?

There remains more to learn about our finding that stars from portability-oriented firms do not suffer a performance penalty when they move. Specifically, it would be worthwhile to explore whether outcomes differ with the portability orientation and/or the quality of the destination firm. More generally, it could be revealing to look more deeply at the effects on portability of different configurations and move strategies, such as moving from a portability-oriented firm to a nonportability-oriented developmental firm, or from one nonportabilility-oriented firm to another. Tracing the effect on stars with portable skills of taking on performance-eroding roles (initiating new coverage) might also be revealing.

The powerful effect on portability of moving with a team raises a number of questions about how this effect might vary depending on various characteristics of the firm of origin and the destination firm. How does the incidence of team moves correlate with a portability or developmental orientation at the original firm? What is the optimal size of a team? What team configurations retain the most value? For instance, is it more portability protecting to move with colleagues in client-facing roles or with colleagues who primarily support the team leader's own work?

Similarly, it could be enlightening to explore the striking portability of women's performance in light of the orientation toward portability or firm-specificity of the firm of origin and the destination firm. Because women's portability appears to stem from their minority and marginalized status in the industry, it could also be productive to examine whether members of other minority groups—by virtue of race, age, or educational or career factors—have strategically protected their portability in similar ways.

Finally, when we turn to qualitative data, a deeper and more thorough understanding of individuals' decision making about how much firm-specific human capital to seek or to accept would enrich the discourse about questions of performance portability.

Individual Decision Making and Firm-Specific Human Capital

Several meta-questions remain. Do individuals and firms think strategically about portability and its determinants? How would an individual go about appraising his or her portable and nonportable skills? Are firms strategic in the amount of firm-specific human capital they impart to their workers? How do firms influence individuals' thinking about portability? Answers to these questions will ultimately change how individuals view their own knowledge and skills and how firms manage their human capital.

Investment in firm-specific human capital may have high costs or formidable benefits. For a star analyst, investing heavily in firm-specific human capital severely limits portability. However, firm-specific capabilities can significantly enhance her or his productivity. For the employing firm, restricting portability can be a source of competitive advantage. But as we have seen, few firms think hard about how much specific human capital they bestow on their analysts or about how to use the development of human capital strategically. Similarly, star analysts often fail to think explicitly about their firm-specific human-capital investments and often overestimate their endowments of general human capital. This misperception can have disastrous results. Early work on firm-specific and general human capital was conducted in a period when firm-specific human capital was more often hard or product-oriented than soft. It was thus less important for workers and firms to think strategically about human capital and portability; the questions to be answered were somewhat clear to all parties.[4] Hard and product-oriented nonportability are self-evident; it is easy for workers to recognize that the machines they work on at one factory differ from those they would work on elsewhere. A significant body of work in the human-capital domain was thus built on the assumptions (1) that firms and individuals *do* understand how much firm-specific human capital they possess, (2) that they make decisions in such a way as to maximize career benefits, and (3) that neither workers nor firms need to work at predicting and explaining their own patterns of behavior or scrutinizing others' actions and consequences to extract lessons.[5]

As the workplace environment evolved, so too did the theory, which was eventually designated "social economics."[6] Since the 1950s and 1960s hard nonportability has declined. Office systems have become more standardized; nearly every office uses Microsoft packages. Meanwhile, information about competing firms has become more accessible, because of the information explosion generated by the Internet and because of the increased acceptability of poaching talent. If Company X wants to know what Company Y is up to, it is easy enough to hire away some of Company Y's employees and find out. As hard and product-oriented nonportability have receded, soft nonportability has commanded a bigger slice of the pie. And soft nonportability—particularly the web of relationships—is both less visible and less predictable. Hence both workers and firms must pay closer attention to their own actions and those of others in order to think strategically about portability.

Our interviews suggest that the degree to which a given individual relies on firm-specific human capital is unclear not only to others but also in many cases to the individual in question, who may never have considered the question.[7] An analyst who changes firms, obviously, learns certain lessons about his or her portability. "People that have moved before are a lot more thoughtful about what makes them successful," noted Steve Balog, "and are more likely to attribute some of their success to the firm."

The public nature and geographical compactness of the analyst labor market means that analysts are well placed to observe each other's moves and to draw lessons accordingly—particularly about which banks foster mobility and which do not. To put the point another way, a star analyst who is contemplating moving to another firm is likely to observe the outcomes of other analysts' moves. For example, if a star analyst moves to a competing firm and her performance improves or remains unchanged, other star analysts at her former firm may conclude that they, too, possess portable skills. Thus individuals often use others' actions and their consequences as a metric by which to measure their own general and firm-specific human capital.

Of course, the mobile analyst is likely to assess the private information revealed by the move more accurately than others do—there is no better way to find out how portable your own skills are than to switch jobs. As other researchers have noted, each decision influences future decisions because prior choices have revealed previously unknown information.[8]

But analysts could still gain valuable information about portability by observing the success rates of other job-switchers. If a star analyst who moved from Goldman Sachs to Morgan Stanley failed, for example, former colleagues at Goldman Sachs might attribute the star's success there to firm-specific human capital that was only useful at Goldman Sachs. But if the mobile analyst succeeded at Morgan Stanley, that success might be taken as evidence of the portability of Goldman Sachs analysts. An analyst could glean such lessons from observing moves to and from his or her home firm and by following industry gossip in newspapers and trade publications.

That analysts do engage in such observation is readily apparent. The extent to which they derive accurate information from their observations is less clear and a fruitful area for further study. Given (1) the prevailing disinclination to think about portability at all and (2) the typical biases people manifest in social reasoning, particularly in assessing their own skills and likely futures, it is unlikely that analysts are drawing the correct conclusions from their labor-market observations.

A few individuals on Wall Street clearly did grasp what was at issue in moves from one employer to another: some seasoned top search consultants. Those we interviewed had guided, observed, and reflected on multiple moves, successful and otherwise, and drawn experience-based conclusions about cultures and work styles and the limits of human adaptability.

"You wouldn't recruit the same person, to take an extreme example, to Salomon, when Salomon was a freestanding firm, that you would to Morgan Stanley," said search consultant Abram Claude. "Morgan Stanley is very buttoned-down, white-shoe: Yale/Harvard/Princeton/Stanford backgrounds and style and way of functioning. Salomon was a rough-and-tumble in-your-face kind of environment. And people don't flourish in environments that are uncomfortable for them." A senior search consultant pointed out further differences that would affect the fit between an analyst and a firm. "Some research departments are very political, and some are much more collegial," he observed. "In some places research analysts are independent and the work they do is very transportable. Other places it's much more of a group effort."

Tony Cashen, who recruited for Jack Rivkin and Fred Fraenkel at Lehman Brothers, noted the unpredictable aspect of transition from one type of firm to another:

> If you got a star out of a smaller firm or one of the regional firms, there would always be a question: would they succeed? Or had they been successful because they were big fish in a small pond? So while we were successful giving somebody a better and bigger platform to play on, it was always something we looked at very carefully. Bear Stearns was different than DLJ was different than Morgan Stanley was different than Merrill Lynch—but those people knew those firms. If you brought somebody in from Minneapolis or Fort Worth or Dallas, they didn't know. So that was always a question.

Even with the active participation of attentive and thoughtful search consultants strongly motivated to engineer successful matches, equity analysts and research departments on Wall Street stumbled into many mismatches and fiascoes.

Few of the firms we studied understood that they were creating firm-specific human capital in their employees or thought strategically about the competitive advantage that doing so could create for them. Those few that did—notably Goldman Sachs and Sanford C. Bernstein—deliberately emphasized the creation and communication of nonportability. Their example suggests that using firm-specific, nonportable human capital as a strategic advantage is not something that successful companies can do in a halfhearted way. The magnitude of the investment calls for full commitment; otherwise the return on investment might be low.

Building up a firm's specific human capital takes a long time, and maintaining it requires constant reinforcement. Analysts have little a priori motivation to invest heavily in firm-specific human capital, especially if the firm is performing poorly. And even when analysts do invest in firm-specific human capital, the firm cannot reap full benefit from the investment unless it can communicate to its analysts that their success depends in part on their firm-specific human capital and on the firm's capabilities.

Goldman Sachs was perhaps the most adept of all the firms in our study at communicating to its analysts the nonportable nature of their human capital. Executives at Goldman Sachs worked hard at "internal marketing" (dubbed "brainwashing" by its competitors) to convince employees that their success was almost entirely built on specific human capital. Analysts were told that they would fail at another firm because so much of their knowledge and skills were nonportable. "At Goldman Sachs," said Steve Balog, "they convince you that if you move it's going to be bad for you, bad for your kids, bad for your grandkids, and bad for your neighbors." When we asked Goldman Sachs analysts what made them successful, nearly all of them attributed their success to the firm.

Sanford C. Bernstein employed a similar approach. Analysts invested heavily in nonportability when they produced their signature blackbooks, since the process of writing these signature Bernstein products was not portable. And Bernstein was careful to communicate to its analysts that they were dependent on the firm for success. As research director Lisa Shalett said, "We drum into people early that we're playing a different game. We're not here to sell stock picks or sell models." Bernstein executives even recruited for nonportability. As Shalett said, "The people we recruit to our platform are people who are at an age or stage in their career who would not ever be able to get to Wall Street."

Applicability to Other Professions

When we turn to other professions and other settings, more evidence is needed. There have been few comparable studies of professions like law, accounting, consulting, engineering, architecture, or publishing, no doubt in part because of the structural hindrances noted in chapter 2. The few exceptional research projects to study portability are thus intriguing.

One compelling and well-designed study of portability of performance looked at the specialized skills of cardiac surgeons. This great investigation is of particular interest because it examined performance of a single task in different settings at a point in time.[9] The study found that increases in the volume of surgeons' procedures at a particular hospital improved their performance *at that hospital,* but not their performance of the same procedure at a different hospital. The authors concluded that performance depends on familiarity with the assets of a given organization. Noting the "limits to transferring knowledge or expertise across firms," they generalized their findings to urge managers to "take a more critical eye to the practice of building firm capabilities through the 'best-athlete' strategy of hiring."[10]

Several other studies have confirmed the contribution of context to the quality of performance. These studies offer two broad explanations for the importance of context: some point to resources while others focus on tacit knowledge. To a considerable degree these two interpretations appear to fit the populations that gave rise to them. The studies that pinpointed institutional resources looked at scientists and mutual-fund managers, both populations that depend heavily on the financial, informational, and supportive resources of their parent institutions.[11] Those that emphasized tacit knowledge studied surgeons and basketball players, both professions that count on well-oiled team interactions.[12] The study of cardiac surgeons described above underlined "familiarity with critical assets," a formulation that conjoins resources and tacit knowledge.[13]

The consistency of these findings about the primacy of context, particularly institutional quality, in top individual performance is the key argument for competitive knowledge-based organizations to build resource-rich environments that will retain the loyalty and performance of their most talented employees.

Numerous studies have found that free agency tends to mean that individuals can capture the lion's share of their market value for themselves rather than sharing it with their employers.[14] This phenomenon and the mind-set it generates undoubtedly contribute to the temptation to respond to overtures from competing employers. But star knowledge workers who misinterpret the inputs to their market value by appropriating all of the credit to themselves run the risk of eroding their market value by abandoning resources that have contributed to their performance.

Different professions foster or allow for different degrees of portability. Basketball players, for example, are dependent on other members of their teams to perform well. Most scientists depend on the technical and human resources of their laboratories. In other professions, some roles are firm- or team-specific and others are not. When we looked at star football players, we found that punters (who perform independently) showed no significant decline in short- or long-term performance when they changed teams. Wide receivers, whose performance depends on team-specific tacit knowledge, performed less well for a year after changing teams.[15]

Similar patterns have been found in the corporate world. Claudio Fernandez Araoz of the executive-search firm Egon Zehnder International analyzed *stick rates*—the length of time a new hire stays with a company, either in the original position or a higher one—for C-level jobs. Positions in which team-specific knowledge is particularly critical tended to have lower stick rates, suggesting less portability and lower chances of success for an outsider. Presidents and non-executive chairmen, who work part-time and are not responsible for execution, had the highest stick rates. CTOs/CIOs (chief technical officers/chief information officers) and CFOs (chief financial officers), whose positions resemble those of punters in football in that they perform somewhat independently and are not highly dependent on internal relationships or knowledge of particular markets, had stick rates nearly close to those of CEOs. Positions that call for knowledge of a specific market and/or integration with many other internal functions, such as CMO (chief marketing officer), had lower stick rates. The position with the lowest stick rate was that of COO (chief operating officer), who could be characterized as the wide receiver of the corporate world. For a COO, good fit with the company and the CEO is paramount, and fit tends to be a matter of possessing a large store of applicable tacit company knowledge. The job is also often ill defined. In practice, the title of COO can be applied to many roles—bad guy or good guy to complement the CEO, team member, implementer, change agent, and so forth—and inaccurate assumptions about the role can generate poor fit and thus rapid turnover.

Returning to the arena of sports, one pertinent study found that some roles are team-specific and others are not: pitchers, catchers, and shortstops, whose positions call for close interaction with other team members, moved to other teams less frequently than outfielders, who function more independently.[16]

Habits of Mind

Star equities analysts are justly celebrated for their ability to think strategically about the sources of value in the companies they cover. Why is it so hard for them to think strategically about the sources of value in their own careers? Those who discount the importance of environment (the presence of high-quality colleagues, their firms' resources and reputation) when accounting for their own success are exhibiting two traits, overoptimism and egocentrism, long studied by psychologists. David Dunning, Chip Heath, and Jerry M. Suls have documented the evidence that people consistently overestimate their own abilities and the psychological mechanisms that lead them to do so.[17] People consistently tend to attribute positive events (such as being ranked by *II*) to internal, stable, and global causes—in other words, to believe that good fortune happened because of aspects of the self that are permanent and general enough to reliably foster more good things in the future. For instance, people are more likely to attribute their own academic success to being broadly "intelligent" than to being more narrowly "good at math." Negative events tend to elicit attributions to temporary, highly specific causes external to the individual. Considerable evidence suggests that this bias helps maintain mental health—at least in Western countries, where beliefs about the nature of the self and the concomitant sources of self-regard are primarily individualistic.[18]

People can assess their abilities more accurately when they receive frequent and objective feedback—but even in sports, which offers instant, frequent, and objective feedback, there is still only a moderately strong correlation between people's self-estimation and reality.[19] In more subjective fields, the correlation is much lower.[20] Dunning and colleagues reviewed a large array of reasons for people's poor self-assessment and prediction skills, several of which are relevant to the analysts in our study.

> *Mispredicting their own emotional reactions to situations.* People are surprisingly bad at predicting how they will respond to a situation emotionally, which leads them to make decisions based on erroneous beliefs about what will or will not make them happy. For example, analysts may discount the stress that changing jobs will

invariably entail; they may also overestimate the satisfaction they will derive from increased income.

Ignoring concrete and situational details and background circumstances. When imagining the future, people are likely to concentrate only on their own behavior and its immediate consequences and to ignore the role of chance, random situational variables, or the actions of others: "People also mispredict because their imagined scenarios concentrate too much on the behavior in question and not about seemingly irrelevant swirls and eddies of everyday life that are not conceptually related to the behavior but that may still interfere with their capacity to perform that behavior."[22] Any change will have unintended consequences, yet people are unlikely to factor a quotient of randomness into their predictions of the future. What if the research director at the new firm leaves? What if the industry sector has a downturn? Analysts are unlikely to consider these types of worst-case scenarios before moving.

Ignoring the lessons of experience (one's own and others'). People display a consistent disinclination to evaluate events based on prior similar events, preferring instead to think only of their own (usually overestimated) abilities and the immediate task at hand. In other words, analysts who witness other analysts' post-move declines are highly likely to think, "Yes, but I'm different," rather than learning an object lesson from this vicarious experience. Unrealistic optimism can be moderated by negative events, but this moderation is usually highly domain-specific and short-lived.

Newly ranked stars might be expected to be particularly vulnerable to these dynamics as a result of the immense psychological impact of ranking for the first time.[22]

Finally, is there something peculiarly American about the tendency of otherwise shrewd strategic thinkers not to think strategically about their own careers? Alexis de Tocqueville would not have been surprised by the rise of "free agent nation." In *Democracy in America*, published in 1835, that prescient commentator on the American character predicted that the middle class in a democratic society would "form the habit of thinking of themselves in isolation and imagine that their whole destiny is in their hands."[23] Long before the age of television and multitasking, Tocqueville observed that Americans tend not to be good strategic thinkers, a condition he blamed on the demands and opportunities of life in a mobile society. Americans tended to be *serious* thinkers, Tocqueville pointed out, because their thoughts have consequences, but the broad array of things they need to think about means that they cannot pay attention to any particular thought or choice in great depth: "The habit of inattention has to be regarded as the greatest defect of the democratic character."[24]

Implications for Employers

Lessons from experience for managers are scattered through these pages, mostly embedded in the analysis and in perceptive quotes from research directors, analysts, and astute observers of the industry and the analyst community. These observations address such fundamental managerial issues as how to make good hiring choices, how to think about compensation and integration, how to mentor and train stars, how to promote collaboration, and how to elicit loyalty. But picking them out for mention here would imply a general applicability that does not exist. These are not universal principles; their applicability depends on the particulars of an organization's orientation and mission. If not firm-specific, they are at least relevant to particular types of enterprises, with particular orientations and missions.

The broadly applicable lessons that we can specify have largely to do with hiring. Our evidence strongly suggests the wisdom of hiring from firms with similar orientations and of hiring from firms of lesser or equivalent quality. Specifically, good hiring strategy maximizes matching on different types of human capital. Hiring from organizations far more resource-rich than one's own increases the likelihood that the incoming star will suffer a performance decline and prove to be a disappointment. Our findings also argue for being frank and thorough in presenting the firm to prospective candidates in the interest of maximizing goodness of fit.

Hiring a star should be a well-thought-out strategic decision, undertaken to fulfill a specific operational aim. For firms that look to the labor market for fully formed talent, in preference to taking the development route, it is a high priority to guard against incurring a winner's curse. It is all too easy even for experienced negotiators to overpay: stars are well positioned in such negotiations to appropriate the lion's share of the added value they will generate, and it has been demonstrated that the greater an individual's endowment of general human capital, the more on a relative basis it will cost to engage his or her services. It is also easy to underestimate the risk of demoralizing the star's new colleagues, existing employees who will feel undervalued when the new, highly compensated star comes onboard. These are among the reasons that developmentally oriented firms opt to train, develop, and seek to retain a cadre of talented up-and-coming employees in the conviction that they will ultimately contribute greater and more reliable value to the firm.[25] These firms also tend to focus more on the interplay among colleagues and resources and less on being preoccupied with individual stars.

It is noteworthy that companies that spend lavishly on promoting themselves to clients and potential clients in the form of marketing rarely expend comparable—or, often, any—money and effort on communicating their value proposition to their own employees. A company that offers its valued employees a convincing counterargument to the prevailing superficial and formulaic thinking about portability stands to gain a great deal.

Finally, firms have a clear self-interest in retaining their best and brightest employees. Retention in turn appears to be a function of organizational factors like first-rate colleagues, suggesting that talent tends to attract and keep other talent in a self-reinforcing manner. We found consistently lower turnover at firms that provide higher-quality (better-performing) colleagues.

As we have seen, companies like Sanford C. Bernstein and Lehman Brothers successfully developed many stars. Development of this kind is not a matter of pampering, crude incentives, or lavish outlays. It involves a joint recognition on the part of the firm and the promising star-in-the-making that they need each other's capabilities and can both benefit from making the most of each other's resources.

Implications for Individual Careers

To shed light on individual behavior during job changes, we conducted a survey of over 400 search consultants from more than 50 industries in mid-2008. The respondents, 67 percent of whom had more than ten years of experience and 70 percent of whom recruited stars at the senior-executive level or higher, were asked to specify the most common mistakes individuals make when contemplating a job change and the reasons for such mistakes. Also, over 500 C-level executives were interviewed from more than 40 countries in late 2008 about their experiences managing *their own* human capital.[26] Finally, we posed similar questions to the heads of human resources at 15 multinational companies in mid-2009.[27]

The job-change mistakes most frequently identified by recruiters were (1) doing inadequate research; (2) being swayed excessively by money; (3)

moving "from" rather than "to"; (4) overestimating oneself; and (5) thinking short term.

These mistakes are also often intertwined. Causality can flow in many directions: assigning excessive importance to money, for instance, can lead to lack of research (because the salary trumps other information), and lack of research can in turn lead to overemphasis on money (in the absence of other data on which to base a decision). One can easily imagine job seekers making all five mistakes at once: because they overvalue themselves, they feel unjustly treated at bonus time and leap at the first company that promises a signing bonus without doing due diligence on the company's long-term prospects. Lack of self-awareness was often cited as a reason for both overvaluing money and overestimating oneself; thinking that the grass is greener elsewhere was associated with inadequate research. Thus these tendencies can lead to a vicious cycle of maladaptive behaviors: dissatisfaction, unrealistic hope, ill-considered moves, and further dissatisfaction. That all three groups of respondents pinpointed the same pattern of behavior suggests that this cycle underlies many dysfunctional job changes.

Mistake 1: Doing Inadequate Research

By far the most frequently mentioned mistake was insufficient research on the company or job in question. Four types of research were mentioned: basic market and industry research; the "hard areas," or the company's financials, business plan, and model; the "soft areas," or cultural factors; and the job-skills requirements of the specific position. On the broadest level, many job seekers—including senior executives—are not fully literate in the job-market realities of their industries and functions. Job seekers often fail to "sufficiently [research] the field to know where they might make a good fit," one recruiter said. "They haven't taken stock of their strengths and weaknesses."

Recruiters also described job seekers who neglected due diligence on companies they were thinking of joining. Job seekers are often guilty of "not doing a thorough background investigation of that firm to ascertain how solid the foundation really is," one recruiter noted. "I have witnessed firms that knew there was trouble, and would hire in spite of it."

Recruiters repeatedly observed that people fail to request specific performance metrics, assuming that the job title sufficiently describes the job. Companies sometimes sweeten job titles to attract top talent—and new recruits at badly managed companies could find themselves in ill-defined jobs whose formal titles are meaningless.

Mistake 2: Leaving for Money

Changing employers solely for financial reasons was the mistake that recruiters analyzed the least: perhaps the reasons a person might do so seemed too obvious to need explication. Occasional executives admitted to this mistake in judgment: "I was doing the identical role for $10K more, but leaving behind the relationships and connections was just not worth it in hindsight," said the vice president of talent and engagement at an international casino company.

Money is a scorecard, and people who lack awareness of their true priorities and success factors can be blinded by it. "[Job seekers] get consumed by compensation and not by fit, so they keep moving, mistaking compensation for recognition, personal satisfaction, et cetera," one recruiter pointed out. "They don't take any time for introspection to understand why they are unhappy where they are."

Mistake 3: Moving "From" Rather than "To"

The third mistake identified by recruiters is allowing discontent in one's present position build to the point that, as one recruiter put it, "instead of planning their career moves, they lurch from one crisis to the next." Candidates desperate to believe that the grass is greener elsewhere skimp on due diligence and fail to look strategically at their current companies or to recognize opportunities there. Such emotional reactivity increases self-perceived time pressure, which promotes other biases and bad practices (notably inadequate research and short-term thinking).

Mistake 4: Overestimating Oneself

The fourth mistake recruiters mentioned was self-aggrandizement: an inflated assessment of their own skills, prospects, and, occasionally, culpability. That is, job candidates often fail to pinpoint the reasons for their dissatisfaction. They are "looking at the current company as being the problem and not acknowledging that they themselves may be a part of the problem," one recruiter said. Another concurred: "People fail to be realistic sometimes [and] to be self-critical, and [they therefore think] that external circumstances and environments have more to do with their frustrations or failures than their own issues."

An inflated self-image also leads job seekers to overestimate their capacity to cope in the new position. Many executives' self-admitted worst mistakes involved taking on unrealistic challenges, notably underestimating the difficulty of creating change in large organizations. A software CFO regretted taking a job at a large multinational he found "so much bigger, more unwieldy, difficult to make an impact, and impersonal. No matter what I did, it didn't make a difference."

Mistake 5: Not Taking a Long-Term Perspective

Failing to look at the long term is a mistake that is implicated in all the mistakes discussed above. A job seeker who performs slapdash research before accepting a position is thinking only of the short term or behaving in such a way that solely short-term rewards are likely. Leaving for money—especially inflated first-year salary projections—embodies a short-term perspective. Short-term thinking can also play into the "moving-from" scenario if unhappiness at work blinds one to the possibility of change. And overestimating oneself can lead one to feel deserving of rewards *now*, not five years down the line.

Recruiters offered three main explanations for a self-sabotaging short-term focus. The first is cognitive: candidates who might have been open to taking a longer-term point of view may have simply been unequipped to do research and ask questions that would enable them to assess long-term prospects. The second is emotional, composed of greed, impatience, and what one recruiter calls "a deterioration of the philosophy of deferred gratification." Finally, there is simple time pressure: a candidate may simply be forced to decide before amassing enough information.

Executives did not blame short-term thinking for their worst decisions but often praised a long-term perspective for the best. Several said that willingness to sacrifice short-term rewards, though sometimes mystifying to their peers, had ultimately resulted in long-term opportunity. "I gave up the short-term economic and social status reward," one executive said, "for being a part of a project in which I believed and where I thought I was going to have much better professional and personal development."

Opting for a tantalizing offer of a 50 percent increase in compensation, for instance, could turn out to be ultimately value-destroying. Our finding that stars move to competitors less frequently than do non stars (though they probably receive more overtures) suggests that those who have a record of performance to protect may be more cautious, at least in this respect, than those who are still on the ascent and possibly impatient to prove themselves.

Routes to Outstanding Job Performance

For ambitious professionals it clearly makes sense to affiliate with, and stick with, the highest-quality organizations. That it is far easier to achieve stardom in the first place at certain employers is an important observation with obvious applicability to individual careers. We also found that though longevity at an employer promotes better performance, the quality of the employer is very important when it comes to fostering first-rate performance. Furthermore, those who moved from lesser firms to superior firms were able to maintain their performance without penalty, while those who left the best firms suffered the greatest declines. Taken together, these findings strongly suggest that choosing an organization that offers high-quality colleagues and first-rate technical and supportive resources is of decisive importance in achieving and maintaining outstanding performance.

But neither our findings nor others' should be taken as condemnation of job-changing on the part of individuals or of seeking talent in the labor market on the part of hiring organizations. External hiring can enrich a work environment by introducing new capabilities and preventing ossification.[28] Several studies have pointed out that mobility is inherent in the process of seeking a good fit between personal capabilities and preferences on the one hand and the culture, resources, and inclinations of an employer on the other. Most such mobility is concentrated in the early years of individuals' careers,[29] but our study of former GE executives demonstrates that matching is also pertinent to the maintenance of high performance on the part of experienced stars. Thus the portability of human assets continues to be an active question throughout the careers of outstanding performers.

Many highly talented people are more than willing to trade portability for a nurturing environment and productive interactions. As an editor-in-chief of the *Harvard Business Review* put it, "The longer I stay in an organization, the more the knowledge I have is developed in the context of that organization. . . . Part of the value of human capital is not just 'How great I am,' but 'How great I am when I'm part of this particular team in this particular company.' "[30] Employees of firm-specific organizations who are weighing other opportunities should subject themselves to hardheaded assessment of the employer's contribution to their personal performance and the likely duration of the detrimental effects of its loss on performance at a new employer.

Exceptional performers who are contemplating changing employers would do well to emulate the star female analysts whose careful methods of exploring overtures from rival firms were described in chapter 8. They concentrated on assuring themselves that the prospective employer would be welcoming and supportive and that the particulars of the job would be a good fit for their styles; they were not lured by the promise of lavish compensation to make rash and ill-advised decisions. Because changing firms is risky for a professional whose skills are at least partly firm-specific, due diligence of this kind is imperative.

In conclusion, we hope that this book will enrich the conceptual vocabulary available to firms and individual professionals, as well as to scholars. It will have done its job if it has offered some new concepts useful for thinking about job performance, competitive advantage, human-capital strategies and their consequences, portability, mobility, hiring, retention, compensation, and the nature of talent, helping make these complex phenomena more amenable to systematic, realistic, and strategic thinking and the lessons of experience.

Appendix

This section elaborates on analyses of the portability of star performance, the main focus of this book. Thus the sections that follow cover this topic. Readers who are interested in more data on portability tests or robustness tests can refer to the academic articles cited in chapters 3–8. Readers interested in more detailed analysis of turnover and compensation are encouraged to read the papers listed in the first endnote for the corresponding chapters (chapters 10 and 11 for turnover analyses and chapter 12 for compensation analysis).

Research Approach

We tested our hypotheses by looking at the job histories and performance records of star Wall Street security analysts.[1] To test whether research analysts possessed firm-specific human capital, we examined whether changing employers had an effect on their short-term and long-term performance. Determining whether a given individual's performance changed when he or she changed firms was problematic, in that we could not control for what *would have happened* to an individual's performance had he or she stayed put. Our data do, however, capture the performance of many "stayers." Hence, we can compare a mover's performance to that of a comparable individual who stayed at the mover's original firm (i.e., a control group). This approach has been used to address a similar empirical problem in research on labor migration.

If performance is primarily driven by firm-specific skills, a decline in performance could be expected when an individual changed jobs because it takes time to develop skills specific to the new firm.

Yet changes in performance may reflect either the loss of firm-specific human capital or the new employer's different capabilities. Only when the original and destination firms possess equal capabilities can we assert that a decline in performance confirms the contribution of firm-specific skills to productivity. Thus, we compared the performance of stayers and movers to firms with equal capabilities. We also tested whether moving with colleagues affects subsequent performance.

Furthermore, workers do not move at random. Changing employers is endogenous if the decision to do so correlates with unobservables that affect performance. Prior studies have demonstrated the importance of accounting for self-selection in estimating returns to migration. Therefore our econometric methodology takes into account the self-selection process by which workers become movers or stayers, permitting consistent estimates of the performance of both groups. (See our academic articles for methods and analyses.)

Finally, the best way to determine whether the acquisition or loss of a high-performing worker is value-reducing or value-enhancing for a firm would be to calculate a profit-and-loss statement for each worker. The unavailability of detailed compensation data makes this method unfeasible. In its stead we used the event study methodology to determine how the stock market treated the share price of an investment bank in reaction to news of its unforeseen loss or acquisition of a star analyst. Stock-market movement is a well-established proxy for the value created or lost for a given firm in reaction to a specific event. This measure has been successfully used in research in accounting, finance, law, and strategic management. It has also been used to measure the effects on firm value of announced changes in top management. We used stock-price movement to assess whether acquiring firms gained or lost value when they hired a star analyst. Finally, we examined stock reactions by the type of hiring announcements.

Data

From the annual All-America Research Team issues of *Institutional Investor* published between 1988 and 1996, we collected the following information for equity analysts (ranked in October) and fixed-income analysts (ranked in August): name; industry specialty/sector; type (equity or fixed income);

rank; year of the ranking; and company affiliation. The nine-year period of the study produced a total of 4,200 analyst-year combinations (3,514 in equity and 686 in fixed income). If each analyst were counted only once, the list would include 799 equity analysts and 254 fixed-income analysts. Ranked analysts were employed by 78 investment banks; the 24 firms employing the most number of ranked analysts accounted for 4,036 ranked analyst-year combinations (96 percent). To collect information on analysts' tenure with their current employers and total industry experience, we searched databases maintained by Lexis-Nexis, the National Association of Securities Dealers, and Dow Jones News. Data on analysts' tenure at their firms were available for 3,639 analyst-year combinations (87 percent), and information on analysts' experience was collected for 3,653 analyst-year combinations (87 percent).

We accounted for every ranked analyst who left or joined an investment bank within one year of being ranked during the period 1988–96. Each of these incidents was identified an "analyst-year move." Analysts' affiliations in the year subsequent to being ranked and the specific dates of their moves were identified using the databases of Nelson's Directory of Investment Research, Lexis-Nexis, and Dow Jones News Service. We identified 546 analyst-year moves: 500 were from one firm to another, and 46 were promotions or transfers to non-research positions within the same investment bank. Of the 500 analyst-year moves from one firm, 134 were exits from research altogether.[2] The remaining 366 moves (made by 316 individual analysts) were switches to competitors' research departments.

News announcements on the hiring of ranked analysts indicated that ranked analysts occasionally moved in teams. Of the 366 analyst moves, 100 involved such colleagues as other ranked analysts, junior analysts, institutional salespeople, and traders.

Variables

Dependent Variable

The dependent variable in this study is the analyst's performance, operationalized as rank in the *Institutional Investor* All-America Research Team poll, $Rank_{t+1}$. Each year the magazine's editor sends a letter asking institutional investors to rank the analysts who "have been most helpful to you and your institution in researching U.S. equities over the past twelve months." Voters are asked to evaluate analysts using six criteria: earnings estimates, servicing initiatives, accessibility and responsiveness, stock selection, industry knowledge, and written reports. The respondents award a single overall numerical score to each analyst in each industry sector. Votes are cumulated using weights based on the size of the voting institution. The identities of the respondents and their institutions are kept confidential. A very small percentage of analysts achieve rankings in multiple sectors. Some, but not all, stars in a given year continue to be ranked in subsequent years. In each sector, there are five levels of the dependent variable (categorical and ordinal): the first, second, third, runner-up, and unranked.

Independent Variables

Switching Firms

We tested whether the analyst's movement across firms had an effect on his or her *Institutional Investor* ranking. The independent variable of interest is the analyst's mobility. The *Analyst move* variable is 1 if a ranked analyst switched to another sell-side research department and 0 if a ranked analyst did not move during the year.

Firm Capability

For each of the 366 job changes, we determined whether the destination firm had lesser, equivalent, or better capabilities relative to the originating firm by using the bulge-bracket distinction. Bulge-bracket investment banks are those responsible for the bulk of securities underwritten in the United States; historically, the six bulge firms were Credit Suisse First Boston, Goldman Sachs, Lehman Brothers, Merrill Lynch, Morgan Stanley, and Salomon Brothers. These banks and their employees enjoyed a competitive edge due to the firms' exceptional capabilities: economies of scale in marketing, sales, and technology; a broad product base; a wide distribution network for its services, including analysts' research products; and specialized units (investment banking, sales, trading, and research) capable of solving complicated customer problems.

We assigned the job changes of ranked analysts to three groups: better firm capability, equal firm capability, and lesser firm capability. The *Firm capability direction* categorical variable took the value "no move" if a ranked analyst did not move during the year, "moving to a weaker firm" if the move was from a bulge to a non-bulge firm, "moving to a better firm" if the move was from a non-bulge to a bulge firm, and "moving to a comparable firm" if the move was from bulge to bulge or non-bulge to non-bulge.

Team Movement

We also tested the effects of moving with a team of colleagues. The *Coworker move* categorical variable took the value of "no move" if a ranked analyst did not move in a given year, "moving solo" if the analyst switched to another sell-side research department solo, and "moving in teams" if he or she made such a move with other professionals (junior and senior research analysts, institutional salespeople, or traders).

Hiring for Exploitation/Exploration

We tested whether joining a new firm for exploitation or exploration had an effect on an analyst's *Institutional Investor* ranking. Of the stars hired by investment banks in the period we studied, 61 percent were hired into existing sectors and 39 percent initiated new coverage.

The *Hired for exploitation/exploration* variable was coded by creating variables: "no move" if a ranked analyst did not move in a given year, "hired for exploitation" if the analyst was hired to work in a sector already covered by the firm, and "hired for exploration" if the analyst was hired to begin coverage of a sector not previously covered by the firm.

Team Movement for Exploitation/Exploration

We also examined the effects of moving with one or more colleagues for exploitation or exploration.

The effect of moving with coworkers was tested by creating the "Coworker move for exploitation/exploration" variable: "no move" if an analyst did not move in a given year, "hired solo for exploitation" if an analyst switched to another sell-side research department solo to work in a sector already covered by the firm, "hired as a team for exploitation" if an analyst moved with colleagues to work in a sector already covered by the firm, "hired solo for exploration" if an analyst switched to another sell-side research department solo to initiate coverage of a new sector, and "hired as a team for exploration" if an analyst moved with colleagues to begin coverage of a new sector.

Control Variables

The variables included in the model were operationalized into four categories: individual, firm, sector, and macroeconomic.

Individual Analyst Variables

Firm tenure and overall experience are important variables to control for when analyzing performance. *Analyst firm tenure* is the number of years an analyst had worked at a given firm at the end of each year. *Analyst experience* is the number of years an analyst had worked as an analyst at the end of each year. We also controlled for *Analyst type,* because equity and fixed-income analysts pursued different activities and had different customer bases.

Analysts' prior performance has an effect on their future performance. Some analysts were able to repeat their outstanding performance and rank again in subsequent years. Others were not. To control for prior performance, we collected information on the number of years a ranked analyst had been ranked as of the end of the year and created the *Analyst star tenure* variable. Finally, the *Analyst rank dummy $t = 0$,* which represents an analyst's rank in the year $t = 0$, controlled for rank-specific effects on analysts' rankings.

Firm Variables

We used *Firm dummy* to control for effects specific to firms, since research points to differences in forecasting performance across banks.

Sector Variables

The *Sector dummy* variable controlled for effects specific to the sectors that analysts cover. We identified sectors using Nelson's Investment Research Database.

Macroeconomic Variables

To control for intertemporal changes, we used the *Year dummy* variable.

Model Specifications

The Ordered Probit Model

We used an ordered probit model because the dependent variable, analysts' *Institutional Investor* rankings, was categorical and ordinal in nature. The model was estimated using panel data on ranked analysts for the nine-year period 1988–96. Heterogeneity across individual analysts was modeled using the robust clustered estimators of variance—Huber/White or sandwich estimator—because it produces "correct" standard errors (in the measurement sense).[3]

Event Study Data Set and Methodology

We used the event study methodology to determine whether and how the stock market reacted to the unexpected news of the departure or hiring of a star analyst. The dates on which analyst departures or hirings were first announced were chosen as the event dates. We conducted a short window study of daily excess returns over the event period of -1 to +1 days (the actual announcement date plus the days prior to and after the announcement date). The data set consisted of 269 observations for ranked analysts leaving publicly listed firms and 228 observations of analysts joining such firms. Subsidiaries of larger diversified firms that generated less than 50 percent of those companies' revenues were then excluded. The reduced data set consisted of 188 observations for analysts leaving and 156 observations for analysts joining investment banks. The data set was then checked for confounding announcements in the event period. The event window was examined for the following confounding effects: restructuring/divestiture, dividend/earnings announcements, buy/hold/sell recommendations by investment banks, joint ventures, acquisitions, new products, litigation/labor unrest, major executive changes, forecasted changes in earnings or sales, layoffs, debt- or equity-related events, and contract awards. Sixty-four observations for analysts leaving and 47 data points for analysts joining firms were deleted for confounded effects. Furthermore, 13 observations on the leaving side and 8 observations on the joining side were excluded because they overlapped in time and involved identical companies. The final data set consisted of 111 exit announcements and 101 hiring announcements. Stock-returns data were provided by the Center for Research in Security Prices (CRSP) at the University of Chicago.

Empirical Tests and Results

We first determined whether, controlling for individual, firm, sector, and intertemporal variables, ranked analysts' movement across firms affected their performance ($Rank_{t+1}$, $Rank_{t+2}$, $Rank_{t+3}$, $Rank_{t+4}$, and $Rank_{t+5}$).

Switching Firms and Ranked Analysts' Performance

The portability of ranked analysts' performance is examined by focusing on the sign and the significance level of the *Analyst move* variable. In models M1 through M5 (table 3.1 in chapter 3, more fully presented in table A.1), we examine the effects of switching firms on analysts' short-term and long-term performance, controlling for individual (*Analyst type, Analyst firm tenure, Analyst experience, Analyst star tenure, Analyst rank dummy t = 0*), firm (*Firm dummy*), sector (*Sector dummy*), and intertemporal (*Year dummy*) characteristics. Coefficients in these models are similar. Consequently, unless otherwise noted, the following comments apply to all models.

In model M1, the *Analyst move* coefficient is negative and significant, suggesting that ranked analysts' short-term performance declined after switching jobs.[4] Findings from models M2 through M5 suggest that ranked analysts' movement across firms had a significant negative effect on their long-term performance.[5] The *Analyst move* coefficient is negative and significant in models M2 ($Rank_{t+2}$), M3 ($Rank_{t+3}$), M4 ($Rank_{t+4}$), and M5 ($Rank_{t+5}$). Even after spending five years at a new firm, ranked analysts were unable to recapture their pre-move performance levels.

In chapters 3–8, we only report coefficients for our independent variables using the same control variables. For a more detailed description of the study's methodology, statistical findings, control variables, robustness check, and analysis relating to endogeneity, see the sources cited in the first endnote to each chapter.

Table A.1
Effect of Switching Firms on Ranked Analysts' Short-Term and Long-Term Performance

Variable	1988–96 Ordered probit regressions				
	M1 rank $(t+1)$	M2 rank $(t+2)$	M3 rank $(t+3)$	M4 rank $(t+4)$	M5 rank $(t+5)$
Year dummy	yes	yes	yes	yes	yes
Sector dummy	yes	yes	yes	yes	yes
Firm dummy	yes	yes	yes	yes	yes
Analyst rank dummy $t = 0$	yes	yes	yes	yes	yes
Analyst type	0.174 *	0.086	0.101	0.266 *	0.341 *
	(0.094)	(0.116)	(0.129)	(0.152)	(0.190)
Analyst firm tenure	0.000	0.006	0.000	0.000	−0.003
	(0.005)	(0.006)	(0.008)	(0.010)	(0.011)
Analyst experience	0.007	0.008	0.007	0.007	0.003
	(0.000)	(0.000)	(0.000)	(0.000)	(0.000)
Analyst star tenure	−0.024 ***	−0.032 ***	−0.042 ***	−0.048 ***	−0.051 ***
	(0.004)	(0.006)	(0.007)	(0.008)	(0.010)
Analyst move	−0.340 ***	−0.263 ***	−0.229 **	−0.218 **	−0.263 **
	(0.076)	(0.089)	(0.098)	(0.111)	(0.130)
Predicted probabilities for analysts who do not move					
First rank	0.106	0.150	0.156	0.157	0.154
Second rank	0.234	0.215	0.199	0.186	0.187
Third rank	0.356	0.279	0.237	0.211	0.193
Runner-up	0.238	0.252	0.258	0.256	0.258
Unranked	0.066	0.105	0.150	0.191	0.207
Marginal change in probabilities for analysts who move					
First rank	−0.050	−0.053	−0.049	−0.047	0.054
Second rank	−0.064	−0.040	−0.033	−0.029	−0.036
Third rank	−0.013	−0.008	−0.010	−0.011	−0.014
Runner-up	0.071	0.046	0.031	0.022	0.022
Unranked	0.056	0.056	0.060	0.065	0.083
Avg. effect	0.051	0.041	0.036	0.035	0.042
Cut Point 1	−0.960	−1.194	−1.209	−0.882	−0.624
Cut Point 2	0.030	−0.307	−0.407	−0.141	0.106
Cut Point 3	0.954	0.408	0.197	0.398	0.602
Cut Point 4	1.791	1.098	0.837	1.000	1.212
Log (likelihood)	−4413.808	−4006.221	−3381.890	−2844.371	−2075.233
No. of observations	3511	2966	2451	2033	1501
Pseudo–R^2	0.211	0.157	0.140	0.125	0.130

Source: Adapted from Boris Groysberg, Linda-Eling Lee, and Ashish Nanda, "Can They Take It with Them? The Portability of Star Knowledge Workers' Performance: Myth or Reality," *Management Science* 54, no. 7 (July 2008): 1213–30, p. 1223.

Notes: The marginal effect of the *Analyst move* variable is calculated as the discrete change in F(x) as this variable changes from 0 to 1: F(x = 1) − F(x = 0). The categorical and ordinal dependent variable (*Rank$_t$*) is represented by first rank, second rank, third rank, runner-up, and unranked. Models 1–5 examine the impact of switching firms on ranked analysts' short-term and long-term performance. Each model is a robust cluster ordered probit specification with ranked analysts as clusters in which the dependent variable is analysts' *Institutional Investor* rankings. This table presents coefficients for the *Analyst Move* variable for ranked analysts, controlling for individual, firm, sector, and intertemporal variables. Only adjusted robust standard errors are reported.

*p < .10; **p < .05; ***p < .01

Notes

Introduction

1. Jay B. Barney, "Organizational Culture: Can It Be a Source of Sustained Competitive Advantage?" *Academy of Management Review* 11, no. 3 (1986): 656–65; Jay Barney, "Firm Resources and Sustained Competitive Advantage," *Journal of Management* 17, no. 1 (1991): 99–120.
2. Margaret A. Peteraf, "The Cornerstones of Competitive Advantage: A Resource-Based View," *Strategic Management Journal* 14, no. 3 (March 1993): 179–91.
3. See Amanda Paige Cowen, Boris Groysberg, and Paul Healy, "Which Types of Analyst Firms Are More Optimistic?" *Journal of Accounting and Economics* 41, nos. 1–2 (April 2006): 119–46.

1 | Moving On

1. Much of this chapter's discussion of Josie Esquivel is adapted from Boris Groysberg and Laura Morgan Roberts, "Leading the Josie Esquivel Franchise (A & B)," HBS nos. 404-054 and 405-027 (Boston: Harvard Business School Publishing, 2003).
2. Don Tapscott, *The Digital Economy* (New York: McGraw-Hill, 1996).
3. Daniel E. Hecker, "Occupational Employment Projections to 2014," *Monthly Labor Review* 128, no. 11 (November 2005): 70–101.
4. Peter F. Drucker, *On the Profession of Management* (Cambridge, MA: Harvard Business School Press, 1998), ix.
5. Oliver E. Williamson, ed., "Transaction-Cost Economics: The Governance of Contractual Relations," *Journal of Law and Economics* 22, no. 2 (April 1979): 233–61, p. 257.

6. The knowledge-based economy has given rise to a new class of "free-agent" employees. The profound implications of this shift have led some to proclaim the death of firm loyalties and the "career employee." See Melanie Seligman, "The Talent Wars," *New Zealand Management* (October 2000): 52–56, for a prototypical example of popular writing on the topic. The accuracy of such predictions aside, some conclusions are undeniable. Although defining "free agents" is tricky—some are pure freelancers, others "permatemps," while others have part-time jobs but derive the majority of their income and professional identity from free-agent work—Daniel Pink estimated, conservatively, in 2001 that about 16.5 million American workers were "soloists." He also noted that Fortune 500 firms employ fewer than 10 percent of the total workforce. See Daniel H. Pink, *Free Agent Nation: How America's New Independent Workers Are Transforming the Way We Live* (New York: Warner, 2001). Knowledge workers constitute much of this mobile pool of skilled labor, committed only to their individual careers and unlikely to develop deep loyalties to the firms or even the industries that employ them. As Charles Woodruffe put it: "The rise of the power of knowledge and the pivotal role of the knowledge worker means that the basis of competition between organizations moves to these people. They can put their firms at a competitive advantage. It is their skills, abilities and commitment that will determine the long-term success of their organizations. . . . The knowledge worker is well aware of having been given a source of power and freedom by their possession of the knowledge that is so vital to organizations. . . . This independence is partly attributable to the fact that the knowledge worker owns the means of production, or can acquire them for a relatively modest sum from the local computer store." Woodruffe, *Winning the Talent War: A Strategic Approach to Attracting, Developing and Retaining the Best People* (New York: John Wiley, 1999), 10–11. Also see Woodruffe's discussion of the importance of retaining human resources, including knowledge workers, on pp. 29–31.
7. Philip H. Mirvis and Douglas T. Hall, "Psychological Success and the Boundaryless Career," *Journal of Organizational Behavior* 15, no. 4 (July 1994): 365–80; Robert H. Waterman, Judith A. Waterman, and Betsy A. Collard, "Toward a Career-Resilient Workforce," *Harvard Business Review* 72, no. 4 (July/August 1994): 87–95; Kenneth R. Brousseau, Michael J. Driver, Kristina Eneroth, and Rikard Larsson, "Career Pandemonium: Realigning Organizations and Individuals," *Academy of Management Executive* 10, no. 4 (November 1996): 52–66; Pink, *Free Agent Nation*.
8. Woodruffe, *Winning the Talent War*, 24.
9. Michael B. Arthur, "The Boundaryless Career: A New Perspective for Organizational Inquiry," *Journal of Organizational Behavior* 15, no. 4 (July 1994): 295–306; Woodruffe, *Winning the Talent War*.
10. Margaret M. Blair and Thomas A. Kochan, eds., *The New Relationship: Human Capital in the American Corporation* (Washington, DC: Brookings Institution Press, 2000); Norman Bowers and Paul Swain, "Recent Trends in Job Train-

ing," *Contemporary Economic Policy* 12, no. 1 (January 1994): 79–88; Arthur, "The Boundaryless Career."

11. See Ben Phillips, "Free at Last?" *Institutional Investor* 31, no. 8 (August 1997): 48–55, for an analysis of the rise of free agency in the investment industry.

12. The shift to a transactional relationship is not entirely driven by a change in workers' perspectives; downsizing and corporations' refusal to commit to their workers has led the societal shift in attitudes toward employment. Bruce Tulgan, *Winning the Talent Wars: How to Build a Lean, Flexible, High-Performance Workplace* (New York: Norton, 2002).

13. R. Greenwood, C. R. Hinings, and J. Brown, "'P²-Form' Strategic Management: Corporate Practices in Professional Partnerships," *Academy of Management Journal* 33, no. 4 (1990): 725–55; R. Greenwood, C. R. Hinings, and J. Brown, "Merging Professional Service Firms," *Organization Science* 5, no. 2 (1994): 239–57.

14. Timothy M. Gardner, "Interfirm Competition for Human Resources: Evidence from the Software Industry," *Academy of Management Journal* 48, no. 2 (2005): 237–56.

15. Peter Cappelli, *The New Deal at Work: Managing the Market Driven Workforce* (Boston: Harvard Business School Press, 1999).

16. Brook Manville, "Talking Human Capital with Professor Gary S. Becker, Nobel Laureate," *LiNE Zine*, Spring 2001, http://www.linezine.com/4.1/interviews/gbbmthc.htm (accessed February 14, 2008).

17. For contemporary reviews of human resources considered strategically, see Boyan Jovanovic, "Job Matching and the Theory of Turnover," *Journal of Political Economy* 87, no. 5 (1979): 972–90; Oliver Williamson, *The Economic Institutions of Capitalism* (New York: Free Press, 1985); David Kreps, "Corporate Culture and Economic Theory," in *Firms, Organizations and Contracts: A Reader in Industrial Organization*, ed. Peter J. Buckley and Jonathon Michie (New York: Oxford University Press, 1996); Barney, "Organizational Culture"; Ingemar Dierickx and Karel Cool, "Asset Stock Accumulation and Sustainability of Competitive Advantage," *Management Science* 35, no. 12 (December 1989): 1504–11; Gary S. Hansen and Birger Wernerfelt, "Determinants of Firm Performance: The Relative Importance of Economic and Organizational Factors," *Strategic Management Journal* 10 (1989): 399–411; Lee Dyer, "Bringing Human Resources into the Strategy Formulation Process," *Human Resource Management* 22, no. 3 (Fall 1983): 257–71; Mark A. Huselid, "The Impact of Human Resource Management Practices on Turnover, Productivity, and Corporate Financial Performance," *Academy of Management Journal* 38, no. 3 (June 1995): 635–72; Andrew O. Manzini, "Integrating Human Resource Planning and Development: The Unification of Strategic, Operational, and Human Resource Planning Systems," *Human Resource Planning* 11, no. 2 (1988): 78–94; Stella M. Nkomo, "Human Resource Planning and Organizational Performance: An Exploratory Analysis," *Strategic Management Journal* 8 (1987): 387–92; Dave Ulrich, "Strategic Human Resource Planning: Why and How?"

Human Resource Planning 10, no. 1 (March 1987): 37–56; Peteraf, "The Cornerstones of Competitive Advantage."

18. C. A. O'Reilly and J. Pfeffer, *Hidden Value: How Great Companies Achieve Extraordinary Results with Ordinary People* (Boston: Harvard Business School Press, 2000).

19. Jeffrey Pfeffer and Robert I. Sutton, *Hard Facts, Dangerous Half-Truths, and Total Nonsense: Profiting from Evidence-Based Management* (Cambridge, MA: Harvard Business Review Press, 2006).

20. Calculated from "Nelson's Top 25 U.S. Research Firms—Ranked by Total Number of U.S. Companies Covered." Numbers are not adjusted for mergers. *Nelson's Catalog of Institutional Research Reports, 1988–1996* (Port Chester, NY: Nelson Publications).

21. This section is adapted from Ashish Nanda, Boris Groysberg, and Lauren Prusiner, "Lehman Brothers (A): Rise of the Equity Research Department" (HBS case no. 9-906-037, 2007).

22. Adam Smith, *An Inquiry into the Nature and Causes of the Wealth of Nations* (1776; New York: Random House, 1994); Albert Rees, *The Economics of Work and Pay* (New York: Harper and Row, 1973). Rosen argued that even small differences in talent can lead to large differences in compensation; see Sherwin Rosen, "The Economics of Superstars," *American Economic Review* 71, no. 5 (1981): 845–58.

23. This usage goes back to Charles Spearman, *The Abilities of Man* (New York: MacMillan, 1927).

24. John E. Hunter and Frank L. Schmidt, "Intelligence and Job Performance: Economic and Social Implications," *Psychology, Public Policy, and Law* 2, no. 3/4 (1996): 447–72. According to Hunter and Schmidt, general mental ability or intelligence accounts for the bulk of differences in worker productivity. As an employee ages, furthermore, intelligence becomes an even stronger predictor of performance than job tenure. Hunter and Schmidt explicitly encouraged employers to hire based on mental ability. See also Malcolm J. Ree and James A. Earles, "Intelligence Is the Best Predictor of Job Performance," *Current Directions in Psychological Science* 1, no. 3 (June 1992): 86–89; and John E. Hunter, "Cognitive Ability, Cognitive Aptitudes, Job Knowledge, and Job Performance," *Journal of Vocational Behavior* 29, no. 3 (December 1986): 340–62.

25. Hunter and Schmidt, "Intelligence and Job Performance."

26. For a cogent critique of attempts to assess *g* by standardized testing, see David C. McClelland, "Testing for Competence Rather than 'Intelligence,'" *American Psychologist* 28, no. 1 (1973): 1–14. Other definitions of intelligence have also been proposed. Sternberg and Hedlund, for example, defined "practical intelligence" as "the ability that individuals use to find a more optimal fit between themselves and the demands of the environment through adapting to the environment, shaping (or modifying) the environment, or selecting a new environment in the pursuit of personally-valued goals." R. J. Sternberg and J. Hedlund, "Practical Intelligence, *g*, and Work Psychology," *Human Perfor-*

mance 15 (2002): 145. Such practical intelligence is often based on tacit knowledge; tests of tacit knowledge, interestingly, only "exhibit trivial to moderate correlations with measures of *g*" (150). As Sternberg and Hedlund's review describes it, the practical ability to acquire tacit knowledge may be largely innate; tacit knowledge is by definition not explicitly taught but rather "picked up" intuitively by the learner. Also, measures of tacit knowledge correlate with each other. The scores of undergraduates who were tested in two domains in which they had no previous knowledge (tacit-knowledge tests developed for academic psychologists and business managers) were correlated at .58. See R. K. Wagner, "Tacit Knowledge in Everyday Intelligent Behavior," *Journal of Personality and Social Psychology* 52 (1987): 1236–47. Howard Gardner, critiquing single-factor theories of intelligence, developed the theory of "multiple intelligences." See Gardner, *Frames of Mind: The Theory of Multiple Intelligences* (New York: Basic Books, 1983). Conceptions of intelligence also vary significantly by culture. See R. J. Sternberg and E. L. Grigorenko, "Cultural Intelligence and Successful Intelligence," *Group and Organizational Management* 31, no. 1 (2006): 27–39.

27. Daniel Goleman, "What Makes a Leader?" *Harvard Business Review* (November–December 1998): 93–102. Goleman's formulation of emotional intelligence has been challenged by other researchers, who have defined the construct and its measurement differently. See Peter Salovey and John D. Mayer, "Emotional Intelligence," *Imagination, Cognition and Personality* 9, no. 3 (1989): 185–211; John D. Mayer, Peter Salovey, and David R. Caruso, "Emotional Intelligence: Theory, Findings, and Implications," *Psychological Inquiry* 15, no. 3 (2004): 197–215. What does not appear to be open to debate, however, is that emotional intelligence does exist and does have a strong impact on success.

28. David C. McClelland, "Identifying Competencies with Behavioral-Event Interviews," *Psychological Science* 9, no. 5 (1998): 331–39.

29. David Keith Simonton, "Talent and Its Development: An Emergenic and Epigenetic Model," *Psychological Review* 106, no. 3 (1999): 435–57.

30. K. Anders Ericsson, Neil Charness, Paul J. Feltovich, and Robert R. Hoffman, eds., *The Cambridge Handbook of Expertise and Expert Performance* (Cambridge: Cambridge University Press, 2006).

31. For a review, see K. Anders Ericsson and A. C. Lehmann, "Expert and Exceptional Performance: Evidence of Maximal Adaptation to Task Constraints," *Annual Review of Psychology* 47 (1996): 273–305.

32. Robert Kelley and Janet Caplan, "How Bell Labs Create Star Performers," *Harvard Business Review* (July–August 1993): 128–39.

33. McClelland, "Identifying Competencies with Behavioral-Event Interviews"; Richard Boyatzis, *The Competent Manager: A Model for Effective Performance* (New York: Wiley-Interscience, 1982).

34. Gary S. Becker, *Human Capital* (New York: Columbia University Press, 1964); Gary S. Becker, "Investment in Human Capital: A Theoretical Analysis," *Journal of Political Economy* 70 (1962): 9–42. In a 2001 interview, Becker stated, "I

also think the best companies will set up human-capital accounting systems. In order for a company to know more about just what human capital is costing and what the payoff is, they want to track and assess the return on investment. I can also foresee [companies] publicly reporting what they spend and invest in this area. In this age when human capital is such an important form of capital, how could they not want to do that?" Manville, "Talking Human Capital with Professor Gary S. Becker."

35. Manville, "Talking Human Capital with Professor Gary S. Becker."
36. Becker, *Human Capital.*
37. Ibid.
38. Edward P. Lazear, "Firm-Specific Human Capital: A Skill-Weights Approach" (National Bureau of Economic Research working paper no. 9679, revised, 2004).
39. Nanda and Groysberg, "Lehman Brothers (A)," p. 14.
40. Ron Cooper, "Lehman's Equity Division Stunned by Loss of Chief," *Investment Dealer's Digest,* August 31, 1992, pp. 6–8.
41. John E. Hunter, Frank L. Schmidt, and Michael K. Judiesch, "Individual Differences in Output Variability as a Function of Job Complexity," *Journal of Applied Psychology* 75, no. 1 (1990): 28–42.
42. Kelley and Caplan, "How Bell Labs Create Star Performers."
43. Francis Narin and Anthony Breitzman, "Inventive Productivity," *Research Policy* 24 (1995): 507–19.
44. A. J. Lotka, "The Frequency Distribution of Scientific Productivity," *Journal of the Washington Academy of Sciences* 15 (June 1926): 317–23; Derek Price de Solla, *Little Science, Big Science . . . and Beyond* (1963; New York: Columbia University Press, 1986). Lotka is known for Lotka's Law, which attributes to scientists an "inverse-square law of productivity" (38). Essentially, according to Lotka's Law, for every 100 authors who finish a single paper within a given time period, 25 produce two, 11 produce three, and so forth.
45. Jonathan R. Cole and Stephen Cole, *Social Stratification in Science* (Chicago: University of Chicago Press, 1973); Paul D. Allison and John A. Stewart, "Productivity Differences among Scientists: Evidence for Accumulative Advantage," *American Sociological Review* 39, no. 4 (August 1974): 596–606.
46. Simonton, "Talent and Its Development," 435.
47. Shinobu Kitayama, Hazel Rose Markus, Hisaya Matsumoto, and Vinai Norasakkunkit, "Individual and Collective Processes in the Construction of the Self: Self-Enhancement in the United States and Self-Criticism in Japan," *Journal of Personality and Social Psychology* 53 (1997): 636–47.
48. Jin Li, "A Cultural Model of Learning: Chinese 'Heart and Mind for Wanting to Learn,'" *Journal of Cross-Cultural Psychology* 33, no. 3 (2002): 248–69; Jin Li, "U.S. and Chinese Cultural Beliefs about Learning," *Journal of Educational Psychology* 95, no. 2 (2003): 258–67; Harold W. Stevenson, "Learning from Asian Schools," *Scientific American* 267 (1992): 70–76.
49. Alfred Marshall, *Principles of Economics*, 8th ed. (New York: Macmillan for the Royal Economic Society, 1920).

50. Large differences in earnings could coincide with small differences in talent, Rosen pointed out, because (a) lesser talent is not a good substitute for top talent and (b) the cost of production does not rise in proportion to the size of a seller's market. (For instance, a research analyst exerts roughly equal effort whether ten or three thousand clients attend his presentation.) As substitutability narrows at the upper reaches of stardom, both demand for stars and their earnings increase more than proportionally. Thus the combination of advanced joint-consumption technology and imperfect substitution allows a few superstars to dominate very large markets and command large incomes. Rosen, "The Economics of Superstars," 845. Tournament theory holds that small differences in productivity among top-ranked executives can lead to huge differences in pay. See Edwin P. Lazear and Sherwin Rosen, "Rank-Order Tournaments as Optimum Labor Contracts," *Journal of Political Economy* 89, no. 5 (October 1981): 841–64; Sherwin Rosen, "Prizes and Incentives in Elimination Tournaments," *American Economic Review* 76, no. 4 (September 1986): 701–15; and Brian G. M. Main, Charles A. O'Reilly, and James Wade, "Top Executive Pay: Tournament or Teamwork?" *Journal of Labor Economics* 11, no. 4 (October 1993): 606–28.

51. Barney, "Firm Resources and Sustained Competitive Advantage"; Peteraf, "The Cornerstones of Competitive Advantage."

52. Albert Rees, in *The Economics of Work and Pay* (New York: Harper and Row, 1973), posited that skilled workers are unlikely to migrate to jobs outside their professions because they would earn much less. Rees proposed that job mobility depends on the skill specialization within an industry or at a given employer: "Where skills are specialized to one employer, voluntary mobility will be extremely low, and a worker may spend his entire career with the same employer" (103).

53. Barney, "Firm Resources and Sustained Competitive Advantage"; Peteraf, "The Cornerstones of Competitive Advantage."

54. Jeffrey Pfeffer, *Competitive Advantage through People* (Boston: Harvard Business School Press, 1994), 124–27; Jeffrey Pfeffer, *The Human Equation: Building Profits by Putting People First* (Boston: Harvard Business School Press, 1998).

55. Peteraf, "The Cornerstones of Competitive Advantage," 187.

56. Michael Santoli, "Morgan Stanley Reworks Mgmt of Research amid Global Growth," Dow Jones News Service, September 14, 1994.

57. "Morgan Stanley Planning Major Push to Top of Research Rankings," *Securities Week* 21, no. 33 (August 15, 1994): 1.

58. Laurie Meisler, "The Complex World of Global Research," *Institutional Investor*, December 1997, pp. 127–40.

59. Tulgan, *Winning the Talent Wars*; Stan Davis and Christopher Meyer, *Blur: The Speed of Change in the Connected Economy* (Reading, MA: Perseus Books, 1998).

60. This book is the first to look at the portability of performance in knowledge workers, but a number of studies have been done on related issues—free agency and team-specific human capital—among professional athletes. Like research analysts, athletes represent an excellent population for study in

that their performance is publicly observable and quantifiable. This research stream found that players are not equally productive on all teams, and a version of firm-specific human capital and goodness of fit clearly influences the success of individuals and teams. Chapman and Southwick concluded that the performance of major league baseball managers was heavily influenced by the match between the manager and the players. See Kenneth Chapman and Lawrence Southwick Jr., "Testing the Matching Hypothesis: The Case of Major League Baseball," *American Economic Review* 81, no. 5 (December 1991): 1352–60. Borland and Lye, examining coaches in Australian rules football, came to the same conclusion: a winning record was dependent on the degree of match between coach and team. See Jeff Borland and Jenny Lye, "Matching and Mobility in the Market for Australian Rules Football Coaches," *Industrial and Labor Relations Review* 50, no. 1 (October 1996): 143–58. Looking at the effects of team-specific skills and job matching on turnover in major league baseball, Glenn, McGarrity, and Weller found that the positions requiring the most teamwork—shortstop, second baseman, and catcher—have the lowest turnover due to acquisition of team-dependent skills. To put it simply, the success of a shortstop depends on his working interactions with the second baseman. Thus as a shortstop's job tenure and team-specific skills increase, he is less likely to be traded or to leave the team as a free agent. Outfielders rely primarily on general skills and have the highest turnover because their positions require minimal teamwork. See Andrew Glenn, Joseph P. McGarrity, and Jim Weller, "Firm Specific Human Capital, Job-Matching, and Turnover: Evidence from Major League Baseball, 1900–1992," *Economic Inquiry* 39, no. 1 (January 2001): 86–93. For further exploration of the relationship between individual performance and team wins, see Michael Lewis, *Moneyball* (New York: Norton, 2003), in which the author analyzes the Oakland A's' attempt to win a championship despite a small budget. In a similar vein, David J. Berri, Martin B. Schmidt, and Stacey L. Brook try to pinpoint what actions lead to wins in professional sports in *The Wages of Wins* (Palo Alto: Stanford University Press, 2006).

61. David H. Maister, *Managing the Professional Service Firm* (New York: Free Press, 1993); Richard P. Castanias and Constance E. Helfat, "Managerial Resources and Rents," *Journal of Management* 17, no. 1 (March 1991): 155–71; Eccles and Crane, *Doing Deals*; Michael B. Mikhail, Beverly R. Walther, and Richard H. Willis, "The Development of Expertise: Do Security Analysts Improve Their Performance with Experience?" *Journal of Accounting Research* 35 (1997): 131–57; Ronald J. Gilson and Robert H. Mnookin, "Coming of Age in a Corporate Law Firm: The Economics of Associate Career Patterns," *Stanford Law Review* 41, no. 3 (February 1989): 567–95; Joel F. Henning, *Maximizing Law Firm Profitability: Hiring, Training, and Developing Productive Lawyers* (New York: Law Journal Seminars-Press, 1993); Kevin A. Kordana, "Law Firms and Associate Careers: Tournament Theory versus the Production-Imperative Model," *Yale Law Journal* 104, no. 7 (May 1995): 1907–34.

1. Sidney B. Lurie, "What Makes a Good Analyst?" *Institutional Investor*, July 1967, p. 42.
2. Ibid., 44.
3. Godfrey Howard, "What Makes a Good Analyst? Well . . . ," *Institutional Investor* 1 (May 1967): 12–13.
4. Scott Stickel, "Reputation and Performance among Security Analysts," *Journal of Finance* 47 (December 1992): 1811–36. The impact on security prices of ranked analysts' large upward forecast revisions was 0.21 percent greater than that of similar revisions by unranked analysts. First-ranked analysts had the largest impact, 0.65 percent; second-ranked analysts impacted security prices by an incremental 0.09 percent. Stickel found no significant difference in impact on security prices between ranked and unranked analysts' large downward revisions.
5. Lurie, "What Makes a Good Analyst?"
6. "The 20th Annual All-America Research Team," *Institutional Investor*, October 1991, p. 82.
7. Danielle Sessa, "All-Star Analysts 1999 Survey: Early Mornings, Late Nights Mark an Analyst's Days," *Wall Street Journal*, June 29, 1999, p. R13.
8. Jeffrey Laderman, "Who Can You Trust? Wall Street's Spin Game," *BusinessWeek*, October 5, 1998, 148–56.
9. A. Chacar and R. Coff, "Deconstructing a Knowledge-Based Advantage: Rent Generation, Rent Appropriation and 'Performance'" (London Business School working paper, SLRP WP71/1999, February 14, 2000).
10. Ford Harding, *Creating Rainmakers* (Holbrook, MA: Adams Media Corporation, 1998), x–xi.
11. John P. Kotter, *The General Managers* (New York: Free Press, 1982). Kotter's study of general managers' performance found "no evidence . . . that training programs, after graduate school, played an important role in helping any of the fifteen GMs" (137). Rather than dismissing in-house training programs, Kotter argued that successful programs must aim to guide rising stars to the most important business information, help kindle strong intrafirm relationships through mentorship, and teach up-and-comers to think systematically about their career development.
12. Some researchers even assert that starmaking is more central than rainmaking to a firm's long-term success. As two distinguished scholars put it, "Starmaking is an organization's competency at attracting, retaining, developing, and motivating star talent—the future professionals and leaders who build the firm from generation to generation. Just as there are individual rainmakers, there are partners who become starmakers—people especially adept at building star capacity within a firm. They, and the star-making firms they work for, understand *the* basic fact of life in professional services: *The people you pay are more important over time than the people who pay you.*" Jay W. Lorsch and Thomas J. Tierney, *Aligning the Stars: How to Succeed When Professionals Drive Success* (Boston: Harvard Business School Press, 2002), 64.

13. Greenwich Associates and the *Wall Street Journal* also compiled annual rankings. Greenwich Associates' poll ranked research departments and sectors rather than individual analysts. The survey was not made public, but the standings reached the press through the brokerage houses that received the results. Like *II*, Greenwich Associates asked three thousand money managers at mutual-fund companies and money-management firms to name their primary sources of equity research. Greenwich Associates also conducted a similar annual survey of more than five hundred chief investment officers at buy-side firms. The *Wall Street Journal*'s All-Star Survey ranked individual research analysts and their departments. In each industry, five individuals were chosen in two categories: stock picking and earnings estimates. The *Wall Street Journal* survey also ranked firms based on the number of their analysts who made the All-Star list. The *Wall Street Journal* and Greenwich polls were less influential than the *Institutional Investor* poll.

14. "The 1996 All-America Research Team," *Institutional Investor* 30, no. 10 (October 1996): 68.

15. Michael Siconolfi, "Shearson Research Analysts Finish First on 'All-America Team' for Third Year," *Wall Street Journal*, October 13, 1992, p. C18; Lawrence D. Brown and David Chen, "How Good Is the All-America Research Team in Forecasting Earnings?" *Journal of Business Forecasting Methods and Systems* 9 (Winter 1990–91): 14–18; Stickel, "Reputation and Performance among Security Analysts."

16. Stickel, "Reputation and Performance among Security Analysts"; Brown and Chen, "How Good Is the All-America Research Team in Forecasting Earnings?"

17. Stickel, "Reputation and Performance among Security Analysts," 1836.

18. Ibid., 1835.

19. Companies preferred to have ranked analysts follow their stocks, particularly companies preparing to issue initial public offerings. Thus promising that an *II*-ranked analyst will follow a company gave an investment bank an advantage in landing deals.

20. Professional athletics may be the best alternative example of a profession that employs standardized performance measurements. Glenn, McGarrity, and Weller, "Firm Specific Human Capital, Job-Matching, and Turnover"; Anthony C. Krautmann and Margaret Oppenheimer, "Free Agency and the Allocation of Labor in Major League Baseball," *Managerial and Decision Economics* 15 (1994): 459–69; Chapman and Southwick, "Testing the Matching Hypothesis."

21. Siconolfi, "Shearson Research Analysts Finish First on 'All-America Team' for Third Year."

22. Robert Gibbons and Lawrence F. Katz, "Layoffs and Lemons," *Journal of Labor Economics* 9, no. 4 (1991): 351–80.

23. Edward P. Lazear, "Raids and Offer Matchers," in *Research in Labor Economics*, ed. Ronald G. Ehrenberg (Greenwich, CT: JAI Press, 1986), 141–65.

24. Ibid., 152.

25. Myra H. Strober, "Human Capital Theory: Implications for HR Managers," *Industrial Relations* 29, no. 2 (Spring 1990): 214–39. This article provides an excellent outline of studies of human-capital theory and analyzes their theoretical underpinnings. Strober concluded that, due to the difficulty of empirically testing competing theories, "several theories continue in contention" (237). In view of a rapidly evolving services-based labor market, Strober foresaw much to learn from future studies of the "behavior of managers and workers under these new labor market conditions" (239). We view our study of analysts as a fulfillment of Strober's prediction: this study allows us to test human-capital theory on multiple levels—individual, firm, and market—against easily measured outputs.

26. Chacar and Coff, "Deconstructing a Knowledge-Based Advantage."

27. "The 20th Annual All-America Research Team." See pages 87–145 for clients' comments on ranked analysts.

28. Executive-recruitment firms operated on two economic models: retainer and contingency. A retained firm—like many search consultants for investment banks—was paid an up-front retainer fee to fill a given position. Retained search was an exclusively client-driven process: job candidates did not hire retainer firms, and during negotiations recruiters did not represent the candidate. Money first changed hands when the client bank asked the search firm to represent it in a specific search. Retained search firms kept the initial retainer even if the search was unsuccessful. Unlike retainer firms, contingency firms had no formal relationship with potential employers. Recruiters from such firms submitted information on potential candidates when they received an order from the manager or learned through the grapevine that a position was open. The firm was paid nothing unless the manager hired its candidate. Recruiters who worked on retainer argued that they conducted more sustained and painstaking research and recruiting efforts. They were highly motivated to keep longstanding clients happy by conducting exhaustive searches. Contingency recruiters, they said, could not devote comparable time and attention given their business model. The ethical and legal implications of the two models also differed. When a recruiting firm was on a retainer, it was obligated not to introduce the same candidate to other firms; a contingency recruiter had no such obligation. Contingency recruiters were bound by the same obligation not to poach from clients but often found ways to circumvent this restriction on the grounds that the lack of trust inherent in contingency-fee relationships justified doing so. (Finlay and Coverdill mentioned strategies like setting a time limit after which a customer was no longer considered a client, defining loyalty as owed to a specific contact or department rather than the client organization as a whole, and declaring it acceptable to poach a candidate from a client if the candidate had made the initial overture. See W. Finlay and J. E. Coverdill, "Risk, Opportunism, and Structural Holes: How Headhunters Manage Clients and Earn Fees," *Work and Occupations* 27, no. 3 [2000]: 377–405). Retained recruiters, on the other hand, were unlikely to risk losing a client to attract even the most promising candidate.

29. Clifford Geertz, "The Bazaar Economy: Information and Search in Peasant Marketing," *American Economic Review* 68 (1978): 28–32. Also see Finlay and Coverdill, "Risk, Opportunism, and Structural Holes"; M. Granovetter, *Getting a Job*, 2nd ed. (Chicago: University of Chicago Press, 1995); and R. Khurana, "Market Triads: A Theoretical and Empirical Analysis of Market Intermediation," *Journal for the Theory of Social Behaviour* 32, no. 2 (2002): 239–62.

30. Some data used in this book came from a data set compiled by Boris Groysberg and Ashish Nanda in 2006, on ranked and unranked analysts; Industrial Brokers' Estimate System; Greenwich Associates; *Institutional Investor*; Nelson's Investment Research Database; and First Call. This research was funded by the Division of Research at Harvard Business School. We are grateful for research assistance from Sarah Eriksen, Kathleen Ryan, and James Schorr.

3 | The Limits of Portability

1. This chapter draws on Boris Groysberg, "The Portability of Star Knowledge Workers: Evidence from the Analyst Market" (Ph.D. diss., Harvard Business School, 2002); Boris Groysberg, Linda-Eling Lee, and Ashish Nanda, "Can They Take It with Them? The Portability of Star Knowledge Workers' Performance: Myth or Reality," *Management Science* 54 (July 2008): 1213–30; Boris Groysberg and Ashish Nanda, "When Superstars Switch Allegiance: Ranked Analyst Turnover in Investment Banks" (working paper); Boris Groysberg, Ashish Nanda, and Nitin Nohria, "The Risky Business of Hiring Stars," *Harvard Business Review*, May 2004. In particular, the quantitative findings in this chapter (regressions and some exhibits) are based on and drawn from these articles.

2. Tulgan, *Winning the Talent Wars*; Woodruffe, *Winning the Talent War*.

3. Kordana, "Law Firms and Associate Careers."

4. Arthur, "The Boundaryless Career."

5. Blair and Kochan, *The New Relationship*; Bowers and Swain, "Recent Trends in Job Training"; G. A. Callanan and J. H. Greenhaus, "Personal and Career Development: The Best and Worst of Times," in *Evolving Practices in Human Resource Management: Responses to a Changing World of Work*, ed. A. I. Kraut and A. K. Korman (San Francisco: Jossey-Bass, 1999), 146–71.

6. Stefanie R. Schmidt, "Long-Run Trends in Workers' Beliefs about Their Own Job Security: Evidence from the General Social Survey," *Journal of Labor Economics* 17, no. 4, part 2 (October 1999): S127–S141; David Neumark, Daniel Polsky, and Daniel Hansen, "Has Job Stability Declined Yet? New Evidence from the 1990s," *Journal of Labor Economics* 17, no. 4, part 2 (October 1999): S29–S64; Robert G. Valletta, "Declining Job Security," *Journal of Labor Economics* 17, no. 4, part 2 (October 1999): S170–S197.

7. Adverse selection is a central factor in predicting labor-market outcomes when an individual's abilities are not public knowledge. See Dan Bernhardt and David Scoones, "Promotion, Turnover, and Preemptive Wage Offers,"

American Economic Review 83, no. 4 (September 1993): 771–91; Bruce C. Greenwald, "Adverse Selection in the Labor Market," *Review of Economic Studies* 53, no. 3 (July 1986): 325–47; Bruce C. Greenwald, *Adverse Selection in the Labor Market* (New York: Garland Press, 1979); Paul Milgrom and Sharon Oster, "Job Discrimination, Market Forces, and the Invisibility Hypothesis," *Quarterly Journal of Economics* 102, no. 3 (August 1987): 453–76; Michael Waldman, "Up-or-Out Contracts: A Signaling Perspective," *Journal of Labor Economics* 8, no. 2 (April 1990): 230–50. In asymmetric-information models, employees and employers at a given firm possess an informational advantage over other firms about employees' productivity levels, leading less-able workers to predominate among those changing jobs. See Greenwald, "Adverse Selection in the Labor Market"; Greenwald, *Adverse Selection in the Labor Market*. The existence of a winner's curse is an outcome of several asymmetric models (see Greenwald, "Adverse Selection in the Labor Market"; Greenwald, *Adverse Selection in the Labor Market*; Milgrom and Oster, "Job Discrimination, Market Forces, and the Invisibility Hypothesis"). In contrast to Greenwald, Lazear examined claims that higher visibility increases the probability of competition for top-rated employees. See Lazear, "Raids and Offer Matchers."

8. Becker, *Human Capital*; Becker, "Investment in Human Capital"; Jacob Mincer, *Schooling, Experience, and Earnings* (New York: Columbia University Press, 1974).

9. Manville, "Talking Human Capital with Professor Gary S. Becker."

10. Cheryl L. Maranto and Robert C. Rodgers, "Does Work Experience Increase Productivity? A Test of the On-the-Job Training Hypothesis," *Journal of Human Resources* 19, no. 3 (Summer 1984): 341–57; Robert Topel, "Specific Capital, Mobility, and Wages: Wages Rise with Job Seniority," *Journal of Political Economy* 99, no. 11 (1991): 145–76.

11. Topel, "Specific Capital, Mobility, and Wages."

12. David Krackhardt and Jeffrey R. Hanson, "Informal Networks: The Company behind the Chart," *Harvard Business Review* (July–August 1993): 104–11.

13. Krackhardt and Hanson, "Informal Networks."

14. John J. Gabarro, "When a New Manager Takes Charge," *Harvard Business Review* (May–June 1985): 110–23.

15. Meryl Reis Louis, "Surprise and Sense Making: What Newcomers Experience in Entering Unfamiliar Organizational Settings," *Administrative Science Quarterly* 25, no. 2 (June 1980): 226–51.

16. Harry J. Holzer, Richard N. Block, Marcus Cheatham, and Jack H. Knott, "Are Training Subsidies for Firms Effective? The Michigan Experience," *Industrial and Labor Relations Review* 46, no. 4 (July 1993): 625–36; Ann P. Bartel, "Productivity Gains from the Implementation of Employee Training Programs," *Industrial Relations* 33, no. 4 (October 1994): 411–25.

17. Becker, "Investment in Human Capital"; Jacob Mincer and Boyan Jovanovic, "Labor Mobility and Wages," in *Studies in Labor Markets*, ed. Sherwin Rosen (Chicago: University of Chicago Press, 1981).

18. Molly Baker, "Heard on the Street: Some Analysts Enter Land of Big Bucks," *Wall Street Journal*, July 2, 1996, p. C1.

19. Organizational resources can affect knowledge workers' ability to sustain top performance. See Ikujiro Nonaka, "A Dynamic Theory of Organizational Knowledge Creation," *Organization Science* 5, no. 1 (February 1994): 14–37; and Robert M. Grant, "Towards a Knowledge-Based Theory of the Firm," *Strategic Management Journal* 17 (Winter 1996): 109–22. Because professionals depend on acquiring high-quality information and accessing sources of ideas, one important resource that organizations provide is colleagues with whom to share important information. See Pfeffer, *Competitive Advantage through People*, and Pfeffer, *The Human Equation*.

    Colleagues also provide information that an individual might not encounter on his or her own. Colleagues working on a different team might have access to different information. See Jay R. Galbraith, *Organization Design* (Reading, MA: Addison Wesley, 1977); James G. March and Herbert A. Simon, *Organizations* (New York: John Wiley, 1958); M. Davis and Paul R. Lawrence, *Matrix* (Reading, MA: Addison Wesley, 1977); Kim B. Clark and Takahiro Fujimoto, *Product Development Performance: Strategy, Organization, and Management in the World Auto Industry* (Boston: Harvard Business School Press, 1991); Ronald S. Burt, "Social Contagion and Innovation: Cohesion versus Structural Equivalence," *American Journal of Sociology* 92, no. 6 (May 1987): 1287–1335; Eccles and Crane, *Doing Deals*.

20. John Cassidy, "The Firm," *The New Yorker*, March 8, 1999, p. 30.

21. Nanda, Groysberg, and Prusiner, "Lehman Brothers (A)," 12.

22. "1996 All-America Research Team."

23. Boris Groysberg and Anahita Hashemi, "Sanford C. Bernstein: Growing Pains" (HBS case no. 9-405-011) (Boston: Harvard Business School Publishing, 1993), 19.

24. Barbara Donnelly, "Tough Times for Research Directors," *Wall Street Journal*, May 28, 1991, p. C1.

25. Ibid.

26. Participation in investment-banking deals represents a particular threat to analysts' intellectual independence. A number of research departments have created the position of investment-banking officer to help analysts handle this delicate and often adversarial relationship. The 2003 Global Research Analyst Settlement entered into by ten investment banks, the Securities and Exchange Commission, the New York Stock Exchange, and securities regulators aimed to resolve conflict-of-interest issues by insulating research from investment banking. The settlement allows analysts to make technical contributions to investment-banking deals but not to help solicit such deals. These requirements were not in effect during the period of our study, which made the role of the research director in protecting the analyst's independence more crucial than it is today. Then, a firm's corporate finance department could ask an analyst for information to help construct a deal or twist the analyst's arm to attend business pitches. "Analysts are often pressured to trash their franchises

to help get a deal done," one analyst complained in 1990 (Debbie Galant, "The Hazards of Negative Research Reports," *Institutional Investor*, July 1990, p. 74). At some firms, analysts were even expected to bring in investment-banking deals themselves. Fred Fraenkel said about that environment, "You're literally getting deals because the CEO likes the analyst at a certain place, thinks he's smart, thinks he's got industry knowledge, thinks he's going to make their stock price go up and their cost of capital go down." Analysts were also sometimes expected to help sustain existing corporate finance relationships, expectations that could jeopardize analysts' reputation and performance. According to Michael Culp, ex-director of research at Prudential, when an analyst is "viewed as a mouthpiece for investment banking, their career is over. The best mark of an analyst is having two managements that want you dead" (Ellen E. Schultz, "Wall Street Grows Treacherous for Analysts Who Speak Out," *Wall Street Journal*, April 5, 1990, p. C1).

27. Mary Rowland, "The New Power of the Research Director," *Institutional Investor*, December 1983, p. 87.

28. The popular explanation for analysts' failure to serve as unbiased financial intermediaries is to attribute their research optimism to incentives associated with underwriting activities. In response to regulatory alarm about overoptimistic research at leading investment banks, ten of the largest U.S. investment banks agreed in 2003 to (1) implement a series of reforms, (2) pay $900 million in fines and disgorgement of profits, (3) pay $85 million for investor education, and (4) pay $450 million over five years to acquire three independent research reports on every company they cover and to distribute them along with their own reports. A subsequent study of research optimism found analysts at firms with underwriting business to actually be *less* optimistic than those at pure brokerage houses, which perform no underwriting. The less optimistic forecasts of underwriting firms are not fully explained by bank reputation or by the types of clients they serve (retail or institutional). The study concludes that the use of trading to fund research creates powerful incentives for analyst optimism. These findings are important for regulators that require sanctioned underwriters to supplement their own research with research from three independent sources. See Amanda Paige Cowen, Boris Groysberg, and Paul Healy, "Which Types of Analyst Firms Are More Optimistic?" *Journal of Accounting and Economics* 41, nos. 1–2 (April 2006): 119–46.

29. Donnelly, "Tough Times for Research Directors."

30. Reba White, "How Two Research Departments Can Add Up to One," *Institutional Investor*, September 1976, pp. 28–29.

31. Ibid.

32. Ibid., 29.

33. Jacob Mincer compared investment in on-the-job training with investment in formal education and attempted to determine the rate of return for each. His findings show that on-the-job training accounts for over half of total investment in education in the United States. Rates of return were quite similar, though formal education sometimes produced a better return than on-the-job

training. See Mincer, "On-the-Job Training: Costs, Returns, and Some Implications," *Journal of Political Economy* 70, no. 5 (October 1962): 50–79. Using the National Longitudinal Survey of Youth, which examines the job training of 4,614 men and women from 1986 to 1990, Jonathan R. Veum attempted to pinpoint the wage impact of different training programs such as company training programs, apprenticeships, business schools, vocational and technical institutes, correspondence courses, and seminars outside the workplace. Total time spent in training did not significantly affect 1990 wage levels, but company training and seminars outside work did have a positive effect on wage levels and wage changes between 1986 and 1990. See Veum, "Sources of Training and Their Impact on Wages," *Industrial and Labor Relations Review* 48, no. 4 (July 1995): 812–26.

34. In an interesting piece on intrafirm networks, Krackhardt and Hanson explain the process of mapping advice-and-trust networks within an organization. A visual representation of workplace communication patterns can help a manager identify such problems as irregular communication and overdependence. See Krackhardt and Hanson, "Informal Networks." Management guru Peter F. Drucker underscores the need for drastic change in the profession of management to meet the needs of the information age. Drucker encourages knowledge workers to take "relationship responsibility"—to learn how to communicate effectively with colleagues and to teach colleagues how to reciprocate. Drucker, *Management Challenges for the 21st Century*.

35. Groysberg, Lee, and Nanda, "Can They Take It with Them?"; Boris Groysberg and Linda-Eling Lee, "Hiring Stars and Their Teams: Exploration and Exploitation in Professional Service Firms," *Organization Science* 20, no. 4 (July–August 2009): 740–58; Boris Groysberg and Linda-Eling Lee, "The Effects of Colleague Quality on Top Performance: The Case of Security Analysts," *Journal of Organizational Behavior* 29, no. 8 (November 2008): 1123–44.

36. Groysberg and Roberts, "Leading the Josie Esquivel Franchise (B)," 2.

37. Ibid.

38. Thomas J. Peters and Robert H. Waterman, *In Search of Excellence: Lessons from America's Best-Run Companies* (New York: Harper and Row, 1982), 79.

39. Groysberg, Lee, and Nanda, "Can They Take It With Them?"; and Groysberg and Lee, "Hiring Stars and Their Teams."

40. We defined the overall quality of a department as the percentage of institutional clients who rate it among the ten best research departments in a given year. The quality of colleagues was defined as the percentage of star colleagues on a given analyst's team. The quality of the portfolio strategist and the sales staff were both defined by the percentage of institutional clients who rated the firm as offering the best portfolio strategy and sales support, respectively.

41. Boris Groysberg, "Stardom: Effects of Context & Tenure: The Case of Equity Analysts" (Working paper, 2008).

42. Anne Cummings and Greg R. Oldham have pointed out that creative employees need complex jobs, supportive supervisors, and stimulating coworkers in

order to produce. See Cummings and Oldham, "Enhancing Creativity: Managing Work Contexts for the High Potential Employee," *California Management Review* 40, no. 1 (Fall 1997): 22–38.

43. The quality of colleagues exerted a variable effect on stars. Lower-ranked stars appeared to benefit most from higher-quality colleagues; high-quality colleagues contributed less to the performance of higher-ranked analysts. Groysberg and Lee have demonstrated the strategic importance of retaining higher-quality human assets. Their study shows how organizations that enjoy superior means of supporting high-quality human assets accrue and maintain performance advantages over organizations with fewer such means. Firms without a large stable of star performers have a harder time supporting the few stars they do have. Groysberg and Lee wrote: "Our study suggests that professionals in different roles and areas of the organization complement one another in creating and delivering highly intangible outputs to clients. Hence, although top performers in these markets appear to 'own' their reputational and other advantages, they may owe part of their performance to colleagues who spark ideas, provide information, and position their service with clients." See Groysberg and Lee, "The Effects of Colleague Quality on Top Performance." This study also connects to the literature on professional business services. See Royston Greenwood et al., "Biggest Is Best? Strategic Assumptions and Actions in the Canadian Audit Industry," *Canadian Journal of Administrative Sciences* 10, no. 4 (December 1993): 308–32; Henning, *Maximizing Law Firm Profitability*; and Kordana, "Law Firms and Associate Careers." Related research on organizational status in academic careers has demonstrated a Matthew effect. See Robert K. Merton, "The Matthew Effect in Science," *Science* 159, no. 3810 (January 5, 1968): 56–63; and Cole and Cole, *Social Stratification in Science*.

44. See Eccles and Crane, *Doing Deals*.

45. The six bulge-bracket firms were Credit Suisse First Boston, Goldman Sachs, Lehman Brothers, Merrill Lynch, Morgan Stanley, and Salomon Brothers. These firms underwrote the bulk of the equities sold in the United States. Bulge-bracket firms had large and well-financed research departments, and their distribution capabilities, specialized units, and economies of scale in marketing, sales, and technology enabled them to provide richer resources than the other seventy-two firms we studied. These resources and capabilities gave them a competitive edge. Prior studies have found that analysts employed by large departments tend, on average, to be better forecasters.

46. "The 1978 All-America Research Team," *Institutional Investor*, October 1978, p. 30.

47. James G. March, "Exploration and Exploitation in Organizational Learning," *Organization Science* 2 (1991): 71–87.

4 | Do Firms Benefit from Hiring Stars?

1. This chapter draws on Groysberg, "The Portability of Star Knowledge Workers"; Groysberg, Lee, and Nanda, "Can They Take It with Them?"; Groysberg

and Lee, "Hiring Stars and Their Teams"; Groysberg and Nanda, "When Superstars Switch Allegiance"; Groysberg, Nanda, and Nohria, "The Risky Business of Hiring Stars." In particular, quantitative findings (regressions and some exhibits) are based on and drawn from these articles.

2. "The 1998 All-America Research Team," *Institutional Investor International Edition*, October 1998, pp. 99–187.

3. Woodruffe, *Winning the Talent War*, 101.

4. Gary Hamel and C. K. Prahalad, *Competing for the Future* (Boston: Harvard Business School Press, 1994), 52–56.

5. Northcraft and Neale looked at the processes of scientific collaboration and found that teams composed of collaborators with diverse and varied skill sets are more likely to succeed. See Gregory B. Northcraft and Margaret A. Neale, "Negotiating Successful Research Collaboration," in *Social Psychology in Organizations: Advances in Theory and Research*, ed. J. Keith Murnighan (Englewood Cliffs, NJ: Prentice Hall, 1993), 204–24. Peters and Waterman (*In Search of Excellence*) have shown how some of the most successful U.S. companies, like 3M and Hewlett-Packard, used strategic hires and small acquisitions to build a new skill. Also see John Bramham, *Human Resource Planning* (London: Institute of Personnel and Development, 1994).

6. "The 1997 All-America Research Team," *Institutional Investor*, October 1997, p. 82.

7. Ibid.

8. Philip Maher, "Gross Expectations: Wall Street's Endless Pay Demands May Finally Have Gone over the Top," *Investment Dealer's Digest*, May 5, 1997, p. 22.

9. "Pay Packages and Demand Continued to Soar for Top Analysts during First Half of 1994," *Securities Week*, July 4, 1994, p. 1; "Pay Continues to Soar for Top Research Analysts," *Securities Week*, September 5, 1994, p. 8.

10. Groysberg, Nanda, and Nohria, "The Risky Business of Hiring Stars."

11. "1997 All-America Research Team," 81.

12. The winner's curse was first identified in the context of bidding for oil-drilling rights and gas leases. See E. C. Capen, R. V. Clapp, and W. M. Campbell, "Competitive Bidding in High-Risk Situations," *Journal of Petroleum Technology* 23 (June 1971): 641–53. "If one wins a tract against two or three others, he may feel fine about his good fortune," the authors commented. "But how should he feel if he won against 50 others? Ill" (645). According to Capen, Clapp, and Campbell, as quoted by Thaler, "He who bids on a parcel what he thinks it is worth, will, in the long run, be taken for a cleaning." See Richard H. Thaler, "Anomalies: The Winner's Curse," *Journal of Economic Perspectives* 2, no. 1 (Winter 1988): 191–202, p. 201. Examining bidding behavior on oil and gas leases by eighteen firms, Hendricks, Porter, and Boudreau found that firms overpaid for development rights. In fact, some firms tended to consistently overvalue tracts. See Kenneth Hendricks, Robert H. Porter, and Bryan Boudreau, "Information, Returns, and Bidding Behavior in OCS Auctions: 1954–1969," *Journal of Industrial Economics* 35, no. 4 (June 1987): 517–42. Smith explained the winner's curse: "In the auction of any item whose

value is uncertain, there is a possibility that the winning bidder is led to that position because he has most overestimated the item's true value. In retrospect, the winner will revalue the item in accordance with the revealed bids of his rivals, all of whom bid lower than himself. Consequently, the winner's appraisal may be diminished by the very act of winning. If the firm does not respect the underbidding rule . . . , it may enter a bid that exceeds its final appraisal of the item's value, even though the bid started out well below the initial (pre-auction) estimate. In this unfortunate event, the firm would regret its action immediately upon winning the auction, and could be said to have experienced the winner's curse." See James L. Smith, "Non-Aggressive Bidding Behavior and the Winner's Curse," *Economic Inquiry* 19, no. 3 (July 1981): 383–84. Thaler elaborated that "the winner can be said to be 'cursed' in one of two ways: (1) the winning bid exceeds the value of the tract [bidding item], so the firm loses money; or (2) the value of the tract [or any other object] is less than the expert's estimate, so the winning firm is disappointed." See Richard H. Thaler, *The Winner's Curse: Paradoxes and Anomalies of Economic Life* (New York: Free Press, 1992), 192.

13. The existence of a winner's curse has been confirmed in laboratory experiments. See Max H. Bazerman and William F. Samuelson, "I Won the Auction But Don't Want the Prize," *Journal of Conflict Resolution* 27, no. 4 (December 1983): 618–34; William F. Samuelson and Max H. Bazerman, "The Winner's Curse in Bilateral Negotiations," *Research in Experimental Economics* 3 (1985): 105–37; John H. Kagel and Dan Levin, "The Winner's Curse and Public Information in Common Value Auctions," *American Economic Review* 76, no. 5 (December 1986): 894–920; and John H. Kagel, Dan Levin, and Ronald M. Harstad, "Judgment, Evaluation, and Information Processing in Second-Price Common Value Auctions" (unpublished manuscript, Department of Economics, University of Houston, 1987). Brannman, Klein, and Weiss found evidence of the winner's curse phenomenon in their examination of bidding behavior in several auction markets. See Lance Brannman, Douglass J. Klein, and Leonard W. Weiss, "The Price Effects of Increased Competition in Auction Markets," *Review of Economics and Statistics* 69, no. 1 (February 1987): 24–32. Brown found the winner's curse in investment projects. The most overestimated returns were viewed as the most acceptable projects. See Keith Brown, "A Note on the Apparent Bias of Net Revenue Estimates for Capital Investment Projects," *Journal of Finance* 29, no. 4 (September 1974): 1215–16. Kagel and Levin ("The Winner's Curse and Public Information in Common Value Auctions") discovered that the severity of the winner's curse in auctions increases with the participation of more rivals. To their surprise, after examining whether feedback and relevant experience helped avoid the winner's curse, Foreman and Murnighan concluded that "experience had little impact and that additional feedback reduced overbidding but never extinguished the winner's curse; instead it was pervasive and highly resistant to learning" and that "high endowments and limited feedback, in particular, led to the most extreme curses." See Peter Foreman and J. Keith Murnighan, "Learning to Avoid

Winner's Curse," *Organizational Behavior and Human Decision Processes* 67, no. 2 (August 1996): 170. Even individuals who understand the winner's curse in one setting consistently fail to avoid it in other situations. See Thaler, *The Winner's Curse*.

The existence of the winner's curse in the labor market context has also been studied by Lazear, "Raids and Offer Matchers"; Greenwald, "Adverse Selection in the Labour Market"; Milgrom and Oster, "Job Discrimination, Market Forces, and the Invisibility Hypothesis"; Waldman, "Up-or-Out Contracts"; and Gibbons and Katz, "Layoffs and Lemons."

14. In *Book Publishing*, Dessauer claimed that many auctioned book manuscripts fail to earn back their advances because publishing companies' experts overestimate their "true" market value. See John P. Dessauer, *Book Publishing: What It Is, What It Does* (New York: Bowker, 1981). In a study of major league baseball, Cassing and Douglas demonstrated that owners systematically pay more for free agents than their actual value to the team. See James Cassing and Richard W. Douglas, "Implications of the Auction Mechanism in Baseball's Free Agent Drafts," *Southern Economic Journal* 47, no. 1 (July 1980): 110–21. Oorlog also found that free agents were overpaid relative to their impact on the team. See Dale R. Oorlog, "Marginal Revenue and Labor Strife in Major League Baseball," *Journal of Labor Research* 16, no. 1 (Winter 1995): 25–42. In the film industry, Ravid found that Oscar winners captured most of their expected value added. In fact, hiring stars did not increase return on investment for movie projects. Ravid concludes: "This article presents two alternative explanations for the role of stars in motion pictures. Either informed insiders signal project quality by hiring an expensive star, or stars capture their expected rent. These approaches are tested on a sample of movies produced in the 1990s. Means comparisons suggest that star-studded films bring in higher revenues. However, regressions show that any big-budget investment increases revenue. Sequels, highly visible films and 'family oriented' ratings also contribute to revenues. A higher return on investment is correlated with G or PG ratings and marginally with sequels. This is consistent with the 'rent capture' hypothesis" (463). See S. Abraham Ravid, "Information, Blockbusters and Stars: A Study of the Film Industry," *Journal of Business* 72, no. 4 (October 1999): 463–92. In a similar study, Elbrese also concludes that movie stars capture all of their value added to a film. See Anita Elberse, "The Power of Stars: Do Star Actors Drive the Success of Movies?" *Journal of Marketing* 71, no. 4 (October 2007).

15. Examining why firms consistently overpay for target acquisitions, Roll assumes that all information in a potential deal is symmetric. The only logical reason why the deal is still pursued, Roll hypothesizes, is hubris or arrogance on the part of the acquirer. See Richard Roll, "The Hubris Hypothesis of Corporate Takeovers," *Journal of Business* 59, no. 2, part 1 (April 1986): 197–216.

16. The existence of a winner's curse in the corporate-takeover context has been extensively studied and empirically confirmed in various domestic and inter-

national markets. See Michael C. Jensen and Richard S. Ruback, "The Market for Corporate Control—The Scientific Evidence," *Journal of Financial Economics* 11 (1983): 5–50; Roll, "The Hubris Hypothesis of Corporate Takeovers," 197–221; and Nikhil P. Varaiya, "The 'Winner's Curse' Hypothesis and Corporate Takeovers," *Managerial and Decision Economics* 9, no. 3 (September 1988): 209–19. For example, a winner's curse has been identified in banks' acquisitions of their failed counterparts. See Richard H. Pettway and Jack W. Trifts, "Do Banks Overbid When Acquiring Failed Banks?" *Financial Management* 14, no. 2 (Summer 1985): 5–15. Increased competition drove up the winning bids and the bid levels of all participants. Furthermore, bidders failed to adjust for the winner's curse. See Michael S. Giliberto and Nikhil P. Varaiya, "The Winner's Curse and Bidder Competition in Acquisitions: Evidence from Failed Bank Auctions," *Journal of Finance* 44, no. 1 (March 1989): 59–75. For relevant topics, see Nikhil P. Varaiya and Kenneth R. Ferris, "Overpaying in Corporate Takeovers: The Winner's Curse," *Financial Analysts Journal* 43, no. 3 (May/June 1987): 64–70. Dickie, Michel, and Shaked claim that an informational disadvantage is why acquirers suffer the winner's curse. See Robert Dickie, Allen Michel, and Israel Shaked, "The Winner's Curse in the Merger Game," *Journal of General Management* 12, no. 3 (Spring 1987): 32–51; Gregg A. Jarrell, James A. Brickley, and Jeffry M. Netter, "The Market for Corporate Control: The Empirical Evidence since 1980," *Journal of Economic Perspectives* 2, no. 1 (Winter 1988): 49–68. In his extensive review of the merger-and-acquisition literature, Sirower claims that on average abnormal returns for acquiring firms are negative. See Mark L. Sirower, *The Synergy Trap: How Companies Lose the Acquisition Game* (New York: Free Press, 1997). Acquiring firms' overpayments are often offered as explanations for negative bidder returns. See Michael Bradley, Anand Desai, and Han E. Kim, "Synergistic Gains from Corporate Acquisitions and Their Division between the Stockholders of Target and Acquiring Firms," *Journal of Financial Economics* 21, no. 1 (May 1988): 3–40; and Paul Asquith, Robert F. Bruner, and David W. Mullins Jr., "The Gains to Bidding Firms from Merger," *Journal of Financial Economics* 11 (April 1983): 121–39. Roll argues that acquiring firms overpay for their targets because their managers overestimate their own ability to create value after acquisitions. See Roll, "The Hubris Hypothesis of Corporate Takeovers," 197–216. Morck, Shleifer, and Vishny claim that managers sacrifice shareholder value to receive substantial personal benefits and rewards. See Randall Morck, Andrei Shleifer, and Robert W. Vishny, "Do Managerial Objectives Drive Bad Acquisitions?" *Journal of Finance* 45, no. 1 (March 1990): 31–48; Andrei Shleifer and Robert W. Vishny, "Value Maximization and the Acquisition Process," *Journal of Economic Perspectives* 2, no. 1 (1988): 7–20; and Andrei Shleifer and Robert W. Vishny, "Management Entrenchment: The Case of Manager-Specific Investments," *Journal of Financial Economics* 25, no. 1 (November 1989): 123–39.

17. Chacar and Coff, "Deconstructing a Knowledge-Based Advantage."
18. Robert Wilson, "Auditing: Perspectives from Multi-Person Decision Theory," *Accounting Review* 58, no. 2 (April 1983): 305–18.

19. Roll, "The Hubris Hypothesis of Corporate Takeovers," 197–216. See note 16 for further discussion.

20. Newcomers' uneasy adjustment has been extensively studied by sociologists and psychologists. See Louis, "Surprise and Sense Making"; and Nigel Nicholson and Michael A. West, *Managerial Job Change: Men and Women in Transition* (New York: Cambridge University Press, 1988). Newcomers' success depends on their ability to develop new firm-specific skills. They acquire such skills through education, training, and experience, using performance feedback as a guiding mechanism. See A. T. Welford, *Skilled Performance: Perceptual and Motor Skills* (Glenview, IL: Scott Foresman, 1976). Over time, newcomers' acquisition of skills, rules, and attitudes results in improved performance in their new work environments. See Irwin L. Goldstein, *Training and Development in Organizations* (San Francisco: Jossey-Bass, 1989). However, newly hired stars might be the most resistant to change because of their previous success. In fact, a star may experience a particularly slow transition from newcomer to insider status. Throughout the process, Van Maanen and Schein point out, "newcomers must first be tested either informally and formally as to their abilities, motives, and values before being granted inclusionary rights" (222). See Josh Van Maanen and Edgar H. Schein, "Towards a Theory of Organizational Socialization," in *Research in Organizational Behavior*, vol. 1, ed. B. M. Straw and L. L Cummings (Greenwich, CT: JAI Press, 1979): 209–64.

21. Woodruffe, *Winning the Talent War*, 86.

22. Ibid.

23. Harding, *Creating Rainmakers*, 207–8. In a detailed look at excellent salespeople in professional-service firms, Harding concluded that firms should identify talented individuals early, set long-term goals, provide resources to attain those goals, and monitor the developing star's performance. Harding argued for internal star development because star hires are destructive to the performance of the organization.

24. Danny Miller, *The Icarus Paradox: How Exceptional Companies Bring about Their Own Downfall* (New York: Harper Business, 1990); Rosabeth Moss Kanter, Barry A. Stein, and Todd D. Jick, *The Challenge of Organizational Change: How Companies Experience It and Leaders Guide It* (New York: Free Press, 1992); Michael Hammer and James Champy, *Reengineering the Corporation: A Manifesto for Business Revolution* (New York: Harper Business, 1993); David K. Hurst, *Crisis and Renewal: Meeting the Challenge of Organizational Change* (Boston: Harvard Business School Press, 1995); and Howard E. Aldrich, *Organizations Evolving* (London: Sage, 1999). New stars who are not given time to integrate into a group are especially resistant to change even if they are mentored by other stars. As Lewin points out, "it is usually easier to change individuals formed into a group than to change any one of them separately" (210). See Kurt Lewin, "Group Decision and Social Change," in *Readings in Social Psychology*, ed. Eleanor E. Maccoby, Theodore M. Newcomb, and Eugene L. Hartley (New York: Holt, Rinehart and Winston, 1958), 197–211.

25. Groysberg, Nanda, and Nohria, "The Risky Business of Hiring Stars," p. 3.

26. Harding, *Creating Rainmakers*.

27. Kanter points out that people need organizational power to obtain necessary resources, and that organizations are more willing to give resources to those with outstanding track records. See Rosabeth Moss Kanter, *The Change Masters: Innovation for Productivity in the American Corporation* (New York: Simon and Schuster, 1983). In his study of the capital resource allocation process, Bower shows that the reputation and track record of high-performing employees allow them to obtain significant organizational resources for investment projects. See J. L. Bower, *Managing the Resource Allocation Process: A Study of Corporate Planning and Investment* (Boston: Harvard Business School Division of Research, 1970). In corporate venturing, champions' prior track records, status, and networks enable them to identify, acquire, mobilize, and deploy resources. See Robert A. Burgelman, Clayton M. Christensen, and Steven C. Weelwright, *Strategic Management of Technology and Innovation* (Homewood, IL: Irwin, 1988); and Patricia G. Greene, Candida G. Brush, and Myra M. Hart, "The Corporate Venture Champion: A Resource-Based Approach to Role and Process," *Entrepreneurship Theory and Practice* 23, no. 3 (Spring 1999): 103–22. In investment banking, Smith and Walter report on the disproportional allocation of resources to the best and brightest, because firms believe that their success or failure is dependent on stars' actions. See Roy C. Smith and Ingo Walter, *Street Smarts: Linking Professional Conduct with Shareholder Value in the Securities Industry* (Boston: Harvard Business School Press, 1997). When investment banks enter new markets or introduce new products, many choose a shortcut strategy of hiring star experts from the competition. These stars are richly rewarded and receive superior human and financial resources in the pursuit of organizational goals. See Eccles and Crane, *Doing Deals*. The star's irreplaceability and his or her perceived power are also important factors in negotiations for limited organizational resources. See E. P. Hollander, "Legitimacy, Power and Influence: A Perspective on Relational Features of Leadership," in *Leadership Theory and Research: Perspectives and Directions*, ed. M. M. Chemers and R. Ayman (San Diego: Academic Press, 1992), 29–43.

A firm's hiring rate, especially for high-level jobs, also affects opportunities for promotion at the firm and the psychological contract between existing workers and their employers. See L. C. Gratton, "Management of High Potential," in *Blackwell Encyclopedia of Management: Organizational Behavior*, ed. N. Nicholson, vol. 6 (Cambridge, MA: Blackwell, 1995), 312–14. Given a limited number of opportunities for promotion, additions of newcomers intensify competition for advancement. Though the firm's employees are ordinarily in a better position to be promoted than new hires, newly hired stars restrict existing employees' chances of being promoted because stars usually enter fast-track positions. See James E. Rosenbaum, *Career Mobility in a Corporate Hierarchy* (Orlando, FL: Academic Press, 1984); James E. Rosenbaum, "Organization Career Systems and Employee Misperceptions," in *Handbook of Career Theory*, ed. M. B Arthur, D. T. Hall, and B. S. Lawrence (Cambridge: Cambridge University Press, 1989).

28. An organization that hires stars who differ from existing employees and receive conspicuous rewards upon joining might find that many of its employees perceive the distribution of rewards as unfair. These employees' job satisfaction then decreases, dragging their performance down with it. Their desire to exit the organization might also increase. Specifically, the decreased motivation associated with a perception of unfair distribution of resources has a disproportionate impact on the performance of higher-ability people. See Victor H. Vroom, *Work and Motivation* (New York: John Wiley, 1964).

    Furthermore, the arrival of highly prized newcomers who receive disproportional rewards for their contributions might force others to start comparing themselves to their new peers, which often results in the pain of inequity. See Jerald Greenberg, "Approaching Equity and Avoiding Inequity in Groups in Organizations," in *Equity and Justice in Social Behavior*, ed. Jerald Greenberg and Ronald L. Cohen (San Diego: Academic Press, 1982), 389–435. The social-comparison theory might also provide insights into existing employees' self-esteem and jealousy. See Jerry Suls and Thomas Ashby Wills, "Commentary: Neo-Social Comparison Theory and Beyond," in *Social Comparison: Contemporary Theory and Research*, ed. Jerry Suls and Thomas Ashby Wills (Hillsdale, NJ: Erlbaum, 1991), 395–411.

29. See Greenberg, "Approaching Equity and Avoiding Inequity in Groups in Organizations"; Jerald Greenberg, "Employee Theft as a Reaction to Underpayment Inequity: The Hidden Cost of Pay Cuts," *Journal of Applied Psychology* 75, no. 5 (October 1990): 561–68; John P. Meyer et al., "Organizational Commitment and Job Performance: It's the Nature of the Commitment That Counts," *Journal of Applied Psychology* 74, no. 1 (February 1989): 152–56; John P. Meyer and Natalie J. Allen, "A Three-Component Conceptualization of Organizational Commitment," *Human Resource Management Review* 1, no. 1 (Spring 1991): 61–89; see also Stephen Fineman, *Emotion in Organizations* (Newbury Park, CA: Sage, 1993).

30. Harding, *Creating Rainmakers*.

31. Woodruffe, *Winning the Talent War*, 75.

32. Vroom, *Work and Motivation*.

33. Harding, *Creating Rainmakers*.

34. For use of stock-market reaction methodology to measure the effects of mergers and joint ventures, see Jensen and Ruback, "The Market for Corporate Control"; Jarrell, Brickley, and Netter, "The Market for Corporate Control"; John J. McConnell and Timothy J. Nantell, "Corporate Combinations and Common Stock Returns: The Case of Joint Ventures," *Journal of Finance* 40, no. 2 (June 1985): 519–36; Jeongsok Koh and N. Vekatraman, "Joint Venture Formations and Stock Market Reactions: An Assessment in the Information Technology Sector," *Academy of Management Journal* 34, no. 4 (December 1991): 869–92; and Partha Mohanram and Ashish Nanda, "Stock Market Reaction to Joint Venture Announcement" (HBS working paper no. 96-028, 1996). For a comparison of event study methods, see Thomas Dyckman, Donna Philbrick, and Jens Stephan, "A Comparison of Event Study Methodologies Using Daily Stock

Returns: A Simulation Approach," *Journal of Accounting Research* 22, supplement (1984): 1–30; Grant McQueen and V. Vance Roley, "Stock Prices, News and Business Conditions," *Review of Financial Studies* 6, no. 3 (1993): 683–707; Paul Asquith and David W. Mullins Jr., "Equity Issues and Offering Dilution," *Journal of Financial Economics* 15, no. 1–2 (January–February 1986): 61–89; and Mark Mitchell and Jeffry M. Netter, "The Role of Financial Economics in Securities Fraud Cases: Applications at the Securities and Exchange Commission," *Business Lawyer* 49, no. 2 (February 1994): 545–90.

35. Jerold B. Warner, Ross L. Watts, and Karen H. Wruck, "Stock Prices and Top Management Changes," *Journal of Financial Economics* 20 (1988): 461–92.

36. Twenty move announcements appeared on days when the stock market was closed. Thus, we changed the event dates to the next trading day.

37. The event window was examined for the confounding effects of these kinds of announcements and events: restructuring/divestiture, dividend/earnings announcements, buy/hold/sell recommendations by investment banks, joint venture, acquisitions, new products, litigation/labor unrest, major executive changes, forecasted changes in earnings or sales, layoffs, debt- or equity-related events, and contract awards.

38. "The 1997 All-American Research Team," 81.

39. Ibid., 82.

40. "County NatWest Hires Trader from Steinhardt to Complement Research," *Securities Week*, October 29, 1990, p. 5.

41. For examples of hires of star analysts reported in the financial press, see the *Securities Week* column "People People" on September 24, 1990, and March 19, 1990.

42. We categorized research departments as strong or weak using the results of an annual poll of three thousand buy-side analysts, conducted by Greenwich Associates, about the research they relied on most for investment ideas. For these purposes, the Greenwich rankings are a more appropriate filter than the distinction between bulge-bracket and other firms that we used to characterize the direction of analysts' job changes. However, it is not available for fixed-income research departments. The bulge-bracket designation is a proxy for the reputation and resources of the entire firm; the Greenwich rankings are a measure of the recent performance of research departments themselves, as assessed by users of their research.

43. Alternatively, a star might be worth the price to the new firm if he or she creates some positive externalities despite poor individual performance. In interviews, upon reflection, some executives nevertheless still indicated their awareness that they paid star new hires more than their performance merited.

5 | Stars and Their Galaxies: Firms of Origin and Portability

1. This chapter draws on Groysberg, "The Portability of Star Knowledge Workers"; Groysberg, Lee, and Nanda, "Can They Take It with Them?"; Groysberg and Nanda, "When Superstars Switch Allegiance"; Groysberg, Nanda, and Nohria, "The Risky Business of Hiring Stars." In particular, the quantitative

findings in this chapter (regressions and some exhibits) are based on and drawn from these articles. Several sections of this chapter draw on publications I coauthored with colleagues, many published by Harvard Business School Publishing. The section on soft nonportability: Boris Groysberg, Scott Snook, and David Lane, "Leadership Development at Goldman Sachs" (HBS no. 9-406-002, 2005). The section on product-based nonportability: Boris Groysberg and Anahita Hashemi, "Sanford C. Bernstein: The Fork in the Road (A)" (HBS case no. 404-001); and Groysberg and Hashemi, "Sanford C. Bernstein: Growing Pains." The discussion of Lehman Brothers' research department draws on a series of Harvard Business School case studies. The sections on creating a vision and on soft, hard, and product-based nonportability: Nanda, Groysberg, and Prusiner, "Lehman Brothers (A)." The section on reorganization and decline: Ashish Nanda, Boris Groysberg, and Lauren Prusiner, "Lehman Brothers (B): Exit Jack Rivkin" (HBS case no. 9-906-035, 2007), and Ashish Nanda and Boris Groysberg, "Lehman Brothers (C): Decline of the Equity Research Department" (HBS case no. 9-902-003, 2007). The section on rebuilding the department: Boris Groysberg and Ashish Nanda, "Lehman Brothers (D): Reemergence of the Equity Research Department" (HBS case no. 9-406-090, 2007).

2. Some of this material on DLJ draws on Ashish Nanda, Thomas J. DeLong, and Sarah Thorp, "Jill Greenthal at Donaldson, Lufkin & Jenrette: The TCI/AT&T Deal (A)" (HBS case no. 9-800-213) (Boston: Harvard Business School Publishing, 2001).

3. Ibid., 4.

4. Ida Picker, "The Perils of Prosperity at DLJ," *Institutional Investor* 28, no. 8 (August 1994): 28.

5. Nanda, DeLong, and Thorp, "Jill Greenthal at Donaldson, Lufkin & Jenrette," 5.

6. Some of this material on Montgomery Securities draws on Thomas DeLong, Ashish Nanda, Scott Landry, Matthew C. Lieb, and Boris Groysberg, "Thomas Weisel Partners (A)" (HBS case no. 9-800-215) (Boston: Harvard Business School Publishing, 2005).

7. Ibid., 2.

8. Scott McMurray, "What Makes Montgomery Run?" *Institutional Investor* 31, no. 2 (February 1997): 46–53.

9. Ibid.

10. Robert Clow, "Allen Wheat's Unfinished Symphony," *Institutional Investor* 34, no. 9 (September 2000): 117.

11. Ibid., 120.

12. Some of this material on Salomon Brothers draws on Lynn Sharp Paine, "Salomon Brothers (A)" (HBS case no. 9-305-019) (Boston: Harvard Business School Publishing, 2005).

13. Michael Lewis, *Liar's Poker: Rising through the Wreckage on Wall Street* (New York: Norton, 1989), 38, 109, 127.

14. This section draws heavily on Groysberg, Snook, and Lane, "Leadership Development at Goldman Sachs." Many quotes and data are taken directly from this case.

15. In their study of professional-service firms, Lorsch and Tierney assert: "Culture is a dominant force—if not the dominant force—in determining how the members of the firm actually behave toward one another and toward their clients" (*Aligning the Stars*, 145). Furthermore, they argue, "Culture can emerge as the defining competitive advantage, in part because it is impossible to copy. Individuals in great firms rally around a powerful cultural core, while in other firms, they obsess over their personal circumstances as their business flounders" (153).

16. *The 1978 Directory of Securities Research Information* (New York: Nelson Communications, 1978).

17. This section draws heavily on Groysberg and Hashemi, "Sanford C. Bernstein: The Fork in the Road (A)" and "Sanford C. Bernstein: Growing Pains." Many quotes and data are taken directly from this case.

18. H. W., "Morgan Stanley Study Recommends Research Department Delivers 'Goldman Quality without the Arrogance,'" *Securities Week* 21, no. 51 (December 19, 1994).

19. This section draws heavily on a series of Harvard Business School case studies of Lehman Brothers. Many quotes and data are taken directly from the following specific cases: Nanda, Groysberg, and Prusiner, "Lehman Brothers (A)"; Nanda, Groysberg, and Prusiner, "Lehman Brothers (B)"; Nanda and Groysberg, "Lehman Brothers (C)"; and Groysberg and Nanda, "Lehman Brothers (D)."

6 | Integrating Stars: The Hiring Firm and Portability of Performance

1. This chapter draws on Groysberg, "The Portability of Star Knowledge Workers"; Groysberg and Lee, "Hiring Stars and Their Teams"; Groysberg, Lee, and Nanda, "Can They Take It with Them?"; Groysberg and Nanda, "When Superstars Switch Allegiance"; and Groysberg, Nanda, and Nohria, "The Risky Business of Hiring Stars." In particular, quantitative findings in this chapter (regressions and some exhibits) are based on and drawn from these articles.

2. This process of assimilation, known as "organizational socialization," has four broad components: organizational culture, group values, job skills, and personal change. See Cynthia D. Fisher, "Organizational Socialization: An Integrative Review," in *Research in Personnel and Human Resources Management*, vol. 4, ed. K. M. Rowland and G. R. Ferris (Greenwich, CT: JAI Press, 1986), 101–45. The *culture* of an organization encompasses its mission, values, goals, dress code, humor, jargon, and the like. *Group values* encompass relationships and norms such as how interactions are structured in a group. This can be one of the hardest and most frustrating aspects of integration for new analysts. To develop effective relationships with other analysts, sales personnel, and the research director, a star analyst must first figure out the tacit assumptions governing interaction within each group. *Job skills* are simply the knowledge and know-how needed to perform a task, which star analysts have clearly mastered unless it requires firm-specific skills. Finally, the integration process typically calls for *personal change* in new hires' identity to reflect those of the organization. See Gerald R. Salancik and Jeffrey Pfeffer, "A Social Information

Processing Approach to Job Attitudes and Task Redesign," *Administrative Science Quarterly* 23 (1978): 224–50. Socialization takes place in distinct stages. See John Van Maanen, "Breaking In: Socializing to Work," in *Handbook of Work, Organization, and Society*, ed. R. Dubin (Chicago: Rand McNally, 1976); Edgar H. Schein, *Career Dynamics: Matching Individual and Organizational Needs* (Reading, MA: Addison-Wesley, 1978); Daniel Charles Feldman, "The Multiple Socialization of Organization Members," *Academy of Management Review* 6 (1981): 309–18; Arthur P. Brief et al., "Anticipatory Socialization and Role Stress among Registered Nurses," *Journal of Health and Social Behavior* 20 (June 1979): 161–66.

3. John Van Maanen and Edgar H. Schein ("Towards a Theory of Organizational Socialization") have developed a model to characterize how firms integrate inexperienced newcomers and to pinpoint the benefits and drawbacks of specific organizational socialization tactics. Van Maanen and Schein specify six continua across which firms' integration strategies vary: collective vs. individual, formal vs. informal, sequential vs. variable or random, fixed vs. variable, serial vs. disjunctive, and investiture vs. divestiture. Their classic work proposed a comprehensive theory of organizational socialization and laid the foundation for analysis of the structure, stages, and tactics of socialization. See also Talya Niehaus Bauer, Elizabeth Wolfe Morrison, and Ronda Roberts Callister, "Organizational Socialization: A Review and Directions for Future Research," *Research in Personnel and Human Resources Management* 16 (1998): 149–214; David G. Allen, "Do Organizational Socialization Tactics Influence Newcomer Embeddedness and Turnover," *Journal of Management* 32, no. 2 (April 2006): 237–56; Natalie J. Allen and John P. Meyer, "Organizational Socialization Tactics: A Longitudinal Analysis of Links to Newcomers' Commitment and Role Orientation," *Academy of Management Journal* 33, no. 4 (1990): 847–58; Blake E. Ashforth and Alan M. Saks, "Socialization Tactics: Longitudinal Effects on Newcomer Adjustment," *Academy of Management Journal* 39, no. 1 (1996): 149–78.

4. Relatively few studies of organizational socialization have examined experienced individuals who switched firms. One such study found that experienced professionals who switched employers required extensive adjustment but did not explore specific integration strategies. See Georgia T. Chao et al., "Organizational Socialization: Its Content and Consequences," *Journal of Applied Psychology* 79, no. 5 (1994): 730–43.

5. Integration can be especially challenging when newcomers have vast previous experience and training and have developed entrenched beliefs and attitudes. In these circumstances, organizations count on training, mentoring, and rules as socialization tactics. Lehman Brothers' research department under Rivkin and Fraenkel, for instance, used morning meetings to communicate knowledge and the values of the organization. Some firms in our study simply escorted the new analyst to an office and told him or her to start producing; for better or worse, this, too, is a "socialization" tactic.

6. Failure to adequately socialize or integrate a newcomer is associated with high turnover and the loss of significant investment in recruitment and training. See Fisher, "Organizational Socialization: An Integrative Review"; and John D. Kammeyere-Mueller and Connie R. Wanburg, "Unwrapping the Organizational Entry Process: Disentangling Multiple Antecedents and Their Pathways to Adjustment," *Journal of Applied Psychology* 88, no. 5 (October 2003): 779–94. Successful integration, by contrast, leads to high organizational commitment and job satisfaction. See Allen, "Do Organizational Socialization Tactics Influence Newcomer Embeddedness and Turnover." It is thus surprising that few firms in our study implemented an explicit assimilation strategy.

7. Chatman found that the amount of time interviewers spend with an applicant significantly affects the subsequent quality of the match between the newcomer and the organization. See Jennifer Chatman, "Matching People and Organizations: Selection and Socialization in Public Accounting Firms," *Administrative Science Quarterly* 36 (1991): 459–84. Simply put, the more time a firm spends interviewing candidates, the less likely it is to hire people who do not share its values and beliefs. We observed this phenomenon at a number of firms, including DLJ, Lehman Brothers, Goldman Sachs, and Sanford C. Bernstein. At Lehman Brothers, five features of the hiring process contributed to the amount of time a recruit spent interviewing: (1) candidates were interviewed by a committee, (2) every member of the committee had to agree on the hiring decision, (3) representatives from other functions (e.g., sales and trading) participated in the process, (4) the culture of the firm was thoroughly explained, and (5) hiring decisions were debated at length. See Nanda, Groysberg, and Prusiner, "Lehman Brothers (A)." Such painstaking hiring familiarizes the firm and the newcomer with each other and—just as important—ensures that the new hire will be accepted by his or her colleagues. But few firms pursued recruiting this way, possibly in the belief that stars' jobs are identical at every firm and that most firms—and star analysts—are roughly interchangeable.

8. Fit is typically analyzed during the interview process. See Daniel M. Cable and Charles K. Parsons, "Socialization Tactics and Person-Organization Fit," *Personnel Psychology* 54 (2001). Essentially, applicants and organizations choose each other in part on the strength of similar goals and values. See Daniel M. Cable and Timothy A. Judge, "Interviewers' Perceptions of Person-Organization Fit and Organizational Selection Decisions," *Journal of Applied Psychology* 82, no. 4 (1997): 546–61. New hires whose values and beliefs are in keeping with the organization's values socialize more quickly and report greater job satisfaction. See Chatman, "Matching People and Organizations." It is possible that a high *II* ranking could cloud the ability of a hiring committee to accurately assess fit, however, resulting in a poor match that negatively impacts performance.

9. For the seven stages of the interview process, see Claudio Fernandez-Araoz, Boris Groysberg, and Nitin Nohria, "The Definitive Guide to Recruiting in Good Times and Bad," *Harvard Business Review* 87, no. 5 (May 2009): 74–84.

10. Haspeslagh and Jemison's classic work on mergers and acquisitions (M&A) offers a comprehensive overview of the integration process when one firm acquires another. The authors' central thesis is that successful integration is the major source of value creation in M&A. See Philippe C. Haspeslagh and David B. Jemison, *Managing Acquisitions: Creating Value through Corporate Renewal* (New York: Free Press, 1991). Furthermore, as we shall see, research departments' motives for hiring ranked analysts roughly parallel companies' strategies for pursuing acquisitions. For related literature from mergers and acquisitions, see Jaeyong Song, Paul Almeida, and Geraldine Wu, "Learning-by-Hiring: When Is Mobility More Likely to Facilitate Interfirm Knowledge Transfer?" *Management Science* 49, no. 4 (2003): 351–65; Holger Ernst and Jan Vitt, "The Influence of Corporate Acquisitions on the Behaviour of Key Inventors," *R&D Management* 30 (2004): 105–19; and S. Chaudhuri and B. Tabrizi, "Capturing the Real Value in High-Tech Acquisitions," *Harvard Business Review* 77 (1999): 123–30.

11. Drucker, *Management Challenges for the 21st Century*, 166.

12. Linda A. Hill, *Becoming a Manager: Mastery of a New Identity* (Cambridge, MA: Harvard Business School Press, 1992).

13. In his seminal 1991 article, March describes the difference thus: "Exploration includes things captured by terms such as search, variation, risk taking, experimentation, play, flexibility, discovery, innovation. Exploitation includes such things as refinement, choice, production, efficiency, selection, implementation, execution" ("Exploration and Exploitation in Organizational Learning," 71). Both tasks are necessary for an organization to survive: overreliance on exploitation will ensure a company's ultimate obsolescence, but exploration is risky because its returns are "systematically less certain, more remote in time, and organizationally more distant from the locus of action and adaption" (73).

14. Some researchers have questioned whether service firms can be said to practice innovation because services by definition are hard to measure and subjective, meaning it can be difficult to determine when a service firm has innovated. See Jon Sundbo, "Management of Innovation in Services," *Service Industries Journal* 17 (1997): 432–56. Others have suggested that innovation in service-based firms might have different dynamics than innovation in product-based firms. See Stefan Thomke, *Experimentation Matters: Unlocking the Potential of New Technologies for Innovation* (Boston: Harvard Business School Press, 2003).

   What a professional-service firm sells to its clients is frequently less the services of the firm per se than the services of specific individuals (or teams of individuals). Hence, for professional-service firms, hiring stars is a valid lens through which to look at exploration and exploitation. Because people are the product in professional-service firms, a firm is entering a new market and/or offering a new product when it hires a professional in a new specialty. Hiring someone to round out existing competencies is a way to exploit the firm's existing capacities and reputation. See Song, Almeida, and Wu, "Learning-by-Hiring"; and Udo Zander and Bruce Kogut, "Knowledge and the Speed of the Transfer and Imitation of Organizational Capabilities," *Organization Science* 6 (1995): 76–92. For a review of innovation in professional services, with a focus on investment banking, see Richard K. Lyons, Jennifer A. Chatman, and Caneel K. Joyce, "Innovation in Services: Corporate Culture and Investment Banking," *California Management Review* 50, no. 1 (2007): 174–91. The authors characterize five key distinctions between innovation in services and innovation in manufacturing as strongly rooted in human capital and the organization's ability to manage it: "First, innovation in services is distributed throughout the organization. Second, it is fluid and continuous in pace. Third, it is far more relevant to hiring and promotion decisions. Fourth, it is influenced by formal reward systems and culture at the firm-wide level. Finally, it is strongly influenced by leaders' behavior" (181). They also note that a strong organizational culture can encourage innovation if it fosters social norms that support creative activity.

Though DLJ, Lehman Brothers, and Sanford C. Bernstein were all very different from one another, there is a limit to how much diversity of organizational culture can exist in any given industry. Cultures within a given industry will not tend to vary excessively, as industry characteristics (e.g., technology complexity, degree of government regulation, rates of growth) act as constraints. Jennifer A. Chatman and Karen A. Jehn, "Assessing the Relationship between Industry Characteristics and Organizational Culture: How Different Can You Be?" *Academy of Management Journal* 37, no. 3 (1994): 522–53.

15. We used the dynamic probability that a newly acquired star would be ranked again after changing employers as a measure of integration.

16. M&A research has found similar short-term and long-term effects on the share price of the acquiring firm. See Robert F. Bruner, *Applied Mergers and Acquisitions* (Hoboken, NJ: John Wiley, 2004). The clear winner in mergers and acquisitions is the target firm. This pattern may also apply to star analysts. The firm that acquires a star almost invariably experiences either no gain in value or value destruction. The star, like the target firm, is often able to extract much of the value from the transaction. Much of this discussion builds on arguments presented in chapter 4.

7 | Liftouts (Taking Some of It with You): Moving in Teams

1. This chapter draws on Groysberg, "The Portability of Star Knowledge Workers"; Groysberg, Lee, and Nanda, "Can They Take It with Them?"; Groysberg and Lee, "Hiring Stars and Their Teams"; Groysberg, Nanda, and Nohria, "The Risky Business of Hiring Stars"; Boris Groysberg and Robin Abrahams, "Liftouts: How to Acquire a High-Functioning Team," *Harvard Business Review* 84, no. 12 (2006): 133–40. In particular, quantitative findings in this chapter (regressions and some exhibits) are based on and drawn from these articles. Several sections of this chapter draw on publications I coauthored with colleagues, many published by Harvard Business School Publishing: Boris Groysberg, Anahita Hashemi, and Brendan Reed, "Drexel Burnham Lambert (A): "The Smartest People on Wall Street Can be Had" (HBS case no. 9-406-

107) (Boston: Harvard Business School Publishing, 2006); Boris Groysberg, "Drexel Burnham Lambert (B): Kirsch's Talent Sale" (HBS supplement 9-406-057) (Boston: Harvard Business School Publishing, 2006); Boris Groysberg and Robin Abrahams, "Drexel Burnham Lambert (A): The Smartest People on Wall Street Can Be Had (TN)."

2. A sticky definitional problem arises in any discussion of team hiring: what is a team? As *Financial News* put it, "Multiple recruits do not always amount to a team." Sarah Butcher, "Team Defections Are Back with a Vengeance," *Financial News*, June 19, 2005. Even in cases of people who clearly work in unison and depend on each other's skills, is it reasonable to expect the same principles to apply, say, to a senior analyst and her junior and to an eighty-member department? Richard Hackman has specified four criteria for a group of people to be considered a team: a clear task, clear boundaries around team membership, authority to manage their own work, and membership stability over time. Hackman, *Leading Teams: Setting the Stage for Great Performances* (Boston: Harvard Business School Press, 2002). These criteria accommodate shades of gray. In general, we can posit that the more closely a group resembles a true team, the more likely it is to operate efficiently—and the more insular it is apt to be and thus the more likely it is to resist full integration into a new firm.

3. When colleagues on a team of knowledge workers are capable and possess expertise, they can access each other's knowledge to frame their own problems and ideas. See J. Lave, *Cognition in Practice* (Cambridge: Cambridge University Press, 1988); and K. E. Weick, *Sensemaking in Organizations* (Thousand Oaks, CA: Sage, 1995). Furthermore, proximity and frequency of interaction may facilitate transfer of tacit knowledge from high-performing members to their coworkers. See M. Polanyi, *The Tacit Dimension* (Garden City, NY: Anchor Press, 1967). Performance based on tacit knowledge is considered a particularly strong source of competitive advantage, in that it is by definition not transferable; if such knowledge could be codified, it would no longer be tacit. See S. L. Berman, J. Down, and C. W. Hill, "Tacit Knowledge as a Source of Competitive Advantage in the National Basketball Association," *Academy of Management Journal* 45, no. 1 (2002): 13–31; and B. Kogut and U. Zander, "Knowledge of the Firm and the Evolutionary Theory of the Multinational Corporation," *Journal of International Business Studies* 24, no. 4 (1993): 625–46.

4. Some relationships among some analysts, bankers, and salespeople are strong enough that the departure of one team member leads to industry-wide rumors about his or her colleagues. This was the case when UBS banker Richard Barrett defected to DLJ along with twenty-two members of his team in 1998. Speculation immediately ensued that high-profile banking analyst Thomas Hanley would also leave UBS to join Barrett, despite Hanley's repeated denials. "UBS Analysts, Investment Bankers Poised to Depart Ahead of Merger," Dow Jones Online News, March 27, 1998.

5. This research is reported in Groysberg and Abrahams, "Liftouts."

6. This section draws heavily on ibid.; Groysberg, Hashemi, and Reed, "Drexel Burnham Lambert (A)"; Groysberg, "Drexel Burnham Lambert (B)."

7. Recent work by Timothy Gardner has suggested that firms compete for valuable human capital much as they compete for customers and revenue. Gardner noted that competitive practices, including poaching talent in groups, can "deplete rivals' human capital pools by 'cherry-picking' employees with strong performance" and that "interfirm personnel moves may result in the transfer of knowledge about operations, strategies, and customers from firms to their industry competitors" (237). See Gardner, "In the Trenches at the Talent Wars: Competitive Interaction for Scarce Human Resources," *Human Resource Management* 41 (2002): 225–37; Gardner, "Interfirm Competition for Human Resources."

8. Jena McGregor, "I Can't Believe They Took the Whole Team," *BusinessWeek*, December 18, 2006.

9. David Ivanovich, "Prodigal Analysts Come Home," *Houston Chronicle*, June 17, 1995, sec. 2, p. 3.

10. Stephanie Strom, "Two Analysts Returning to CS First Boston," *New York Times*, June 17, 1995, p. 35.

11. "Observer: Tit 4 Tat," *Financial Times*, April 18, 2000, p. 23. Gardner has noted that poaching of highly valuable employees is likely to spur defensive retaliation—such as poaching similarly valuable employees in return—by the losing firm, particularly when it is clear that the hire was deliberately intended to inflict damage. Gardner, "Interfirm Competition for Human Resources."

12. R. Batt, "Work Organization, Technology, and Performance in Customer Service and Sales," *Industrial and Labor Relations Review* 52, no. 4 (1999): 539–64; also see Henning, *Maximizing Law Firm Profitability*; Kordana, "Law Firms, Associate Careers"; and Maister, *Managing the Professional Service Firm*.

13. Butcher, "Team Defections Are Back with a Vengeance."

14. Having moved en masse once, a team may find it easier to contemplate doing so again. A *BusinessWeek* article on liftouts quoted the CEO of a recruitment firm: "It's kind of like having an affair with a married woman. If you marry her, remember she cheated on her ex. So don't be surprised if she cheats on you." See McGregor, "I Can't Believe They Took the Whole Team."

15. For a look at the dynamics of team hirings—and firings—in football coaching, see C. Edward Fee, Charles J. Hadlock, and Joshua R. Pierce, "Promotions in the Internal and External Labor Market: Evidence from Professional Football Coaching Careers," *Journal of Business* 79, no. 21 (2006): 821–59.

16. In a dramatic example from the medical profession, a liver-transplant team performed a joint liver-kidney transplant only a few months after moving from Boston's Beth Israel Deaconess Medical Center to the Lahey Clinic. The surgery, involving three operating rooms and more than twenty professionals, required a level of teamwork unlikely to be found in a newly assembled group. "Lahey Clinic's New Liver Transplantation Team Performs First Transplant," PR Newswire, June 25, 1999.

17. Butcher, "Team Defections Are Back with a Vengeance."

18. Companies can lower their risk of losing teams to liftouts by creating strong relationships between (as well as within) teams and by preventing teams from being self-isolating. Autonomous teams are at considerable risk of being wooed away by another company. For an economic model of wage setting and the retention of employee networks, see G. J. Mailath and A. Postlewaite, "Workers versus Firms: Bargaining over a Firm's Value," *Review of Economic Studies* 57, no. 3 (1990): 369–80. Even if only some members of a team choose to leave together, the strategic advantage of the team's collective knowledge may be lost. See O. Chillemi and B. Gui, "Team Human Capital and Worker Mobility," *Journal of Labor Economics* 90, no. 4 (1997): 1034–54. Thus teams should be strongly connected to other in-house groups, both for reasons of retention and for the strategic advantage that cross-team relationships can provide. See W. M. Cohen and D. A. Levinthal, "Absorptive Capacity: A New Perspective on Learning and Innovation," *Administrative Science Quarterly* 35, no. 1 (1990): 128–52; and K. M. Eisenhardt and J. A. Martin, "Dynamic Capabilities: What Are They?" *Strategic Management Journal* 21, no. 10/11 (2000): 1105–21.

19. Greater attachment to coworkers than to the organization—i.e., greater team-specific than firm-specific human capital—is also apparent when a team disperses after the departure of one member. One study of managerial turnover has shown that when one executive leaves, complementary executives are also likely to leave. Having examined alternative hypotheses, the authors suggested that the loss of firm-specific human capital when a coworker with complementary skills leaves makes staying in the job less desirable. See R. M. Hayes, P. Oyer, and S. Schaefer, "Co-worker Complementarity and the Stability of Top Management Teams" (Stanford Graduate School of Business Research Paper no. 1846, 2004). Related work on CEO and non-CEO dismissals has suggested that "the value of a manager to his firm very much depends on the identity of those who are around him" (35), supporting what the authors called a team-specific human-capital hypothesis of managerial turnover. See C. E. Fee and C. J. Hadlock, "Management Turnover across the Corporate Hierarchy," *Journal of Accounting and Economics* 37 (2004): 3–38.

20. P. Maher and A. Schwimmer, "The End of the Gravy Train," *Investment Dealers' Digest*, May 6, 1996, pp. 14–19.

21. Individuals prefer teammates who have demonstrated or are known for high performance. See P. J. Hinds, K. M. Carley, D. Krackhardt, and D. Wholey, "Choosing Work Group Members: Balancing Similarity, Competence, and Familiarity," *Organizational Behavior and Human Decision Processes* 81, no. 2 (2000): 226–51. Even so, the extent to which individuals attribute their success to team-specific human capital is unclear. Do analysts who move in teams do so strategically to preserve performance by taking some of their firm-specific human capital with them? Or is the decision made on the basis of affinity and good chemistry, without conscious awareness of safeguarding performance? The evidence is mixed. Evidence from baseball suggests that players recognize their team-specific human capital; players whose positions require coordination with other team members are less likely to be traded—

or, if free agents, to move to another team—than players whose positions are relatively independent. See Glenn, McGarrity, and Weller, "Firm-Specific Human Capital, Job Matching, and Turnover." But network theory suggests that professionals are not fully aware of the strategic benefits of their relationships and do not realize that different network configurations convey different benefits. See R. S. Burt, "The Gender of Social Capital," *Rationality and Society* 10, no. 1 (1998): 5–46.

22. The exception is a 2006 *Harvard Business Review* article by Boris Groysberg and Robin Abrahams, on which this chapter draws, proposing a four-stage model for successful liftouts. See Groysberg and Abrahams, "Liftouts."

23. Drexel Burnham Lambert was a small but highly successful investment bank that during the late 1980s was notoriously associated with funding many hostile takeovers and junk bonds, courtesy of Michael Milken, head of the West Coast division. Huge profits were not the only consequence of Milken's activities: in 1989 he was indicted on multiple counts of fraud and racketeering. Drexel agreed to plead guilty to six felony counts and pay $650 million in penalties and fines. Drexel consisted of two distinct entities: Drexel West, in California, the home of Milken's high-yield department, had brought down the firm; Drexel East, in New York, which housed the equity division, including the fourth-ranked research department, was largely untouched by the scandals.

24. Two further pairs of analysts left Drexel for the same bank, but they do not meet our criteria for team moves; the analysts who moved to Smith Barney did not move at the same time, and one of the analysts who moved to Merrill Lynch was hired as a consultant and retained his primary job at Harvard Business School.

25. We are not strictly following Richard Hackman's definition of a "team." Some of these exits were moves of groups.

26. Thirty-two of Drexel's fifty senior equity analysts had been named to the 1989 *Institutional Investor* All-America Research Team. Drexel's equity research department was ranked fourth among all U.S. firms that year; in 1988 it had ranked second. The equity group also employed top-rated institutional salespeople and traders in the United States and Europe. Groysberg, Hashemi, and Reed, "Drexel Burnham Lambert (A)," 5.

27. Groysberg, "Drexel Burnham Lambert (B)," 9.

28. Groysberg, Hashemi, and Reed, "Drexel Burnham Lambert (A)," 7.

29. Jessica Sommar, "The Culture Clash at County NatWest," *Investment Dealers' Digest*, March 22, 1993, pp. 14–19.

30. Jessica Sommar, "How County NatWest Plans to Make Money in Equity: An Interview with Arthur Kirsch," *Investment Dealers' Digest*, May 28, 1990, p. 27.

31. Ibid.

32. Compared to commercial banks, investment banks tend to exhibit flatter networks, employ a more bottom-up approach to designing strategy, award bonuses as a significant fraction of compensation, and have greater involvement by senior management. Eccles and Crane, *Doing Deals*.

33. Patrick Harverson, "U.K. Banks Seek New Identity on Wall Street," *Financial Times*, February 23, 1994, p. 32.

34. "Barclays de Zoete Continues Hiring Former Drexel Burnham Analysts," *Securities Week*, April 9, 1990, p. 3.

35. For example, *Institutional Investor* reported that "There are signs that BZW's Drexel recruits will inject new life into the firm's stodgy research format." Debbie Galant, "Britain's Wall Street Beachhead," *Institutional Investor*, August 1990, p. 100.

36. Anne Schwimmer, "Drexel Diaspora: The People Who Drove the Juggernaut, One Year Later," *Investment Dealers' Digest*, February 11, 1991, p. 20.

37. Ashish Nanda and Kristin Lieb, "Abby Joseph Cohen: A Career Retrospective" (HBS case no. 903-118) (Boston: Harvard Business School Publishing, 2003), 7.

38. "Barclays de Zoete Ends U.S. Equities Trading after a Year's Activity," *Wall Street Journal*, April 24, 1991, sec. C, p. 19; and "View from City Road—Accountability Needed at BZW," *London Independent*, February 1, 1991, p. 23.

39. Justin Schack, "The Pioneers (The Three Founders of Donaldson, Lufkin and Jenrette)," *Institutional Investor*, October 1, 2001, p. 104.

40. Tom Pratt, "The Very Private World of Donaldson, Lufkin & Jenrette," *Investment Dealers' Digest*, September 21, 1992, pp. 16–21.

41. Anne Schwimmer, "Home Improvement?" *Investment Dealers' Digest*, October 30, 1995, p. 15.

42. Schwimmer, "Drexel Diaspora."

43. Pre-hire and ongoing integration efforts are particularly vital at team-oriented cultures such as Goldman Sachs, where the performance not just of the individual new hire but of the team itself may be at stake. Richard Hackman notes the importance of stability in group membership for maintaining high performance. A new team member will always lead to new process losses; proactive integration efforts are necessary to offset these losses. Hackman, *Leading Teams*.

44. The courtship phase of a liftout somewhat resembles the decision-making phase of an acquisition, during which the leadership of the acquiring company decides whether and how to make the acquisition. Haspeslagh and Jemison have identified four problems common during the decision-making phase that we have also noted in many less-than-successful team moves: "fragmented perspectives of many specialists during analysis and decision making; increasing momentum to consummate the transaction; ambiguous expectations about key aspects of the acquisition between both sides in the negotiation; [and] multiple motives among hiring managers" (*Managing Acquisitions*, 58).

45. The urgency felt by both the hiring companies and the Drexel professionals may seem hard to fathom—why would such highly compensated employees be in such a rush to find new jobs?—but it was a logical response to the situation. Most Drexel employees had considerable net worth tied up in Drexel stock, which had became almost worthless overnight. It is also difficult for analysts to get back in the game after several months of being out of contact with the industries they cover; the longer an analyst is unemployed, the less

attractive he or she is. The early 1990s were not a good time on the Street, furthermore, and dire predictions about the fate of the Drexel workers were bandied about in the media: "Perrin Long, a securities industry analyst at Lipper Analytical Services Inc., believes only 10% of Drexel's employees may find work," reported the *Wall Street Journal*. See Laurie P. Cohen and Randall Smith, "Many Employees at Drexel Face Loss of Savings along with Jobs," *Wall Street Journal*, February 15, 1990, sec. C, p. 17. Despite such predictions, hiring companies approached the Drexel talent bonanza with a sense of urgency. Drexel talent flooded the market all at once, which meant that careful deliberation posed a risk of seeing the best employees snatched up by faster-moving competitors. In this gold-rush, bargain-basement atmosphere, there was little careful research or planning on either side.

46. Sommar, "The Culture Clash at County NatWest."

47. As has been noted, certain aspects of a given work environment become apparent only after an employee has begun work there. See Jovanovich, "Job Matching and the Theory of Turnover." Jovanovich discusses individual hires; the same point has also been made about acquisitions. See Haspeslagh and Jemison, *Managing Acquisitions*.

48. Haspeslagh and Jamison, for example, note that managing integration is essential to create value in an acquisition. According to their research, there is no single right way to integrate: multiple paths to integration can be successful. But they do specify critical factors necessary for all successful integrations: "adapting pre-acquisition views to embrace reality, an ability to create the atmosphere necessary for capability transfer, the leadership to provide a common vision, and careful management of the interactions between the organizations" (*Managing Acquisitions*, 11). These factors appear in our framework as well, particularly in the leadership-integration phase.

49. For insight into team moves, we interviewed Roberto Casati, an Italian law partner who has experienced both mergers and liftouts. Casati described his own experience as a team leader with considerable nuance: "The best thing you have to do to make sure that you smoothly merge or integrate with the new organization is to step back as a leader of the team a little bit, make sure that you do not position yourself as the point of difference or defender of the team, and manage in a way that the team recognizes that there are other leaders in that organization that they can turn to and look at as being as good and as reliable as the original leader. And at the same time, I think, the other members of the existing organization that accepts the new team have to play a very delicate balancing act of respect and deference to the leader of the new team coming in, so that it is perceived at all levels that we all want to merge together and we all respect each other. And the old leader has to expand his leadership within the new organization by establishing this leadership by conduct, by intelligence, by superior commitment to whoever already is working with the new organization."

50. A well-integrated leader can also help ensure that the team maintains optimal autonomy in its new corporate home. Most mobile teams move with the

intention of continuing to work as a unit, not to be dispersed in ones and twos throughout the new organization. Autonomy is also usually necessary in order for a team to retain its value. Haspeslagh and Jemison, writing about acquisitions, describe the situation thus: "One of the paradoxes in acquisitions is that the pursuit of capability transfer itself may lead to the destruction of the capability being transferred. Whereas capability transfer requires different degrees of boundary disruption or dissolution, the preservation of capabilities requires boundary protection and, hence, organizational autonomy" (*Managing Acquisitions*, 142). Thus a balance must be struck between integration and autonomy; a leader who is detached from the team or (more commonly) insufficiently integrated into the new firm is in a poor position to maintain this delicate balance.

51. Haspeslagh and Jemison also emphasize the role of strong leadership in successful post-acquisition integration. They cite the need for credible gate-keepers to provide a buffer between the two organizations and communicate expectations. Gatekeepers from the acquired firm (a role akin to the team leader in a liftout) provide resources to their workers and help them acculturate to the new organization. Gatekeepers from the acquiring organization need to guard against turning their attention elsewhere after the acquisition and instead continue to provide resources, communication, and guidance. See Haspeslagh and Jemison, *Managing Acquisitions*. For more on the role of team leaders as boundary spanners, see D. G. Ancona, "Outward Bound: Strategies for Team Survival in the Organization," *Academy of Management Journal* 33 (1990): 334–65; and D. G. Ancona and D. F. Caldwell, "Bridging the Boundary: External Activity and Performance in Organizational Teams," *Administrative Science Quarterly* 37 (1992): 634–65.

52. Some integration difficulties in transnational liftouts resemble those typical of international joint ventures. See D. C. Hambrick, J. Li, K. Xin, and A. S. Tsui, "Compositional Gaps and Downward Spirals in International Joint Venture Management Groups," *Strategic Management Journal* 22, no. 11 (2001): 1033–1105.

53. We studied several successful liftouts of regional legal teams. Continuity in the content of their work was almost always mentioned as crucial to success. Michael Schilling, who facilitated the liftout of an Eastern European law firm, described the continuity his team enjoyed: "We essentially changed the names on the doors and we were still in the same space, still doing the same work for the same clients with the same people. And that helped, in the sense that people didn't feel they lost their identity or they lost their roles, or that expectations changed radically overnight."

54. A similar honeymoon period characterized the case of Richard Sandor, a futures expert and former executive vice president at Drexel, who joined the French investment bank Banque IndoSuez U.S. in early 1990 as chief executive of the newly formed Indosuez International Capital Markets Corporation (ICM). Like Kirsch, Sandor brought a team of Drexel talent with him.

Business went relatively smoothly for about a year, and senior management was pleased with the profits. But issues began to appear. IndoSuez veterans resented the high profile and high salaries of their Drexel coworkers; U.S.-French cultural differences proved hard to navigate; Sandor's refusal to relocate to Paris, even part-time, caused hard feelings and logistical headaches; and disagreement persisted in the senior ranks about what skills, exactly, the Drexel team was supposed to have brought to the table. In mid-1991, Sandor left IndoSuez. Most of his group stayed but foundered without executive support and direction.

55. Hackman has pointed out the need for expert coaching and regular interventions to keep teams on track over time. See Hackman, *Leading Teams*.

56. The importance of the "soft" or relational aspects of team integration should not be underestimated. A sense of psychological safety—confidence that it is acceptable to take interpersonal risks, such as asking for help or admitting a mistake—is necessary if teams are to learn and has been shown to affect team performance strongly. Since the learning curve will become steeper in a new environment, psychological safety will be particularly decisive following a liftout. The behavior of the team leader is crucial in the creation of a psychologically safe environment. See Amy Edmondson, "Psychological Safety and Learning Behavior in Work Teams," *Administrative Science Quarterly* 44, no. 2 (1999): 350–83.

8 | Women and Portability: Why Is Women's Performance More Portable than Men's?

1. Some researchers have noted that women build up less firm-specific human capital than do men. Because of their role as primary caregiver in the family, women choose to invest less in firm-specific human capital and to rely more on general skills that can withstand the career interruption of childrearing. See J. Mincer and S. Polachek, "Family Investments in Human Capital: Earnings of Women," *Journal of Political Economy* 82 (1974): S76–S108; and C. Goldin and S. Polachek, "Residual Differences by Sex: Perspectives on the Gender Gap in Earnings," *American Economic Review* 77, no. 2 (1987): 143–51. Because women's labor is divided between the workplace and the home, they receive poorer returns on their labor than do men. See G. S. Becker, *A Treatise on the Family* (Cambridge, MA: Harvard University Press, 1981); and G. S. Becker, "Human Capital, Effort, and the Sexual Division of Labor," *Journal of Labor Economics* 3 (1985): 33–58. Another research stream attributes women's less firm-specific human capital not to their own choices but to employers' reluctance to make investments in women based on the belief that women feel less attachment to their jobs. See E. Lazear and S. Rose, "Male-Female Wage Differentials in Job Ladders," *Journal of Labor Economics* 8, no. 1 (1990): S1-06–S123. Some recent work has disputed this claim, suggesting that women do in fact build up firm-specific human capital. See, for instance, T. F. Crossley, S.R.G. Jones, and P. Kuhn, "Gender Differences in Displacement Costs: Evidence and Implications," *Journal of Human Resources* 29, no. 2 (1994): 461–80.

The women in our study would have liked to accumulate firm-specific human capital as their male colleagues did, but they had trouble doing so in an inhospitable environment and opted, instead, for strategic alternatives.

2. Ibarra and Smith-Lovin have pointed out that even when men and women have identical job titles, the nature of their jobs is different because of women's lower status in society, different expectations of gender-role behavior, and extra-work responsibilities. "Consequently, men and women holding structurally equivalent formal positions may be viewed as operating in different social contexts that require different network configurations to accomplish similar goals." H. Ibarra and S. L. Smith-Lovin, "New Directions in Social Network Research on Gender and Careers," in *Creating Tomorrow's Organizations: A Handbook for Future Research in Organizational Behavior*, ed. Susan E. Jackson and Cary L. Cooper (Hoboken, NJ: John Wiley, 1997), 361–83, p. 366.

3. Traditionally and with few exceptions, scholarly work on gender and organizations has taken a naive view of sex differences, relying on tautologies, stereotypes, and the assumption that organizational practices are gender neutral. See R. Ely and I. Padavic, "A Feminist Analysis of Organizational Research on Sex Differences," *Academy of Management Review* 32, no. 4 (October 2007): 1121–43.

4. Rosabeth Moss Kanter, *Men and Women of the Corporation* (1977; New York: Basic Books, 1993), 9.

5. Louise Marie Roth, "Making the Team: Gender, Money, and Mobility in Wall Street Investment Banks" (Ph.D. diss., New York University, September 2000, UMI number 9985275).

6. Janet Lewis, "The Rise of Woman Power," *Institutional Investor*, December 1989: 176–81, p. 180.

7. Diana B. Henriques, "Ms. Siebert, Still on the Barricades," *New York Times*, July 5, 1992, p. 15.

8. Carol R. Mathews, "The Ladies on the Street," *Institutional Investor*, November 1967, pp. 21–23.

9. Solveig Jansson and Linda Franke, "The Silent Women of Wall Street," *Institutional Investor*, May 1972, pp. 37–39.

10. Ibid.

11. It is possible that these women's minority status helped them. Jennifer Chatman and colleagues have shown that being the sole member of an opposite-sex team can enhance an individual's performance if that individual is working on a task considered stereotypically appropriate for his or her gender. See Jennifer A. Chatman, Alicia D. Boisnier, Sandra E. Spataro, Cameron Anderson, and Jennifer L. Berdahl, "Being Distinctive versus Being Conspicuous: The Effects of Numeric Status and Sex-Stereotyped Tasks on Individual Performance in Groups," *Organizational Behavior and Human Decision Processes* 107 (2008): 141–60.

12. Lewis, "The Rise of Woman Power," p. 178.

13. Beth McGoldrick and Gregory Miller, "Wall Street Women: You've Come a Short Way, Baby," *Institutional Investor*, June 1985, pp. 85–96.

14. *Hegemonic masculinity* is a term used by Rosabeth Moss Kanter to refer to excessive valorization of stereotypical masculine traits and the belief that these traits—including "a tough-minded approach to problems; analytic abilities to abstract and plan; a capacity to set aside personal, emotional considerations in the interests of task accomplishment; and a cognitive superiority in problem-solving and decision-making"—are necessary for success in the business world. In a hegemonically masculine culture, a woman can possess these admired traits and even be recognized as having them, but her identity as a woman may be thrown into question. Hegemonic masculinity thus leaves women in a double bind: either their gender identity or their professional identity will be suspect. Kanter, *Men and Women of the Corporation*, 22.

15. Debbie Galant, "Can Wall Street Women Have It All?" *Institutional Investor*, July 1996, p. 143.

16. Sue Herera, *Women of the Street: Making It on Wall Street—The World's Toughest Business* (New York: John Wiley, 1998). Members of disadvantaged groups, such as women and minorities, often prefer and do better in environments in which performance is externally and objectively measured. As Kanter points out (*Men and Women of the Corporation*), under conditions of uncertainty, in which it is difficult to tell who the best performers are, managers and coworkers often fall back on subjective measures of trust—which nearly always means preferential treatment for those who are most like the group in power. As it becomes more possible to measure productivity objectively, it becomes easier for the dominant or majority group to trust and tolerate outsiders. Hence, the highly visible and quantifiable nature of analysts' work at investment banks might make the career particularly inviting to women. Elvira and Graham have shown that women are not discriminated against in terms of salary if a job is characterized by objective performance metrics but are discriminated against in terms of discretionary bonuses. See M. Elvira and M. E. Graham, "Not Just a Formality: Pay System Formalization and Sex-Related Earnings Effects," *Organization Science* 13, no. 6 (2002): 601–17. Work by Baron and Newman has also suggested that the more ambiguous the performance measures, the more women workers in particular suffer a salary penalty. See J. N. Baron and A. E. Newman, "For What It's Worth: Organizations, Occupations, and the Value of Work Done by Women and Nonwhites," *American Sociological Review* 55 (1990): 155–75.

17. Galant, "Can Wall Street Women Have It All?" p. 144.

18. Explaining discrimination in hiring has long been a contentious issue in labor economics. See G. S. Becker, *The Economics of Discrimination* (Chicago: University of Chicago Press, 1957); S. Oster, "Industry Differences in the Level of Discrimination against Women," *Quarterly Journal of Economics* 89 (1975): 215–29; B. R. Bergman, "Does the Market for Women's Labor Need Fixing?" *Journal of Economic Perspectives* 3, no. 1 (1989): 43–60.

19. Lewis, "The Rise of Woman Power."

20. Nanda, Groysberg, and Prusiner, "Lehman Brothers (A)," 14. Fraenkel's assumption that simply deciding not to discriminate against women would

automatically lead to a gender-neutral process may have been too optimistic. Extensive research has shown that women are discriminated against in situations where explicit sexism is unlikely to be the sole reason. For instance, a study done in Sweden—a country generally credited with strong egalitarian values—showed that when applying for research grants, female scientists had to be a remarkable 2.5 times more productive than men to be judged equally competent. See C. Wennerås and A. Wold, "Nepotism and Sexism in Peer-Review," *Nature* 387, no. 6631 (1997): 341–43. The "John and Joan McKay" study performed in 1983 showed that judges—both male and female—rated scholarly articles higher if the author's name was male rather than female. See M. A. Paludi and W. D. Bauer, "Goldberg Revisited: What's in an Author's Name," *Sex Roles* 9 (1983): 387–90. An extensive longitudinal study on women in academia led Long, Allison, and McGinnis to conclude that "women are expected to meet higher standards for promotion" in academia than men are. See J. S. Long, P. D. Allison, and R. McGinnis, "Rank Advancement in Academic Careers: Sex Differences and the Effects of Productivity," *American Sociological Review* 58 (1993): 703–22, p. 720. More than goodwill may be necessary to reverse these perhaps unconscious tendencies. A well-known example of a process to reduce discrimination is symphony orchestras' use of "blind auditions" in which musicians perform behind screens, invisible to the judges. (Auditioners even go barefoot so that their footsteps cannot reveal their gender.) When orchestras use blind auditions, female musicians are hired in larger numbers. See C. Goldin and C. Rouse, "Orchestrating Impartiality: The Impact of 'Blind' Auditions on Female Musicians," *American Economic Review* 90, no. 4 (2000): 715–40. This is not an exhaustive review of discrimination against women in hiring and advancement but merely a brief summary of some high-profile studies. Given this evidence, Fraenkel may have found women analysts to be better than men because, despite his efforts to recruit equally, women had to clear a higher bar to be hired.

21. Lewis, "The Rise of Woman Power," p. 180.
22. Ibid.
23. Roth, "Making the Team."
24. Because of investment banks' high profiles and deep pockets, they are likely targets for discrimination suits. Hence discrimination may play out in more subtle ways. See Roth, "Making the Team." For how gender discrimination manifests in subtle ways that disadvantage women, see R. J. Ely and D. E. Meyerson, "Theories of Gender: A New Approach to Organizational Analysis and Change," in *Research in Organizational Behavior*, vol. 22, ed. B. Staw and R. Sutton (Oxford: Elsevier Science & Technology Books, 2000), 105–53.
25. Kanter developed a "taxonomy of representation" that can help predict at what concentration minority status will cease to be problematic. In terms of gender representation, most functions in investment banking fall between "uniform" (no minorities) and skewed (15 percent minority). Equity research falls between skewed and "tilted" (35 percent minority) representation. When minority representation reaches 35 percent, the minority can initiate a coalition and

many of the problematic dynamics of minority status begin to recede. Equity research has yet to reach that point, and a "balanced" representation of 40–50 percent women seems unlikely in the near future. Kanter, *Men and Women of the Corporation.*

26. The apparent contradiction in Becker's statements is not surprising. Both women and men in our sample may have been psychologically invested in downplaying the sexism of the institution. To acknowledge persistent sexism may cause cognitive dissonance for men who do not wish to see themselves as oppressors (or beneficiaries of discrimination rather than as individuals who have succeeded entirely on their own merits) and for women who wish to see themselves as strong and self-determined rather than victims of discrimination. For an engaging example of the "narrative management" used by men and women to reconcile sex-role ideology with actual behavior and circumstances—in this case, sharing housework—see A. Hochschild and A. Machung, *The Second Shift: Working Parents and the Revolution at Home* (New York: Viking Press, 1998).

27. Kanter, noting that minorities are highly visible and attract attention, has asserted that "accepting notoriety and trading on it" (*Men and Women of the Corporation*, 219) was not likely to succeed in the conservative corporate environment she studied. Such a strategy would, however, be extremely viable in the high-profile, attention-seeking world of star analysts—a fact not lost on some of the women we interviewed.

28. Because we did not collect quantitative data on analysts' networks, this study's contribution to research on organizational networks is limited. Nevertheless, research in this field can shed light on our findings. Interviews with analysts revealed that research analysts, male and female, have networks of similar size: all analysts have the same approximate number of clients and cover approximately the same number of companies, and salespeople represent all analysts. Hence, differences reside primarily in the quality or strength of the relationships rather than the size of the networks. Research on workplace networks suggests that relationships can convey multiple benefits, depending on the individual's needs and goals and the organizational structure. Some networks, such as those explored by Burt (*Structural Holes: The Social Structure of Competition* [Cambridge, MA: Harvard University Press, 1992]), provide the most benefit when they are rich in "structural holes" that allow the worker to bridge gaps, gain nonredundant information from multiple sources, and exploit entrepreneurial opportunities. Smaller and denser networks do not afford these entrepreneurial opportunities but create "a sense of personal belonging within a collectivity and clear normative expectations associated with one's role" (674). See J. M. Podolny and J. N. Baron, "Resources and Relationships: Social Networks and Mobility in the Workplace," *American Sociological Review* 62, no. 5 (1997): 673–93. Similarly, Ibarra and Andrews found that people with highly central networks (people to whom many other people in the organization are connected) are comfortable taking risks and feel accepted and aware of what is going on in the organization. See H. Ibarra

and S. B. Andrews, "Power, Social Influence and Sense Making: Effects of Network Centrality and Proximity on Employee Perceptions," *Administrative Science Quarterly* 38, no. 2 (1993): 277–303. There is not necessarily a "best" kind of network, but our data suggest that women in equity research may by default develop more entrepreneurial, wide-ranging networks while men develop stronger, denser, and less portable ones. Podolny and Baron have also noted that some relationships retain value over the course of a career while others do not. Relationships that are primarily focused on a worker's specific job—for example, a salesperson-analyst relationship—do not withstand career changes. Relationships that provide strategic information (such as industry information) and social support, however, can be maintained when an individual changes jobs or even workplaces. It appears that women build more of these portable relationships. Still, the authors note, the lack of dense, central networks can create problems for women: "It is especially important for women . . . to forge clear organizational identities and to internalize a coherent set of normative expectations about their organizational roles. . . . Resolving identity concerns may be of greater moment than maximizing access to information, resources, and brokerage opportunities" (690). Subsequent research by Ibarra differentiated between the networks of women identified as having high potential for advancement and those identified as low potential. The high-potential women forged networks with more close ties and more ties across different business units than did women with less potential and high-performing men. H. Ibarra, "Paving an Alternate Route: Gender Differences in Network Strategies for Career Development," *Social Psychology Quarterly* 60, no. 1 (1997): 91–102. This evidence suggests, again, that there may be multiple paths to success.

29. As Kanter has pointed out (*Men and Women of the Corporation*), the entrance of "tokens" into a profession makes the members of the majority group seem more alike by contrast and may elicit more solidarity among them than had previously existed. The entry of minorities can also tend to heighten role-typical behavior on the part of the majority—for example, overt displays of aggression and/or sexuality in the case of men.

30. Ibid., 225.

31. In a study of investment bankers (who did not work in equities research), Ibarra found that successful career transitions depend on three interdependent elements: competencies and experience, relationships (internal and external), and a successfully managed image. Early success can lead to cumulative advantage; lack of success, likewise, can start a vicious cycle of underachievement. Women have particular issues with image development and creating strong in-house relationships (especially finding mentors). In-house relationships are especially important in the early phase of a career, when superiors largely control a junior's visibility to clients. Women had a harder time forming initial deep mentor/sponsor relationships, which made it difficult for them to develop a breadth of networks throughout the firm. Part of this was the difficulty of attracting a mentor, but part of it also appeared to be the

junior women's expectations. Women were more likely than men to look for a "perfect" mentor who was not only successful but whom they also admired personally, whereas men took a more pragmatic approach and were willing to learn from a mentor, or seek his sponsorship whether or not they liked, respected, or identified with him. Women were also less likely to engage in self-promotion efforts or "politics," to their detriment, assuming that the quality of their work would speak for itself. See H. Ibarra, "Women, Investment Banking, and the Problem of Style" (working paper).

32. Kathy Kram, *Mentoring at Work: Developmental Relationships in Organizational Life* (Glenview, IL: Scott Foresman, 1985).

33. R. J. Burke, "Mentors in Organizations," *Group & Organization Studies* 9, no. 3 (1984): 353–72. This study found role modeling to be a distinct function; Kram, by contrast, included it in psychosocial support. Among the reasons for considering it a separate function, the most important is that role modeling does not require a direct relationship.

34. A protégé's failure reflects badly on the mentor, and in professions in which women are a minority, their failures tend to attract a good deal of attention. For both of these reasons, mentors of women choose their protégées carefully and defer establishing relationships with them until they have proven themselves. D. A. Newton and L. W. Fitt, "When the Mentor Is a Man and the Protégée a Woman," *Harvard Business Review* 59 (1981): 56–60.

35. Galant, "Can Wall Street Women Have It All?" p. 143.

36. Nanda and Lieb, "Abby Joseph Cohen," 10.

37. B. R. Ragins and D. B. McFarlin, "Perceptions of Mentor Roles in Cross-Gender Mentoring Relationships," *Journal of Vocational Behavior* 37 (1990): 321–39.

38. This expectation can be a difficult hurdle for professional women. It affects how pregnant women and mothers are treated on Wall Street, regardless of their actual child-care arrangements. One female investment-banking professional described the situation as follows: "When you come back from maternity leave, your commitment to the job is questioned. When you're not at your desk, it's assumed that you're doing something with the baby. When a man's not at his desk, it's assumed that he's in a meeting." See H. Ibarra and B. Harrington, "Impossible Selves: Image Strategies and Identity Threat in Professional Women's Career Transitions" (working paper, 1997). Research has also suggested that experienced women in investment banking may not serve as good role models for how to balance work and family life. In Roth's study, young women noted that senior women often "appropriated traditionally masculine family behaviors in order to demonstrate that their primary commitments were to their careers, *not* to their families." See Roth, "Making the Team," 297. Ely also found that women associates at firms with few women partners believed that women were poor role models in part because they did not have families. See R. J. Ely, "The Effects of Organizational Demographics and Social Identity on Relationships among Professional Women," *Administrative Science Quarterly* 39, no. 2 (June 1994): 203–38.

39. A similar dynamic has been found in cross-race mentoring relationships, which also tend to provide less psychosocial support. See D. A. Thomas, "The Impact of Race on Managers' Experiences of Developmental Relationships," *Journal of Organizational Behavior* 11 (1990): 479–92. Thomas found that a key variable is whether or not the protégé and mentor take the same attitude toward racial differences—either ignoring them in an attempt to be "color-blind" or acknowledging and discussing them openly. See D. A. Thomas, "Racial Dynamics in Cross-Race Developmental Relationships," *Administrative Science Quarterly* 38, no. 2 (1993): 169–94. If the same thing holds true for cross-gender relationships, the mentoring relationships most likely to provide psychosocial support would be those in which both parties were comfortable discussing gender issues. While it is possible to attempt to be blind to race, gender is not easily overlooked, as a revealing quote from one of Thomas's subjects makes clear: asked if race played any part in his relationship with his black protégé, he responded, "I never really thought of Michael as anything other than *a man* doing a job" (181; emphasis added). A complicating factor is that cross-gender mentoring relationships run the risk of sparking gossip about sexual involvement, which can be damaging to both parties. In part to discourage such talk, protégés with cross-gender mentors tend to socialize less with their mentors. See Ragins and McFarlin, "Perceptions of Mentor Roles in Cross-Gender Mentoring Relationships."

40. Kanter has noted that sponsors and mentors are an important source of mobility. Their role transcends helping protégées polish skills and involves fighting for the protégée, recommending her for opportunities, helping her bypass hierarchies, serving as a source of reflected power, and the like. Ultimately, mentorship is about plugging the protégée into the wider organization. Similarly, writing about advice networks, Ibarra and Andrews have pointed out that the main function of such networks is to "regulat[e] access to information, resources, and legitimacy, and not [to expose] focal actors to the views of those they seek out for advice." See Ibarra and Andrews, "Power, Social Influence and Sense Making," 296.

41. Burt in particular has noted that for members of "illegitimate"—underrepresented or otherwise suspect—groups, a mentor provides both legitimacy and a network that the protégé can "borrow." Mentors without good networks cannot help with advancement, regardless of their individual skills. Burt stresses that the importance of a borrowed network is not a gender issue per se but involves the different needs of insiders and outsiders. See Burt, "The Gender of Social Capital." Other research indicates that a mentor needs to be connected to the protégé's bosses and workplace clients (individuals who exercise "fate control") in order to be helpful. A mentor who is not connected to people with "fate control" is actually a liability to a protégé. See Podolny and Baron, "Resources and Relationships."

42. Research has shown that successful women tend to have differentiated networks, deriving social support and friendship from women and advice and organizational "clout" from men. Homophily (a preference for one's own

kind) either had no effect on men's networks or improved the quality of the network; it decreased the quality of women's networks. In other words, men who prefer to build their networks primarily with other men experience no ill effects or are rewarded for that choice; women who build networks primarily with other women or primarily with men suffer for it. They need both instrumental support from men and psychosocial role-modeling support from women. See H. Ibarra, "Homophily and Differential Returns: Sex Differences in Network Structure and Access in an Advertising Firm," *Administrative Science Quarterly* 37 (1992): 422–47.

43. Women who are underrepresented in the senior ranks of an organization may be prone to sexism of their own. According to Robin Ely, women at law firms with few senior women are less likely to identify positively with other women, to perceive senior women as role models with legitimate authority, or to find support in relationships with other women, and they are more likely to perceive competition with other women. See Ely, "The Effects of Organizational Demographics and Social Identity on Relationships among Professional Women."

44. Hill has explained that some stars created a "personal board of directors"— an apt metaphor for an individual's network of developmental relationships. See Linda A. Hill, "Developing the Star Performer," in *Leader to Leader*, ed. F. Hesselbein and P. M. Cohen (San Francisco: Jossey-Bass, 1999).

45. Baugh and Scandura used data on high-ranking female managers and executives and their male peers to study the potential for enhanced mentoring outcomes with multiple mentors. Their results suggested that "having one or more mentoring relationships in the workplace may result in greater commitment to the organization, greater job satisfaction, enhanced career expectations, increased perceptions of alternative employment, and lower ambiguity about one's work role" (514). They also found that "the effects of mentoring relationships may be somewhat stronger if the protégé has had a previous mentoring relationship," leading to the inference that "more [mentors] may be better in some ways" (514). See S. Gayle Baugh and Terri A. Scandura, "The Effect of Multiple Mentors on Protégé Attitudes toward the Work Setting," *Journal of Social Behavior and Personality* 14, no. 4 (1999): 503–21.

46. Lewis, "The Rise of Woman Power," p. 182.

47. Kanter, *Men and Women of the Corporation*, 200.

48. Ibid., 199.

49. This may not be the case in all professions. In research on a large advertising firm, Ibarra found that men's professional networks became more powerful as they rose in rank and as their professional activity increased. Such "bureaucratic investments" did not enhance women's networks. See Ibarra, "Homophily and Differential Returns."

50. See M. E. Meitzen, "Differences in Male and Female Job-Quitting Behavior," *Journal of Labor Economics* 4, no. 2 (1986): 164; and J. G. Miller and K. G. Wheeler, "Unraveling the Mysteries of Gender Differences in Intentions to Leave the Organization," *Journal of Organizational Behavior* 13, no. 5 (1992): 465–78.

51. In labor economics, the "perspicacious peregrinator" model suggests that workers continuously scan the labor market and move to optimal locations. The decision to migrate depends on an individual's traits and experiences and on the quality and content of information about alternate locations. Acquiring information about a new location incurs a cost. See S. W. Polachek and F. W. Horvath, "A Life Cycle Approach to Migration: Analysis of the Perspicacious Peregrinator," in *Research in Labor Economics*, vol. 1, ed. Ronald G. Ehrenberg (Greenwich, CT: JAI Press, 1977), 103–50. The cost of acquiring this information might be higher for women than it is for men because women also need to learn if a given firm is good for women. However, costs may be outweighed by perceived benefits. If, in a given market, location is a key predictor of success, perspicacious peregrinators would be motivated to learn the terrain in order to move to the best place. Women analysts appear to be more aware than men of the role that the firm plays in their success; they also know that there are fewer optimal locations for a woman analyst than for her male counterpart. Hence the increased cost of vigilance is a rational investment.

52. A vivid example of the cavalier attitude with which male professionals in investment banking approach the job search was offered by star telecommunications analyst Whitney Johnson: "A few weeks ago I was asked to interview a research sales candidate. He told me that he excelled at promoting analysts—getting their ideas into the marketplace, generating commission-dollar votes for them. I then asked what he knew about Merrill Lynch's analysts. His answer: nothing. I parried: 'Then how do you know that you want to work here?' His response (and this is important): 'Across the bulge-bracket, all of the analysts are pretty much the same.'" Although the interviewee was a sales representative rather than an analyst, we have encountered a similar attitude in the male analysts we interviewed. Whitney L. Johnson, address to the Merrill Lynch Women's Development Forum, April 30, 2004.

53. Laboratory experiments using artificially created minority/majority groups have shown that members of minority groups take into account more secondary, peripheral information than majority members do when making social judgments and that they look past the information provided to evaluate a situation. This tendency was attributed to feeling less in control of the situation and thus more motivated to increase control through accuracy of perception. Majority members were more likely to take information at face value. Because minority/majority status was assigned by the experimenter and not correlated with the subjects' actual social attributes, the study provided evidence that structural factors, not merely innate factors or socialization, have a strong impact on social perception and behavior. See A. Guinote, M. Brown, and S. T. Fiske, "Minority Status Decreases Sense of Control and Increases Interpretive Processing," *Social Cognition* 24, no. 2 (2006): 169–86.

54. Ely has noted that the self-perceptions of professional women in male-dominated professional firms tend to fall into four categories: accommodators, who consciously model their behavior on men's and disassociate from other women, a stance they view as either appropriate or necessary; resisters,

who actively defy hegemonic masculine values and tend to foresee a short career trajectory; self-blamers, who neither conform to nor actively reject masculine norms; and minimizers, who do not see gender as an issue. Women in more gender-integrated firms were characterized as "integrators," who "drew on both traditionally masculine and traditionally feminine images when describing themselves and felt reasonably confident that doing so enhanced their ability to succeed in their firms" (623). We found both accommodators and minimizers in our study (self-blamers and resisters were probably unlikely to reach the top ranks of competitive equity research), but it seems safe to say that most of the women interviewed preferred an environment in which they could be integrators. See R. J. Ely, "The Power of Demography: Women's Social Constructions of Gender Identity at Work," *Academy of Management Journal* 38 (1995): 589–634.

55. Cohen's observation echoes Ely's finding that a key determinant of the quality of a woman's organizational experience is not simply the percentage of professional women in the firm but the percentage of women in its senior ranks. Organizations in which men and women are sorted into jobs that replicate existing social hierarchies—male lawyers and female secretaries, for example—are more likely to promote sexism and stereotypes (Ely, "The Power of Demography").

56. Lewis, "The Rise of Woman Power," p. 178.

57. Women often speak of having to manage themselves carefully in order to be perceived as competent but not aggressive or threatening. This double bind has been explored by social psychologists, who in multiple studies have found that stereotypes break down across two dimensions: competence and warmth. Women, defined generally, are often considered both competent and warm. But when the category of women is subdivided, traditional women (e.g., housewives) are rated as high warmth/low competence, and "career women" and "feminists" are rated as high competence/low warmth. This research replicates women's experience that there is a trade-off to be made between appearing competent and appearing likable. Achievement does not always reduce prejudice but can exacerbate it: "High-status out-groups may elicit an envious mixture of admiration . . . plus intense dislike motivated by a sense of threat (for dangerous competitors). Thus, a person's belief that Asian Americans, Jews, and businesswomen are competent (perhaps even hypercompetent) may only add fuel to the fire of prejudice." See S. T. Fiske et al., "A Model of (Often Mixed) Stereotype Content: Competence and Warmth Respectively Follow from Perceived Status and Competition," *Journal of Personality and Social Psychology* 82 (2002): 899.

58. According to a line of reasoning developed by sociologists like Erving Goffman, the notion of "being oneself" is naive at best. The "self" is always a social construct, consciously or semiconsciously performed with an eye toward making the desired impression on others. See Erving Goffman, *The Presentation of Self in Everyday Life* (Garden City, NY: Doubleday, 1959). For women in a male-dominated profession, self-presentation is a minefield. Such women

often develop a defensive self-presentation style, relying less on charisma and confidence to create an impression of competence and more on technical mastery, extensive prep work, and long-term relationships in which assertive attempts to "impress" the other party gradually become less necessary. Women in such professions note that it is hard to determine exactly what the social rules and expectations are, in part because the assertive strategies necessary for male success are often deemed inappropriate for women and because their male colleagues are unable to convey or model tacit social expectations clearly. Finally, once a self-presentation style has been developed, it is difficult to change. A woman who has chosen a self-protective style early in her career may need to move to another employer to create a bolder, more confident "self." See Ibarra and Harrington, "Impossible Selves." Star analyst Whitney L. Johnson described her own battles with perfectionism: "In building relationships, not only with external clients but also with internal clients like sales and sales/traders, I find myself not willing to pick up the phone or go down to the trading floor because I don't have something important enough to say. I'm realizing that it's not about waiting to have something perfect to say, but to connect." Johnson, address to the Merrill Lynch Women's Development Forum, April 30, 2004.

59. It may be easier for minorities, including women in a male-dominated industry, to succeed in organizational cultures that emphasize interdependence, to the benefit of both the individual and the firm. Drawing on a business-simulation experiment conducted with MBA students, Jennifer Chatman, Jeffrey T. Polzer, and Margaret C. Neale concluded that "the purported benefits of demographic diversity are more likely to emerge in organizations that, through their culture, make organizational membership salient and encourage people to categorize one another as having the organization's interests in common, rather than those that emphasize individualism and distinctiveness among members." In particular, organizations with a more collectivistic orientation (those that "highlight members' common fate and interdependence," like Lehman Brothers and Goldman Sachs) enjoyed enhanced creativity: the "highest total creative output was achieved by dissimilar people in collectivistic cultures." Thus it is not enough for people to have novel ideas; the firm must provide them an environment in which those ideas can be safely shared. Jennifer A. Chatman, Jeffrey T. Polzer, and Margaret A. Neale, "Being Different Yet Feeling Similar: The Influence of Demographic Composition and Organizational Culture on Work Processes and Outcomes," *Administrative Science Quarterly* 43 (1998): 749–80, p. 749.

60. Research has indicated that people in power are more likely to use stereotypes to assess subordinates, both because they are not particularly motivated to be accurate in their assessments (whereas subordinates are highly motivated to assess their superiors correctly) and to reinforce the status quo in their own minds. "Negatively stereotyping subordinates can justify one's power position, the status of one's social groups, and the broader system of power relations between groups." See S. A. Goodwin, A. Gubin, S. T. Fiske, and V. Y. Yzerbyt,

"Power Can Bias Impression Processes: Stereotyping Subordinates by Default and by Design," *Group Processes and Intergroup Relations* 3, no. 3 (2000): 227–56, p. 230.

61. Lewis, "The Rise of Woman Power," p. 178.

62. Research has suggested that this is a wise criterion to use. Women tend to do better in terms of both compensation and promotion in environments with objective or formal methods for payment and promotion. In the absence of objective standards or bureaucratic procedures, there is more room for stereotypes and discrimination to operate. See B. Reskin, "The Proximate Causes of Employment Discrimination," *Contemporary Sociology* 29, no. 2 (2000): 319–28. Organizations that have a formal promotional system, for example, are thirteen times more likely to have a female CEO than those that do not. See D. Guthrie and L. M. Roth, "The State, Courts, and Equal Opportunities for Female CEOs in U.S. Organizations: Specifying Institutional Mechanisms," *Social Forces* 78 (1999): 511–42. Ambiguous occupations, in which performance criteria are difficult to specify, are those in which women are most likely to be discriminated against or in which a predominance of women is likely to depress wages. See E. R. Auster and R. Drazin, "Sex Inequality at Higher Levels in the Hierarchy: An Intraorganizational Perspective," *Sociological Inquiry* 58 (1988): 216–27; and Baron and Newman, "For What It's Worth." Women earn higher wages in environments with formalized work practices. See D. G. Anderson and D. Tomaskovic-Devey, "Patriarchal Pressures: An Exploration of Organizational Processes That Exacerbate and Erode Gender Earnings Inequality," *Work & Occupations* 22 (1995): 328–56; and Elvira and Graham, "Not Just a Formality."

63. The American Management Association reported annual turnover rates of 22 percent in business and professional services and 19 percent in the typical private firm in 2000. See Itworld.com (accessed September 11, 2000) and govexec.com (accessed October 1, 2001).

64. Data on the overall turnover rates of female workers are mixed. See J. L. Cotton and J. M. Tuttle, "Employee Turnover: A Meta-Analysis and Review with Implications for Research," *Academy of Management Review* 11, no. 1 (1986): 55–70. Overall, women quit jobs at a higher rate then men do. But when these data are broken down by job and personal characteristics, job-quit likelihood is very similar for both sexes. See F. Blau and L. Kahn, "Race and Sex Differences in Quits by Young Workers," *Industrial and Labor Relations Review* 34 (1981): 563–77; and A. B. Royalty, "Job-to-Job and Job-to-Unemployment Turnover by Gender and Education Level," *Journal of Labor Economics* 16, no. 2 (1998): 392–443. Other researchers have noted that the major contributor to differences in job-quit rate is the first year of employment, when women are far more likely to quit than men are. After the first year, there are no significant differences in quitting behavior. See W. K. Viscusi, "Sex Differences in Worker Quitting," *Review of Economics and Statistics* 62 (1980): 388–98. Other data show that gender has played a much less determinant role in job attachment since 1980 than it did previously. See A. Light and M. Ureta, "Panel Estimates of Male and Female Job Turnover:

Can Female Nonquitters Be Identified?" *Journal of Labor Economics* 10, no. 2 (1992): 156–81; and F. Walsh and E. Strobl, "Changes in the Gender Wage Gap and the Returns to Firm Specific Human Capital" (working paper, University College, Center for Economic Research, Dublin, 1999). Brown and Woodbury found further evidence that women's turnover is largely based on structural factors, showing that the higher quit rates of female faculty in academia were due to their more frequent appointment to temporary (non-tenure-track) positions. See B. W. Brown and S. A. Woodbury, "Gender Differences in Faculty Turnover" (Upjohn Institute staff working paper, Michigan State University, 1995).

65. G. Ichheiser, "Projection and the Mote-Beam Mechanism," *Journal of Abnormal & Social Psychology* 42, no. 1 (1947): 131–33.

66. As one study noted, employers are likely to see young women as at high risk for quitting their jobs. This is true, but young men are also at high risk for quitting—young workers in general "job shop" for optimal matches. However, the stigma of being a potential quitter seems to attach itself only to women. See Light and Ureta, "Panel Estimates of Male and Female Job Turnover Behavior."

67. The demographic information we collected also suggests that male and female stars might manage their careers differently. Specifically, female stars as a group were 4.5 years younger than their male counterparts: the women's average age was 37.3, the men's 41.8. Women had also achieved stardom earlier in their careers, having put in less time as analysts (9.4 years versus men's 10.8 years) and less time at their firms (6.5 years versus 7.3 years) before achieving *II* ranking. Both men and women had averaged 1.7 prior jobs as analysts. Our interviews suggest that women may be in more of a hurry to make their mark and then to capitalize on the broader career options that stardom brings in its wake.

Many young women anticipate and then meet an inflection point in their career paths that their male colleagues typically sail past: parenthood. Anticipation of parenthood and preparation to arrange one's work life to make room for children could explain the stepped-up pace at which female analysts achieve stardom. One female analyst quoted in *Institutional Investor* commented that on Wall Street "there's very little room for life's getting in the way. There's a saying, 'You want a friend on Wall Street? Buy a dog.'" Galant, "Can Wall Street Women Have It All?" p. 145. This familiar quip is usually taken as a comment on the Street's hard-edged values; this woman reinterpreted it as a reference to job demands that give short shrift to private life.

Josie Esquivel pointed out a possible difference in men's and women's assumptions about the availability and suitability of a preconceived career path: "Women, of my age anyway, learned early on that we had to work in a man's world but needed to go outside the box to really make a difference. My male colleagues typically felt that they had a ladder to climb, and if they took a misstep there was always another ladder waiting around the corner. My thought is that women tend to want to make that ladder work. . . . Personally, I tried to make the ladder work for some time while a number of my male colleagues just did not want to deal with the issues and looked for greener pastures. And I was not the lone female staying put."

68. Many women in finance see their career paths as "unusual and marked by flukes and accidents" (1349), according to one study, often due to a shortage of role models. Interestingly, the same study suggests that as women appeared in greater numbers in a profession, career trajectories became more rigid and marked by external expectations. To some extent, then, minorities enjoy a certain freedom that is lost when integration is achieved. See M. Blair-Loy, "Career Patterns of Executive Women in Finance: An Optimal Matching Analysis," *American Journal of Sociology* 104, no. 5 (1999): 1346–97.

69. According to Kanter (*Men and Women of the Corporation*), workers who have encountered a glass ceiling or whose advancement has been blocked are more likely to socialize and build networks downward and outward within their organizations. *Outward* means building networks with peers/customers—internally and/or externally, depending on the job—as opposed to networking "up" to superiors.

70. It may be particularly important for women to treat everyone in their environment well to avoid being considered coldly ambitious (a designation that may be perceived positively in a man but negatively in a woman). Star analyst Whitney L. Johnson advised, "Treat your assistant well. Not just because it's the right thing to do. For women in particular, people are watching how we treat those junior to us." Johnson, address to the Merrill Lynch Women's Development Forum, April 30, 2004.

71. Lorsch and Mathias describe the difficulties faced by professionals who move into a managerial role. The training and assimilation needed to turn a producer into an effective producing manager are problematic even for men rich in firm-specific human capital—which, the authors make clear, is central to success. "Managers . . . deal with a more complicated web of relationships—with superiors, peers, and subordinates—and they all need continual attention. . . . The glue that holds the units together is not tight control by top management but the personal relationships among the producing managers themselves. . . . Successful professionals who have the respect of their peers are the best candidates." One particular difficulty is that the role of manager tends to have less clear and objective goals than that of producer—a situation difficult for anyone but one that puts women particularly at risk. See J. W. Lorsch and P. F. Mathias, "When Professionals Have to Manage," *Harvard Business Review* 65 (1987): 78–83, pp. 79–81.

72. External networks can facilitate effective internal management if the external ties can be leveraged for organizational goals. Ibarra and Hunter have noted that people making the "leadership transition" from functional manager to business leader need to use their networks, which provide both valuable information and political leverage, in order to succeed. Their study showed that both men and women have a hard time with this transition, for reasons ranging from time management to lack of immediate rewards to introversion to the belief that networking is somehow unethical. One of the best ways to

become comfortable networking, they found, is to develop a mentor who does it well and ethically. As previously cited researchers have noted, finding such a mentor may be particularly difficult for women. H. Ibarra and M. Hunter, "How Leaders Create and Use Networks," *Harvard Business Review* 85, no. 1 (2007): 40–47.

73. Research in the very different environment of a customer-service call center also suggests that multiple routes to excellence are possible, even in a far more constrained, less knowledge-based environment. The managers of the call center agreed that their two best representatives were a man and a woman. The man was "polite . . . quick, focused," and his calls were "a series of clear, efficient, but somewhat curt interactions." The woman was "relatively leisurely . . . warm . . . kind and gentle" and "foster[ed] customer loyalty." The fact that both styles of excellence were strongly gendered was not lost on the study's authors. See R. M. Fernandez and M. L. Sosa, "Gendering the Job: Networks and Recruitment at a Call Center," *American Journal of Sociology* 111, no. 3 (2005): 859–904.

74. As Robin Ely, Debra Meyerson, and Laura Wernick have noted, "an organization's standard practice is not always best practice" (455). Examining and trying to solve the problems faced by a minority group in an organization can create an organizational-learning opportunity that enhances productivity for everyone: "When any group, such as women, has trouble entering an organization or moving through its ranks, the organization has an opportunity to examine how its cultural and operational conditions, its basic assumptions, norms, and work practices, as well as its values and incentives, may be inhibiting more than simply the advancement of a particular group of people: they may also be inhibiting effectiveness" (455). Ely, Meyerson, and Wernick suggested that in male-dominated professions, many accepted behaviors and practices are ultimately constructed more to reinforce stereotypical gender norms than to respond appropriately to organizational needs and goals. Deconstructing these behaviors and practices and refocusing the organizational culture on occupationally relevant—rather than gender-normed—ways of conducting business creates an environment in which women can succeed and men can expand their skill set. See Robin Ely, Debra Meyerson, and Laura Wernick, "Disrupting Gender, Revising Leadership," in *Women and Leadership: The State of Play and Strategies for Change*, ed. D. Rhode and B. Kellerman (San Francisco: Jossey-Bass, 2007): 453–73. This approach to organizational change, known as "the dual agenda," has been used at the Center for Gender in Organizations at Simmons Graduate School of Management as a way to both improve access for disadvantaged groups and enhance organizational effectiveness and learning. See Lotte Bailyn and Joyce K. Fletcher, "The Equity Imperative: Reaching Effectiveness through the Dual Agenda," *CGO Insights* 18 (July 2003), and D. Kolb et al., *CGO Insights no. 1: Making Change: A Framework for Promoting Gender Equity in Organizations* (Boston: Simmons Graduate School of Management, 1998).

75. Research on learning in organizations has suggested that learning takes place through relationships, particularly when there are multiple and diverse networks in place. Cohen and Levinthal, for example, defined "absorptive capacity" as "the ability to recognize the value of new information, assimilate it, and apply it to commercial ends" ("Absorptive Capacity," 128). This ability, a key source of advantage, is not achieved simply by putting together a collection of clever and competent workers; it resides throughout the firm in the relationships between individuals, units, and "boundary spanners" who can link the firm to the external environment—as female analysts typically do. Burt made a similar point about the ability to exploit "structural holes," or serve as a bridge between diverse groups, as a key source of advantage for the individual; this is an ability women analysts tend to develop. See R. S. Burt, "The Contingent Value of Social Capital," *Administrative Science Quarterly* 42, no. 2 (1997): 339–65; and Burt, "The Gender of Social Capital." Clearly, an individual with such relationships would also be a strategic asset to the firm. Similarly, research on "dynamic capabilities" has emphasized the ability to recombine relationships as a resource for maintaining advantage and the value of workers who can create links to the external environment. See, for instance, Eisenhardt and Martin, "Dynamic Capabilities." Given female analysts' tendency to develop strong external relationships and unconventional in-house alliances, they would be well suited to lead their organizations to learn and adapt to a dynamic environment.

76. As Kanter has noted, when judgments must be made under conditions of uncertainty, people fall back on "social bases for trust" (*Men and Women of the Corporation*, 49). Trust is easier to develop with people like oneself, a dynamic that leaves minorities disadvantaged. The more objectively productivity and performance are measured, the more heterogeneity can be sustained.

77. In the academic life sciences, for example, women do not tend to form external relationships with scientists working in industry. This is one factor in their relatively low patent rate compared to that of male life scientists in academia. See W. W. Ding, F. Murray, and T. E. Stuart, "Gender Differences in Patenting in the Academic Life Sciences," *Science* 313 (2006): 665–67.

78. This pattern is in line with research suggesting that men tend to be more overconfident than women in financial domains, which often leads them to greater losses. See B. M. Barber and T. Odean, "Boys Will Be Boys: Gender, Overconfidence, and Stock Investment," *Quarterly Journal of Economics* 116 (2001): 261–92.

9 | Star Formation: Developmental Cultures at Work

1. Research indicates that a working environment that supports the development of talent can become a source of competitive advantage for a firm. McCall, *High Flyers*; Hill, "Developing the Star Performer"; Christina A. Douglas and Cynthia D. McCauley, "Formal Developmental Relationships: A Survey of Organizational Practices," *Human Resource Development Quarterly* 10, no. 3 (Fall

1999): 203–20. The relative rarity of such development programs, especially in investment banking during the years of our study, increased the competitive advantage that they conferred. Such programs were not only valuable in themselves but also served as a way for firms to differentiate themselves from their competitors.

2. This chapter focuses on equity-research analysts (not fixed-income analysts) because a richer body of information is available about them.

3. We designated any research department that made deliberate and consistent efforts to develop its analysts as having a "developmental culture." This definition does not distinguish among firms on the basis of the type or intensity of developmental efforts. Given the small number of firms in investment banking that engaged in any developmental efforts at all and the prevailing belief in the pointlessness of such endeavors, the similarities among firms that developed their analysts far outweighed their differences. We limit our attention to the culture of the research department, not that of the bank as a whole, because in some cases these differed. Some firms had developmental cultures; others did not. Lehman Brothers, for instance, did not have a strong culture of development overall, though its research department did.

4. Similar terminology has been employed by others in articles that also describe the difficulties of and internal barriers to creating such cultures. Conger has noted that "The culture of an organization can be positive and supportive, or threatening and destructive. A career development culture helps address productivity, competitiveness, affirmative action, and succession planning. It helps people redefine their talents to realize the full potential of their jobs. Supervisors should play a key role in creating a career development culture, but many feel their careers are going nowhere and see career development efforts to be an added burden. Supervisors seldom do performance appraisals properly because they are afraid of their workers and the workers are virtually paranoid about the slightest negative note on their files. A better way is to organize a system of mentorship. Evaluation of initiatives can be calculated on the basis of savings that can be attributed to the program and its actual costs. A managed career development culture can pay great rewards to an organization and the people working in it." See Stuart Conger, "Fostering a Career Development Culture: Reflections on the Roles of Managers, Employees, and Supervisors," *Career Development International* 7, no. 6/7 (2002): 371–75, p. 375. Simonsen also explored development culture as a response to the "radically changing world of work" in her instructional guide for practitioners: "The approach to career development must align with, or support, the organization's new or desired culture to make the greatest impact. Without understanding the forces driving the culture or a goal to create a development culture, many companies have tried to implement career development or other programs that came to be referred to as 'the flavor of the month.' While well meaning, they weren't sustained because the components didn't fit the new culture or cause enough change to contribute to the development of a new or desired culture." See Peggy Simonsen, *Promoting a Development Culture in Your Orga-*

nization: Using Career Development as a Change Agent (Palo Alto, CA: Davies-Black, 1997), 15.

5. They are DLJ, Goldman Sachs, Lehman Brothers, Morgan Stanley, Prudential, Sanford C. Bernstein, and Schroder Wertheim.

6. We excluded from this category firms that experimented with training and development programs for a year or two and subsequently dropped them.

7. Turnover to competitors among non-star analysts was lower at developmental firms than at nondevelopmental firms. These findings are consistent with much of the literature on the effects of employee development on retention. On the effects of mentoring, Payne and Huffman found, in a study of one thousand U.S. Army officers, that mentoring increased protégés' emotional attachment and involvement with the organization, commitment to continue with the organization, and awareness of the cost of leaving; mentorship also reduced turnover by 38 percent. See Stephanie C. Payne and Ann H. Huffman, "A Longitudinal Examination of the Influence of Mentoring on Organizational Commitment and Turnover," *Academy of Management Journal* 48, no. 1 (2005): 158–68. These trends also seem to be confirmed in the workplace more generally: according to a 1999 Emerging Workforce Study by Interim Services and Louis Harris and Associates, 35 percent of employees who did not receive regular mentoring planned to seek another job within a year, compared to only 16 percent of those with good mentors. See Jennifer Reingold and Robert McNatt, "Why Your Workers Might Jump Ship," *BusinessWeek*, March 1, 1999, p. 8. Training programs have also been shown to have a positive impact on retention. A study of soldiers in the Israeli Air Force found that both program and occupational turnover were reduced by career "decision-making training" in which soldiers were trained to use a five-step plan to evaluate different career options within the organization. See Asya Pazy, Yoav Ganzach, and Yariv Davidov, "Decision-Making Training for Occupational Choice and Early Turnover: A Field Experiment," *Career Development International* 11, no. 1 (2006): 80–91. Similar effects were found in survey data obtained through the Institute for Employment Research: researchers Garloff and Kuckulenz noted that "there are both a negative correlation of training with job change and a negative effect of training on job change." Alfred Garloff and Anja Kuckulenz, "Training, Mobility, and Wages: Specific versus General Human Capital," *Jahrbücher für Nationalökonomie und Statistik* 226, no. 1 (January 2006): 69.

8. Laurie Meisler, "The 1997 All-America Research Team," *Institutional Investor* 31, no. 10 (October 1997): 79.

9. Groysberg and Hashemi, "Sanford C. Bernstein," 14.

10. Nanda, Groysberg, and Prusiner, "Lehman Brothers (A)," 11.

11. Ibid., 2.

12. While career-development efforts are most commonly thought of as efforts to help new professionals learn the ropes, research suggests that it is important through all stages of the career. In particular, professionals who have moved into leadership positions (formal or informal) have found that coaching helped them broaden their focus from individual excellence to leading others.

Hill (*Becoming a Manager*), for example, has explained that leaders must build skills in three key areas: interpersonal judgment (influencing others without relying on formal authority, conflict management, and balancing individual needs with team goals), self-awareness (understanding one's own strengths and weaknesses), and learning ability (continuously developing leadership skills). See also Lorsch and Mathias, "When Professionals Have to Manage."

13. The literature on mentorship is vast, and it is beyond the scope of this chapter to provide a comprehensive review. Mentoring is itself a complex phenomenon. As Kram points out in her seminal 1985 book, the term *mentor* is "derived from Greek mythology, [implying] a relationship between a younger adult and an older, more experienced adult [who] helps the younger individual learn to navigate the adult world and the world of work" (*Mentoring at Work*, 2). Research on traditional dyadic mentoring dates to the late 1970s, when scholars began exploring how relationships between younger and older adults affect career development. See, for example, Daniel J. Levinson, Charlotte N. Darrow, Edward B. Klein, Maria H. Levinson, and Braxton McKee, *The Seasons of a Man's Life* (New York: Knopf, 1978); Kanter, *Men and Women of the Corporation*; Gene W. Dalton, Paul H. Thompson, and Raymond L. Price, "The Four Stages of Professional Careers," *Organizational Dynamics* 6, no. 1 (Summer 1977): 19–42; Eileen C. Shapiro, Florence P. Haseltine, and Mary P. Rowe, "Moving Up: Role Models, Mentors and the 'Patron System,'" *Sloan Management Review* 19, no. 3 (Spring 1978): 51–58. For a meta-analytic overview of this early work, see Tammy Allen, Lillian T. Eby, Mark L. Poteet, Elizabeth Lentz, and Lizzette Lima, "Career Benefits Associated with Mentoring for Protégés: A Meta-Analysis," *Journal of Applied Psychology* 89, no. 1 (2004): 127–36.

14. We collected data on the educational backgrounds of 30 percent of star analysts over nine years (317 out of 1,053). They attended 120 different universities as undergraduates; finance, accounting, and economics were the most common majors, followed by engineering. The typical route to research was via business school: 70 percent held MBAs or other master's degrees. By contrast to their undergraduate degrees, the sources of star analysts' MBAs were highly concentrated. Five schools accounted for 55 percent of all stars with graduate degrees: New York University (42), Columbia University (26), Harvard University (25), University of Pennsylvania (21), and University of Chicago (10). Nearly 11 percent of star analysts held Ph.D.s or other advanced degrees, many in economics or finance but some in technical fields like geochemistry and molecular biology. Thirty percent had worked in the industries they covered.

15. Research suggests that mentoring at the beginning of one's career has persistent beneficial effects. Chao's 1997 longitudinal study of the career development of alumni from a large midwestern university and a small private institute found "differences between mentored and nonmentored individuals, regardless of whether the protégés were in current or former mentorships. Although all groups continued to learn and be better socialized in their organizations, the advantages of the mentored groups did not dissipate greatly

over time. Significant differences were still observed on four of the nine outcome measures in the last year of study. Consistent with Orpen's findings, these results suggest that the effects of mentoring on outcomes like income and organizational socialization endure over a long term." Georgia T. Chao, "Mentoring Phases and Outcomes," *Journal of Vocational Behavior* 51 (1997): 15–28, p. 24; see also Christopher Orpen, "The Effects of Mentoring on Employees' Career Success," *Journal of Social Psychology* 135 (1995): 667–68. The finding that the beneficial effects of mentoring are lasting lends support to our observation in this chapter that companies that supported mentoring tended to benefit in a sustained way.

16. Simply having a mentor is not sufficient to reap the benefits of mentorship; one must have a *good* mentor. Certain mentoring relationships are more effective than others. Research on the determinants of successful mentoring is consistent with the comments of our interview subjects, who stressed the importance of functional and positive mentoring. In a survey-based study of social workers, engineers, and journalists, Ragins, Cotton, and Miller found satisfaction with a mentoring relationship to have a stronger impact on attitudes than "the presence of a mentor, whether the relationship was formal or informal, or the design of formal mentoring program." Belle Rose Ragins, John L. Cotton, and Janice S. Miller, "Marginal Mentoring: The Effects of Type of Mentor, Quality of Relationship, and Program Design on Work and Career Attitudes," *Academy of Management Journal* 43, no. 6 (2000): 1177–94, p. 1177. Interpersonal comfort is another element of a good mentoring relationship. See Tammy D. Allen, Rachel Day, and Elizabeth Lentz, "The Role of Interpersonal Comfort in Mentoring Relationships," *Journal of Career Development* 31, no. 3 (Spring 2005): 155–69.

17. Although such cases exist, fear that mentoring will lead to training one's own competition is probably exaggerated. As we have seen, mentoring is likely to promote retention; an analyst well mentored at Goldman Sachs is unlikely to decamp for Merrill Lynch. Mentored analysts are also likely to build up levels of firm- and team-specific human capital that will not be portable when they change employers. Hence mentoring can reduce the likelihood that a junior analyst will become a competitor to the senior (given that he or she is provided with opportunities in a firm): the junior will be less likely to leave and less likely to succeed if he or she does so.

18. Much research supports a positive stance on the value of informal mentoring. In a survey-based study of social workers, engineers, and journalists, for example, Ragins and Cotton found that "protégés with informal mentors received greater benefits than protégés with formal mentors." Belle Rose Ragins and John L. Cotton, "Mentor Functions and Outcomes: A Comparison of Men and Women in Formal and Informal Mentoring Relationships," *Journal of Applied Psychology* 84, no. 4 (August 1999): 529–50, p. 544. Similarly, Noe's study of a comprehensive development program involving educators and administrative mentors found that "organizations should not expect protégés

to obtain the same type of benefits from an assigned mentoring relationship as they would receive from an informally established, primary mentoring relationship." Raymond A. Noe, "An Investigation of the Determinants of Successful Assigned Mentoring Relationships," *Personnel Psychology* 41, no. 3 (1988): 457–79, p. 473. Chao, Walz, and Gardner found that protégés who were informally mentored reported more support and higher compensation than individuals who were formally mentored. However, the differences between these two groups were small. The largest differences were between the mentored and nonmentored groups, which differed significantly in organizational socialization, satisfaction, and compensation. Georgia T. Chao, Pat M. Walz, and Philip D. Gardner, "Formal and Informal Mentorships: A Comparison on Mentoring Functions and Contrast with Nonmentored Counterparts," *Personnel Psychology* 45, no. 3 (Autumn 1992): 619–36.

19. A meta-analysis of forty-three empirical studies of mentoring showed that the benefits of mentoring pertained primarily to subjective factors; mentored individuals were significantly more likely than nonmentored individuals to report higher career satisfaction, job satisfaction, career commitment, and expectations for advancement. The relationship of mentoring to objective outcomes such as promotions and compensation is, unsurprisingly, stronger for individuals who receive career mentoring than for those who receive psychosocial mentoring. Even in the former case, however, the relationship between mentoring and promotion or compensation is relatively weak. This finding does not discredit mentoring; as the authors point out, "[S]alary increases and promotions can also be contingent on the financial solvency and hierarchical structure of the organization in which the employee works. In addition, it may take a greater amount of time for objective benefits to accrue than for affective reactions such as job satisfaction to be impacted by a mentoring experience" (Allen et al., "Career Benefits Associated with Mentoring for Protégés"). This finding could suggest that the most immediate benefits of mentoring accrue to the *organization* given its more satisfied and committed workers.

20. Attentive readers may have noted that this chapter quotes heavily from female analysts, who as a group have less access to mentorship (as reported in chapter 8). The apparent explanation for this paradox is that, in our interviews, women appeared to be more reflective about the role mentors had played in their careers; men find it easier to find mentors, but they are less likely to discuss the experience in depth. The major difference we found between male and female analysts' mentoring experiences was that women had much leaner mentorship networks, often consisting of a single key champion within the organization who provided primarily career-related advice. Men were more likely to have a diverse network of mentors who provided both career and psychosocial support.

21. Businesses have become increasingly dependent on training programs to help employees deal with the frequent organizational changes necessary to maintain competitiveness. Paul T. Thayer, "A Rapidly Changing World: Some Implications for Training Systems in the Year 2001 and Beyond," in *Training*

in the 21st Century: Applications of Psychological Research, ed. M. A. Quinones and A. Dutta (Washington, DC: APA Press, 1997). Annual corporate investment in training worldwide has been estimated at $200 billion, 30 percent of which is spent on training the technical workforce. Joseph F. McKenna, "Take the 'A' Training," *Industry Week* 239, no. 10 (1990): 22–29. Investment banks, clearly, were behind the curve in this trend, perhaps because of their prevailing belief in the "nature" hypothesis. The efficacy of training to promote development is by now widely accepted by practitioners and academics alike. A 2003 meta-analysis of training and development literature published between 1960 and 2000 found a moderate to strong effect for individual training, noting that the "effectiveness of organizational training appears to vary as a function of the specified training delivery method, the skill or task being trained, and the criterion used to operationalize effectiveness." Winfred J. Arthur, Winston Bennett Jr., Pamela S. Edens, and Suzanne T. Bell, "Effectiveness of Training in Organizations: A Meta-Analysis of Design and Evaluation Features," *Journal of Applied Psychology* 88, no. 2 (2003): 234–45, p. 243. Other studies have confirmed the positive effects of training on productivity. See Thomas Zwick, "The Impact of Training Intensity on Establishment Productivity," *Industrial Relations* 45, no. 1 (January 2006): 26–46.

22. Mentoring has been adopted as a systematized human-resources practice by companies like General Electric and Johnson and Johnson, and by numerous government agencies. Lisa C. Ehrich and Brian Hansford, "Mentoring: Pros and Cons for HRM," *Asia Pacific Journal of Human Resources* 37, no. 3 (1999): 92–107, http://www.management-mentors.com/MentoringvsCoaching.aspx (accessed December 2006).

23. Parts of this section are drawn from several cases: Nanda, Groysberg, and Prusiner, "Lehman Brothers (A)"; Nanda, Groysberg, and Prusiner, "Lehman Brothers (B)"; Nanda and Groysberg, "Lehman Brothers (C)"; and Groysberg and Nanda, "Lehman Brothers (D)."

24. Nanda, Groysberg, and Prusiner, "Lehman Brothers (A)," 11.

25. These are metrics used to calculate a company's profitability. EVA signifies "economic value added"; EBIT, "earnings before interest and taxes"; and EBITDA, "earnings before interest, taxes, depreciation, and amortization." Different models are appropriate for different companies and industries.

26. Nanda, Groysberg, and Prusiner, "Lehman Brothers (A)," 11.

27. Groysberg and Roberts, "Leading the Josie Esquivel Franchise (A)," 7.

28. Scholarship supports the beneficial effects of peer-to-peer training, which are similar to mutual mentoring. Kram and Isabella, for example, have asserted that "peer relationships offer an important alternative to conventional mentoring relationships by providing a range of developmental supports of personal and professional growth at each career stage." Kathy E. Kram and Lynn A. Isabella, "Mentoring Alternatives: The Role of Peer Relationships in Career Development," *Academy of Management Journal* 28, no. 1 (March 1985): 110–32, p. 116. Bryant's study of employees at a large software firm who had been trained in basic peer-mentoring skills suggested that peer mentoring

may benefit the organization. He found that "peer mentoring holds promise for increasing organizational knowledge creation and sharing." Scott E. Bryant, "The Impact of Peer Mentoring of Organizational Knowledge Creation and Sharing: An Empirical Study in a Software Firm," *Group and Organization Management* 30, no. 3 (June 2005): 319–38, p. 331; see also Babette Raabe and Terry A. Beehr, "Formal Mentoring versus Supervisor and Coworker Relationships: Differences in Perceptions and Impact," *Journal of Organizational Behavior* 24, no. 3 (May 2003): 271–93. These findings inform our understanding of how and why the Accelerated Marketing Training program and similar programs were so successful.

The sharing of mistakes, in particular, may have been a particularly valuable learning opportunity. Research departments are not teams per se, but studies of team learning have shown the importance of psychological safety or a "shared belief held by members of a team that the team is safe for interpersonal risk taking." In a study of work teams at a manufacturing company, Edmondson found that "structural and interpersonal characteristics both influence learning and performance in teams" ("Psychological Safety and Learning Behavior in Work Teams," 379). Specifically, "psychological safety is a mechanism that helps explain how previously studied structural factors, such as context support and team leader coaching, influence behavioral and performance outcomes" (379). Developmental cultures seem not only to prompt more individuals to contribute to team- and organizational-level learning but also to create an environment in which such learning is more likely given the contribution of a nurturing culture to psychological safety.

29. Nanda, Groysberg, and Prusiner, "Lehman Brothers (A)," 11.
30. Ibid., 10.
31. Ibid., 11.
32. Groysberg and Nanda, "Lehman Brothers (D)," 10.
33. Mentoring by the research director resembles a phenomenon known as supervisory career mentoring (SCM). For example, a study of employed MBA students at a private southeastern university found that "respondents with supervisory mentors reported higher career mentoring compared with those for whom the mentor was not a supervisor . . . [and that] employees reporting SCM had the most positive work attitudes and career expectations." See Terri A. Scandura and Ethlyn A. Williams, "Mentoring and Transformational Leadership: The Role of Supervisory Career Mentoring," *Journal of Vocational Behavior* 65, no. 3 (December 2004): 448–68, p. 462.
34. Ibid., 10.
35. Groysberg and Hashemi, "Sanford C. Bernstein: Growing Pains," 8.
36. Ibid., 14.
37. Ibid., 19.
38. Ibid.
39. Much of the significance of such networks may flow from the support provided by multiple mentors. Understandably, the benefits of having a mentor has prompted inquiry into the possible benefits of multiple mentors. Van

Eck Peluchette and Jeanquart found that among faculty members at two U.S. research institutions, "assistant professors with multiple sources of mentors yielded significantly higher levels of both objective and subjective career success than did those with single sources or no mentor." Joy Van Eck Peluchette and Sandy Jeanquart, "Professionals' Use of Different Mentor Sources at Various Career Stages: Implications for Career Success," *Journal of Social Psychology* 140, no. 5 (October 2000): 549–64, p. 549.

More recent research has stated this case even more strongly. Higgins and Thomas, for example, performed a longitudinal study of the effects of lawyers' developmental relationships. They found that "while the quality of one's primary developer affects short-term career outcomes such as work satisfaction and intentions to remain with one's firm, it is the composition and quality of an individual's entire constellation of developmental relationships that account for long-run protégé career outcomes such as organizational retention and promotion." Monica C. Higgins and David A. Thomas, "Constellations and Careers: Toward Understanding the Effects of Multiple Developmental Relationships," *Journal of Organizational Behavior* 22, no. 3 (2001): 223–47, p. 223. Further studies have reinforced these findings: Van Emmerick, in a survey study of university employees in the Netherlands, examined the effects of mentoring on intrinsic career success and the incremental effects of development networking. The study found mentoring to be positively associated with both career satisfaction and intrinsic job satisfaction. "After controlling for having a mentor, the relationship between development network diversity was found to be related to intrinsic outcomes. Specifically, size of the advice network was found to be positively related to . . . intrinsic career success." I. J. Hetty Van Emmerick, "The More You Can Get the Better: Mentoring Constellations and Intrinsic Career Success," *Career Development International* 9, no. 6 (2004): 578–94, p. 588. Such results led to a reassessment of Baugh and Scandura's earlier exploration ("The Effect of Multiple Mentors") of whether "more is better"; Van Emmerick concluded that it is indeed.

40. Many scholars have also drawn attention to the contribution to mentoring and development of what have been called "relationship constellations" and "developmental networks." Kram, *Mentoring at Work*; Baugh and Scandura, "The Effect of Multiple Mentors"; Monica C. Higgins, "The More the Merrier? Multiple Developmental Relationships and Work Satisfaction," *Journal of Management Development* 19 (2000): 277–96; and David A. Thomas and Monica C. Higgins, "Mentoring and the Boundaryless Career: Lessons from the Minority Experience," in *The Boundaryless Career: A New Employment Principle for a New Organizational Era*, ed. M. B. Arthur and D. M. Rousseau (New York: Oxford University Press, 1996), 268–81.

41. Monica C. Higgins and Kathy E. Kram, "Reconceptualizing Mentoring at Work: A Developmental Network Perspective," *Academy of Management Review* 26, no. 2 (April 2001): 262–88, p. 264.

42. Mentoring programs could also facilitate recruiting efforts: in a study of undergraduates seeking jobs, "the availability of a formal mentoring program

[could] significantly influence organizational attraction." Tammy D. Allen and Kimberly E. O'Brien, "Formal Mentoring Programs and Organizational Attraction," *Human Resource Development Quarterly* 17, no. 1 (Spring 2006): 43–58, p. 53.

43. Groysberg and Hashemi, "Sanford C. Bernstein: The Fork in the Road," 12.

44. In general, the more experienced the mentor, the more adept he or she becomes at passing on knowledge. Interestingly, the more experienced protégé also benefits the most. See Nigel Nicholson, Randall S. Schuler, and Andrew H. Van De Ven, eds., "Mentoring," *The Blackwell Encyclopedic Dictionary of Organizational Behavior* (Cambridge: Blackwell, 1995), 323–24.

45. Research on the effects of proximity on the strength of ties has shown that mere physical nearness increases the strength of a tie. See Leon Festinger, Stanley Schachter, and Kurt Back, *Social Pressures in Informal Groups: A Study of Human Factors in Housing* (Palo Alto, CA: Stanford University Press, 1950), cited by Higgins and Kram, "Reconceptualizing Mentoring at Work."

10 | Turnover: Who Leaves and Why

1. This chapter draws on Boris Groysberg, Ashish Nanda, and M. Julia Prats, "Does Individual Performance Affect Entrepreneurial Mobility? Empirical Evidence from the Financial Analysis Market," *Journal of Financial Transformation* 25 (March 2009): 95–106; Boris Groysberg and Linda-Eling Lee, "Star Power: Colleague Quality and Turnover," *Industrial and Corporate Change*, forthcoming; Groysberg, "The Portability of Star Knowledge Workers"; Boris Groysberg and Ashish Nanda, "Does Stardom Affect Job Mobility? Evidence from Analyst Turnover in Investment Banks" (HBS working paper); and Groysberg and Nanda, "When Superstars Switch Allegiance." In particular, the quantitative findings in this chapter (regressions and some exhibits) are based on and drawn from these articles. Also, some descriptions are taken directly from these papers.

2. See Cindy Krischer Goodman, "Dollars and Sense of Flexible Work: A Small But Growing Number of Companies Are Documenting the Financial Benefits of Work/Life Initiatives Such as Flexible Schedules," Knight Ridder Tribune Business News, May 31, 2006, p. 1; Steve Hillmer, Barbara Hillmer, and Gale McRoberts, "The Real Costs of Turnover: Lessons from a Call Center," *Human Resource Planning* 27, no. 3 (2004): 34–41; and J. D. Phillips, "The Price Tag on Turnover," *Personnel Journal* 69, no. 12 (1990): 58–62. Cascio and Pinkovitz have identified the three major costs of turnover as separation (severance pay, administrative overhead, etc.), replacement (not only the salary of a new hire but the expense of recruiters, advertisement, time spent on interviews, and the like), and training. See F. W. Cascio, *Managing Human Resources: Productivity, Quality of Work Life and Profits* (New York: McGraw Hill, 1991); and W. H. Pinkovitz, "How Much Does Your Employee Turnover Cost?" *Small Business Forum* 14, no. 3 (1997): 70–71. However, as other researchers have noted, this financial formula does not take into account harder-to-quantify but important side effects of turnover—especially turnover of top perform-

ers—including reduced productivity, disruption of the corporate culture, loss of morale among remaining staff, disruption of client relationships, loss of institutional knowledge, and inefficiencies as remaining workers cover for the departed employee. For examinations of how these dynamics play out in particular industries, see Phani Tej Adidam, "Causes and Consequences of High Turnover by Sales Professionals," *Journal of American Academy of Business, Cambridge* 10, no. 1 (2006): 137–41; and J. Deane Waldman, Frank Kelly, Sanjeev Arora, and Howard L. Smith, "The Shocking Cost of Turnover in Health Care," *Health Care Management Review* 29, no. 1 (2004): 2–7; see also Aharon Tznier and Assa Birati, "Assessing Employee Turnover Costs: A Revised Approach," *Human Resource Management Review* 6, no. 2 (1996): 113–22, for an updated formula for assessing turnover costs. For a human-capital perspective on turnover costs—tangible and intangible—see Gregory G. Dess and Jason D. Shaw, "Voluntary Turnover, Social Capital, and Organizational Performance," *Academy of Management Review* 26, no. 2 (2001): 446–56. Dess and Shaw argued that in a knowledge-based company, the loss incurred by turnover of key employees is not monotonic but exponential: "Social capital . . . is created through combining and leveraging resources. As such, it may yield exponential performance benefits for organizations, but it also increases the potential downside risk exposure should something go wrong (e.g., voluntary turnover of key network members)" (450). In other words, a firm that has lost a star oil analyst has lost not only that key player but also the productivity boost to other analysts that the star's knowledge provided.

3. "Bernard Picchi Named New Director of Lehman's U.S. Research," *Securities Week*, April 3, 1995, p. 4.

4. Becker, *Human Capital*; Becker, "Investment in Human Capital"; and Lazear, "Raids and Offer Matchers."

5. The dynamics of turnover that we have captured may be more applicable to the high-performing end of the market because of the disproportionate presence of high performers at our twenty-four firms.

6. We examined 385 moves by ranked equity analysts (269 moves to competitors and 116 exits from the profession) and 1,392 moves by unranked senior equity analysts (796 moves to competitors and 596 exits from the profession).

7. In studies of research-and-development productivity, star inventors were dependent on firm-specific resources for the number of patents they produced. See Holger Ernst, Christopher Leptien, and Jan Vitt, "Inventors Are Not Alike: The Distribution of Patenting Output among Industrial R&D Personnel," *IEEE Transactions on Engineering Management* 47, no. 2 (May 2000): 184–99; and Ernst and Vitt, "The Influence of Corporate Acquisitions on the Behavior of Key Inventors."

8. See Groysberg, Nanda, and Prats, "Does Individual Performance Affect Entrepreneurial Mobility?"; Groysberg and Lee, "Star Power"; Groysberg and Nanda, "Does Stardom Affect Job Mobility?"; Groysberg, "The Portability of Star Knowledge Workers"; Groysberg and Nanda, "When Superstars Switch Allegiance".

9. Becker, *Human Capital*; Becker, "Investment in Human Capital."

10. Among non-elite workers, Sicherman found that women initially exhibit a higher turnover rate than men but that turnover rates converge as women gain more job experience. Sicherman also discovered that women leave their jobs much more often than men for non-market-related reasons like home duties or family illness. Higher turnover rates were also linked to less job training. See Nachum Sicherman, "Gender Differences in Departures from a Large Firm," *Industrial & Labor Relations Review* 49, no. 3 (April 1996): 484–505. Lynch has demonstrated that women in private industry receive less training than men, which may lead to higher turnover and lower wages. See Lisa M. Lynch, "Private-Sector Training and the Earnings of Young Workers," *American Economic Review* 82, no. 1 (March 1992): 299–312. Hill discovered that women who received more training were likely to remain in the workforce longer. See Elizabeth T. Hill, "Labor Market Effects of Women's Post-School-Age Training," *Industrial & Labor Relations Review* 49, no. 1 (October 1995): 138–49. Finally, Becker and Lindsay found gender differences in tenure to be more acute for younger women. See Elizabeth Becker and Cotton M. Lindsay, "Sex Differences in Tenure Profiles: Effects of Shared Firm-Specific Investment," *Journal of Labor Economics* 12, no. 1 (1994): 98–118.

11. It has been shown that job tenure is longer at larger firms. See Henry L. Moore, *Laws of Wages: An Essay in Statistical Economics* (New York: Augustus M. Kelley, 1911); and Todd L. Idson, "Employer Size and Labor Turnover," *Research in Labor Economics* 15 (1996): 273–304.

12. Dan Dorfman, "Why Can't Research Directors Hold Their Jobs?" *Institutional Investor* 7, no. 10 (October 1973): 48–50, 102–3.

13. D. P. Schwab, "Contextual Variables in Employee Performance-Turnover Relationships," *Academy of Management Journal* 34, no. 4 (1991): 966–75.

14. Regression results are similar if we use a firm's stock performance instead of its investment-banking performance. But because stock-price performance is available for far fewer firms because many analysts worked for non-public firms, the predictive power of regressions is lower.

15. For a detailed explanation of this measure, see Groysberg, Nanda, and Prats, "Does Individual Performance Affect Entrepreneurial Mobility?"

16. Eugene Kandel and Edward P. Lazear, "Peer Pressure and Partnerships," *Journal of Political Economy* 100, no. 4 (August 1992): 801–17.

17. "The 1997 All-American Research Team," 81.

18. DiPrete and Nonnemaker have noted that workers enjoy greater opportunities during market expansions, resulting in increased mobility. During periods of contraction, more workers are pushed out of employment altogether. Those with limited labor resources are more affected by these economic changes. See Thomas A. DiPrete and K. Lynn Nonnemaker, "Structural Change, Labor Market Turbulence, and Labor Market Outcomes," *American Sociological Review* 62, no. 3 (June 1997): 386–404.

19. March and Simon, *Organizations*; J. M. Carsten and P. E. Spector, "Unemployment, Job Satisfaction and Employee Turnover: A Meta-Analytic Test of the

Muchinsky Model," *Journal of Applied Psychology* 72 (1987): 374–81; and C. O. Trevor, "Interactions among Actual Ease-of-Movement Determinants and Job Satisfaction in the Prediction of Voluntary Turnover," *Academy of Management Journal* 44, no. 4 (2001): 621–38.

20. Performance has been found to relate to turnover positively (R. M. Marsh and H. Mannari, "Organizational Commitment and Turnover: A Prediction Study," *Administrative Science Quarterly* 22 [1977]: 57–75; T. N. Martin, J. L. Price, and C. W. Mueller, "Job Performance and Turnover," *Journal of Applied Psychology* 66 [1981]: 116–19), negatively (M. Argyle, G. Gardner, and F. Cioffi, "Supervisory Methods Related to Productivity, Absenteeism, and Labour Turnover," *Human Relations* 11 [1958]: 32–40; R. H. Turner, "Sponsored and Contest Mobility and the School System," *American Sociological Review* 25 [1960]: 855–67), or not at all (J. E. Sheridan and D. J. Vredenburgh, "Predicting Leadership Behavior in a Hospital Organization," *Academy of Management Journal* 21 [1978]: 679–89). To clarify the relationship between employees' performance and turnover, researchers used meta-analysis. In their meta-analysis of turnover drivers that focused more on the turnover of knowledge workers than did any previous studies, Griffeth, Hom, and Gaertner documented that high performers were less likely to quit than were low performers. R. W. Griffeth, P. W. Hom, and S. Gaertner, "A Meta-Analysis of Antecedents and Correlates of Employee Turnover: Update, Moderator Tests, and Research Implications for the Millennium," *Journal of Management* 26 (2000): 463–88.

21. Laurie Meisler, assistant managing editor, *Institutional Investor*, personal communication, June 15, 1999. Chain-reaction turnover might also raise turnover rates among third-ranked and runner-up analysts. If a first- or second-rank analyst quits the industry, his or her firm might try to fill the opening with another ranked analyst.

11 | A Special Case of Turnover: Stars as Entrepreneurs

1. This chapter draws on Groysberg, Nanda, and Prats, "Does Individual Performance Affect Entrepreneurial Mobility?"; Boris Groysberg, Ashish Nanda, and Julia Prats, "Entrepreneurship among Knowledge Workers: Evidence from Equity Analyst Market" (working paper); Groysberg, "The Portability of Star Knowledge Workers"; and Groysberg and Nanda, "Does Stardom Affect Job Mobility?" In particular, the quantitative findings in this chapter (regressions and some exhibits) are based on and drawn from these articles.

2. Dan Dorfman, "The Rise of the Entrepreneurial Analyst," *Institutional Investor*, July 1974, pp. 43–106; John W. Milligan, "The Boutiques Are Making It Big," *Institutional Investor*, November 1985, pp. 274–75; Thomas Kostigen, "Captain of Your Own Ship," *Investment Dealers' Digest*, February 12, 1990, pp. 22–29; and Phillips, "Free at Last?"

3. Kostigen, "Captain of Your Own Ship," 22.

4. Gilbert Probst, Steffen Raub, and Kai Romhardt, *Managing Knowledge: Building Blocks for Success* (New York: John Wiley, 2000), 227.

5. Edward O. Welles, "How to Get Rich in America," *Inc.*, January 1993, pp. 50–55; Anise Wallace, "The New Entrepreneurs," *Institutional Investor*, September 1981, pp. 83–90.

6. The literature on entrepreneurship is vast, and it is beyond the scope of this chapter to provide a comprehensive review of it. We selectively cite works as they relate to a very narrow focus on of this chapter as a special case of turnover. This chapter incorporates some of our quantitative findings but mostly focuses on the qualitative evidence provided by our subjects.

In his very influential work, Schumpeter argued that entrepreneurship is the engine of "creative destruction." See Joseph A. Schumpeter, *The Theory of Economic Development* (Cambridge, MA: Harvard University Press, 1934). Schumacher claimed that people dislike working for big firms and that it is part of human nature to be entrepreneurial. See E. F. Schumacher, *Small Is Beautiful: Economics as if People Mattered* (New York: Harper and Row, 1973).

Entrepreneurship has been a topic of study in a number of fields, including economics, psychology, sociology, history, and administrative theory. See David C. McClelland, *The Achieving Society* (Princeton: Van Nostrand, 1961); Max Weber, *The Protestant Ethic and the Spirit of Capitalism* (New York: Routledge, 1904); Arthur Harrison Cole, *Business Enterprise in Its Social Setting* (Cambridge, MA: Harvard University Press, 1959); Howard H. Stevenson, "A Perspective on Entrepreneurial Management" (HBS working paper no. 9-384-131, 1983).

Early studies focused on identifying specific traits of entrepreneurs in an effort to determine whether entrepreneurs differ from non-entrepreneurial individuals and whether such differences are innate. See McClelland, *The Achieving Society*; Alan K. Carsrud, Kenneth W. Olm, and George G. Eddy, "Entrepreneurship: Research in Quest of a Paradigm," in *The Art and Science of Entrepreneurship*, ed. Donald L. Sexton and Raymond W. Smilor (Cambridge, MA: Ballinger, 1986), 367–78; Robert H. Brockhaus and Pamela S. Horwitz, "The Psychology of the Entrepreneur," in *The Art and Science of Entrepreneurship*, ed. Donald L. Sexton and Raymond W. Smilor (Cambridge, MA: Ballinger, 1986), 25–48; Sari Scheinberg and Ian C. MacMillan, "An 11 Country Study of Motivations to Start a Business," in *Frontiers of Entrepreneurship Research*, ed. B. Kirchoff, W. McMullan, K. Vesper, and W. Wetzel (Wellesley, MA: Babson College, 1988), 337–56; Paul D. Reynolds and Brenda Miller, *1987 Minnesota New Firms Study* (Minneapolis: Center for Urban and Regional Affairs, University of Minnesota, 1988); Arnold C. Cooper, Carolyn Y. Woo, and William C. Dunkelberg, "Entrepreneurship and the Initial Size of Firms," *Journal of Business Venturing* 4 (1989): 317–32; Carolyn Y. Woo, Arnold C. Cooper, and William C. Dunkelberg, "The Development and Interpretation of Entrepreneurial Typologies," *Journal of Business Venturing* 6, no. 2 (March 1991): 93–114; and Connie Marie Gaglio, "Opportunity Identification: Review, Critique and Suggested Research Directions," *Advances in Entrepreneurship, Firm Emergence and Growth* 3 (1997): 139–202.

Research has also attempted to explain entrepreneurial behavior as dependent on individual risk tolerance, access to information, and social relationships. See Frank H. Knight, *Risk Uncertainty and Profit* (1921; New York: Harper and Row, 1965); Scott Shane, "Prior Knowledge and Discovery of Entrepreneurial Opportunities," *Organization Science* 11, no. 4 (July 2000): 448–69; Howard Aldrich and Catherine Zimmer, "Entrepreneurship through Social Networks," in *The Art and Science of Entrepreneurship*, ed. Donald L. Sexton and Raymond W. Smilor (Cambridge, MA: Ballinger, 1986), 3–23; Howard E. Aldrich, *Organizations Evolving* (London: Sage, 1999); and Thomas Dunn and Douglas Holtz-Eakin, "Financial Capital, Human Capital and the Transition to Self-Employment: Evidence from Intergenerational Links," *Journal of Labor Economics* 18, no. 2 (April 2000): 282–305. For social ties, see Andrea Larson, "Network Dyads in Entrepreneurial Settings: A Study of the Governance of Exchange Relationships," *Administrative Science Quarterly* 37, no. 1 (March 1992): 76–104; Ranjay Gulati and Monica C. Higgins, "Which Ties Matter When? The Contingent Effects of Interorganizational Partnerships on IPO Success," *Strategic Management Journal* 24, no. 2 (February 2003): 127–44; and Toby E. Stuart, Ha Hoang, and Ralph C. Hybels, "Interorganizational Endorsements and the Performance of Entrepreneurial Ventures," *Administrative Science Quarterly* 44, no. 2 (June 1999): 315–49.

Other researchers have found that characteristics like age, education, prior entrepreneurial experience, intellectual ability, knowledge, contacts, and prestige can predict whether or not someone chooses self-employment. See Zhengxi Lin, Garnett Picot, and Janice Compton, "The Entry and Exit Dynamics of Self-Employment in Canada," *Small Business Economics* 15, no. 2 (September 2000): 105–25; Michael A. Hitt et al., "Direct and Moderating Effects of Human Capital on Strategy and Performance in Professional Service Firms: A Resource-Based Perspective," *Academy of Management Journal* 44, no. 1 (February 2001): 13–28.

Researchers also looked at the importance of the amount of financial and human capital an individual possesses and his or her decision to become an entrepreneur. See David S. Evans and Linda S. Leighton, "Some Empirical Aspects of Entrepreneurship," *American Economic Review* 79, no. 3 (June 1989): 519–35; Douglas Holtz-Eakin, David Loulfaian, and Harvey S. Rosen, "Entrepreneurial Decisions and Liquidity Constraints," *RAND Journal of Economics* 25, no. 2 (Summer 1994): 334–47; David G. Blanchflower and Andrew J. Oswald, "What Makes an Entrepreneur?" *Journal of Labor Economics* 16, no. 1 (January 1998): 26–60; Robert E. Lucas Jr., "On the Size and Distribution of Business Firms," *Bell Journal of Economics* 9, no. 2 (Autumn 1978): 508–23; and Evans and Leighton, "Some Empirical Aspects of Entrepreneurship."

Researchers have also found that the institutional context is an important factor in the decision to become an entrepreneur. See Timothy Bates, "Analysis of Survival Rates among Franchise and Independent Small Business Startups," *Journal of Small Business Management* 33, no. 2 (April 1995): 26–36; William J. Baumol, *Entrepreneurship, Management, and the Structure of Payoffs*

(Cambridge, MA: MIT Press, 1993); Paul A. Gompers and Josh Lerner, *The Venture Capital Cycle* (Cambridge, MA: MIT Press, 1999); Lowell W. Busenitz, Caroline Gomez, and Jennifer W. Spencer, "Country Institutional Profiles: Unlocking Entrepreneurial Phenomena," *Academy of Management Journal* 43, no. 4 (October 2000): 994–1003; and Lloyd Steier and Royston Greenwood, "Entrepreneurship and the Evolution of Angel Financial Networks," *Organization Studies* 21, no. 1 (2000): 163–92. For economic conditions, see Lin, Picot, and Compton, "The Entry and Exit Dynamics of Self-Employment in Canada."

Researchers have also examined the origins of entrepreneurial firms and the process of starting a new firm. See Jack W. Brittain and John Freeman, "Entrepreneurship in the Semiconductor Industry" (unpublished paper, University of California, Berkeley, 1986); Arnold C. Cooper, William C. Dunkelberg, Carolyn Y. Woo, and W. J. Dennis Jr., *New Business in America: The Firms and Their Owners* (Washington, DC: NFIB Foundation, 1990); Arnold C. Cooper and F. Javier Gimeno Gascon, "Entrepreneurs, Processes of Founding, and New-Firm Performance," in *State of the Art in Entrepreneurship*, ed. Donald L. Sexton and John D. Kasarda (Boston: PWS-Kent, 1992), 301–40; John Freeman, "Entrepreneurs as Organizational Products: Semiconductor Firms and Venture Capital Firms," *Advances in the Study of Entrepreneurship, Innovation, and Economic Growth*, ed. Gary Libecap, 1 (1986): 33–52; M. Diane Burton, Jesper B. Sorensen, and Christine Beckman, "Coming from Good Stock: Career Histories and New Venture Formation" (HBS working paper no. 99-010, 1999).

7. Many researchers have noted the difficulty of conducting empirical research on entrepreneurship. See William B. Gartner, "Who Is an Entrepreneur? Is the Wrong Question," *Entrepreneurship Theory and Practice* 13, no. 4 (Summer 1989): 47–68; Howard E. Aldrich and Ted Baker, "Blinded by the Cites? Has There Been Progress in Entrepreneurship Research?" in *Entrepreneurship 2000*, ed. Donald L. Sexton and Raymond W. Smilor (Chicago: Upstart, 1997), 377–400; and Amar Bhide, *The Origin and Evolution of New Businesses* (New York: Oxford University Press, 2000). Groysberg, Nanda, and Prats have noted "two criticisms commonly leveled against existing empirical research in entrepreneurship, that the analysis is (a) cross-sectional and (b) single-level. Cross-sectional data are simultaneously too restrictive in underrepresenting failures and too broad in assuming similar entrepreneurial efforts across industries. Cross-sectional analysis is susceptible to self-selection bias since it underrepresents individuals who attempt, but fail in, entrepreneurial pursuits" ("Does Stardom Affect Job Mobility?" 96). Longitudinal data would allow for more thorough analysis of entrepreneurial activity. See Evans and Leighton, "Some Empirical Aspects of Entrepreneurship."

Entrepreneurship research has also been faulted for looking exclusively at either the individual or the external environment, but rarely both. See Aldrich and Baker, "Blinded by the Cites?" By contrast, our data allowed us to analyze entrepreneurship at the individual, firm, sector, and macroeconomic levels. As we examined each driver, we were able to control for the other variables, re-sulting in a truer representation of entrepreneurial activity. This is also, to our knowledge, the first study that links an individual's prior job performance to the decision to become an entrepreneur. Our data also allowed us to observe entrepreneurship among knowledge workers. The only other studies to ana-lyze this important facet of the modern economy have dealt with physicians, accountants, and scientists. See Douglas R. Wholey, Jon B. Christianson, and Susan M. Sanchez, "The Effect of Physician and Corporate Interests on the Formation of Health Maintenance Organizations," *American Journal of So-ciology* 88, no. 1 (July 1993): 164–200; Alvin E. Headen Jr., "Wage, Returns to Ownership, and Fee Responses to Physician Supply," *Review of Economics and Statistics* 72, no. 1 (February 1990): 30–37; Johannes M. Pennings, Kyngmook Lee, and Arjen can Wittelloostuijn, "Human Capital, Social Capital and Firm Dissolution," *Academy of Management Journal* 41, no. 4 (August 1998): 425–40; Lynne G. Zucker, Michael R. Darby, and Marilyn B. Brewer, "Intellectual Human Capital and the Birth of U.S. Biotechnology Enterprises," *American Economic Review* 88, no. 1 (March 1998): 290–306; and Dante Di Gregorio and Scott Shane, "Why Do Some Universities Generate More Start-Ups than Oth-ers?" *Research Policy* 32, no. 2 (February 2003): 209–27.

8. One study found that nearly 40 percent of new firms still existed after six years; of those that had grown, the success rate was over 65 percent. Bruce Phillips and Bruce Kirchoff, "Formation, Growth and Survival; Small Firm Dynamics in the U.S. Economy," *Small Business Economics* 1 (1989): 65–74. Subsequent research using data from the Business Information Tracking Se-ries corroborated these findings: about half of new firms remained in business for over four years. Brian Headd, "Redefining Business Success: Distinguish-ing between Closure and Failure," *Small Business Economics* 21 (2003): 51–61. Using Census Bureau data on 20,000 small businesses formed in 1984–87, Bates found a 72 percent survival rate after five years for new professional and services ventures. Bates, "Analysis of Survival Rates among Franchise and In-dependent Small Business Startups."

9. In this study, we measured new ventures' survival rate by identifying those that still existed three years after their formation. For a review of the literature on the use of "discontinuance of a business" as a proxy for failure, see John Watson and Jim E. Everett, "Do Small Businesses Have High Failure Rates? Evidence from Australian Retailers," *Journal of Small Business Management*, October 1996, pp. 45–62.

10. Much research has investigated factors affecting the success or failure of a new firm. For example, initial start-up capital and access to further funding greatly impact failure rates. See David S. Evans and Boyan Jovanovic, "An Estimated Model of Entrepreneurial Choice under Liquidity Constraints," *Journal of Political Economy* 97, no. 4 (August 1989): 808–27; Evans and Leigh-ton, "Some Empirical Aspects of Entrepreneurship"; Holtz-Eakin, Loulfaian, and Rosen, "Entrepreneurial Decisions and Liquidity Constraints"; and Dunn and Holtz-Eakin, "Financial Capital, Human Capital and the Transition to

Self-Employment." Other models have looked at the personal characteristics of the entrepreneur. See Evans and Leighton, "Some Empirical Aspects of Entrepreneurship"; Andrew E. Burke, Felix R. FitzRoy, and Michael A. Nolan, "When Less Is More: Distinguishing between Entrepreneurial Choice and Performance," *Oxford Bulletin of Economics & Statistics* 62, no. 5 (December 2000): 565–87. Other researchers looked at social capital. See Scott Shane and Toby Stuart, "Organizational Endowment and the Performance of University Start-Ups," *Management Science* 48, no. 1 (January 2002): 154–70.

11. Looking specifically at analysts who left to pursue self-employment, we found that high performers were more likely to leave than low performers. Many factors can be linked to this characteristic of star performers. For example, stars gain credibility from their public recognition in *Institutional Investor*, and potential clients view ranking as a sign of quality. This stature helps the star attract resources to initiate a new venture. See A. Stinchcombe, "Social Structure and Organizations," in *Handbook of Organizations*, ed. James G. March (Chicago: Rand McNally, 1965), 142–93; and Stevenson, "A Perspective on Entrepreneurial Management." General ability has also been linked to entrepreneurship. See Thomas J. Holmes and Jason A. Schmitz, "A Theory of Entrepreneurship and Its Application to the Study of Business Transfers," *Journal of Political Economy* 98, no. 2 (April 1990): 265–94.

12. Economic conditions heavily influence the likelihood of choosing entrepreneurship. See Jeanne M. Carsen and Paul E. Specter, "Unemployment, Job Satisfaction, and Turnover: A Meta-Analytic Test of the Muchinsky Model," *Journal of Applied Psychology* 72, no. 3 (August 1987): 374–81; Stinchcombe, "Social Structure and Organizations"; Blanchflower and Oswald, "What Makes an Entrepreneur?"

13. A knowledge worker's reputation depends on such factors as personal characteristics and position as well as the firm and associations to which he or she belongs. See Joseph Berger, P. Cohen, and Morris Zelditch Jr., "Status Characteristics and Expectation States," in *Sociological Theories in Progress*, ed. Joseph Berger, Morris Zelditch Jr., and Bo Anderson (Boston: Houghton Mifflin, 1966), 29–46; Eliot Freidson, *Professional Powers: A Study of the Institutionalization of Formal Knowledge* (Chicago: University of Chicago Press, 1986); Michael Useem and Jerome Karabel, "Pathways to Top Corporate Management," *American Sociological Review* 51, no. 2 (April 1986): 184–200; Matthew L. A. Hayward and Warren Boeker, "Power and Conflicts of Interest in Professional Firms: Evidence from Investment Banking," *Administrative Science Quarterly* 43, no. 1 (March 1998): 1–22; and Freeman, "Entrepreneurs as Organizational Products."

14. During the six-year period 1972–77, a total of 1,274 star analysts appeared on the *Institutional Investor* All-America Research list; 247 of those 1,274 stars left their firms, for a turnover rate of 19.39 percent. Over the nine-year period 1988–96, 489 out of 4,200 star analysts moved, for a turnover rate of 11.6 percent. Six stars in the earlier period and 30 in the later period founded their own firms. These numbers correspond to rates of turnover to entrepreneur-

ship of 0.47 percent in 1972–77 and 0.71 percent in 1988–96. In the 1988–96 period about 6 percent of all mobile stars became entrepreneurs, compared to about 2 percent in the first period. It is interesting to note the gender distribution of entrepreneurial star analysts in the two periods: there were 59 ranked female analysts in the 1972–77 period (4.6 percent) but no entrepreneurial female stars. Eighteen percent of all stars in the 1988–96 period were female, but only 4 out of 30 entrepreneurial star analysts (13 percent) were female.

15. Paul D. Reynolds, "Who Starts New Firms? Preliminary Explorations of Firms-in-Gestation," *Small Business Economics* 9 (1997): 449–67.

16. Over the course of nine years, only thirty star analysts—twenty-eight from the top twenty-four banks and two from smaller banks—chose entrepreneurship.

17. Ann Monroe, "A Business Tailor-Made for Local Boutiques," *Investment Dealers' Digest* 61, no. 20 (May 15, 1995): 15.

18. James M. Clash, "Dr. Biotech (Fund Manager Brandon Fradd)," *Fortune*, May 19, 1997, p. 264.

19. Phyllis Berman, "Gas-Fired: These Rainwater Acolytes Did Well in Natural Gas Even When It Flamed Out," *Money & Investing*, November 13, 2000; "Natural Gas Partners," *Oil & Gas Investor,* July 1, 2000; Toni Mack and Phyllis Berman, "Making Money on Flat Prices," *Forbes*, November 12, 1990.

20. Dorfman, "The Rise of the Entrepreneurial Analyst."

21. Woodruffe, *Winning the Talent War*; Mike Johnson, *Winning the People Wars: Talent and the Battle for Human Capital* (London: Financial Times, 2000); and Tulgan, *Winning the Talent Wars*.

22. Stephens Taub, "Shakeout Time for Hedge Funds," *Financial World*, January 21, 1992, p. 9.

23. Louis Uchitelle, "2 Leading Economists Moving on Wall St.," *New York Times*, March 21, 1991, sec. D, p. 4.

24. Hill, *Becoming a Manager*; Boris Groysberg, Andrew L. McLean, and Nitin Nohria, "Are Leaders Portable," *Harvard Business Review* 84, no. 5 (May 2006): 92–100; and Lorsch and Tierney, *Aligning the Stars*.

12 | Measuring and Rewarding Stars' Performance

1. In particular, some quantitative findings in this chapter (regressions and some exhibits) are based on and drawn from Boris Groysberg, Paul M. Healy, and David Maber, "What Drives Sell-Side Analyst Compensation at High-Status Banks?" (HBS working paper).

2. Kerr and Slocum discussed corporate rewards in terms of hierarchy-based "clan culture" versus performance-based "market culture." Clan cultures are "a control system based on socialization and internalized values and norms" (101). In such cultures, tacit knowledge is a key to success and tenures are typically long. Rewards are bestowed on teams, not individuals, and performance reviews are geared more toward development than evaluation. Bonuses are a relatively small proportion of compensation at these firms. By contrast, performance-based market cultures emphasize short-term performance, quantitative results (with minimal attention to how those results

were achieved), autonomy of managers, little cross-divisional or team-based collaboration, and "a system of control in which behaviors are constrained by negotiated terms of exchange" (103). Bonuses typically play a larger role in market-culture firms. Kerr and Slocum noted that either kind of corporate culture can be effective but that all practices within a given culture need to be aligned coherently, and that the overall thrust of the culture needs to make sense strategically in the market within which it operates. The nonportability-oriented firms in our sample exhibited many more attributes of the clan cultures. See J. Kerr and J. W. Slocum, "Managing Corporate Culture through Reward Systems," *Academy of Management Executive* 1, no. 2 (1987): 99–108.

3. The idea that compensation systems need to be integrated into a coherent corporate culture may be the only point on which researchers in the field agree. Psychologist Alfie Kohn, known for his work on the unintended negative effects of rewards on motivation, is perhaps the most radical critic of the use of compensation (and nonmonetary rewards) as a motivator. Kohn has argued that rewards "typically undermine the very processes they are intended to enhance." External incentives merely change temporary behavior patterns, not underlying motivation or commitment. See Alfie Kohn, "Why Incentive Plans Cannot Work," *Harvard Business Review* 71, no. 5 (1993): 54–63, p. 54. While not all scholars or managers would agree with Kohn's formulation that rewards are inherently ineffective, even destructive, many would agree with his criticism that incentive systems tend to work in a vacuum as the only way employers motivate and direct employees. According to Kohn, incentive systems are too often used in the workplace as inadequate substitutes for providing feedback, creating a collaborative environment, investigating the underlying causes of performance problems, and soliciting employee feedback on workplace issues. Beer characterized this as perhaps Kohn's most salient criticism: "Managers tend to use compensation as a crutch," he pointed out (39). In the same article (a series of responses to Kohn), Lebby argued that what matters is not the use of financial incentives per se but how employees interpret them; when asked what was rewarding about a financial reward, most employees characterized the reward as "a tacit acknowledgement of the outstanding nature of their contribution" (40). Amabile also emphasized the *interpretation* of rewards, arguing that if workers are intrinsically motivated, external rewards need not undermine motivation and can provide recognition and a sense of freedom (if the reward allows the worker access to previously unattainable resources). See T. Amabile, E. Appelbaum, G. P. Baker III, et al., "Rethinking Rewards," *Harvard Business Review* 71, no. 6 (1993): 37–49. For more on the effect of framing on how rewards are perceived, see C. Heath, "On the Social Psychology of Agency Relationships: Lay Theories of Motivation Overemphasize Extrinsic Incentives," *Organizational Behavior and Human Decision Processes* 78, no. 1 (1999): 25–62.

4. Much of the research on the effects of incentives (such as pay-for-performance or bonuses) assumes that firms offer rewards to encourage behavior that employees might not otherwise pursue. This is designated as *the principal-agent*

problem phenomenon in which the goals of agents—in this case, employees—are at odds with those of the principal. Compensation and contracts are used to align the goals of principal and agent. The public nature of the market for analysts affects this equation in that the goals of principal and agent are impacted, at least in terms of *II* rankings, by market forces: the rewards of an *II* ranking accrue to the individual as well as the institution. See K. Eisenhardt, "Agency Theory: An Assessment and Review," *Academy of Management Review* 14, no. 1 (1989): 57–74. Also see M. Bloom and G. T. Milkovich, "Relationships among Risk, Incentive Pay, and Organizational Performance," *Academy of Management Journal* 41, no. 3 (1998): 283–97. In addition to being rewards, bonuses paid to star analysts function as attraction-and-retention mechanisms. Beer and Katz assert that attraction and retention are the most salient functions of bonuses, regardless of the performance-enhancing rationales put forth for their use. See M. Beer and N. Katz, "Do Incentives Work? The Perceptions of a Worldwide Sample of Senior Executives," *Human Resource Planning* 26, no. 3 (2003): 30–44.

5. Management & Capital Partners undertook an exhaustive study of appraisal and compensation in the equity-research market in spring 2001. The firm performed in-depth interviews with 219 analysts, research managers, institutional equities managers, and general managers at twenty-seven sell-side firms, including most of the bulge-bracket firms. The study, *Equity Research at a Crossroad*, was undertaken as a utility for M&CP's clients and is not publicly available.

6. Lawrence J. Fraser and James S. Peterson, *Equity Research at a Crossroad*, (New York: Management & Capital Partners, 2001).

7. One significant change in compensation practices since the period of our study is the effect of the 2003 global settlement on the portion of compensation previously linked to analysts' participation in investment-banking deals. The global settlement entered into by ten investment banks (two other firms settled later), the SEC, the North American Securities Administrators Association, the NYSE, the New York attorney general, and state securities regulators specifies thirteen criteria that can be used to determine analysts' compensation. The agreement, whose purpose is to insulate research from firms' pursuit of investment-banking business, prohibits analysts from participating in such pursuits and from receiving compensation for investment-banking activities directly. Thus the thirteen approved criteria specifically exclude input from investment-banking personnel. During the period of our study, prior to the settlement, analysts were routinely compensated for helping attract deals.

The investment-banking arm of a firm can still contribute to the research department's budget. Analysts can be compensated for substantive technical contributions during the execution of investment-banking deals but can no longer participate in soliciting such deals. One industry insider spelled out the practical consequences: "Analysts are still very much involved in the capital-formation process, but their role is that they do not call on investment-banking clients, so they do not solicit that kind of business. And they're not brought over the wall until much later in the process, but they are asked on behalf of the firm to issue an opinion about the security. And hypothetically that opinion is independent of their compensation, but the fact that they took the time to do the work is a consideration, as I understand it, in many of the large security firms."

8. Research has shown that incentive programs appear to work better the longer they are in place. S. J. Condly, R. E. Clark, and H. D. Stolovitch, "The Effects of Incentives on Workplace Performance: A Meta-Analytic Review of Research Studies," *Performance Improvement Quarterly* 16, no. 3 (2003): 46–63.

9. Findings are drawn from Groysberg, Healy, and Maber, "What Drives Sell-Side Analyst Compensation at High-Status Banks?"

10. The compensation findings reported in this chapter are derived from different data sets; there is no uniform data set on analyst compensation.

11. Choosing a compensation system is difficult. Multiple decisions must be made, and they must all reinforce one another. The economic literature treats compensation as inherently problematic because of the principal-agent problem, but the principal-agency problem is itself a controversial formulation. One interesting criticism of it has come from social psychology. Heath posited the existence of an "extrinsic incentives bias": people believe others to be motivated primarily by external rewards (such as money) while they themselves are motivated by intrinsic rewards (such as learning). Therefore, Heath argued, principals may offer inappropriate and nonmotivating deals to agents ("On the Social Psychology of Agency Relationships").

12. For a review of compensation choices, see M. S. Salter, "Tailor Incentive Compensation to Strategy," *Harvard Business Review* 51, no. 2 (1973): 94–102; and S. H. Applebaum and L. Mackenzie, "Compensation in the Year 2000: Pay for Performance?" *Health Manpower Management* 22, no. 3 (1996): 31–40. For an economic analysis of similar issues, see also G. Baker, M. Jensen, and K. Murphy, "Compensation and Incentives: Practice vs. Theory," *Journal of Finance* 43 (1988): 593–616.

13. To the best of our knowledge, very few investment banks based bonuses on team results. They might have considered doing so: one meta-analytic review found that team-based incentives had a more powerful effect on performance than did individual incentives, regardless of industry, the structure of the system (paying only the highest performers versus paying everyone whose performance improves), performance outcome, or whether the study was a laboratory or field study. See Condly, Clark, and Stolovitch, "The Effects of Incentives on Workplace Performance."

14. In addition to its effects on workers, compensation can also be a signal to the market that a firm is attentive to performance issues. See R. M. Brooks, D. O. May, and C. S. Mishra, "The Performance of Firms Before and After They Adopt Accounting-Based Performance Plans," *Quarterly Review for Economics and Finance* 41 (2001): 205–22.

15. One of the banks in our study conducted a statistical analysis and determined that the opinions of the sales force were highly correlated with those of clients.

16. Though the amount of attention lavished on performance data varied from firm to firm, the basic decision about how to measure performance was always given prolonged and serious thought, and the ultimate choice was always justified on a logical basis (as opposed to one of convenience). The magnitude of analyst bonuses, not to mention the publicity they elicited, created an incentive for research directors to be highly accurate. For more about the effect of cost on the accuracy of employee evaluations, see Baker, Jensen, and Murphy, "Compensation and Incentives."

17. *Institutional Investor* had several major competitors. Greenwich Associates also polled buy-side firms about sell-side analysts, but it was less influential because it was private (not published) and because it rated groups rather than individuals. The *Wall Street Journal* published an annual list of "All-Star Analysts" that concentrated on analysts' stock-picking ability and earnings-forecasting accuracy. StarMine, a San Francisco–based firm, recently began doing the same. Though research management and individual analysts paid attention to all three guides, none came close to challenging *II*'s standing as an arbiter of analysts' skills.

18. Nanda and Groysberg, "Lehman Brothers (D)," p. 7.

19. Fraser and Peterson, *Equity Research at a Crossroad.*

20. Commissions per share had shrunk since deregulation in 1975 and were not sufficient in themselves to support a large research department. At most full-service firms, revenues from investment banking and retail brokerage helped support research.

21. Using multiple and qualitative performance metrics might have encouraged managers to maintain a long-term focus on performance as opposed to thinking in terms of immediate, short-term rewards. See Salter, "Tailor Incentive Compensation to Strategy."

22. Baker, Jensen, and Murphy have noted that pay-for-performance can be *too* motivating: "Strong pay-for-performance motivates people to do exactly what they are told to do" ("Compensation and Incentives," 597). If performance measures were unclear, pay-for-performance could cause morale problems and stimulate extensive lobbying by employees, tying up managerial resources. However, many firms were convinced that some subjectivity was inevitable when assessing creative or risk-taking performance, a stance that made trust and transparency in the assessment process all the more salient.

23. This paragraph is drawn from Groysberg, Nanda, and Prusiner, "Lehman Brothers (A)," 5.

24. An excess of metrics can easily become unmanageable. Reporting on research by two consulting firms, *Strategic Finance* noted that "scorecards" were used effectively less than 20 percent of the time. A key reason was the inclusion of too many metrics: "Companies report an average of 132 measures to senior management each month . . . which is nearly nine times the number in effective scorecards." See K. Williams, "What Constitutes a Successful Balanced Scorecard?" *Strategic Finance* 86, no. 5 (2004): 19.

25. Fraser and Peterson, *Equity Research at a Crossroad*, 27.

26. Ibid.

27. The heavy use of performance bonuses in analyst compensation may have been related to this trend. Beer and Katz noted a positive correlation in a variety of industries between compensation dispersion and the use of bonuses in executive pay ("Do Incentives Work?").

28. High levels of pay dispersion are not inherently good or bad; they must be assessed in the context of the overall work climate and the behaviors that compensation is designed to encourage. To be effective, high dispersion in pay *must* be accompanied by the conviction that performance is assessed and compensation is awarded in an unbiased fashion. Pay dispersion is apt to be accepted and to have positive effects when it is seen as the legitimate outcome of differences in performance and when the nature of the work is largely independent rather than cooperative. See J. D. Shaw, N. Gupta, and J. E. Delery, "Pay Dispersion and Workforce Performance: Moderating Effects of Incentives and Interdependence," *Strategic Management Journal* 23 (2002): 491–512. Research in academia has shown that high pay dispersion erodes faculty job satisfaction, productivity, and collaboration. See J. Pfeffer and N. Langton, "The Effect of Wage Dispersion on Satisfaction, Productivity, and Working Collaboratively: Evidence from College and University Faculty," *Administrative Science Quarterly* 38 (1993): 382–407. Negative effects of pay dispersion on cooperation and collaboration have also been found in the high-technology sector. See P. A. Seigel and D. C. Hambrick, "Pay Disparities within Top Management Groups: Evidence of Harmful Effects on Performance of High-Technology Firms," *Organization Science* 16, no. 3 (2005): 259–74.

29. Startlingly, a 2003 survey of 205 executives found that "no aspect of a company's pay plan design predicts the company's performance. The only variable that significantly predicts company performance is teamwork." See Beer and Katz, "Do Incentives Work?" This finding, in conjunction with several studies demonstrating the negative effects of pay disparity on teamwork, suggests that research directors who are concerned about pay disparity are right to be worried. A 1999 study on the effects of pay dispersion in major league baseball found that extreme pay dispersion had significant negative effects on player and team performance. See M. Bloom, "The Performance Effects of Pay Dispersion on Individuals and Organizations," *Academy of Management Journal* 42, no. 1 (1999): 25–40. This is a particularly interesting finding in that the market for baseball players is similar in many ways to that of analysts: both are highly visible achievement-oriented professionals. For a review of the effects of secrecy versus openness about pay and of salary dispersion versus compression, see "Compensation Systems: Forms, Bases, and Distribution of Rewards," in J. N. Baron and D. M. Krep, *Strategic Human Resources: Frameworks for General Managers* (New York: John Wiley, 2000).

30. "Heard on the Street," *Wall Street Journal*, October 29, 1991.

31. Nanda and Groysberg, "Lehman Brothers (C)," 2.

32. Boris Groysberg, Nitin Nohria, and Derek Haas, "The 1995 Release of the *Institutional Investor* Research Report" (Boston: Harvard Business School

Publishing, 2005). Balog may have been underestimating the corporate-culture advantage. A 1998 study of companies with non-traditional compensation schemes (such as Men's Wearhouse, Southwest Airlines, and the SAS Institute) suggested that a healthy corporate culture—one in which employees are respected, offered opportunities to solve engaging problems with intelligent colleagues, and allowed to have fun on the job—is the key to retention. The SAS Institute was a particularly notable example: even during the heyday of the high-tech boom, the company did not pay individual bonuses or offer stock options to employees, practices that most software firms considered obligatory to attract and retain the best and brightest. Pfeffer also noted that tinkering with compensation plans can be perceived as an easy fix compared to the harder work of changing a company's culture. Creating a culture of motivated, collaborative employees is harder than adopting the latest compensation scheme—but this very difficulty can be a virtue, in that cultural advantages are harder for competitors to imitate. See J. Pfeffer, "Six Dangerous Myths about Pay," *Harvard Business Review* 76, no. 3 (1998): 109–19.

33. See Baker, Jensen, and Murphy, "Compensation and Incentives."

34. Fairness is a more complicated issue than it may appear to be. In a 2004 article on perceived fairness in compensation practices, Bloom described three types of justice/fairness: *distributive justice*, or fairness in the allocation of pay itself (the "outcome" factor discussed earlier in this chapter); *procedural fairness*, or the way compensation is determined (the "input" and "process" factors); and *interactional justice*, which is "concerned with interpersonal treatment, especially the treatment people receive by those who set and carry out organizational policies and procedures." According to Bloom, perceptions of procedural fairness are more important than perceptions of distributive justice and "have a strong impact on whether employees view their managers and their organization as trustworthy, whether they feel that their organization values them as a person, and whether they believe that their employment exchange is simply an economic transaction or a trust-based relationship involving mutuality." See M. Bloom, "The Ethics of Compensation Systems," *Journal of Business Ethics* 52, no. 2 (2004): 149–52.

13 | Lessons from Wall Street and Elsewhere

1. Groysberg, McLean, and Nohria, "Are Leaders Portable?"

2. A variation of this point applies to the professions as well. A great deal of the human capital possessed by professionals is profession-specific but not firm-specific. A lawyer and a physicist may share general attributes like literacy and diligence, but very little of the knowledge base of their respective professions is held in common. Within a given profession, furthermore, the general human capital of particular specialties diverges markedly. The skills of a tax lawyer differ from that of a bankruptcy lawyer; so do those of a civil engineer and an aeronautical engineer. The same pattern characterizes all professions and academic fields.

3. We computed abnormal returns, a measure of corporate performance, with an asset-pricing model widely used in the field of finance. The model controls for four factors: market, size, book-to-market, and price momentum. Thus, a firm's abnormal returns show how well it performs in comparison to the market and to similar firms. We calculated abnormal returns from day two following the new CEO's hire through the next three years of his tenure. We have replicated the analysis using other performance measures and found results that are consistent with those reported here.

4. Gary S. Becker, *The Economic Approach to Human Behavior* (Chicago: University of Chicago Press, 1976); Gary S. Becker and Kevin M. Murphy, *Social Economics: Market Behavior in a Social Environment* (Cambridge, MA: Belknap Press of Harvard University Press, 2000).

5. Becker and Murphy, *Social Economics.*

6. Ibid.

7. In Becker's words: "The economic approach does not assume that decision units are necessarily conscious of their efforts to maximize or can verbalize or otherwise describe in an informative way reasons for the systematic patterns in their behavior" (*The Economic Approach to Human Behavior*, 7).

8. Sushil Bikhchandani, David Hirshleifer, and Ivo Welch, "A Theory of Fads, Fashion, Custom, and Cultural Change in Informational Cascades," *Journal of Political Economy* 100, no. 5 (June 1992): 992–1026.

9. Robert S. Huckman and Gary P. Pisano, "The Firm Specificity of Individual Performance: Evidence from Cardiac Surgery," *Management Science* 52, no. 4 (April 2006): 473–88.

10. Ibid., 486.

11. Paul D. Allison and John A. Stewart, "Productivity Differences among Scientists: Evidence for Accumulative Advantage," *American Sociological Review* 39, no. 4 (August 1974): 596–606; Paul D. Allison and J. Scott Long, "Departmental Effects on Scientific Productivity," *American Sociological Review* 55, no. 4 (August 1990): 469–78; Klaas P. Baks, "On the Performance of Mutual Fund Managers" (unpublished paper, Wharton School, University of Pennsylvania); and John Jacob, Thomas Z. Lys, and Margaret A. Neale, "Expertise in Forecasting Performance of Security Analysts," *Journal of Accounting and Economics* 28 (1999): 51–82.

12. Shawn L. Berman, Jonathan Down, and Charles W. L. Hill, "Tacit Knowledge as a Source of Competitive Advantage in the National Basketball Association," *Academy of Management Journal* 45, no. 1 (2002): 13–31; Huckman and Pisano, "The Firm Specificity of Individual Performance."

13. Huckman and Pisano, "The Firm Specificity of Individual Performance," 485; Allison and Stewart, "Productivity Differences among Scientists"; Allison and Long, "Departmental Effects on Scientific Productivity"; and J. Scott Long and Robert McGinnis, "Organizational Context and Scientific Productivity," *American Sociological Review* 46, no. 4 (August 1981): 422–42.

14. Oorlog, "Marginal Revenue and Labor Strife"; Ravid, "Information, Blockbusters, and Stars"; Cassing and Douglas, "Implications of the Auction

Mechanism in Baseball's Free Agent Draft"; and Elberse, "The Power of Stars."

15. Boris Groysberg, Lex Sant, and Robin Abrahams, "When 'Stars' Migrate, Do They Still Perform Like Stars?" *MIT Sloan Management Review* 50, no. 1 (Fall 2008): 41–46.

16. Glenn, McGarrity, and Weller, "Firm-Specific Human Capital, Job Matching, and Turnover."

17. David Dunning, Chip Heath, and Jerry M. Suls, "Flawed Self-Assessments: Implications for Health, Education, and the Workplace," *Psychological Science in the Public Interest* 5 (2007): 69–106. The article focuses on the real-world domains of health, education, and the workplace, with an eye toward the negative consequences of inaccurate self-assessment: "[W]hether people decide well in life depends, at least in part, on whether their self-assessments are accurate. . . . To the degree that people judge themselves accurately, they make decisions, big and small, that lead to better lives. However, to the extent that people misjudge themselves, they may suffer costly consequences by pursuing wrong paths and missing opportunities to take advantage of special skills and resources they truly own" (70).

18. Amy H. Mezulis, Lyn Y. Abramson, Janet S. Hyde, and Benjamin L. Hankin, "Is There a Universal Positivity Bias in Attributions? A Meta-Analytic Review of Individual, Developmental, and Cultural Differences in Self-Serving Attributional Bias," *Psychological Bulletin* 130 (2004): 711–47. See also Bertram F. Malle, "The Actor-Observer Asymmetry in Attribution: A (Surprising) Meta-Analysis," *Psychological Bulletin* 132 (2006): 895–919.

19. Paul A. Mabe and Stephen G. West, "Validity of Self-Evaluation of Ability: A Review and Meta-Analysis," *Journal of Applied Psychology* 67 (1982): 280–96.

20. Feedback can help reduce overoptimistic biases, but only if it is unambiguous, timely, and objective. Lessons from feedback are often unclear. People are also more likely to overestimate themselves on broadly defined traits and abilities (e.g., sophistication) than on more objective measures (e.g., punctuality). David Dunning, Judith A. Meyerowitz, and Amy D. Holzberg, "Ambiguity and Self-Evaluation: The Role of Idiosyncratic Trait Definitions in Self-Serving Assessments of Ability," *Journal of Personality and Social Psychology* 57 (1989): 1082–90; see also Jerry Suls, Katherine Lemos, and H. Lockett Stewart, "Self-Esteem, Construal, and Comparisons with the Self, Friends, and Peers," *Journal of Personality and Social Psychology* 82 (2002): 252–61. Thus the feedback provided by the *II* rankings might not be sufficient to keep analysts from overestimating their abilities. The rankings only come out once a year and only provide information for those who are ranked.

21. Dunning, Heath, and Suls, "Flawed Self-Assessments," 77.

22. "Illusion of control" is the term used to characterize people's belief that they have greater control over events—or the ability to predict events accurately—than they in fact do. The term was initially defined as "an expectancy of a personal success probability greater than the objective probability would warrant." Ellen J. Langer, "The Illusion of Control," *Journal of Personality and*

Social Psychology 32, no. 2 (1975): 311–28, p. 313. Initial positive experiences or feedback—such as being ranked by *II*—can heighten the illusion of control. Paul K. Presson and Victor A. Benassi, "Illusion of Control: A Meta-Analytic Review," *Journal of Social Behavior and Personality* 11 (1996): 493–510.

23. Alexis de Tocqueville, *Democracy in America and Two Essays on America*, trans. Gerald E. Bevan (1835–40; London: Penguin, 2003), 589.

24. Ibid., 709.

25. O'Reilly and Pfeffer, *Hidden Value*.

26. The interviews with executives were conducted by students in Boris Groysberg's 2008 Managing Human Capital class at Harvard Business School.

27. This section about the five most frequent job-change mistakes is drawn and some descriptions and quotes taken directly from Boris Groysberg and Robin Abrahams, "A Seeker Born Every Minute: Top Five Career Transition Mistakes, Why People Make Them, and How to Avoid Them" (working paper).

28. Nico Lacetera, Iain M. Cockburn, and Rebecca Henderson, "Do Firms Change Capabilities by Hiring New People? A Study of the Adoption of Science-Based Drug Discovery" (MIT working paper, 2003).

29. Dale T. Mortensen, "Matching: Finding a Partner for Life or Otherwise," *American Journal of Sociology* 94, supplement (1988): S215–S240, and Borland and Lye, "Matching and Mobility in the Market for Australian Rules Football Coaches."

30. "Management's Role in the Knowledge Economy: An Interview with Tom Stewart," 8th Annual Life Long Learning Conference, June 2, 2006, Toronto.

Appendix

1. Most of this appendix (text, table, and endnotes) is reprinted by permission from the Institute for Operations Research and the Management Sciences, B. Groysberg, L.-E. Lee, and A. Nanda, "Can They Take It with Them? The Portability of Star Knowledge Workers' Performance," *Management Science* 54, no. 7 (2008): 1213–30. Copyright 2008, the Institute for Operations Research and the Management Sciences, 7240 Parkway Drive, Suite 300, Hanover, MD 21076.

2. One hundred thirty-four analysts left sell-side research: 69 joined buy-side firms, 30 founded new companies, 20 retired, 8 took non-research positions in the securities industry, 5 joined companies they had covered as analysts, one died in a car accident, and one died of a heart attack.

3. P. J. Huber, "The Behavior of Maximum Likelihood Estimates under Nonstandard Conditions," *Proceedings of the Fifth Berkeley Symposium on Mathematical Statistics and Probability* (Berkeley: University of California Press, 1967), 221–23.

4. The *Analyst move* coefficient might not measure the unbiased impact of analysts' changing firms, as analysts do not move at random, introducing a potential self-selection problem. In particular, treatment effects (decisions to change firms) are present in settings in which individuals themselves decide whether or not they will receive the treatment. In this nonexperimental evalu-

ation of performance differences between ranked analysts who change firms and those who do not, the process by which analysts decide to change firms needs to be modeled. With William Greene's help, we estimated several alternative econometric models to (1) access the robustness of our results and (2) control for the endogeneity of the decision to change firms by modeling the analyst's decision to change firms as a function of the individual, firm, sector, and macroeconomic variables that were found to affect turnover of analysts. The estimates showed that the study's results were robust. Overall, we found that the significance levels of the coefficients and the relative magnitude of the estimates from these models were similar to those from the ordered probit with robust cluster estimation. Furthermore, our analyses showed that the control for sample selection bias was insignificant and selectivity was not a problem, meaning that the two equations could be run separately. Thus, in our subsequent analysis we ignored the selection equation and focused solely on the estimation of analysts' performance using the one-stage ordered probit regressions with robust cluster estimate of variance. See W. H. Greene, *Econometric Analysis*, 4th ed. (Upper Saddle River, NJ: Prentice-Hall, 2000); J. Heckman, "Sample Selection Bias as a Specification Error," *Econometrica* 47 (1979): 153–61; G. S. Maddala, *Limited-Dependent and Qualitative Variables in Economics* (New York: Cambridge University Press, 1983), 117–22; and Russell Davidson and James MacKinnon, *Econometric Theory and Methods* (New York: Oxford University Press, 2004). For a far more detailed description of the study's methodology, statistical findings, control variables, robustness check, and analysis relating to endogeneity, see Groysberg, Lee, and Nanda, "Can They Take It with Them?"

5. The *Analyst star tenure coefficient* was also affected by top-rated analysts' inability to move up in rankings. Furthermore, using the *Analyst new star* variable, we examine if being ranked for the first time affected performance. *Analyst new star* took the value of 1 if an analyst had been ranked for the first time as of the end of the year, 0 otherwise. Newly ranked analysts might be on their way up or might have just gotten lucky one year and are thus expected to lose rankings in the next year. The *Analyst new star* coefficient was positive and insignificant. Finally, in order to reject alternative explanations for our results, we tested whether there were significant interactions between the *Analyst move* and *Analyst firm tenure, Analyst experience, Analyst star tenure, Analyst performance,* and *Analyst new star* variables. None of the interactions was found to be significant.

Index

The letters *e, t, f,* or *n* following a page number indicate an exhibit, table, figure, or note on that page. The number following the *n* indicates the number of the note cited.

Barclays de Zoete Wedd (BZW), Drexel
Burnham team moves and, 155, 157, 159
basketball players, 332, 333
Bear Stearns, 73, 78, 93, 303; newly hired
stars and, 127
Becker, Helane, 22–23, 168, 169, 189, 203–4,
395n26; on building networks, 170, 179;
on departmental culture, 184; on marketing training course, 214; on mentoring, 206; on mentorship, 203, 204; on
Prudential's marketing training program,
209; on the research director, 184–85
Bernstein, Sandy, 107. *See also* Sanford C.
Bernstein (SCB)
Bilotti, Rich, 200
biotechnology sector, 135–36, 200, 214, 260
Black Monday, 21
Blankfein, Lloyd, 104
Blumstein, Michael, 200–201, 229–30;
on bonus calculation, 297; on business
plans, 310
bonuses, 247; collaborative work and,
120; cultural factors and, 425n2, 426n3;
employee behavior and, 426n4; hiring
stars and, 3, 84; investment banks versus
commercial banks and, 387n32; men
versus women and, 181; performance
review and, 304; signing and, 338. *See
also* compensating analysts
book, flow of, 8–12
Booth, Michael, 146
Bronston, Deborah, 208
Brown, Debra, 248–49; on evaluating opportunities, 180–81, 400n52; on hiring
stars, 80; on performance measurement,
185
Buell, Steve, 302; on analysts' value by sector, 315–16; on client-vote system, 292,
293; on individual business plans, 307;
on performance review, 304; on rating
analysts, 296
bulge-bracket firms, 69, 369n45
Business Week, 144
buy-side firms, 39–40, 43, 55, 291, 292,
362n13, 434n2

cardiac surgeons, 332
Casati, Roberto, 389n49
Casesa, John: on Schroder Wertheim,
235–36; on Tarasoff, 237
Cash, Andrew, 145
Cashen, Tony, 330
Cena, Alex, 78
Center for Research in Security Prices
(CRSP), 85, 349
Chasen, Amy Low, 218
Clark, James, 68, 145
Clark, Mayree, 31; on analysts' stock pick-
ing, 299; on client-vote system, 292, 293;
on compensation of analysts, 297–98; on
Morgan Stanley mentoring, 230–31; on
rating analysts, 295–96; on star management, 200
Claude, Abram: on interviewing and hiring,
130; on recruiting strategy, 330; on team
moves, 149; on women on Wall Street,
168
clientelization, 48
client-vote system, 43–44, 291–93
Cobb, Alex, on sales forces, 58
Cohen, Abby Joseph, 101, 188; on departmental culture, 182–83, 401n55; on Drexel
Burnham team move, 155; on evaluating
opportunities, 181; on Goldman Sachs,
104; on mentorship, 173–74; on the
research director, 184
Comeau, Ed, 243; on DLJ, 97–98; on mentoring at DLJ, 208
company-specific skills, 325–26. *See also*
firm-specific human capital
compensating analysts, 274–303, 318–20,
426n3; analyst questionnaire excerpts
and, 281–82; attitudes toward the *II* poll
and, 285; attributes of ranked analysts
and, 283, 286t–89t; budget analysis and,
277–78; business plans and, 307–11; challenges for firms and, 311–15; competitive
analysis of *II* analysts at Lehman Brothers and, 284–85; criteria at a leading
investment bank and, 284; decision
points and, 278–79; dispersion and, 275,

exploitation versus exploration, 133–37, 382n13; findings and, 133–35, 382n14; methodology and, 133–34; types of hires and, 136–37, 347. *See also* findings

Farrell, Bob, 105

findings: choosing and integrating capacities of the new firm and, 73; drivers of turnover and, 243–49; effect of gender on portability and, 74; effect of switching firms on ranked analysts' short-term and long-term performance and, 350, 351t; entrepreneurial exits versus ordinary job changes and, 257–59; financing research and compensating analysts and, 274–303; firm quality and other factors in performance portability and, 68–74; former analysts' survival rates as entrepreneurs and, 255–57; leaving solo versus leaving with a team and, 73–74; market reactions to the hiring of stars and, 84–88; moving solo versus moving in teams and, 141–44; orientation of the analyst's original firm and, 72–73; price of leaving and, 63–68; star development at research departments and, 197–99; stars in new roles: exploitation versus exploration and, 133–37; stock market's response to hiring stars, by gender and, 190–91; stock market's response to hiring stars and, 137–39; turnover at portability-promoting and nonportability-promoting firms and, 241–43; women's performance more portable than men's and, 163–66

firm-specific human capital, 4, 56–63, 157, 190–91, 232, 255–56, 325–26; building of, 109–22; entrepreneurial analysts and, 253, 256; individual decision making and, 109–22, 327–30; liftouts and, 10, 26; portability and, 322; training, and, 208–17; turnover and, 241–43

Fradd, R. Brandon, 263–64

Fraenkel, Fred, 59, 109–22, 208; on departmental culture, 182; on exploitation versus exploration, 135–36; on *II* ranking, 44–45, 280; on Josie Esquivel, 22; on Leh-

man, 113; on marketing training, 209; on portability, 40; on security analysts, 36; on team moves, 149; training program of, 24; on women on Wall Street, 168–69, 181, 393n20

Fraser, Larry: on analysts' compensation, 280; on analysts' value by profitability, 317; on job offers and compensation, 312–13, 314–15

free-agent thesis, 4, 16, 324, 332–34, 354n6; athletes and, 359n60; companies and, 31–32; portability and, 16–17, 32; security analysts and, 40–41

Galbraith, Steve, on sales forces, 58

Garzarelli, Elaine, 167

Gay, Robert, 265, 268

gender. *See* portability, women versus men and; findings; women

General Electric executives, 324–26

generalizability to other professions, 332–34

general management skills, portability of, 324–26

Gilbert, Denise, 87

globalization, nonportability and, 101

global settlement of 2003, 7, 366n26, 427n7

Goldman Sachs: best practices and, 103–4; compensation and, 130–31; globalization and, 101; hiring and socializing stars and, 128–31; institutionalized mentoring and, 217–18; internal marketing and, 331; interviewing and hiring and, 129–30; on job offers and compensation and, 313–14; newly hired stars and, 126; recruitment and training and, 103; team-based culture and, 102

Goldstein, Gary, 168

Greenberg, Edward, 270

Greenthal, Jill, on DLJ, 97

Greenwich Associates, 245–46, 248, 273, 362n13, 429n17

Gutfreund, John, 99

Haggerty, Steve, on Tarasoff, 236–37

Hall, Gordon, 68, 145

Harvard Business Review, 341–42

Hash, Steve, 109, 118–20, 123, 215; on the accelerated marketing training course, 215–16; on analyst's value by sector, 316–17; on business plans, 310; on commitment to training, 201–2; on compensation of analysts, 298, 311–12; on job offers and compensation and, 314; on Lehman's marketing training program and turnover, 233; loyalty, training and, 202; on star development, 199; Tortoriello move from Deutsche Bank to Lehman Brothers and, 160–61

hedge funds, 263–64

hegemonic masculinity, 168, 393n14

Hill, Emma, 205–6

hiring and socializing stars: exploitation versus exploration, 133–37; implications for employers and, 336–37; implications for individual careers and, 337–43; picking and integrating and, 127–32; stock market's response to, 137–39

Hoffmann, John, 198

human capital, nonportable: associate analysts as, 57–58; colleagues, teams, and networks as, 56–63, 366n19; firm-specificity and, 322; investment committee as, 61; IT platforms and corporate systems as, 61; portfolio strategists as, 60; research director as, 59–60, 366n26, 367n28; sales force as, 58; technical analysts as, 60–61; traders as, 59; training and, 53–54, 62–63, 367n33

human capital, portable: analysts' backgrounds and, 39; buy-side clients as, 55; compensation of, 39, 44; data on, 45–46; external information networks as, 56; extraneous factors and, 46–47; free-agent thesis and, 40–41; general human capital and, 53; general training as, 56; industry role of, 39–40; job description of, 361n4; market compactness and transparency, 44–45; public companies and, 48; relationships with companies as, 55; search consultants and, 47–48, 363n28;

standardized performance measures and, 42–45; unique market features of, 42–48; working conditions of, 36–40

human-capital theory, 4, 25–26, 53–54, 321, 363n25; company-specific skills and, 325–26; general versus firm-specific skills and, 26, 431n2; industry human capital and, 325; portfolio model and, 324–26; relationship human capital and, 325; strategic human capital and, 325; work settings and, 54

Hyman, Edward S., International Strategy and Investment Group and, 267

industry human capital, 325

industry sectors, 42; blackbooks and, 106; Esquivel and, 31; interdependency and, 57; rankings and, 21, 42–43; teams and, 57; value to the firm and, 315–17. See also specific sectors

Institutional Investor (II), 6; All-America Research Team and, 21–22; client-vote system, 290–92; compensation of analysts and, 276, 277; on CSFB, 99; data packaged as research product and, 283–84; on DLJ, 97; ranking system of, 42–45; on turnover and sector performance, 248–49; on women on Wall Street, 167, 168

institutional investors. See buy-side firms

intelligence: emotions and, 23; free agency and, 28; "g" and, 23; performance and, 23–24

Internet sector, 135, 168, 328

interviewing and hiring, 129–30, 385n9

Investment Dealers' Digest, 156; on stars as entrepreneurs, 254

James, Tony, 97

job-change mistakes: doing inadequate research, 338–39; leaving for money, 339; moving "from" rather than "to," 339; not taking a long-term perspective, 340–41; overestimating oneself, 339–40

Johnson, Alan, on stars' compensation, 78

Johnson, Whitney L., 405n70
J. P. Morgan, 145

Kahan, Robert, 98
Karlen, Sara, 148, 149, 172; on departmental
    culture, 183–84; on evaluating opportuni-
    ties, 180; on mentorship, 174–75
Keating, Richard, 61
Keegan, Karl, 146
Kimball, Darren, 37–38
Kirnan, Jack, 68
Kirsch, Arthur, 152–54, 158
Kloner, Craig, 206–7
Kotowski, Chris: on his apprenticeship,
    203–4; on rating analysts, 296; on sales
    forces, 59
Krawcheck, Sallie, on SCB, 107
Krutick, Jill: on mentorship, 175–76; on
    relying on the sales force, 178

Lehman Brothers, 15; Accelerated Market-
    ing Class, 208–17; acquisition of E. F.
    Hutton and, 21; culture and commitment
    and, 120–22; female analysts and, 192–93;
    hiring and, 113; innovative analysis and,
    116–17; *Institutional Investor* (*II*) and,
    115–16; leadership and culture and, 111–12;
    newly hired stars and, 127; performance
    and, 109–10; performance evaluation
    and, 115–16; portability and turnover
    and, 243; rebuilding the department and,
    118–20; reorganization and decline and,
    117–18; soft nonportability and, 111–14;
    systematizing processes and, 114–15; team
    approach and, 57; training and, 62, 113–14
Lelon, Elise, 219
Lerner, Teena, 116, 188; on Lehman, 113;
    on marketing training course, 214; on
    performance measurement, 185
Levy, Steven, 78
liftouts, 10, 136–37, 141–62, 327, 384n2,
    384n4; competitive advantage and,
    386n18; courtship stage and, 156–57;
    cultural integration stage and, 160,

161, 391n56; entering new markets and,
    147–48; findings and, 141–43, 162; leader-
    ship integration stage and, 158–59, 161;
    legal matters and, 144; methodology and,
    141–43; notable examples of, 145–46; op-
    erational integration stage and, 159–60,
    161; reasons for, 146–48; rise of, 146–48;
    stages of, 156–60; Tortoriello move from
    Deutsche Bank to Lehman Brothers,
    160–61; why teams move and, 148–49,
    386nn18–19
Lipstein, Richard, on hiring teams, 147
Lobaccaro, Nicholas, 37–39
Lurie, Sidney, B., 36

Management & Capital Partners, 291, 302,
    427n5
Manlowe, David, 145
Maxwell, John, 265
Meehan, Steven, on Drexel Burnham team
    move, 154
Meeker, Mary, 168
Melnick, Andrew: on hiring stars, 78; on
    research associates, 57
mentorship, 203–7, 216–17; informal men-
    toring and, 204–7; junior-analyst system
    and, 203–4; training and, 207–8. *See also*
    developmental cultures, mentorship and
Merrill Lynch, 79, 93, 127; associates and,
    57–58; belief in portability and, 123, 199;
    compensation and, 123; IQ database and,
    105–6; labor market and, 133; newly hired
    stars and, 127; proprietary information
    systems and, 105–6, 122; training and,
    199; turnover and, 241; uniqueness of,
    105, 111
minder-finder-grinder distinction, 254
Montgomery Securities, 98; newly hired
    stars and, 127
Morgan Stanley, 31; compensation of
    analysts and, 297; "Equity Research
    Conference of the Americas" and, 231–32;
    mutual mentoring and, 229–32; 1994
    study and, 107; 1995 liftout and, 145–46

Muratore, Carol, 172, 192, 269–70; on burnout, 261; on client service, 171; on evaluating opportunities, 181; Green Tree Research and, 265; on performance measurement, 185, 403n62; on self-marketing, 269; on starting her own business, 265
Murphy, Charles, 145

National Association of Securities Dealers, 345
Natural Gas Partners, 264
nature versus nurture, outstanding performance and, 41, 201, 302; Einhorn on, 217
Nejmeh, Greg, 27; on Rivkin, 112; on team approach, 57
nonportability, types of, 10. *See also* human capital, nonportable; portability, firms of origin and
nonportability-oriented firms, 10, 100–109, 328–29; hard, 104–6; product-based, 106–9; retention and, 122–23; soft, 101–4
nonportable human capital: associate analysts as, 57–58; colleagues, teams, and networks as, 56–57; firm-specific training as, 62; investment committee as, 61; IT platforms and corporate systems as, 61; portfolio strategist as, 60; research director as, 59–60; sales force as, 58–59; technical analysts as, 60–61; traders as, 59

organizational socialization, 127–28, 379n2, 380n3, 380nn4–5, 381n6
outstanding job performance, routes to, 341–43

Paulson, Henry, on Goldman Sachs, 103
Pedone, Frank, 169
performance management: attributes of ranked analysts and, 286t–89t; client-vote system and, 291–93; compensation choices and, 278–79; external offers and, 312–15; *II* rankings and, 280; incentives versus perceptions of fairness and,

311–12; performance data and, 302–3; performance review process, 304–11; polling the sales force and, 293–96; promotion criteria and, 284–85; value to the firm and, 315–18
performance-review process, 304–11; business plans and, 307–11; data for, 305f
Petrie, Thomas, 263
Petrie Parkman, 263
Philips, Chuck, 200
Plourde, Katharine, 156
portability: determinants of, 323–24; empirical tests and results and, 349–50, 351t; exploitation versus exploration and, 347; firm capability and, 346; firm quality and, 68–72, 368n40, 369n43; gender and, 10–11, 74; general management skills and, 324–26; hiring for exploration versus exploitation and, 347; lessons for firms and, 75–76; lessons for knowledge workers and, 74–75; model specifications and, 348–49; moving to a better firm and, 71–72; moving to a comparable firm and, 70–71; moving to a weaker firm and, 72; new firm's choosing and integrating capacities and, 73; orientation of original firm and, 72–73; prescriptive goal of the study of, 321; research approach and, 343–44; solo versus team moves and, 73–74; switching firms and, 346; team movement and, 347; team movement for exploration versus exploitation and, 347; variables and, 345–48
portability, firms of origin and, 93–94, 99, 327; circumstantial portability and, 98–100; compensation and, 123; firm-specific human capital and, 100–109; general human capital and, 95; hard nonportability and, 104–6; intentional portability and, 96–98; Lehman Brothers and, 109–22; product-based nonportability and, 106–9; retention and nonportability and, 122–24; silos and, 96; soft nonportability and, 101–4

portability, hiring firms and, 125–26; assimilation and, 127–32; DLJ and, 128–31; exploitation versus exploration and, 133–37; findings and, 126–27; integrating new stars and, 131, 382n10; market response and, 137–39, 383n16; records and strategies and, 126–27; rocky transitions and, 131–32

portability, women versus men and, 327, 342; building a research franchise, 169–85, 395n28; departmental culture and, 182–84; divergence from male career paths and, 187–88, 404n67; early years and, 166–67; employment conditions and, 167–69, 393n16; external networks and, 170–80, 405n72; findings and, 163–66, 391n1; implications for organizations, 191–93; importance of compensation and, 181–82; in-house alliances and, 188–89; in-house relationships and, 172–73; internal career progression and, 189–90, 405n71; market response and, 190–91; other knowledge professions and, 193–94; poor mentorship and, 173–76, 396n31, 397n34, 398n39; research directors and, 184–85, 402nn59–60; sales force and, 176–78; scrutinizing prospective employers and, 180, 400n51, 400nn53–54; strategic protection and, 178–80, 399n49; team membership and, 179–80; turnover and, 185–87, 403nn63–64, 404n66

portability-oriented firms, 95–100; circumstantial, 98–100; intentional, 96–98

portable human capital: external information networks as, 56; general training as, 56; relationships with buy-side clients as, 55; relationships with companies as, 55

portfolio model of human capital, 324–26

price of leaving, 63–68; short- and long-term performance and, 64t. *See also* findings

professional athletes, 332, 333–34

Raab, Brian, 219; on sales forces, 59

rate busters, 113, 214

relationship human capital, 325

research analysts as study population, 5–8, 344–45

research approach, 343–44

research tests, 349–50, 351t

research variables, 345–48

retail brokers, 105, 132; women and, 188–89

reward systems. *See* compensating analysts; performance-review process

Rivkin, Jack, 15, 21, 59, 109–22, 123, 201; on analysts' compensation, 280; departure from Lehman and, 27; evaluating analysts and, 301; on *II* ranking, 42; on marketing training course, 214; on recruiting strategy, 192; sports analogy and, 111; training program of, 24; on women on Wall Street, 185

Rose, Charles, 267

Rosen, Benjamin, 254

Ross, Lawrence, 36

sales force: managing across functions and, 58–59; polling of, 279; relationships with female analysts and, 176–78

Salomon Brothers, 68, 73, 122; bulge bracket and, 346; circumstantial portability and, 99–100; turnover and, 241

Sanders, Judy, 113, 115, 183

Sanders, Lewis, 218; on Sanford C. Bernstein's development culture, 234

Sandor, Richard, 390n54

Sanford C. Bernstein (SCB): blackbooks and, 62, 106–9, 218, 309e, 331; culture and, 108–9; evaluation and compensation and, 108; *Guide for New Analysts*, 219–29; hiring and development and, 108; institutionalized mentoring and, 218–29; portfolio strategists at, 60; sales questionnaire regarding analyst, 294e–95e

Santora, Kim, 119; on the accelerated marketing training course, 216

Schroder Wertheim, developmental culture of, 234–37; structured critique and, 235–36; turnover and, 237